Christian Approaches to Other Faiths

Christian Approaches to Other Faiths

A Reader

Edited by
Paul Hedges
and
Alan Race

scm press

© Paul Hedges and Alan Race 2009

Published in 2009 by SCM Press
Editorial office
13–17 Long Lane,
London, EC1A 9PN, UK

SCM Press is an imprint of Hymns Ancient and Modern Ltd
(a registered charity)
St Mary's Works, St Mary's Plain,
Norwich, NR3 3BH, UK
www.scm-canterburypress.co.uk

British Library Cataloguing in Publication data

A catalogue record for this book is available
from the British Library

978 0 334 04115 3

Typeset by Regent Typesetting, London
Printed and bound by
CPI Antony Rowe, Chippenham SN14 6LH

This book is dedicated to

Yue and Raphael (PH)

Christine, Nick, Georgina, Madeleine (AR)

Contents

Part Two Christian Responses to Individual Faiths

Section A: Abrahamic Traditions

Section B: Indic Traditions

Part Three Other Faith Traditions Respond to Christianity

Preface

This Reader accompanies the *SCM Core Text Christian Approaches to other Faiths*, but can also be read as a standalone text to introduce some of the main writers and themes within the area. The reasons for adding more introductory texts within the field are explained in the Core Text, but may briefly be listed here:

- The importance of the subject matter (today, questions of the relations between faiths are increasingly asked).
- The particular relevance for understanding in this area (ignorance and misunderstanding are two great problems).
- To supply a lack in the existing range of texts (no other texts provide up-to-date introductions to both the theories and relations to other faiths, or supply such a range of perspectives across all viewpoints).

With regard to this Reader, several other introductory points are also in order:

- Selection of the texts.
- Presentation of the texts.
- Differences from the Core Text.

In most sections two texts are provided as we have opted to have a range of longer texts rather than many short snippets. The two texts are also aimed at providing a balance in each area, which may include: a classic (older) and a contemporary reading; a 'negative' and 'positive' attitude; two contrasting viewpoints; coverage of major issues; and so on. A short introduction is provided to contextualize the pieces, allowing them to be read as standalone pieces, although they are often main texts discussed in the corresponding chapter in the Core Text. It should also be noted that in addition to reprints of existing material some new works, including some specially commissioned for this Reader, are included.

Second, it has generally been our aim to present the texts as they are found in the original, so no attempt has been made to harmonize spellings (e.g. between British and American English) or the use of foreign words.

However, to some extent they have been reformatted into a 'house style', which means that the numbers of footnotes have changed (being ordered numerically within our chapters), some diacritics (the accents used on foreign words, especially Sanskrit terms) have been simplified, and the layouts have changed – otherwise the book would have appeared a mess with a range of different formats throughout.

Finally, while the main body sections of the Core Text and the Reader are the same, some differences will be found. First, the Reader does not contain sections that correspond to Chapters 1 and 2 of the Core Text (theological concerns and the typology – i.e. the very use of the terms exclusivist, inclusivist, pluralist, etc.) as these are very much 'setting the scene' chapters: the reader is therefore directed to the Core Text for information on these. However, the Reader contains two new chapters, 15 and 16, which broaden the discussion, being responses from those of other faiths to Christian interpretations and the Christian tradition. This is divided into two parts: responses from Abrahamic faiths (Judaism and Islam); and those of 'Eastern' faith traditions (due to limitations of space only Hindu and Buddhist responses are included). These include both direct responses on how Christianity has interpreted their faith, as well as meditations on the person of Jesus from within these faith traditions – which represents a different style of response to Christianity. It was considered important to include this section, as we live in a world where the Christian cannot simply find and interpret the religious other, but must be in interaction with them as responsive traditions, and individuals within traditions, who do and will speak back and interpret the Christian.

We will end with the same words that concluded the Core Text as they express very well our attitude:

> It is our belief that it is imperative that Christians come to realize the very real importance of how Christian faith might respond creatively to our world's religious plurality through theological reflection as well as inter-religious engagement. Our hope is that this book will stimulate involvement in all aspects of the new world which is opening up before us all.

Paul Hedges and Alan Race

Chapter Editors

K. P. Aleaz is Professor of Religions at Bishop's College as well as Professor and Dean of the Doctoral Programme at North India Institute of Post-Graduate Theological Studies, Kolkata, India. He guides doctoral candidates of South Asia Theological Research Institute, Bangalore, India, as well. Author of 20 books and more than 105 articles, he was William Patton Fellow of the Selly Oak Colleges, Birmingham, in 1977, Visiting Professor at Hartford Seminary, USA, as well as the University of South Africa, Pretoria, in 2002, and Teape Lecturer, in the Universities of Cambridge, Birmingham, Bristol and Edinburgh, UK, in 2005.

David Cheetham is Senior Lecturer in Theology and Religion at the University of Birmingham, UK, and specializes in the philosophy and theology of religions. He is the author of *John Hick* (2003) and numerous articles in journals including the *Heythrop Journal, Sophia, New Blackfriars* and *Theology*. He is currently completing a new book entitled *Ways of Meeting and the Theology of Religions*.

Elizabeth Harris is Senior Lecturer in Religious Studies at Liverpool Hope University, with a specialism in Buddhism. Previously, for 11 years, she was the Secretary for Inter-Faith Relations for the Methodist Church in Britain. She is on the advisory group of the European Network of Buddhist–Christian Studies and of Voies d'Orient, Belgium. She has written widely on Buddhist–Christian Relations, and her recent books include *Theravada Buddhism and the British Encounter* (2006) and *What Buddhists Believe* (1996). She is a Reviews Editor for the journal *Interreligious Insight*.

Paul Hedges is a Senior Lecturer at the University of Winchester, UK, and has taught for other British, Canadian and Chinese universities. Publications include *Preparation and Fulfilment* (2001), *SCM Core Text Christian Approaches to Other Faiths* (2008, with Alan Race), and *Controversies in Interfaith Dialogue and the Theology of Religions* (2010). He is on the editorial board of the *Journal of Religious History*. He researches and teaches widely in such areas as: theologies of religions and interreligious theologies; histories of religious encounter; interreligious ethics; modern and contemporary Christian thought; definitions of religion; death and religion; Buddhism; Chinese religion; sacred place and pilgrimage.

Jeannine Hill Fletcher is an Associate Professor of Theology at Fordham University, Bronx, New York. Her research asks whether and how women's interfaith encounters offer new resources for theology. Publications include: *Monopoly on Salvation? A Feminist Response to Religious Pluralism* (2005); 'As Long as We Wonder: Possibilities in the Impossibility of Interreligious Dialogue', *Theological Studies* 68 (2007); 'Women's Voices in Dialogue: A Look at the Parliament of the World's Religions', *Studies in Interreligious Dialogue* 16.1 (2006); and 'Shifting Identity: The Contribution of Feminist Thought to Theologies of Religious Pluralism', *Journal of Feminist Studies in Religion* 19.2 (Fall 2003).

Pan-chiu Lai graduated from the Chinese University of Hong Kong and King's College London (Ph.D., 1991). He is now Professor and Chairman of the Department of Cultural and Religious Studies at the Chinese University of Hong Kong. Research interests include interreligious dialogue, Christian theology and environmental ethics. In addition to publications in Chinese, he published in English *Towards a Trinitarian Theology of Religions: A Study of Paul Tillich's Thought* (1994) and numerous articles in various academic journals. He delivered the Edward Cadbury Lectures 2005/6, Birmingham, UK, on 'Experiments in Mahayana Christian Theology'.

Alan Race is Dean of Postgraduate Studies, St Philip's Centre, and Vicar of St Philip's Church, Leicester, and an Honorary Canon of Leicester Cathedral. He has written two major books, the classic work *Christians and Religious Pluralism: Patterns in the Christian Theology of Religions* (1983 and 1993 revised and enlarged) and *Interfaith Encounter* (2001), and edited several texts, including *Religions in Dialogue*, with Ingrid Shafer (2002). He is Editor-in-Chief of the international journal *Interreligious Insight: A Journal of Dialogue and Engagement*. He has been involved in Christian theological education and training for many years and is also a respected conference speaker around the world.

Perry Schmidt-Leukel earned a doctorate in Buddhist–Christian dialogue (1990), and a habilitation (1996) on the theology of religions (University of Munich). He has taught at the Universities of Munich, Innsbruck, Salzburg, Glasgow and Münster, where he is Professor of Religious Studies and Intercultural Theology. Publications include over 20 books and 100 articles in Buddhist studies, Buddhist–Christian dialogue, Interfaith studies and systematic theology. Recently edited publications include: *War and Peace in World Religions* (2004), *Buddhism and Christianity in Dialogue* (2005), *Understanding Buddhism* (2006), *Islam and Inter-Faith Relations* (2007). A monograph, *God Without Limits*, is forthcoming.

Daniel Strange is Lecturer in Culture, Religion and Public Theology at Oak Hill Theological College, London. His doctoral work (University of Bristol, supervisor: Gavin D'Costa) is published as *The Possibility of Salvation Among the Unevangelised: An Analysis of Inclusivism in Recent Evangelical Theology* (2002). He has published articles and chapters in the area of the theology of religions and systematic theology. He co-edited a series for theology undergraduates, *Keeping Your Balance* (2001); *Getting Your Bearings* (2003) *and Encountering God's Word* (2003), and most recently is co-editing *Engaging with Barth: Contemporary Evangelical Critiques* (2008).

Friedegard Tomasetti is an Honorary Associate of the Department of Studies in Religion at the University of Sydney. He has (with Professor Garry Trompf) published *Religions of Melanesia: A Bibliographic Survey* (2006).

Part One

THEORETICAL AND METHODOLOGICAL RESPONSES

Section A: The 'Classical' Approaches

I

Exclusivisms

DANIEL STRANGE

Introduction

Although inhabiting different times and different academic disciplines, both authors of the following extracts can be located within the Dutch Reformed tradition of Christianity, a confessional community tracing its roots back to the magisterial Reformer, John Calvin. That rare combination of both scholar and practitioner, J. H. Bavinck (1895–1964) served as a missionary in Indonesia for twenty years before occupying the Chair of Missions at the Free University in Amsterdam from 1939 until his death in 1965. For many years his *Introduction to the Science of Mission* was the standard textbook for students of missiology. Presented here is a short chapter in his posthumous book, *The Church between Temple and Mosque* (based on lectures he gave in 1962 to students at an American university), and typical of Bavinck's style: impressionistic and suggestive rather than scholastic; and highlighting both his total commitment to biblical authority and also insights from psychology, a discipline which especially fascinated him. For exclusivists, Romans 1.18–32 has always been a seminal text, and here Bavinck gives us his own exegesis of this passage as it pertains to human religion in God's sight.

Alvin Plantinga (1932–), Professor of Philosophy at the University of Notre Dame, is arguably the most significant and influential analytic philosopher of religion of the last 50 years. He is especially known for his work within epistemology on the subject of 'warrant' (published in a trilogy: *Warrant: The Current Debate* (1993); *Warrant and Proper Function* (1993); and *Warranted Christian Belief* (2000)), his 'freewill defence' concerning the problem of evil, and his 'evolutionary argument against naturalism'. The extract presented here is a part of a longer essay that both defends exclusivism from its 'cultured despisers' and also critiques the self-referential incoherence of pluralism, arguing 'that exclusivism need not involve either epistemic or moral failure and that furthermore something like it is wholly unavoidable, given our human condition' (p. 195).

5

Human Religion in God's Sight

J. H. BAVINCK

We have looked at the fascinating subject of human religions and examined the questions they reply to. But we must go further – we must evaluate what we have found. How must we judge these human religions? Are they merely human fantasy or is there something of God in them? Have these pagan peoples – as we call them – truly searched in their own way for God, or is their religion essentially rebellion against God and a flight from God? Once again many questions arise which must be answered.

The first thing we must do now is listen. So far we have simply looked around and reflected, but now it is necessary to listen to what God says. By merely reasoning we cannot obtain a clear view only God himself can judge all this human religion correctly [sic]. Missionaries from all over the world have become more and more convinced of this since the Conference of Tambaram. We can no longer go by human impressions, and we have learned to begin to listen reverently to God's Word. Hendrik Kraemer, in his books *The Christian Message in a Non-Christian World* and *Religion and the Christian Faith*, strongly advocates listening intelligently, and during the last ten years many other authors have followed his example. When listening to God's Word, we want to formulate our findings very briefly. Within the scope of this study it is not possible to deal with all the Bible texts that speak of human religion. We shall therefore confine ourselves to discussing Romans 1, because a further reflection on what is said there will make the points we want to examine clearer to us.

The best way to proceed is to look at the part where Paul speaks of human religion, and examine it verse by verse. Paul is speaking here of the power of the gospel. In verse 17 he says: 'For therein is revealed a righteousness of God from faith to faith.' Then he goes on in verse 18: 'For the wrath of God is revealed from heaven against all ungodliness and unrighteousness of men, who hinder the truth in unrighteousness.' The New English Bible has the following: 'For we see divine retribution revealed from heaven and falling upon all the godless wickedness of men. In their wickedness they are stifling the truth.'

Several thoughts demand our attention. In the first place, it is obvious that Paul wants to say that God evidently deals with man already in this world and that He retaliates for evil. The Apostle returns to this idea several times later on. In the same chapter he says three times over that 'God gave them up' (vv. 24, 26, 28), that is to say, God gave them up to the dynamics of their own sinful train of thought. That is the divine retribution which Paul discusses in his epistle.

Our second thought concerns the Apostle's statement concerning hindering the truth. In the Greek language St. Paul uses the word *katechein*, literally, 'To keep down.' The King James Version translates it by 'hold,' the New English Bible by 'stifle.' It seems to me that in this case we should translate it by 'repress.' We intentionally choose a word which has a specific meaning in psychological literature. Webster's New Collegiate Dictionary defines the word 'repression' as 'the process by which unacceptable desires or impulses are excluded from consciousness and thus being denied direct satisfaction are left to operate in the unconscious.' This seems to agree with what Paul says here about human life. But we must mention that the word repression has received a wider meaning in more recent psychology.

In Freudian psychology it specifically refers to unconscious desires of a more or less sexual nature. In more recent psychology it is also applied to desires and impulses of a very different nature. The impulses or desires which are repressed may be very valuable. Anything that goes contrary to the accepted patterns of life or to the predominant popular ideas may be repressed. Usually this happens unconsciously; a person does not even know that he is doing it; but it does happen and the results can be far-reaching. We are reminded of this psychological phenomenon recently discovered by Paul's usage of this word. He says that man always naturally represses God's truth because it is contrary to his pattern of life.

Man's wickedness prevents this truth from reaching him; he automatically represses it. In verse 19 the Apostle goes on to say: ' ... because that which is known of God is manifest in them; for God manifested it unto them.' We must observe that the words 'manifest in them' cannot mean that man really sees and understands this. The New English Bible has: 'lies plain before their eyes.' This seems more correct. Whether man comes indeed as far as seeing it is another matter. It is possible that man does not see it because it is automatically repressed, as a rule. Verse 20 has an elaboration on the preceding thought. It shows that what was summed up in verse 19 as 'that which is known of God' can be described as 'His everlasting power and divinity.' These two words are of great importance. The history of religion shows that man seems to be uncertain as to whether God is a 'he' or and 'it' – a person or a power. In primitive religions we observe a distinction between animistic tendencies, which regard all supernatural things as persons, and dynamistic tendencies, which regard them as magical powers.

Therefore it is very instructive that Paul mentions these two things here – the power and the godhead. It seems that he immediately wants to preclude every attempt to reduce God to a mere impersonal power; but at the same time he wants to preclude every attempt to make him a 'High God,' far away in unreachable regions, without any influence on our daily life. Paul says: Through all centuries the fact that God is both a person to whom we can pray and to whom we are responsible, and also everlasting power, forces itself naturally upon man.

These two characteristics of God are 'clearly seen, being perceived through the things that are made.' The New English Bible has: 'have been visible to the eye of reason.' We prefer 'being intelligently observed,' does not refer to seeing with the eyes in this case [*sic*], but neither does it mean that 'seeing God's everlasting power and godhead' is attained by a process of reasoning. It is not a logical conclusion, but a flash that comes in a moment of vision. It comes suddenly to man, it overwhelms him. But still it does not lead to knowledge. Man escapes God's grasp, man represses the truth. Therefore he is 'without excuse.' Verse 21 repeats that man must in fact be regarded as one who knows: 'knowing God, they glorified him not as God, neither gave thanks.' In the day of judgment man cannot claim that he did not know God. He knows God, even though he never comes to real knowledge because he is always busy subtly repressing this knowledge. Man desperately clings to his own egocentric pattern of life. As a result man went further and further astray: 'all their thinking has ended in futility, and their misguided minds are plunged in darkness.' In this connection the Apostle thinks of the pagan religions as he has seen them for himself, with their statues, superstitions, and infatuation. He does not mean to say that these people have consciously or intentionally reflected God's truth.

Generally speaking, they do this unconsciously and unintentionally, but they are nevertheless guilty. The aerial of man's heart can no longer receive the wave length of God's voice, even though it surrounds him on all sides. But in his innermost heart man has turned away from God and now God has vanished out of his sight.

The next part shows what is the result of this attitude. It is remarkable that the Apostle uses the verb 'exchange' (Greek *allasso* or *met'allasso*) three times. In doing this he once again touches upon one of those very remarkable phenomena which recent psychology has pointed out. This phenomenon of replacing, of substituting, is so common that we see it everywhere. It has been discovered that these repressed impulses of which we spoke, which 'are left to operate in the unconscious,' are not dead. They remain strong, and try to reassert themselves again and again. Surely, they play no part in man's conscious life, but they succeed in showing every now and again that they still exist. This has been illustrated by the story of the boy sent out of class at school who kept on throwing stones against the windows of the school to show that he was still there. Freud particularly has called attention to this phenomenon and inaugurated its study. He noticed that the impulses which have been exiled to the unconscious may very well reveal themselves in the errors we make, in our slips of the tongue. But they especially crop up in dreams, for then they get the chance to come to the surface. This does not mean that they appear openly in dreams. The mind retains a certain censorship which causes them to appear only, or at least preferably, disguisedly. Here the process of exchange or substitution comes into the picture. The repressed impulses do come to the surface, but in a changed form, a substituted form. For example, a person may dream about his father but when analyzing the dream he realizes that a sexual inclination or relation lies at the bottom of it, something which he would be ashamed to tell his wife. In dreams things have a distorted form; a certain disguise and exchange takes place. Often symbolic figures appear in dreams which point back to what exists in the unconscious. Therefore psychoanalysis attaches much value to dreams, and they are often used to trace the deeper tendencies, the impulses in exile.

It seems to me that Paul touches upon these things. Man has repressed the truth of the everlasting power and the divinity of God. It has been exiled to his unconscious, to the crypts of his existence. That does not mean, however, that it has vanished forever. Still active, it reveals itself again and again. But it cannot become openly conscious; it appears in disguise, and it is exchanged for something different. Thus all kinds of ideas of God are formed; the human mind as the *fabrica idolorum* (Calvin) makes its own ideas of God and its own myths.

This is not intentional deceit – it happens without man's knowing it. He cannot get rid of them. So he has religion; he is busy with a god; he serves his god – but he does not see that the god he serves is not God Himself. An exchange has taken place – a perilous exchange. An essential quality of God has been blurred because it did not fit in with the human pattern of life, and the image man has of God is no longer true. Divine revelation indeed lies at the root of it, but man's thoughts and aspirations cannot receive it and adapt themselves to it. In the image man has of God we can recognize the image of man himself.

We have already mentioned that the result was that God gave them up. This is said three times in this short passage. In verse 24 we read that God gave them up to the vileness of their own desires and the consequent degradation of their bodies. In verse 26 this is repeated in the words: 'God gave them up unto vile passions.' And in verse 28 the Apostle adds that God gave them up unto a reprobate mind. They could no longer resist the powers within which carried them along. Paul no doubt saw in his days abundant proof of this in the degenerated way of life of the Hellenistic world; he saw what man comes to when God gives him up to his desires and passions. He also saw that mythical religion has no weapon against this degeneration. He had learned what happens when man exchanges the true image of God for all kinds of myths. This weakens man's ethical strength because consciously or unconsciously he then forms an idol according to his own liking.

This in summary is what Paul says in this passage regarding natural man's tendencies and inclinations since the beginning of time. The history of religion illustrates this most convincingly. Now there are still a few points which demand our attention.

(1) It is clear that this passage teaches unmistakably that there is a general revelation. Hendrik Kraemer calls the idea 'general revelation' a 'mislead-

ing term.' He says: 'The whole concept, in its ordinary use, is tainted by all kinds of notions, which are contrary to the way in which the Bible speaks of revelation.'[1] This may be true. The cause, no doubt, is that the concept has been used too often in a philosophical sense. Too often it has been taken for granted that man's reason could lead him to develop a certain natural theology. But the revelation of which Paul speaks in this passage is entirely different. He does not have in mind philosophical conclusions of the human mind nor infantile natural theology. The Bible emphasizes God's everlasting concern for man. We read that God 'left not himself without a witness' (Acts 14:17). Time and again man knows that God exists and that man is actually confronted with Him; yet each time man suppresses these convictions and flees from them. But God still concerns Himself with man in a very concrete and personal way. We cannot explain how God does this. In Romans Paul speaks about the invisible characteristics of God which He manifests in the things He made. In Acts 14 he mentions the rain and fruitful seasons and the gladness with which He fills our hearts. But much more can be said about this. God has created the first year of man in such a way that during his life as a small child he finds peace and safety only in the protecting and sustaining nearness of his mother, and thus He gives a father and mother something of His own image which they retain in later years. God meets man in storm and thunder as well as in the radiant beauty of a glorious summer morning. God occupies Himself with man's conscience, his innermost being. God reminds him again that responsibility and guilt do exist. Who can trace the hidden ways by which God proves His existence to man? God has His own hidden means of approaching man.

(2)   This explains the existence of phenomenon-religion. The man who believes in gods and spirits and bows before his idols shows that he is touched by God and that God is seeking him. But he shows at the same time that he himself is busy suppressing that which is absolutely necessary for a person to come to God. His image of God is distorted; something essential to it is eliminated from it. He does not do this intentionally, but, all the same, he is without excuse. He received his image of God from his parents; he grew up with the religion to which he adheres. That may be true of course, but his religious life contains also something very personal, something belonging only to him – while seeking God earnestly he at the same time tries to escape from Him. His religion is always ambiguous, full of hesitation and discrepancies. In the first chapter we stated that religion, by its very nature, is a response. It is never man seeking and speaking spontaneously; it is always an answer on his part to something that he feels as a revelation. We must now add that all the great religions in history are man's answer embodying this mysterious process of repression. We can show this concretely. In the night of the *bodhi* when Buddha received his great, new insight concerning the world and life, God was touching him and struggling with him. God revealed Himself in that moment. Buddha responded to this

revelation, and his answer to this day reveals God's hand and the result of human repression. In the 'night of power' of which the ninety-seventh sura of the Koran speaks, the night when 'the angels descended' and the Koran descended from Allah's throne, God dealt with Mohammed and touched him. God wrestled with him in that night, and God's hand is still noticeable in the answer of the prophet, but it is also the result of human repression. The great moments in the history of religion are the moments when God wrestled with man in a very particular way. The history of religion contains a dramatic element. It includes the divine approach and human rejection. This rejection is hidden because man apparently is seeking God and serving Him, but the God he seeks is different from the true God because of the uncanny process of repression and exchange that enters in. It seems to me that we can thus formulate the testimony of the Bible concerning human religions.

(3) If this is true, it seems to me that we can make certain distinctions. We can say that natural man is ever busy repressing or exchanging. But does he always succeed to the same degree? That depends on the strength with which God approaches him. God can at times, as it were, stop the noiseless engines of repression and exchange and overwhelm man to such an extent that he is powerless for the moment. There is, also, always the silent activity of the Holy Spirit inside man, even if he resists Him constantly. The way in which Isaiah speaks of Cyrus, the anointed one, who was called by His name and girded by God (Is. 45:4, 5), indicates that the Bible certainly leaves the possibility open for God to anoint those who do not know Him with His Spirit and to gird them for certain tasks to which He calls them. This shows that there are gradations in the history of religion. We always encounter the powers of repression and exchange, but that does not mean that they were always of the same nature and strength. We meet figures in the history of non-Christian religions of whom we feel that God wrestled with them in a very particular way. We still notice traces of that process of suppression and substitution in the way they responded, but occasionally we observe a far greater influence of God there than in many other human religions. The history of religion is not always and everywhere the same; it does not present a monotonous picture of only folly and degeneration. There are culminating points in it, not because certain human beings are much better than others, but because every now and then divine compassion interferes, compassion which keeps man from suppressing and substituting the truth completely.

(4) A final remark we must make in this connection is that this is very important for the fulfillment of the missionary task. When a missionary or some other person comes into contact with a non-Christian and speaks to him about the gospel, he can be sure that God has concerned Himself with this person long before. That person had dealings more than once with God before God touched him, and he himself experienced the two fatal

reactions – suppression and substitution. Now he hears the gospel for the first time. As I have said elsewhere, 'We do not open the discussion, but we need only to make it clear that the God who has revealed His eternal power and Godhead to them, now addresses them in a new way, through our words.' The encounter between God and that man enters a new period. It becomes more dangerous, but also more hopeful. Christ now appears in a new form to him. He was, of course, already present in this man's seeking; and, because He did not leave Himself without a witness, Christ was wrestling to gain him, although he did not know it. John describes this in a most delicate way: the Logos 'lighteth every man' and 'the light shineth in the darkness; and the darkness comprehendeth it not' (John 1:9, 5). In the preaching of the gospel Christ once again appears to man, but much more concretely and in audible form. He awakes man from his long, disastrous dream. At last suppression and substitution cease – but this is possible only in a faithful surrender.

Note

1 Hendrick Kraemer, 1956, *Religion and the Christian Faith*, London: Lutterworth Press, p. 341.

Source: J. H. Bavinck, 1965, *The Church between Temple and Mosque*, Grand Rapids, MI: Eerdmans (pp. 117–28, Chapter 9).

Pluralism: A Defence of Religious Exclusivism

ALVIN PLANTINGA

When I was a graduate student at Yale, the philosophy department prided itself on diversity: and it was indeed diverse. There were idealists, pragmatists, phenomenologists, existentialists, Whiteheadians, historians of philosophy, a token positivist, and what could only be described as observers of the passing intellectual scene. In some ways, this was indeed something to take pride in; a student could behold and encounter real live representatives of many of the main traditions in philosophy. It also had an unintended and unhappy side effect, however. If anyone raised a philosophical question inside, but particularly outside, class, the typical response would be a catalog of some of the various different answers the world has seen: there is the Aristotelian answer, the existentialist answer, the Cartesian answer, Heidegger's answer; perhaps the Buddhist answer; and so on. But the question 'what is the truth about this matter?' was often greeted with disdain as unduly naive. There are all these different answers, all endorsed by people of great intellectual power and great dedication to philosophy; for every argument *for* one of these positions, there is another *against* it: would it not be excessively naive, or perhaps arbitrary, to suppose that one of these is in fact *true*, the others being false? Or, if there really is a truth of the matter, so that one of them is true and conflicting ones false, wouldn't it be merely arbitrary, in the face of this embarrassment of riches, to *endorse* one of them as the truth, consigning the others to falsehood? How could you possibly know which was true?

Some urge a similar attitude with respect to the impressive variety of religions the world displays. There are theistic religions but also at least some nontheistic religions (or perhaps nontheistic strands of religion) among the enormous variety of religions going under the names 'Hinduism' and 'Buddhism'; among the theistic religions, there are strands of Hinduism and Buddhism and American Indian religion as well as Islam, Judaism, and Christianity; and all these differ significantly from one another. Isn't it somehow arbitrary, or irrational, or unjustified, or unwarranted, or even oppressive and imperialistic to endorse one of these as opposed to all the others? According to Jean Bodin, 'each is refuted by all';[1] must we not agree? It is in this neighborhood that the so-called problem of pluralism arises. Of course, many concerns and problems can come under this rubric; the specific problem I mean to discuss can be thought of as follows. To put it in an internal and personal way, I find myself with religious beliefs, and religious beliefs that I realize aren't shared by nearly everyone else. For example, I believe both

(1)   The world was created by God, an almighty, all-knowing, and perfectly good personal being (one that holds beliefs; has aims, plans, and intentions; and can act to accomplish these aims)

and

(2)   Human beings require salvation, and God has provided a unique way of salvation through the incarnation, life, sacrificial death, and resurrection of his divine son.

Now there are many who do not believe these things. First, there are those who agree with me on (1) but not (2): there are non-Christian theistic religions. Second, there are those who don't accept either (1) or (2) but nonetheless do believe that there is something beyond the natural world, a something such that human well-being and salvation depend upon standing in a right relation to it. And third, in the West and since the Enlightenment, anyway, there are people – *naturalists*, we may call them – who don't believe any of these three things. And my problem is this: when I become really aware of these other ways of looking at the world, these other ways of responding religiously to the world, what must or should I do? What is the right sort of attitude to take? What sort of impact should this awareness have on the beliefs I hold and the strength with which I hold them? My question is this: how should I think about the great religious diversity the world in fact displays? Can I sensibly remain an adherent of just one of these religions, rejecting the others? And here I am thinking specifically of *beliefs*. Of course, there is a great deal more to any religion or religious practice than just belief, and I don't for a moment mean to deny it. But belief is a crucially important part of most religions; it is a crucially important part of *my* religion; and the question I mean to ask here is what the awareness of religious diversity means or should mean for my religious beliefs.

Some speak here of a new awareness of religious diversity, and speak of this new awareness as constituting (for us in the West) a crisis, a revolution, an intellectual development of the same magnitude as the Copernican revolution of the sixteenth century and the alleged discovery of evolution and our animal origins in the nineteenth.[2] No doubt there is at least some truth to this. Of course, the fact is all along many Western Christians and Jews have known that there are other religions and that not nearly everyone shares their religion.[3] The ancient Israelites – some of the prophets, say – were clearly aware of Canaanitish religion; and the apostle Paul said that he preached 'Christ crucified, a stumbling block to Jews and folly to the Greeks' (I Cor. 1:23). Other early Christians, the Christian martyrs, say, must have suspected that not everyone believed as they did. The church fathers, in offering defenses of Christianity, were certainly apprised of this fact; Origen, indeed, wrote an eight-volume reply to Celsus, who urged an argument similar to those put forward by contemporary pluralists. Aquinas, again, was clearly aware of those to whom he addresses the *Summa contra gentiles*, and the fact that there are non-Christian religions would have come as no surprise to the Jesuit missionaries of the sixteenth and seventeenth centuries or to the Methodist missionaries of the nineteenth. In more recent times, when I was a child, *The Banner*, the official publication of the Christian reformed Church, contained a small section for children; it was written by 'Uncle Dick', who exhorted us to save our nickels and send them to our Indian cousins at the Navaho mission in New Mexico. Both we and our elders knew that the Navahos had or had had a religion different from Christianity, and part of the point of sending the nickels was to rectify that situation.

Still, in recent years probably more of us Western Christians have become aware of the world's religious diversity, we have probably learned more about people of other religious persuasions, and we have come to see more clearly that they display what looks like real piety, devoutness, and spirituality. What is new, perhaps, is a more widespread sympathy for other religions, a tendency to see them as more valuable, as containing more by way of truth, and a new feeling of solidarity with their practitioners.

There are several possible reactions to awareness of religious diversity. One is to continue to believe what you have all along believed; you learn about this diversity but continue to believe, that is, take to be true, such propositions as (1) and (2) above, consequently taking to be false any beliefs, religious or otherwise, that are incompatible with (1) and (2). Following current practice, I call this *exclusivism*; the exclusivist holds that the tenets or some of the tenets of one religion – Christianity, let's say – are in fact true; he adds, naturally enough, that any propositions, including other religious beliefs, that are incompatible with those tenets are false. Now there is a fairly widespread belief that there is something seriously wrong with exclusivism. It is irrational, or egotistical and unjustified,[4] or intellectually arrogant,[5] or elitist,[6] or a manifestation of harmful pride,[7] or even oppressive and imperialistic.[8] The claim is that exclusivism as such is or involves a vice of some sort: it is wrong or deplorable; and it is this claim I want to examine. I propose to argue that exclusivism need not involve either epistemic or moral failure and that furthermore something like it is wholly unavoidable, given our human condition.

These objections are not to the *truth* of (1) or (2) or any other proposition someone might accept in this exclusivist way (although, of course, objections of that sort are also put forward); they are instead directed to the *propriety* or *rightness* of exclusivism. And there are initially two different kinds of indictments of exclusivism: broadly moral or ethical indictments and broadly intellectual or epistemic indictments. These overlap in interesting ways, as we shall see below. But initially, anyway, we can take some of the complaints about exclusivism as *intellectual* criticisms: it is *irrational* or *unjustified* to think in an exclusivistic way. And the other large body of complaint is moral: there is something morally suspect about exclusivism: it is arbitrary, or intellectually arrogant, or imperialistic. As Joseph Runzo suggests, exclusivism is 'neither tolerable nor any longer intellectually honest in the context of our contemporary knowledge of other faiths.'[9] I want to consider both kinds of claims or criticisms; I propose to argue that the exclusivist is not as such necessarily guilty of any of these charges.

Moral Objections to Exclusivism

I first turn to the moral complaints: that the exclusivist is intellectually arrogant, or egotistical, or self-servingly arbitrary or dishonest, or imperialistic, or oppressive. But first three qualifications. An exclusivist, like anyone else, will probably be guilty of some or all of these things to at least some degree, perhaps particularly the first two; the question is, however, whether she is guilty of these things just by virtue of being an exclusivist. Second, I shall use the term 'exclusivism' in such a way that you don't count as an exclusivist unless you are rather fully aware of other faiths, have had their existence and their claims called to your attention with some force and perhaps fairly frequently, and have to some degree reflected on the problem of pluralism, asking yourself such questions as whether it is or could be really true that the Lord has revealed himself and his programs to us Christians, say, in a way in which he hasn't revealed himself to those of other faiths. Thus my grandmother, for example, would not have counted as an exclusivist. She had, of course, *heard* of the heathen, as she called them, but the idea that perhaps Christians could learn from them, and learn from them with respect to religious matters, had not so much as entered her head; and the fact that it *hadn't* entered her head, I take it, was not a matter of moral dereliction on her part. The same would go for a Buddhist or Hindu peasant. These people are not, I think, plausibly charged with arrogance or other moral flaws in believing as they do. Third, suppose I am an exclusivist with respect to (1), for example, but nonculpably believe, like Thomas Aquinas, say that I proposition that there is such a person as God; and suppose I think further (and nonculpably) that if those who don't believe (1) were to be apprised of this argument (and had the ability and training necessary to grasp it, and were to think about the argument fairly and reflectively), they too would come to believe (1). Then I could hardly be charged with these moral faults. My condition would be like that of Gödel, let's say, upon having recognized that he had a proof for the incompleteness of arithmetic. True, many of his colleagues and peers didn't believe that arithmetic was incomplete, and some believed that it *was* complete; but presumably Gödel wasn't arbitrary or egotistical in believing that arithmetic is in fact incomplete. Furthermore, he would not have been at fault had he nonculpably but *mistakenly* believed that he had found such a proof. Accordingly, I shall use the term 'exclusivist' in such a way that you don't count as an exclusivist if you nonculpably think you know of a demonstration or conclusive argument for the beliefs with respect to which you are an exclusivist, or even if you nonculpably think you know of an argument that would convince all or most intelligent and honest people of the truth of that proposition. So an exclusivist, as I use the term, not only believes something like (1) or (2) and thinks false any proposition incompatible with it; she also meets a further condition C that is hard to state precisely and in detail (and in fact any attempt to do so would involve a long and at present irrelevant discussion of ceteris paribus clauses).[10] Suffice it to say that C includes (1) being rather fully aware of other religions, (2) knowing that there is much that at the least looks like genuine piety and devoutness in them, and (3) believing that you know of no arguments that would necessarily convince all or most honest and intelligent dissenters of your own religious allegiances.

Given these qualifications, then, why should we think that an exclusivist is properly charged with these moral faults? I shall deal first and most briefly with charges of oppression and imperialism: I think we must say that they are on the face of it wholly implausible. I daresay there are some among you who reject some of the things I believe; I do not believe that you are thereby oppressing me, even if you do not believe you have an argument that would convince me. It is conceivable that exclusivism might in some way *contribute to* oppression, but it isn't in itself oppressive.

The important moral charge is that there is a sort of self-serving arbitrariness, an arrogance or egotism, in accepting such propositions as (1) or (2) under condition C; exclusivism is guilty of some serious moral fault or flaw. According to Wilfred Cantwell Smith, 'except at the cost of insensitivity or delinquency it is morally not possible actually to go out into the world and say to devout, intelligent, fellow human beings: "... we believe that we know God and we are right; you believe that you know God, and you are totally wrong".'[11]

So what can the exclusivist have to say for herself? Well, it must be conceded immediately that if she believes (1) or (2), then she must also believe that those who believe something incompatible with them are mistaken and believe what is false. That's no more than simple logic. Furthermore, she must also believe that those who do not believe as she does – those who believe neither (1) nor (2) whether or not they believe their negations – *fail* to believe something that is true, deep, and important, and that she *does* believe. She must therefore see herself as *privileged* with respect to those others – those others of both kinds. There is something of great value, she must think, that *she* has and *they* lack. They are ignorant of something – something of great importance – of which she has knowledge. But does this make her properly subject to the above censure?

I think the answer must be no. Or if the answer is yes, then I think we have here a genuine moral dilemma; for in our earthly life here below, as my Sunday School teacher used to say, there is no real alternative; there is no reflective attitude that is not open to the same strictures. These charges of arrogance are a philosophical tar baby: get close enough to them to use them against the exclusivist, and you are likely to find them stuck fast to yourself. How so? Well, as an exclusivist, I realize I can't convince others that they should believe as I do, but I nonetheless continue to believe as I do: and the charge is that I am as a result arrogant or egotistical, arbitrarily preferring my way of doing things to other ways.[12] But what are my alternatives with respect to a proposition like (1)? There seem to be three choices.[13] I can continue to hold it; I can withhold it, in Roderick Chisholm's sense, believing neither it nor its denial; and I can accept its denial. Consider the third way, a way taken by those pluralists who, like John Hick, hold that such propositions as (1) and (2) and their colleagues from other faiths are literally false although in some way still valid responses to the Real. This seems to me to be no advance at all with respect to the arrogance or egotism problem; this is not a way out. For if I do this, I will then be in the very same condition as I am now: I will believe many propositions others don't believe and will be in condition C with respect to those propositions. For I will then believe the denials of (1) and (2) (as well as the denials of many other propositions explicitly accepted by those of other faiths). Many others, of course, do not believe the denials of (1) and (2), and in fact believe (1) and (2). Further, I will not know of any arguments that can be counted on to persuade those who do believe (1) or (2) (or propositions accepted by the adherents of other religions). I am therefore in the condition of believing propositions that many others do not believe and furthermore am in condition C. If, in the case of those who believe (1) and (2), that is sufficient for intellectual arrogance or egotism, the same goes for those who believe their denials.

So consider the second option: I can instead *withhold* the proposition in question. I can say to myself: 'the right course here, given that I can't or couldn't convince these others of what *I* believe, is to believe neither these propositions nor their denials.' The pluralist objector to exclusivism can say that the right course under condition C, is to *abstain* from believing the offending proposition and also abstain from believing its denial; call him, therefore, 'the abstemious pluralist'. But does he thus really avoid the condition that, on the part of the exclusivist, leads to the charges of egotism and arrogance? Think, for a moment, about disagreement. Disagreement, fundamentally, is a matter of adopting conflicting propositional attitudes with respect to a given proposition. In the simplest and most familiar case, I disagree with you if there is some proposition P such that I believe P and you believe -P. But that's just the simplest case: there are also others. The one that is at present of interest is this: I believe P and you withhold it, fail to believe it. Call the first kind of disagreement 'contradicting'; call the second 'dissenting'.

My claim is that if contradicting others (under the condition C spelled out above) is arrogant and egotistical, so is dissenting (under that same condition). For suppose you believe some proposition P but I don't: perhaps you believe it is wrong to discriminate against people simply on the grounds of race, but I, recognizing that there are many people who disagree with you, do not believe this proposition. I don't disbelieve it either, of course, but in the circumstances I think the right thing to do is to abstain from belief. Then am I not implicitly condemning your attitude, your *believing* the proposition, as somehow improper – naive, perhaps, or unjustified, or in some other way less than optimal? I am implicitly saying that my attitude is the superior one; I think my course of action here is the right one and yours somehow wrong, inadequate, improper, in the circumstances at best second-rate. Also, I realize that there is no question, here, of *showing* you that your attitude is wrong or improper or naive; so am I not guilty of intellectual arrogance? Of a sort of egotism, thinking I know better than you, arrogating to myself a privileged status with respect to you? The problem for the exclusivist was that she was obliged to think she possessed a truth missed by many others; the problem for the abstemious pluralist is that he is obliged to think he possesses a virtue others don't, or acts rightly where others don't. If, in condition C, one is arrogant by way of believing a proposition others don't, isn't one equally, under those reflective conditions, arrogant by way of withholding a proposition others don't?

Perhaps you will respond by saying that the abstemious pluralist gets into trouble, falls into arrogance, by way of implicitly saying or believing that his way of proceeding is *better* or *wiser* than other ways pursued by other people, and perhaps he can escape by abstaining from *that* view as well. Can't he escape the problem by refraining from believing that racial bigotry is wrong, and also refraining from holding the view that it is *better*, under the conditions that obtain, to withhold that proposition than to assert and believe it? Well, yes, he can; then he has no *reason* for his abstention; he doesn't believe that abstention is better or more appropriate; he simply does abstain. Does this get him off the egotistical hook? Perhaps. But then, of course, he can't, in consistency, also hold that there is something wrong with *not* abstaining, with coming right out and *believing* that bigotry is wrong; he loses his objection to the exclusivist. Accordingly, this way out is not available for the abstemious pluralist who accuses the exclusivist of arrogance and egotism.

Indeed, I think we can show that the abstemious pluralist who brings charges of intellectual arrogance against exclusivism is hoist with his own petard, holds a position that in a certain way is self-referentially inconsistent in the circumstances. For he believes

(3) If S knows that others don't believe p and that he is in condition C with respect to p, then S should not believe p.

This or something like it is the ground of the charges he brings against the exclusivist. But, the abstemious pluralist realizes that many do not accept (3); and I suppose he also realizes that it is unlikely that he can find arguments for (3) that will convince them; hence he knows that he is in condition C. Given his acceptance of (3), therefore, the right course for him is to abstain from believing (3). Under the conditions that do in fact obtain – namely his knowledge that others don't accept it and that condition C obtains – he can't properly accept it.

I am therefore inclined to think that one can't, in the circumstances, properly hold (3) or any other proposition that will do the job. One can't find here some principle on the basis of which to hold that the exclusivist is doing the wrong thing, suffers from some moral fault – that is, one can't find such a principle that doesn't, as we might put it, fall victim to itself.

So the abstemious pluralist is hoist with his own petard; but even apart from this dialectical argument (which in any event some will think unduly cute), aren't the charges unconvincing and implausible? I must concede that there are a variety of ways in which I can be and have been intellectually arrogant and egotistic; I have certainly fallen into this vice in the past and no doubt am not free of it now. But am I really arrogant and egotistic just by virtue of believing what I know others don't believe, where I can't show them that I am right? Suppose I think the matter over, consider the objections as carefully as I can, realize that I am finite and furthermore a sinner, certainly no better than those with whom I disagree, and indeed inferior both morally and intellectually to many who do not believe what I do; but suppose it *still* seems clear to me that the proposition in question is true: can I really be behaving immorally in continuing to believe it? I am dead sure that it is wrong to try to advance my career by telling lies about my colleagues; I realize there are those who disagree; I also realize that in all likelihood there is no way I can find to show them that they are wrong; nonetheless, I think they *are* wrong. If I think this after careful reflection – if I consider the claims of those who disagree as sympathetically as I can, if I try level best to ascertain the truth here – and it *still* seems to me sleazy, wrong, and despicable to lie about my colleagues to advance my career, could I really be doing something immoral in continuing to believe as before? I can't see how. If, after careful reflection and thought, you find yourself convinced that the right propositional attitude to take to (1) and (2) in the face of the facts of religious pluralism is abstention from belief, how could you properly be taxed with egotism, either for so believing or for so abstaining? Even if you knew others did not agree with you? So I can't see how the moral charge against exclusivism can be sustained.

Notes

1 *Colloquium Heptaplomeres de rerum sublimium arcanis abditid*, written by 1593 but first published in 1857. English translation by Marion Kuntz (Princeton: Princeton University Press, 1975). The quotation is from the Kuntz translation, p. 256.

2 Thus Joseph Runzo: 'Today the impressive piety and evident rationality of the belief systems of other religious traditions inescapably confronts Christians with a crisis – and a potential revolution,' 'God, Commitment, and Other Faiths: Pluralism vs. Relativism,' *Faith and Philosophy* (October, 1988), 343.

3 As explained in detail in Robert Wilken, 'Religious Pluralism and Early Christian Thought' so far unpublished. Wilken focuses on the third century: he explores Origen's response to Celsus and concludes that there are striking parallels between Origen's historical situation and ours. What is different today, I suspect, is not that Christianity has to confront other religions but that we now call this situation 'religious pluralism'.

4 Thus Gary Gutting: 'Applying these considerations to religious belief, we seem led to the conclusion that, because believers have many epistemic peers who do not share their belief in God ... they have no right to maintain their belief without a justification. If they do so, they are guilty of epistemological egoism.' *Religious Belief and Religious Skepticism* (Notre Dame: University of Notre Dame Press, 1982), p. 90 (but see the following pages for an important qualification).

5 'Here my submission is that on this front the traditional doctrinal position of the Church has in fact militated against its traditional moral position, and has in fact encouraged Christians to approach other men immorally. Christ has taught us humility, but we have approached them with arrogance ... This charge of arrogance is a serious one.' Wilfred Cantwell Smith, *Religious Diversity* (New York: Harper & Row, 1976), p. 13.

6 Runzo, 'Ethically, Religious Exclusivism has the morally repugnant result of making those who have privileged knowledge, or who are intellectually astute, a religious elite, while penalizing those who happen to have no access to the putatively correct religious view, or who are incapable of advanced understanding.' 'God, Commitment, and Other Faiths,' p. 348.

7 'But natural pride, despite its positive contribution to human life, becomes harmful when it is elevated to the level of dogma and is built into the belief system of a religious community. This happens when its sense of its own validity and worth is expressed in doctrines in an exclusive or a decisively superior access to the truth or the power to save,' John Hick, 'Religious Pluralism and Absolute Claims,' in Leroy Rouner, ed., *Religious Pluralism* (Notre Dame: University of Notre Dame Press, 1984), p. 197.

8 Thus John Cobb: 'I agree with the liberal theists that even in Pannenberg's case, the quest for an absolute as a basis for understanding reflects the long tradition of Christian imperialism and triumphalism rather than the pluralistic spirit.' 'The Meaning of Pluralism for Christian Self Understanding,' in Rouner, *Religious Pluralism*, p. 171.

9 'God, Commitment, and Other Faiths,' p. 357.

10 *Ceteris paribus* (Lat.) literally means 'with all other things being equal' and is used in philosophy and elsewhere in relation to assumptions made in claims, statements, etc. (ed.).

11 Smith, *Religious Diversity*, p. 14. A similar statement: 'Nor can we reasonably claim that our own form of religious experience, together with that of the tradition of which we are a part, is veridical whilst others are not. We can of course claim this: and indeed virtually every religious tradition has done so, regarding alternative forms of religion either as false or as confused and inferior versions of itself. Persons living within other traditions, then, are equally justified in trusting their own distinctive religious experience and in forming their beliefs on the basis of it ... let us avoid the implausibly arbitrary dogma that religious experience is all delusory with the single exception of the particular form enjoyed by the one who is speaking.' John Hick, *An Interpretation of Religion* (New Haven: Yale University Press, 1989), p. 235.

12 'The only reason for treating one's tradition differently from others is the very human but not very cogent reason that it is one's own!' Hick, [*An*] *Interpretation of Religion*, p. 235.

13 To speak of choice here suggests that I can simply choose which of these three attitudes to adopt; but is that at all realistic? Are my beliefs to that degree within my control? Here I shall set aside the question whether and to what degree my beliefs are subject to my control and within my power. Perhaps we have very little control over them; then the moral critic of exclusivism can't properly accuse the exclusivist of dereliction of moral duty but he could still argue that the exclusivist's stance is unhappy, bad, a miserable state of affairs. Even if I can't help it that I am overbearing and conceited, my being that way is a bad state of affairs.

Source: Alvin Plantinga, 1995, 'Pluralism: A Defense of Religious Exclusivism', in Thomas D. Senor (ed.), *The Rationality of Belief and the Plurality of Faith*, London: Cornell University Press, pp. 191–215, selection from pp. 191–201.

2

Inclusivisms

DAVID CHEETHAM

Introduction

One of the main challenges that faces inclusivist theologies of religions is how to describe (theologically) the situation or experience of those outside the Christian faith. That is, if the Christian narrative is said to be normative then in what ways can it be said that other traditions are *continuous* with it? In the two readings provided here, both theologians are wrestling with how to give a meaningful account of non-Christian religious experience in light of Christian normativity and, particularly in Amos Yong's case, with how to be meaningful to the non-Christian traditions that are being 'included'.

Karl Rahner (1904–85) was one of the great Roman Catholic theologians of the twentieth century. His thinking on the relationship between Christianity and other religions had an influence on the statements that came out of the Second Vatican Council (1962–5). In this extract, Rahner is expanding on the questions concerning the relationship between anonymous and explicit (i.e. Christian) faith. His thinking emerges out of a unique anthropology that speaks of the 'transcendent character of the human spirit'. Basically, human beings are fundamentally orientated (as an 'inner dynamism') towards God and this forms the background for all human experience whether acknowledged or not. This idea is elaborated further in the extract. Rahner is working out a dogmatic theology (that can later be investigated by an historian of religions *a posteriori*) and his *a priori* concern is to ask how Jesus Christ is present and active in the non-Christian religions. Or, again, what is the relationship between the Holy Spirit that indwells human religion and the Cross as an historical event of grace? As a further extension of his 'anonymous Christians' perspective, Rahner seeks to develop a subtle idea of 'seeking *Memoria*' which he describes as an '*a priori* principle of expectation' within human beings, or a kind of in-built seeking for the 'Absolute Saviour'.

Amos Yong is a Pentecostal theologian who is currently Professor of Systematic Theology at Regent University, Virginia, USA. He has developed a rich and unique theology of religions that concentrates on the working of the Holy Spirit (*pneumatology*). Yong sets up the main problem as a 'Christological impasse'. That is, if Christological categories are given centre-stage in theologies of religions then this means that the theological options are limited and the power to describe the experiences of other religions on their own terms is compromised. Although still fully Trinitarian (and therefore Christological), Yong attempts to outline a theology of religions that concentrates on the distinctive role of the Spirit. In the extract, Yong presents three aspects of a pneumatological theology of religious pluralism: (a) the 'grounding' notion of Acts 2.17 that the Spirit of God is poured out 'upon all flesh'; (b) the idea that a pneumatological approach permits a dynamism towards spiritual experience which moves beyond static notions; (c) an intersubjectivity, facilitated by the Spirit, with regard to religious truth-claims.

Christ in the Non-Christian Religions

KARL RAHNER

The following reflections will deal with this question: What is the exact and concrete meaning of the phrase 'Jesus Christ is present also in non-Christian religions'?[1]

At the very beginning we must make it clear that our approach is not that of a historian or a phenomenologist of religions, but that of a dogmatic theologian. In this field the Christian dogmatic theologian certainly cannot take the place of the historian of religions whose work is done *a posteriori*, whereas the dogmatic theologian's own work is based on the authoritative and binding sources of his faith as unfolded in the Old and New Testaments and even as interpreted by the teaching office of the Church which builds on the Scriptures. These sources, except up to a point the declaration of Vatican II on non-Christian religions, have on the whole been elaborated without direct contact with the majority of non-Christian religions. Therefore the materials supplied by the history of religions which are of importance for our question have never been in any way assimilated. As a consequence these sources, insofar as, from a distance as it were, they deal at all with non-Christian religions, have done so up to now, for understandable reasons, in a somewhat defensive way, stressing rather the differences. Hence on the whole they do not contain much of an answer to our question.

In contrast with the task of the theological historian of religions which is to discover Christ *a posteriori* in non-Christian religions, as far as this is possible, the reflections undertaken here by a dogmatic theologian are *a priori*. They can only serve as a preliminary pointer which may possibly direct and sharpen the searching glance of the historian in his problem, the responsibility for which the dogmatic theologian in no way takes away from him.

Hence our question here is only this: on the basis of dogmatic principles and considerations and prior to a research by the historian of religions, what are the necessary postulates for the formulation of the question of the presence of Christ in non-Christian religions which is likely to yield results? Whether the historian of religions, himself working *a posteriori*, will be able to realise these expectations, or *de facto* will fall short of them or eventually exceed them, is a question that must here remain completely open.

In answer to the dogmatic question limited in this way two presuppositions should be stated. First of all we presuppose a supernatural salvific will of God which is universal and truly operative in the world.[2] This implies the possibility of supernatural faith in God's revelation everywhere, namely in the whole length and breadth of human history. This presupposition has indeed been expressly taught by the second Vatican Council.[3] Admittedly, the Council is extremely reserved with regard to the question *how*, outside the sphere of the Old and the New Testament, such a salvific faith in a true revelation of God in the strict sense of the word comes about. The theologian, however, is not forbidden to ask the question how such a universal possibility of faith can exist – indeed he cannot really be dispensed from asking such a question. The answer, or a possible answer, may be something on the line of Hebrews 11,1–40 (specially verse 6), which however does not yet bring out the Christological character of such salvific faith. Such answer need not be unfolded here but may be presupposed. We should only remark in passing that the elevation of human transcendence by grace realises the concept of a supernatural revelation and, if accepted in freedom, the concept of faith.[4] For through this elevation a supernatural formal object is given even if it is not yet reflected upon or actually objectivised. This can be affirmed even before the question is answered as to what historical and objectivising mediation the acceptance of such a supernatural and revelatory elevation exactly includes.

If we take for granted that the question of the universal possibility of revelation and faith can be answered positively and is already to some extent clarified, then we have only to ask these questions: whether and how such salvific faith in revelation outside the sphere of explicit Christianity can and must attain Christ also, or whether, if this relation to Christ appears impossible, it may perhaps not be required – this would mean that impossibility and good will would dispense from the Christological character of the act of faith which in all other respects would always remain possible.

The question finally remains whether in the coming-to-be of such an act of faith (understood either Christologically or non-Christologically), the non-Christian religions as concrete historical and social phenomena have any positive significance or not. The question of the presence or non-presence of Christ in non-Christian religions will then be answered accordingly.

The second presupposition is this: when a non-Christian gains salvation through faith, hope and love, we cannot accept that the non-Christian religions play no role or only a negative role in that gaining of justification and salvation.[5] By this statement we do not give an altogether definite Christian interpretation and evaluation of a *concrete* non-Christian religion. It is not a question of equating any such religion with the Christian faith in regard to its salvific meaning, or of denying its corrupt aspects, or its preparatory function in the history of salvation. Nor do we dispute that a particular concrete religion may also have a negative effect on the salvation of a concrete non-Christian. All this being presumed, the following must still be stated: if on principle a non-Christian religion could not and ought not to have absolutely any positive influence on the supernatural salvation of a man who is not Christian, then the salvation of such a man would be conceived as totally non-social and non-historical[6] – and this contradicts the historical and social (ecclesial) character of Christianity itself. Special theories of private revelations, extraordinary illuminations (specially at the hour of death) etc. have been proposed to account for divine revelation to a man who has not been reached by Christian preaching. Such postulates are arbitrary and improbable, and one does not see why they should be allowed to come into play only in connection with extraordinary circumstances. Such special interventions contradict the fundamental character of Christian revelation and the nature of man who even in his most personal history is always a being in society whose innermost decisions are mediated by the concreteness of his social and historical life and do not take place in a sphere which on principle is separated from his life.

Add to this that in a theology of salvation history that takes God's universal salvific will seriously and considers equally the enormous time gap between 'Adam' and the Old Testament Mosaic revelation, the whole period in between cannot be thought of as devoid of divine Revelation. (Even the Constitution *Dei Verbum* of Vatican II bypasses this period a little too quickly.[7]) Now, it is not imaginable that such a revelation should simply be divorced from all the history of concrete religions. If we simply leave them out of our consideration we just cannot say any longer where in this world God and his history of Salvation and Revelation can be found. The attempt to bridge the vast distance between 'Adam' and the Mosaic revelation by postulating a 'primitive revelation'[8] is for the same reason very problematic because of the enormous length of human history involved. Moreover, concretely only the historical and socially constituted religions come into question, as being the bearers of such a tradition of 'primitive revelation' which is meant to reach the individual men. They awaken and keep alive the possibility and the obligation which man has to relate himself to the Mystery of Being that presses upon him, whatever be the way in which each religion interprets this ultimate Mystery of Being, and concretises, and may also somewhat vitiate, man's relatedness to It.

Now, if we accept a universal and operative salvific will of God even after the fall and therefore the universal possibility of salvific faith in Revelation at least for the time between 'Adam' and the Mosaic Revelation; and if we accept also that pre-Christian religions at least originally had a positive

salvific role in this, then we see no reason why *a priori* and fundamentally we should or even could deny such positive role, at least partial, to
non-Christian religions for men today who have not been reached by the
Christian message in a way that directly binds them. We have not to discuss
here the concrete ways in which a non-Christian religion can have a positive
function for the possibility of a real faith in Revelation. This question can
remain open.

With these two presuppositions we turn to our real question: how can
Jesus Christ be understood as present and active in non-Christian religions
from the point of view of Christian dogma and thus prior to a description
which would answer this question *a posteriori*? By way of answering this we
must from the beginning soberly and clearly agree that a direct reply must
first be given to the question: how is Jesus Christ present in the *faith* of a
particular non-Christian? Beyond this, namely in relation to non-Christian
religions as social and institutional realities, nothing more will here be said
except for alluding to the preliminary remarks, however regrettable this
may appear. Whatever can eventually be said about the presence of Christ
in non-Christian religions over and above his presence in the salvific faith
of non-Christians is a matter for the theologian who works *a posteriori* as
a historian of religions.

1. With the preliminary remarks and qualifications made above, Christ is
present and active in non-Christian believers (and therefore in non-Christian
religions) through his Spirit. Such a statement is dogmatically self-evident. If
salvific faith can be found in non-Christians and in fact may be expected to
be found in them to a great extent, then it is self-evident that such a faith is
made possible and is sustained by the supernatural grace of the Holy Spirit.[9]
And this is the Spirit who proceeds from the Father and the Son, so that
as the Spirit of the eternal Logos he can and must be called, at least in this
sense, the Spirit of Christ, the Word of God become man. But this dogmatically self-evident statement does not yet bring out the full meaning of and
the justification for the principle formulated above. The question precisely
is whether the supernatural grace of faith and justification coming from the
Holy Spirit as it works in the non-baptised can be called the Spirit of *Jesus*
Christ, and if so what does this exactly mean.

Every Catholic Schoolman will undoubtedly give a positive answer to this
question. He will try to make it intelligible with this explanation – that the
Spirit who makes such a faith possible and who justifies is given always and
everywhere 'intuitu meritorum Christi' (in view of the merits of Christ),[10]
and therefore can rightly be called the Spirit of Jesus Christ. To begin with,
this explanation is surely legitimate and it can also be thought intelligible (at
least to some extent) and therefore can safely serve as the starting point of
our further reflections. But this explanation surely does not answer all the
questions which can be raised here.

First of all, in this statement the relationship between the grace of the

Spirit given everywhere and at all times on the one hand, and on the other hand the historical event of the Cross limited to a point in space and time is not yet as intelligible and clear as it might appear at first sight. One could ask: does the relationship between these two realities just pass through the knowledge and will of God who Himself transcends salvation history so that between the two realities themselves there would exist no actual relationship? Can the event of the Cross be thought of as ('physically' or 'morally') 'influencing' God so that he always pours the grace of the Spirit on the world on the basis of such an influence (obviously always foreknown), which as it were arises from the world and reaches up to Him? But if this cannot strictly be said because God is sovereignly beyond all possible influence, is unmoved and unchangeable, then what would be the meaning of saying that He gives His Spirit because of the merits of Jesus Christ as the moral meritorious cause of this Spirit?

One could say that the statement in question does not connect the Passion of Christ with God as if it was the reason for a change in Him, but with the grace of the Spirit. This would be similar to the case of petitionary prayer which is not the cause of God's decision to answer the petition, but the moral cause (through the free connection on the side of God) of the reality given when God grants the prayer. But even in this case one would have to ask what exactly is the meaning of what is affirmed in relation to the historical event of the cross: for such a moral cause which is within the world and which should not 'influence' God Himself is much later in time than its effect.[11] We may point to the fact that in the second instance, that of petitionary prayer, it would not occur to anybody to come before God and pray for a reality which has already happened earlier – although this also should be meaningful if the popular interpretation of 'intuitu meritorum' were meaningful.

Apart from these questions, we can and must conceive the free salvific will of God as the *a priori* 'cause' (*Ursache*), unconditioned by anything outside God, of even the Incarnation and the Cross of Christ. From this point of view it is not easy to see how the Cross of Christ can be the cause of God's salvific will for other men if this salvific will of God precedes the Cross of Christ as cause, rather than being its effect. And this salvific will of God cannot be thought of but as relating to all men, since a salvific will that would refer only to Christ would on principle be meaningless and contradict the fact that Jesus Christ is absolutely intended to be the redeemer of the world by God's salvific will.

We can escape these and similar dilemmas not mentioned here if we see the Incarnation and the Cross as the 'final cause' (*Finalursache*) – to put it in Scholastic terminology – of God's universal self-communication to the world (called Holy Spirit) which has no other reason (*Grund*) except the very salvific will of God, and consider the Incarnation and the Cross as cause (*Ursache*), in *this* sense, of the communication of the Holy Spirit always and everywhere in the world. This Spirit is always and everywhere from the outset the Entelechy[12] of the *history* of revelation and of salvation, and his communication and acceptance by his very nature never happen in purely abstract Transcendentality but through historical mediation. From this it follows that this mediation, is from the beginning oriented towards a historical event in which the communication and acceptance of the Spirit, though free, are irreversible, and historically tangible in this eschatological victory. This is what happens in what we call the Incarnation, the Cross and the Resurrection of the divine Word. Because the universal activity of the Spirit is from the beginning oriented towards the high point of his historical mediation, in other words because the Christ event is the final cause of the communication of the Spirit to the world, therefore we can say in all truth that this Spirit is from the outset and always the Spirit of Jesus Christ, the Word of God become *man*.

The Spirit communicated to the world has by himself and as such an inner relation to Jesus Christ, and not only in the world-transcending design of God that would be external to him. Jesus Christ is therefore the 'cause' (*Ursache*) of the Spirit, though at the same time, the opposite relationship holds good, as is the case between the efficient cause and the final cause in their unity, difference and mutually conditioned relationship. Because the efficient cause of the Incarnation and the Cross, namely the Spirit, carries in himself his own goal as inner Entelechy and achieves his own essence (as the one communicated to the world) only in the Incarnation and the Cross, he is from the outset the Spirit of Jesus Christ. And because this Spirit brings about always and everywhere justifying faith, such a faith is from the outset, always and everywhere, a faith which comes about in the Spirit of Jesus Christ – the one who is present and operative in this his Spirit wherever there is faith.

2. Jesus Christ is always and everywhere present in justifying faith since this faith is always and everywhere the 'seeking *Memoria*' of the Absolute Saviour, by definition the God-man who was perfected through his Cross and Resurrection.[13] This statement will not be fully explained here in all its aspects as this would lead us too far. Similarly we must not primarily prove any further that the historical Saviour who makes God's gift to the world irreversible and therefore visible is necessarily the Word of God become man, who perfects himself in his earthly existence through his Death and Resurrection.[14]

There is also no need to explain the exact relationship between the first thesis and this second one. Both of them naturally hang together very closely, but the details of this need not occupy us here any longer. For the theme of our reflections we need only to clarify a little what is meant by the thesis that the seeking Memoria of every act of faith, wherever it occurs, goes out towards the Absolute Saviour. In our context we need not deal with the question, either, of how far the goal of this seeking Memoria must be explicit or merely implicit (a question which should be still further differentiated according as whether a collective or an individual consciousness of faith is meant).

At first sight the concept of Memoria seems to be in contradiction with the property which we attribute to it when we say it is a seeking Memoria. In the ordinary understanding of the word, Memoria seems always to refer only to what is already found in the treasure-trove of the past, and not to something that is still to come, either in general or for oneself, and therefore must still be found, and hence is still to be 'sought'. But if we consider Plato's doctrine of Anamnesis[15] or Augustine's doctrine of Memoria, which we cannot do here, one immediately sees that this matter is not so simple as that. Ultimately the whole problematic of the relation between transcendence and history, between the *a priori* and the *a posteriori* elements of knowledge, points to this. One can find and retain what happens to man in history only if there is an *a priori* principle of expectation, search and hope in the subjectivity of the man who finds and retains. In agreement with a tradition that can be traced through the whole history of Western thought, we call this principle Memoria.

This Memoria, however, should not just be understood as a pure faculty of receiving all and everything, as a sort of simple empty space into which a haphazard history would bring in indiscriminately and arbitrarily everything that may ever take place. The Memoria has itself *a priori* structures, which surely do not forestall the free and unexpected of history, but primarily offer the possibility of perceiving in this history itself something that is distinctive and of assigning to it its determined position. Memoria is the *a priori* possibility of historical experience as historical (to be distinguished from the *a priori* condition of the possibility of *a posteriori* knowledge of 'things' in the natural sciences).

This general theory of Memoria can naturally only be indicated here. We insist only on one point: the Memoria is (indeed is *above all*) the anticipation, seeking and searching in history, of the Absolute Saviour. (It is a formal anticipation, and therefore it does not forestall the concrete aspects of history, but is open to its passive experience.) In his transcendence as spirit and as freedom man always experiences his reference to the incomprehensible Mystery which we call God.[16] He experiences in himself a hope, even if he cannot claim a right to it, that this reference to God is so radical that his hope will find its fulfilment in God's direct self-communication – a supernatural grace by which it is sustained, freed and radicalised. But this transcendence of man radicalised through grace is mediated through the historical experience by the content of which man becomes conscious of his own transcendence. This is true in that man reflects at least initially on it and in his freedom accepts or refuses it.

This historical experience, mediating for man his own grace-elevated transcendence, can surely have the most diverse contents. It need not even have necessarily always and everywhere a religious theme, provided only that it mediates man to himself as a person who disposes of himself, as one and whole, in freedom.

As history, which does not consist of simply an amorphous mass of items lying side by side in time and space, the historical experience has a structure. In this structure the different moments, having each their own place in space and time, do not all possess the same significance. The searching anticipation of this structure belongs to the essence of Memoria. All history is a history of freedom, and freedom is not the faculty of choosing always something different but the faculty of decision towards a finality.[17] Hence such decisions belong to the structure of history as it is expected in anticipation by the Memoria, by which (decisions) history's course turns, partly or wholly, from the open plurality of equally valid possibilities to a freely accomplished finality. If we suppose that in the ongoing course of history its finality (that must be worked out within history itself) can as a whole attain really to a historical manifestation and perceptibility, and if we suppose that this manifestation must not simply be identical with the termination of history as a whole, then we can say that the Memoria of the grace-elevated transcendence of man seeks, through hope and anticipation, for that event in history in which the free decision for a salvific outcome of history as a whole is made and becomes tangible – an outcome indeed arising at once from the freedom of God and of mankind and affecting the one history of mankind as a whole.

Now, this event sought and expected in this way by the Memoria is what we call the Absolute Saviour.[18] He is the anticipation of the Memoria given in every act of faith. It is naturally a further question, but one that must finally be answered only *a posteriori* in the history of religions, whether and how far, how explicit or implicit, in mythology or in history, this anticipation of the Absolute Saviour through the Memoria of faith is actually traceable. As it has already been said, at this point the dogmatic theologian must hand over the question to the historian of religions and to his Christian interpretation of this history of religions. From a dogmatic point of view it seems to me that after all it is a secondary question whether the seeking expectation is objectivised in Saviour myths or is projected onto historical figures to whom the character of such a Saviour is acknowledged either as only provisional or as definitive. On the basis of the presuppositions made above the dogmatic theologian can only say that the history of religions should be searched accurately and with sympathy to see whether and how far such Saviour-figures are found in it.[19] He will say that from the dogmatic point of view there is no reason why such a discovery should from the outset be excluded or evaluated in a merely minimising and negative way in order to contrast it with the faith in Jesus, the eschatological and unsurpassable Saviour. The Saviour-figures in the history of religions can indeed be considered as signs that man, always and everywhere moved by grace, looks out in anticipation for that event in which his absolute hope becomes historically irreversible and as such manifested.

With these two theses about the presence of Jesus Christ in justifying faith, which through the grace of God is always and everywhere possible, and, derived from this, about his presence in non-Christian religions, we naturally do not say that all the aspects of the presence and activity of Jesus Christ in the faith of non-Christians and in non-Christian religions have been seen and explained. Perhaps one can have the impression that only obvious statements have been made about our question. But it seems to me first that on this question, if we start purely from Christian dogma, one cannot easily go beyond this answer. It seems to me that the main part in answering our question must be contributed by the historian of religions who interprets his data from a Christian point of view. Were this to be done more clearly and exactly, then the result could well be that this *a posteriori* history of religions and its interpretation of the presence of Christ in all religions might call the attention of the dogmatic theologian to implications for his own teaching of this presence which he has so far overlooked.

Notes

1 The reflexions which will be put forward here are naturally very closely related with the explanations which the author has given regarding the famous catch-word 'anonymous Christians' and also regarding a transcendental Christology. About this much may already be known, although for details one should refer to the appropriate works themselves. Cf. 'Bemerkungen zum Problem des "anonymen Christen"', in *Schriften zur Theologie X*, Einsiedeln 1972, pp. 531–46 (where there are also references to earlier statements), as well as 'Christologie-systematisch und exegetisch' (*Quaestio Disputata 55*), Freiburg/Br. 1972, pp. 15–18.

2 This universal salvific will is more specifically stressed by the second Vatican Council. Cf. *Lumen Gentium*, 16; *Nostra Aetate*, 1; *Ad Gentes*, 7.

3 Cf. on this point the previous note, but also the more general statements in this sense in *Gaudium et Spes*, 2; 10; 22; etc.

4 For a further clarification of this idea, cf. K. Rahner, 'Existence. III: The Existential, B. Theological', in *Sacramentum Mundi* 2, New York/London 1968, pp. 306–7.

5 This idea is in conflict not only with the Vatican II 'Declaration on the Relationship of the Church to non-Christian Religions' but above all with the basic attitude manifested in the document, which goes beyond the Declaration itself and of which a few important aspects will be further worked out in this study.

6 The Vatican II 'Declaration on Religious Freedom' also says this in no. 4: 'The freedom or immunity from coercion in religious matters, which is the endowment of persons as individuals, is also to be recognised as their right when they act in community. For religious communities are a requirement of the social nature both of man and of religion itself'. (Cf. J. Neuner and J. Dupuis, *The Christian Faith* (henceforward: ND), Bangalore 1973, n. 2050.

7 Cf. the 'Dogmatic Constitution on Divine Revelation', no. 3, where the history of revelation is presented in probably too harmless a manner.

8 Cf. on this G. Fries, 'Primitive Revelation', in *Sacramentum Mundi* 5, New York/ London 1970, pp. 355–8, as well as the reflections of the author on 'Revelation. I. Concept of Revelation, B. Theological Interpretation', ibid., pp. 348–53.

9 These statements follow already from the assertions of the Dogmatic Constitution *Dei Filius* of the first Vatican Council, cf. ND 118–19, even though there the doctrine is stated mostly from the point of view of the Christian coming to faith.

10 This expression of the Bull *Ineffabilis Deus* (cf. ND 709) is found in a context that at first sight does not seem to fit in here. Yet the Definition of the Immaculate Conception of Mary has a real significance for our question as it deals with a fact that had its place *before* the historical-categorical salvific work of Jesus Christ, although it is set in immediate relation with Him and is derived from him.

11 The author has made numerous reflections on this point under the title 'Zur Theologie des Todes Jesu von der Auferstehung Jesu her' in K. Rahner and W. Thüsing, *Christologie – systematisch und exegetisch* (*Quaestio Disputata* 55), Freiburg/Br. 1972, pp. 47–50. We must here refer to this work.

12 [Entelechy is used by Aristotle to refer to the actuality as opposed to the potentiality of something; it comes from the Greek *telos* (end/goal/completion) and *exhein* (to have), and thus links to theological teleology – ed.]

13 On the following thoughts, here sketchily exposed, cf. J. B. Metz, 'Erinnerung', in *Handbuch philosophischer Grundbegriffe*, Munich 1973, where the Memoria is specially considered in its comprehensive function.

14 In this connexion attention must be called again to the preliminary remarks made at the beginning of this article.

15 See on this C. Huber, *Anamnesis bei Plato*, Pullacher Philos. Forschungen VI, Munich 1964, and G. Söhngen, 'Der Aufbau der augustinischen Gedächtnislehre', in G. Söhngen, *Die Einheit der Theologie*, Munich 1952, pp. 63–100.

16 With regard to this experience the author has repeatedly taken position from other points of view. We may allude to 'Gotteserfahrung heute', in *Schriften zur Theologie* IX, Einsiedeln 1970, pp. 161–76.

17 Cf. on this K. Rahner, 'Freedom: III Theological', in *Sacramentum Mundi* 2, New York/London 1968, pp. 361–2.

18 See on this point the fundamental exposition of transcendental Christology in 13 theses in K. Rahner and W. Thüsing, *Christologie – systematisch und exegetisch* (*Quaestio Disputata* 55), Freiburg/Br. 1972, pp. 21–4.

19 The division of labour envisaged here between the 'dogmatic theologian' and the 'historian of religions' must naturally not be misunderstood as if the scientific handling of positive material was taken away from systematic and dogmatic theology and as if we wanted thus to proclaim the practical death of positive theology. We rather explain the attitude of the Christian dogmatic theologian vis-à-vis the positive data of non-Christian religions. The suggested approach should moreover be understood only as one possibility among others.

Source: Karl Rahner, 1973, 'Christ in the Non-Christian Religions', in G. Gispert-Sauch (ed.), *God's Word Among Men*, Delhi: Vidyajoti, Institute of Religious Studies, pp. 95–104.

A P(new)matological Paradigm for Christian Mission in a Religiously Plural World

AMOS YONG

I. Elements of a Pneumatological Theology of Religious Pluralism

The turn toward a pneumatological approach in Christian theological reflections on the plurality of religions has been a recent development in response to what I have called the christological impasse.[1] In brief, christological categories at the center of thinking about theology of religions has led to asking if other faiths are (a) opposed to Christ, and hence false (or demonic – the traditional 'exclusivistic' position); (b) fulfilled in some way by Christ (hence pointing to Christ even as the Old Testament points toward the New – the traditional 'inclusivistic' position); or (c) testify in their own ways to the same truth as that to which Christ represents (hence there being diverse testimonies to the truth, in which case 'many roads' lead to the same final destination – the traditional 'pluralist' position). The problem with (c) is that it both assumes a meta-position (which is unavailable to historical creatures like human beings) from which to gauge all religious traditions and it does not take seriously the specific claims of the various religious traditions. The problem with (b) is that it assumes a superiority of Christian faith over that of other religions in an arbitrary way, leading to the impasse because other traditions also assume their superiority to Christianity in turn. The problem with (a) is either that demonizing other religionists is politically and ethically inappropriate, or that such demonization or denunciation is generally done without much attempt to understand those in other traditions on their own terms. Taken together, these difficult questions raise the following dilemma: *either* define other religious traditions on Christian terms but thereby preserve the centrality of Christ in theological reflection on the religions, *or* engage theologically with other religious traditions on their terms but thereby lose the centrality of Christ in Christian reflection on the religions.

But what if Christian theology of religions were to proceed within a more pneumatological (and hence trinitarian) framework instead? Following in the footsteps of others who have sketched the possibility of such a pneumatological theology of religions – e.g., Georges Khodr (Orthodox), Paul Knitter and Jacques Dupuis (Roman Catholic), and Stanley Samartha and Clark Pinnock (Protestant) – I have attempted to develop this idea into a full-fledged model that not only helps with our understanding of religious pluralism (the theological or theoretical dimension) but also enables our engaging with religious otherness (the practical or intersubjective dimension).[2] In brief, a pneumatological theology of religions begins with the doctrine of the Holy Spirit as the universal presence and activity of God, and attempts to understand the world of the religions within that universal framework. Allow me to elaborate on three basic elements of such a pneumatological approach to religious pluralism: its 'grounding' in the Pentecost narrative of Acts 2; its furnishing dynamic categories for comprehending the phenomena of religion and religiosity; and its providing a dialogical and intersubjective means of adjudicating multiple religious truth claims.

Pneumatology and the 'ground' of religious pluralism

First, a pneumatological theology of religions proceeds at least in part from the Pentecost narrative of the Spirit of God being poured out 'upon all flesh' (Acts 2:17).[3] This involves understanding 'all flesh' to have universal application on the one hand, and to include the world of the religions on the other. With regard to the former point, my reading 'all flesh' as having a universal reference is supported *both* by the immediate context of this claim which includes sons and daughters, young and old, and slave and free, *and* by the broader context of the Pentecostal outpouring of the Spirit upon the many who were gathered on the streets of Jerusalem from around the known (Mediterranean) world.[4] While at one (exegetical) level it might be argued that 'all flesh' is limited to the class of Christians drawn from the categories of sons, daughters, etc., at another (theological) level, the sons, daughters, etc., are Christians precisely because they are those upon whom the Spirit is poured out. In this latter reading, the 'all flesh' would not be qualified by 'Christians'. Further, while some might argue that the 'all flesh' is limited to Jews and proselytes to Judaism derived from the Jewish diaspora, this overlooks three more universalistic trajectories embedded in this text: (a) that proselytes are not full converts: rather, being at different stages of their spiritual journeys, they embody in their lives multiple traditions and cultures in various degrees; (b) that the summary list of regions and languages present in Jerusalem symbolize (weaker) or represent (stronger) the breadth of the known first century world; and (c) that Luke's own narrative is guided by a universalistic vision whereby 'all flesh' includes those from Jerusalem, Judea, Samaria, and 'the ends of the earth' (Acts 1:8).[5]

From this universalistic reading of the Pentecost narrative, it is but a short series of steps to understanding the world of the religions in pneumatological perspective. First, it is undeniable that this Pentecost narrative should be read against the narrative of the Tower of Babel (Gen. 11) when human beings were dispersed across the earth through the confusion of their languages. Against this background, the outpouring of the Spirit redeems the diversity of languages, enabling each tongue to become a vehicle to communicate the wondrous works of God. Building on this, the diversity of languages is also correlated with the diversity of cultures (or, nations, tribes, and peoples, to use first century Mediterranean categories; cf. Rev. 7:9 and passim). This is the theological basis for not only accepting but also valuing the plurality of cultures, and is the missiological basis for methods which emphasize the inculturation, indigenization, and contextualization of the gospel. This connection between language and culture is then extended to include the religious dimension of human life. Because the phenomenon of language and of culture cannot be arbitrarily separated from that of religion, the principle of linguistic and cultural diversity necessarily includes that of religious diversity. Hence, the Pentecost narrative can be understood to redeem not only human languages and cultures, but also human religiosity. However, just as this does not mean that all human words and all aspects of human culture are holy without qualification, so also it does not mean that all human religiousness is sanctified. Language, culture, and religion must all be discerned, even as each is potentially a vehicle for mediating the grace of God. But acceptance of this possibility establishes the Day of Pentecost as the narrative 'ground' for understanding the world of the religions in pneumatological perspective.

Pneumatology and the dynamism of religion

The second basic element of a pneumatological approach to religious pluralism is that pneumatology furnishes dynamic categories for comprehending the phenomena of religion and religiosity.[6] Let me explicate this dynamism in terms of a few fundamental religious concepts: conversion, tradition, and praxis. *Conversion* in pneumatological perspective emphasizes the process of salvation in its various dimensions. This understanding complements the classical theological tradition's understanding of conversion as occurring at a point in time. The strength of a pneumatological theology of conversion is precisely its capacity to recognize crisis moments in the spiritual journey without abstracting these from the entire life process. Whereas the classical understanding resulted in asking questions like whether or not, 'once saved, always saved?' – a pneumatological viewpoint emphasizes Christian conversion – i.e., conversion to Christ – as a lifelong path toward being made into the image of Jesus wherein the various dimensions of an individual life (e.g., intellectual, aesthetic, moral, social, and religious[7]) are engaged and transformed over time. Put in theological terms, salvation hence includes the interrelated processes of repentance, justification, sanctification, and glorification. Put in existential terms, 'I was saved, I am being saved, and I will be saved.' Put in religious terms, spiritual life is dynamic rather than static, and religious beliefs and practices are similarly flexible in the ways they operate in lives of devotees to bring about religious transformation. In short, a pneumatological approach to theology of religions would be better sensitized to the unfinished and dynamic character of religiosity (orientations and dispositions), religiousness (states of piety and devotion), and religious life (ritual and praxis), and how each contributes to the religious shaping of human souls.

Tradition is similarly dynamic in pneumatological perspective because it emphasizes how the institutional carriers of religion are themselves continuously in flux. This also complements the classical theological understanding wherein 'tradition' was that which was given once-and-for all (e.g., as an unchanging deposit of revelatory truth). The strength of a pneumatological theology of tradition is precisely its capacity to recognize the givenness and facticity of divine revelation without absolutizing any particular interpretation or expression for all time. So whereas the classical understanding resulted in questions like whether or not the Bible or the patristic fathers *are* normative for Christian theology, a pneumatological viewpoint explores *how* the Bible or patristic fathers, etc., are normative for those in other places and times. Whereas the classical understanding defined the church in static terms, a pneumatological ecclesiology emphasizes the institution of the church as the 'fellowship of the Holy Spirit.' In this pneumatological framework the Christian tradition and church not only *exist*, but are also *becoming*, because the tradition and church are the concrete expressions of human responses to and participation in the Spirit's outpouring upon – presence and activity in – the world. Similarly this pneumatological perspective would more naturally enable recognition of the dynamic character of other religious traditions. In the same way as the Christian tradition can be discerned only through its continually changing empirical manifestations – to see if the Spirit's presence and activity can be detected or if the Spirit is absent in some respect – so also are the traditions of Judaism, Islam, Buddhism, Hinduism, etc., discernible through their ever-changing manifestations. A pneumatological theology of religions would be better equipped to recognize 'religions' and 'religious traditions' not as nouns, but verbs: they are formed by the processes of human 'traditioning'[8] and, thereby, shaped by the various human responses and activities to realities considered transcendent.

Last (for our purposes) but not least (for the point under consideration), religious *praxis* obviously calls attention to the dynamic character of religiosity. In pneumatological perspective, however, praxis becomes just as, if not more, important than beliefs (doctrines) and that precisely because pneumatology calls attention to divine activity rather than divine being. This complements the classical understanding wherein 'praxis' was secondary to 'doctrine' in defining a religious tradition. The strength of a pneumatological theology of tradition is precisely its capacity to recognize the interrelatedness of praxis and doctrine without subordinating either to the other. Rather, praxis is understood to be guided by doctrine even as praxis shapes doctrinal formulations. A pneumatological viewpoint both acknowledges and is able to provide a theological account for the interrelatedness between praxis and doctrine. Hence a pneumatologically informed theology of religions is better able to comprehend religious otherness not only in terms of the category of doctrine but also in terms of other dynamic praxis categories like ritual, piety, devotion, morality, and the like. Unlike previous theologies of religions with their almost exclusive focus on the beliefs of religious others, a pneumatological *theologia religionum* is much better able to account for the diversity of beliefs that are linked to and shaped by different social moral, and religious practices.[9]

Together, these brief discussions of conversion, tradition, and praxis are suggestive of how a pneumatological approach inculcates a more dynamic understanding of the phenomenon of religion. In the same way as pneumatology points to eschatology (the doctrine of things related to the end), so also a pneumatological theology of religions recognizes the openendedness and unfinished character of religious traditions and human religiousness. Certainly, scholars of religion have long been advocates of this more dynamic understanding of human religiosity.[10] The contribution of a pneumatological perspective is a specifically theological (rather than philosophical or empirical) rationale for this kind of dynamic interpretation of religion.

Pneumatology, truth, and the religions

This leads to the third basic element of a pneumatological approach to religious pluralism: its capacity to provide an intersubjective mode of engaging religious truth.[11] Previous approaches to religious doctrines have noticed and, often, emphasized their contradictory quality when explicated in terms of the correspondence theory of truth. So Buddhists believe that death leads either to reincarnation or Nirvana, while Christians believe that death leads either to heaven or hell – in which case, either Buddhists or Christians are right (and the other wrong) since both sets of claims cannot be simultaneously true. The problem here is that claims regarding reincarnation, Nirvana, heaven, or hell are either transcendental or eschatological, resulting in Buddhist and Christian claims and counterclaims without any means of adjudicating the apparent contradictions.

More recent developments seek to emphasize how any particular doctrinal (hence: truth) claim is nested semiotically within a larger web of interlocking doctrines and religious practices, thereby requiring explication in terms of the coherence theory of truth. In this case, Buddhist or Christian claims only make sense within Buddhist or Christian frameworks since doctrines function with regard to religious traditions in ways similar to how grammars function with regard to languages.[12] The problem here is twofold: *either* religious frameworks are incommensurable – based as they are on different semiotic and praxis systems – and hence apparently contrary claims are essentially non-adjudicable; *or* any attempt to adjudicate religious (doctrinal or truth) claims requires that one not only learns about or observes from a distance another tradition but also that one enters into and participates in its semiotic system. The former results in religious relativism: what is true for the Buddhist is not true for the Christian and vice-versa. With regard to the latter option, students of religion recognize the challenges of risking scholarly objectivity when one moves from being an 'outsider' to being an 'insider' of a religious way of life,[13] even as Christian theologians struggle with how one retains one's Christian identity in the process of entering into the beliefs and practices of another faith. Is it then possible to adjudge between contrary claims to truth among the religions?

The pneumatological approach to this dilemma provides a specifically theological (rather than philosophical or politically correct) rationale for holding both correspondence and coherentist theories of truth and methods for their resolution in tension. Let me explicate this claim in three steps. First, going back to the Pentecost narrative, the outpouring of the Spirit enables each one to give witness to the wondrous works of God (Acts 2:11) in and through the diversity of languages. Now insofar as language can only be arbitrarily divorced from culture and from religion, to the same extent, then, cultures and religions are potentially vehicles for mediating the grace and truth of God. More specifically, the Spirit who gives the capacity to speak in a foreign language also can enable, by extension, participation in a foreign culture and even a foreign religion, so that one can experience those realities to some degree 'from within.' From a Christian perspective, this is confirmed by the acknowledgment that 'outsiders' can understand Christian faith only when they enter, by the Holy Spirit, into that faith experience at some level and 'taste and see that the Lord is good' (Psalm 34:8). On the other side, of course, those in other faiths also claim that their truth claims are comprehensible only when we enter into their beliefs and practices at some level. May I suggest that the same Spirit whose outpouring on the Day of Pentecost enabled the speaking in foreign tongues also today enables genuine cross-over into and return from other faiths so as to engage in their claims to truth?

But, second, the Spirit not only enables testimony to be given to the wondrous works of God, but also explicitly to Jesus Christ. This christomorphic aspect is, therefore, not accidental but essential to the identity of the Holy Spirit. With this, of course, we confront once again the 'stumbling block' of Christian tradition. The pneumatological perspective adopted here, however, does not allow the christological norm to act as a conversation terminator. Rather, because a robust pneumatology is *both* christological *and* trinitarian, a robust pneumatological theology *both* points to the particularity of Jesus Christ on the one hand and to the eschatological horizon of the kingdom of God on the other. In faith, Christians believe these two realities are not contradictory. However, in their details, Christians have to wrestle with how they are continuous. The advantage of a pneumatological approach is that it grants theological (read: trinitarian) warrant for holding together the tensions between the historical Jesus and the eschatological

Christ, between the outpouring of the Pentecostal Spirit and the in-breaking of the divine kingdom.

This means, third, a pneumatological approach to the phenomenon of religion empowers a robustly dialogical and intersubjective approach to religious truth. On the one hand (from the Christian perspective), the Spirit graciously enables our entrance into, inhabitation of, and testimony to faith in Jesus Christ. On the other hand (from the theology of religions perspective), this same Spirit also graciously grants understanding of, guides participation in, and empowers engagement with other languages, cultures, and even religious traditions. This dialogical relationship thus means that we engage our own and the other religious tradition both as 'insiders' and as 'outsiders.' We are 'outsiders' even to our own Christian tradition insofar as we are still not yet fully converted to the image of Christ (on this side of the eschaton), and we are 'insiders' even to other faiths insofar as the Spirit enables our cross-over into those traditions. Hence we engage our own and other traditions neither merely 'objectively' (as 'outsiders') nor merely 'subjectively' (as 'insiders'), but intersubjectively – e.g., both within and without each tradition, as individuals and as members of (both) communities, in terms of both beliefs (doctrines) and practices (participation and inhabitation in some respect), in historical reality and yet anticipating eschatological consummation. This dialogical and intersubjective engagement with religious truth therefore neglects neither the criteria of coherence nor of correspondence, but highlights the processes of adjudication as involving the mutual transformation of religious persons and traditions by the power of the eschatological Spirit.

Notes

1 For details, see my *Discerning the Spirit(s): A Pentecostal-Charismatic Contribution to Christian Theology of Religions*, Journal of Pentecostal Theology Supplement Series 20 (Sheffield, UK: Sheffield Academic Press, 2000), esp. ch. 2.

2 Begun in *Discerning the Spirit(s)* and continued in my *Beyond the Impasse: Toward a Pneumatological Theology of Religions* (Grand Rapids, MI: Baker Academic, 2003). For my overviews of the work of others who have explored and attempted to develop the pneumatological path, see *Beyond the Impasse*, chs 4 and 5.

3 Unless otherwise noted, all Scripture quotations will be from the New Revised Standard Version.

4 I presented this argument initially in my essay, '"As the Spirit Gives Utterance ...": Pentecost, Intra-Christian Ecumenism, and the Wider Oekumene,' *International Review of Mission* 92:366 (July 2003): 299–314, esp. 301–03.

5 I develop (b) and (c) in my *The Spirit Poured Out on All Flesh: World Pentecostalism and the Reconstruction of Christian Theology in the 21st Century* (Grand Rapids, MI: Baker Academic, 2005), §4.3.3.

6 I argue this idea of a pneumatological dynamic from exegetical, theological, and philosophical perspectives in my *Spirit-Word-Community: Theological Hermeneutics in*

Trinitarian Perspective (Burlington, VT, and Aldershot, UK: Ashgate Publishing Ltd., 2002), pp. 43–8, and passim.

7 See Donald L. Gelpi, S.J., *The Conversion Experience: A Reflective Process for RCIA Participants and Others* (New York and Mahwah, NJ: Paulist, 1998).

8 See Dale T. Irvin, *Christian Histories, Christian Traditioning: Rendering Accounts*, (Maryknoll, NY: Orbis Books, 1998).

9 On the intrinsic relationship between Christian beliefs and practices, see James William McClendon, Jr., *Systematic Theology*, 3 vols. (Nashville, TN: Abingdon Press, 1986, 1994, 2000); Reinhard Hütter, *Suffering Divine Things: Theology as Church Practice* (Grand Rapids, MI, and Cambridge, UK: Eerdmans, 2000); and Miroslav Volf and Dorothy C. Bass, eds., *Practicing Theology: Beliefs and Practices in Christian Life* (Grand Rapids, MI: Eerdmans, 2002).

10 Going back to Wilfred Cantwell Smith, *The Meaning and End of Religion* (New York: Macmillan, 1962).

11 The following is a synopsis of my article, 'The Spirit Bears Witness: Pneumatology, Truth and the Religions,' *Scottish Journal of Theology* 57:1 (2004): 1–25.

12 E.g., George Lindbeck, *The Nature of Doctrine: Religion and Theology in a Postliberal Age* (Philadelphia: Westminster, 1984), builds on the work of Wittgenstein.

13 E.g., Russell T. McCutcheon, ed., *The Insider/Outsider Problem in the Study of Religion: A Reader* (London and New York: Cassell, 1998), and Elisabeth Arweck and Martin D. Stringer, eds., *Theorizing Faith: The Insider/Outsider Problem in the Study of Ritual* (Birmingham, UK: University of Birmingham Press, 2002).

Source: Amos Yong, 2005, 'A P(new)matological Paradigm for Christian Mission in a Religiously Plural World', *Missiology: An International Review* 33.2, pp. 175–91.

3

Pluralisms

PERRY SCHMIDT-LEUKEL

Introduction

Philosopher of religion and reformed theologian John Hick is one of the 'fathers' of a pluralistic theology of religions which he developed from 1968 onwards in a range of publications, the most significant ones being his *An Interpretation of Religion* (1989; 2nd enl. edn 2004) and *The Metaphor of God Incarnate* (1993; 2nd rev. edn 2005). The article reproduced here was first published (1984) in a festschrift for Wilfred Cantwell Smith, another pioneer of religious pluralism. In it Hick not only explicitly relates his own thinking to Smith's but makes a number of other important points which are often misrepresented by his critics. First, a pluralist theology can only be developed from within a religious tradition – not as a 'God's eye view' above all of them – and is arrived at inductively. Second, the crucial distinction between the Real in itself and its manifestations in human thought and experience, which Hick describes in Kantian terminology, does not depend on Kant's philosophy but has its firm roots in the apophatic traditions of all major religions. Third, the argument of the good 'fruits' of the religions does not involve a conclusion from morality to truth, but serves as a defeater of inclusivism. Fourth, contemporary Christological approaches no longer necessarily support the traditional claim to Christian uniqueness. While Hick feels that such a claim is an implication of 'orthodox' Christology as expressed in the Councils of Nicea and Chalcedon, the Catholic theologian Roger Haight's essay (first published in 2005) argues that the nature of Christ can and indeed needs to be understood in such a way that it is compatible both with its orthodox conception and with a pluralistic theology as well. As a symbol points to something different from itself and thereby renders the symbolized present through itself, Jesus, as a true human, mediates the truly divine reality, to which his whole life points and which it thereby represents. Given the inexhaustible infinity of ultimate reality, this concept of symbolic mediation allows and even requires a plurality and diversity of finite representations. The brief sketch drawn in this essay has been extensively elaborated in Haight's major Christological study, *Jesus: Symbol of God* (1999). A gently critical appraisal by Hick is found in the 2nd edition of his *The Metaphor of God Incarnate*, a factor that illustrates a lively plurality of positions even within a basic acceptance of an overall pluralist theology.

Religious Pluralism

JOHN HICK

The third possible answer to the question of the relation between salvation/ liberation and the cumulative religious traditions can best be called pluralism. As a Christian position this can be seen as an acceptance of the further conclusion to which inclusivism points. If we accept that salvation/liberation is taking place within all the great religious traditions, why not frankly acknowledge that there is a plurality of saving human responses to the ultimate divine Reality? Pluralism, then, is the view that the transformation of human existence from self-centredness to Reality-centredness is taking place in different ways within the contexts of all the great religious traditions. There is not merely one way but a plurality of ways of salvation or liberation. In Christian theological terms, there is a plurality of divine revelations, making possible a plurality of forms of saving human response.

What however makes it difficult for Christians to move from inclusivism to pluralism, holding the majority of Christian theologians today in the inclusivist position despite its evident logical instability, is of course the traditional doctrine of the Incarnation, together with its protective envelope, the doctrine of the Trinity. For in its orthodox form, as classically expressed at the Councils of Nicaea and Chalcedon, the incarnational doctrine claims that Jesus was God incarnate, the Second Person of the Triune God living a human life. It is integral to this faith that there has been (and will be) no other divine incarnation. This makes Christianity unique in that it, alone among the religions of the world, was founded by God in person. Such a uniqueness would seem to demand Christian exclusivism – for must God not want all human beings to enter the way of salvation which he has provided for them? However, since such exclusivism seems so unrealistic in the light of our knowledge of the wider religious life of mankind, many theologians have moved to some form of inclusivism, but now feel unable to go further and follow the argument to its conclusion in the frank acceptance of pluralism. The break with traditional missionary attitudes and long-established ecclesiastical and liturgical language would, for many, be so great as to be prohibitive.

There is however the possibility of an acceptable Christian route to religious pluralism in work which has already been done, and which is being done, in the field of Christology with motivations quite other than to facilitate pluralism, and on grounds which are internal to the intellectual development of Christianity. For there is a decisive watershed between what might be called all-or-nothing Christologies and degree Christologies. The all-or-nothing principle is classically expressed in the Chalcedonian Definition, according to which Christ is 'to be acknowledged in Two Natures', 'Consubstantial with the Father according to his Deity, Consubstantial with us according to his Humanity'. Substance is an all-or-nothing notion, in that A either is or is not composed of the same substance, either has or does not have the same essential nature, as B. Using this all-or-nothing conceptuality Chalcedon attributed to Christ two complete natures, one divine and the other human, being in his divine nature of one substance with God the Father. Degree Christologies, on the other hand, apply the term 'incarnation' to the activity of God's Spirit or of God's grace in human lives, so that the divine will is done on earth. This kind of reinterpretation has been represented in recent years by, for example, the 'paradox of grace' Christology of Donald Baillie (in *God Was in Christ*, 1948) and the 'inspiration Christology' of Geoffrey Lampe (in *God as Spirit*, 1977). In so far as a human being is open and responsive to God, so that God is able to act in and through that individual, we can speak of the embodiment in human life of God's redemptive activity. And in Jesus this 'paradox of grace' – the paradox expressed by St Paul when he wrote 'it was not I, but the grace of God which is in me' (1 Corinthians 15:10), – or the inspiration of God's Spirit, occurred to a startling extent. The paradox, or the inspiration, are not however confined to the life of Jesus; they are found, in varying degrees, in all free human responses to God. Christologies of the same broad family occur in the work of Norman Pittenger (*The Word Incarnate*, 1957), John Knox (*The Humanity and Divinity of Christ*, 1967), and earlier in John Baillie (*The Place of Jesus Christ in Modern Christianity*, 1929), and more recently in the authors of *The Myth of God Incarnate* (1977).

These modern degree Christologies were not in fact for the most part developed in order to facilitate a Christian acceptance of religious pluralism. They were developed as alternatives to the old substance Christology, in which so many difficulties, both historical and philosophical, had become apparent. They claim to be compatible with the teachings of Jesus and of the very early Church, and to avoid the intractable problem, generated by a substance Christology, of the relation between Jesus's two natures. But, as an unintended consequence, degree Christologies open up the possibility of seeing God's activity in Jesus as being of the same kind as God's activity in other great human mediators of the divine. The traditional Christian claim to the unique superiority of Christ and of the Christian tradition is not of course precluded by a degree Christology; for it may be argued (as it was, for example, by both Baillie and Lampe) that Christ was the *supreme* instance of the paradox of grace or of the inspiration of the Spirit, so that Christianity is still assumed to be the *best* context of salvation/liberation. But, whereas, starting from the substance Christology, the unique superiority of Christ and the Christian Church are guaranteed *a priori*, starting from a degree Christology they have to be established by historical evidence. Whether this can in fact be done is, clearly, an open question. It would indeed be an uphill task today to establish that we know enough about the inner and outer life of the historical Jesus, and of the other founders of great religious traditions, to be able to make any such claim; and perhaps an even more uphill task to establish from the morally ambiguous histories of each of the great traditions, complex mixtures of good and evil as each has been, that one's own tradition stands out as manifestly superior to all others.

I think, then, that a path exists along which Christians can, if they feel so drawn, move to an acceptance of religious pluralism. Stated philosophically such a pluralism is the view that the great world faiths embody different perceptions and conceptions of, and correspondingly different responses to, the Real or the Ultimate from within the major variant cultural ways of being human; and that within each of them the transformation of human existence from self-centredness to Reality-centredness is manifestly taking place – and taking place, so far as human observation can tell, to much the same extent. Thus the great religious traditions are to be regarded as alternative soteriological 'spaces' within which, or 'ways' along which, men and women can find salvation/liberation/enlightenment/fulfilment.

But how can such a view be arrived at? Are we not proposing a picture reminiscent of the ancient allegory of the blind men and the elephant, in which each runs his hands over a different part of the animal, and identifies it differently, a leg as a tree, the trunk as a snake, the tail as a rope, and so on? Clearly, in the story the situation is being described from the point of view of someone who can observe both elephant and blind men. But where is the vantage-point from which one can observe both the divine Reality and the different limited human standpoints from which that Reality is being variously perceived? The advocate of the pluralist understanding cannot pretend to any such cosmic vision. How then does he profess to know that the situation is indeed as he depicts it? The answer is that he does not profess to know this, if by knowledge we mean infallible cognition. Nor indeed can anyone else properly claim to have knowledge, in this sense, of either the exclusivist or the inclusivist picture. All of them are, strictly speaking, hypotheses. The pluralist hypothesis is arrived at inductively. One starts from the fact that many human beings experience life in relation to a limitlessly greater transcendent Reality – whether the direction of transcendence be beyond our present existence or within its hidden depths. In theory such religious experience is capable of a purely naturalistic analysis which does not involve reference to any reality other than the human and the natural. But to participate by faith in one of the actual streams of religious experience – in my case, the Christian stream – is to participate in it as an experience of transcendent Reality. I think that there is in fact a good argument for the rationality of trusting one's own religious experience, together with that of the larger tradition within which it occurs, so as both to believe and to live on the basis of it; but I cannot develop that argument here.[1] Treating one's own form of religious experience, then, as veridical – as an experience (how-

ever dim, like 'seeing through a glass, darkly') of transcendent divine Reality
– one then has to take account of the fact that there are other great streams
of religious experience which take different forms, are shaped by different
conceptualities, and embodied in different institutions, art forms, and life-
styles. In other words, besides one's own religion, sustained by its distinctive
form of religious experience, there are also other religions, through each of
which flows the life blood of a different form of religious experience. What
account is one to give of this plurality?

At this point the three answers that we discussed above become available
again: exclusivism, inclusivism and pluralism. The exclusivist answer is that
only one's own form of religious experience is an authentic contact with
the Transcendent, other forms being delusory: the naturalistic interpretation applies to those other forms, but not to ours. This is a logically possible
position; but clearly it is painfully vulnerable to the charge of being entirely
arbitrary. It thus serves the cause of general scepticism, as David Hume
noted with regard to claims that the miracles of one's own religion are genuine whilst those of others are spurious.[2]

Moving to the inclusivist answer, this would suggest that religious experience in general does indeed constitute a contact with the Transcendent,
but that this contact occurs in its purest and most salvifically effective form
within one's own tradition, other forms having value to the varying extents
to which they approximate to ours. This is a more viable position than the
previous one, and less damaging to the claim that religion is not a human
projection but a genuine human response to transcendent Reality. There is
however a range of facts which do not fit easily into the inclusivist theory,
namely the changed and elevated lives, moving from self-centredness towards
Reality-centredness, within the other great religious traditions. Presumably
there must be a strong correlation between the authenticity of the forms of
religious experience and their spiritual and moral fruits. It would then follow from the inclusivist position that there should be a far higher incidence
and quality of saintliness in one tradition – namely, that in which contact
with the Transcendent occurs in 'its purest and most salvifically effective
form' – than in the others. But this does not seem to be the case. There is
of course no reliable census of saints! Nor indeed is the concept of a saint
by any means clear and unproblematic; very different profiles of saintliness
have operated at different times and in different places. But if we look for
the transcendence of egoism and a recentring in God or in the transcendent
Real, then I venture the proposition that, so far as human observation and
historical memory can tell, this occurs to about the same extent within each
of the great world traditions.

If this is so, it prompts us to go beyond inclusivism to a pluralism which
recognises a variety of human religious contexts within which salvation/lib-
eration takes place. But such a pluralistic hypothesis raises many questions.
What is this divine Reality to which all the great traditions are said to be

oriented? Can we really equate the personal Yahweh with the non-personal Brahman, Shiva with the Tao, the Holy Trinity with the Buddhist *Trikāya*, and all with one another? Indeed, do not the Eastern and Western faiths deal incommensurably with different problems?

As these questions indicate, we need a pluralistic theory which enables us to recognise and be fascinated by the manifold differences between the religious traditions, with their different conceptualisations, their different modes of religious experience, and their different forms of individual and social response to the divine. I should like in these final pages to suggest the ground plan of such a theory ...

Each of the great religious traditions affirms that in addition to the social and natural world of our ordinary human experience there is a limitlessly greater and higher Reality beyond or within us, in relation to which or to whom is our highest good. The ultimately real and the ultimately valuable are one, and to give oneself freely and totally to this One is our final salvation/liberation/enlightenment/fulfilment. Further, each tradition is conscious that the divine Reality exceeds the reach of our earthly speech and thought. It cannot be encompassed in human concepts. It is infinite, eternal, limitlessly rich beyond the scope of our finite conceiving or experiencing. Let us then both avoid the particular names used within the particular traditions and yet use a term which is consonant with the faith of each of them – Ultimate Reality, or the Real.

Let us next adopt a distinction that is to be found in different forms and with different emphases within each of the great traditions, the distinction between the Real *an sich* (in him/her/itself) and the Real as humanly experienced and thought. In Christian terms this is the distinction between God in God's infinite and eternal self-existent being, 'prior' to and independent of creation, and God as related to and known by us as creator, redeemer and sanctifier. In Hindu thought it is the distinction between *nirguna* Brahman, the Ultimate in itself, beyond all human categories, and *saguna* Brahman, the Ultimate as known to finite consciousness as a personal deity, Išvara. In Taoist thought, 'The Tao that can be expressed is not the eternal Tao' (*Tao-Te Ching*, 1). There are also analogous distinctions in Jewish and Muslim mystical thought in which the Real *an sich* is called *en Soph* and *al Haqq*. In Mahāyāna Buddhism there is the distinction between the *dharmakāya*, the eternal cosmic Buddha-nature, which is also the infinite Void (*sānyatā*), and on the other hand the realm of heavenly Buddha figures (*śambhogakāya*) and their incarnations in the earthly Buddhas (*nirmānakāya*). This varied family of distinctions suggests the perhaps daring thought that the Real *an sich* is one but is nevertheless capable of being humanly experienced in a variety of ways. This thought lies at the heart of the pluralistic hypothesis which I am suggesting.

The next point of which we need to take account is the creative part that thought, and the range of concepts in terms of which it functions, plays in the formation of conscious experience. It was above all Immanuel Kant who brought this realisation into the stream of modern reflection, and it has since been confirmed and amplified by innumerable studies, not only in general epistemology but also in cognitive psychology, in the sociology of knowledge, and in the philosophy of science. The central fact, of which the epistemology of religion also has to take account, is that our environment is not reflected in our consciousness in a simple and straightforward way, just as it is, independently of our perceiving it. At the physical level, out of the immense richness of structure and detail around us, only that minute selection that is relevant to our biological survival and flourishing affects our senses; and these inputs are interpreted in the mind/brain to produce our conscious experience of the familiar world in which we live. Its character as an environment within which we can learn to behave appropriately can be called its *meaning* for us. This all-important dimension of meaning, which begins at the physical level as the habitability of the material world, continues at the personal, or social, level of awareness as the moral significance of the situations of our life, and at the religious level as a consciousness of the ultimate meaning of each situation and of our situation as a whole in relation to the divine Reality. This latter consciousness is not however a general consciousness of the divine, but always takes specific forms; and, as in the case of the awareness of the physical and of the ethical meaning of our environment, such consciousness has an essential dispositional aspect. To experience in this way rather than in that involves being in a state of readiness to behave in a particular range of ways, namely that which is appropriate to our environment having the particular character that we perceive (or of course misperceive) it to have. Thus to be aware of the divine as 'the God and Father of our Lord Jesus Christ', in so far as this is the operative awareness which determines our dispositional state, is to live in the kind of way described by Jesus in his religious and moral teaching – in trust towards God and in love towards our neighbours.

How are these various specific forms of religious awareness formed? Our hypothesis is that they are formed by the presence of the divine Reality, this presence coming to consciousness in terms of the different sets of religious concepts and structures of religious meaning that operate within the different religious traditions of the world. If we look at the range of actual human religious experience and ask ourselves what basic concepts and what concrete images have operated in its genesis, I would suggest that we arrive at something like the following answer. There are, first, the two basic religious concepts which between them dominate the entire range of the forms of religious experience. One is the concept of Deity, or God, i.e. the Real as personal; and the other is the concept of the Absolute, i.e. the Real as non-personal. (The term 'Absolute' is by no means ideal for the purpose, but is perhaps the nearest that we have.) We do not however, in actual religious experience, encounter either Deity in general or the Absolute in general, but always in specific forms. In Kantian language, each general concept is schematised, or made concrete. In Kant's own analysis of sense-experience the schematisation of the basic categories is in terms of time; but religious experience occurs at a much higher level of meaning, presupposing and going beyond physical meaning and involving much more complex and variable modes of dispositional response. Schematisation or concretisation here is in terms of 'filled' human time, or history, as diversified into the different cultures and civilisations of the earth. For there are different concrete ways of being human and of participating in human history, and within these different ways the presence of the divine Reality is experienced in characteristically different ways.

To take the concept of God first, this becomes concrete as the range of specific deities to which the history of religion bears witness. Thus the Real as personal is known in the Christian tradition as God the Father; in Judaism as Adonai; in Islam as Allah, the Qur'ānic Revealer; in the Indian traditions as Shiva, or Vishnu, or Paramātmā, and under the many other lesser images of deity which in different regions of India concretise different aspects of the divine nature. This range of personal deities who are the foci of worship within the theistic traditions constitutes the range of the divine *personae* in relation to mankind. Each *persona*, in his or her historical concreteness, lives within the corporate experience of a particular faith-community. Thus the Yahweh *persona* exists and has developed in interaction with the Jewish people. He is a part of their history, and they are a part of his; and he cannot be extracted from this historical context. Shiva, on the other hand, is a quite different divine *persona*, existing in the experience of hundreds of millions of people in the Shaivite stream of Indian religious life. These two *personae*, Yahweh and Shiva, live within different worlds of faith, partly creating and partly created by the features of different human cultures, being responded to in different patterns of life, and being integral to different strands of historical experience. Within each of these worlds of faith great numbers of people find the ultimate meaning of their existence, and are carried through the crises of life and death; and within this process many are, in varying degrees, challenged and empowered to move forward on the way of salvation/liberation from self-centredness to Reality-centredness. From the pluralist point of view Yahweh and Shiva are not rival gods, or rival claimants to be the one and only God, but rather two different concrete historical *personae* in terms of which the ultimate divine Reality is present and responded to by different large historical communities within different strands of the human story.

This conception of divine *personae*, constituting (in Kantian language) different divine phenomena in terms of which the one divine noumenon is humanly experienced, enables us to acknowledge the degree of truth within the various projection theories of religion from Feuerbach through Freud to the present day. An element of human projection colours our mental images of God, accounting for their anthropomorphic features – for example, as male or female. But human projection does not – on this view – bring God into existence; rather it affects the ways in which the independently existing divine Reality is experienced.

Does this epistemological pattern of the schematisation of a basic religious concept into a range of particular correlates of religious experience apply also to the non-theistic traditions? I suggest that it does. Here the general concept, the Absolute, is schematised in actual religious experience to form the range of divine *impersonae* – Brahman, the Dharma, the Tao, *nirvāna*, *śānyatā*, and so on – which are experienced within the Eastern traditions. The structure of these *impersonae* is however importantly different from that of the *personae*. A divine *persona* is concrete, implicitly finite, sometimes visualisable and even capable of being pictured. A divine *impersona*, on the other hand, is not a 'thing' in contrast to a person. It is the infinite being-consciousness-bliss (*saccidānanda*) of Brahman; or the beginningless and endless process of cosmic change (*pratītya samutpāda*) of Buddhist teaching; or again the ineffable 'further shore' of *nirvāna*, or the eternal Buddha-nature (*dharmakāya*); or the ultimate Emptiness (*śānyatā*) which is also the fullness or suchness of the world; or the eternal principle of the Tao. It is thus not so much an entity as a field of spiritual force, or the ultimate reality of everything, that which gives final meaning and joy. These non-personal conceptions of the Ultimate inform modes of consciousness varying from the advaitic experience of becoming one with the Infinite, to the Zen experience of finding a total reality in the present concrete moment of existence in the ordinary world. And according to the pluralistic hypothesis these different modes of experience constitute different experiences of the Real as non- or trans-personal. As in the case of the divine *personae*, they are formed by different religious conceptualities which have developed in interaction with different spiritual disciplines and methods of meditation. The evidence that a range of *impersonae* of the one Ultimate Reality are involved in the non-theistic forms of religious experience, rather than the direct unmediated awareness of Reality itself, consists precisely in the differences between the experiences reported within the different traditions. How is it that a 'direct experience' of the Real can take such different forms? One could of course at this point revert to the exclusivism or the inclusivism whose limitations we have already noted. But the pluralist answer will be that even the most advanced form of mystical experience, as an experience undergone by an embodied consciousness whose mind/brain has been conditioned by a particular religious tradition, must be affected by the conceptual framework and spiritual training provided by that tradition, and accordingly takes these different forms. In other words the Real is experienced not *an sich*, but in terms of the various non-personal images or concepts that have been generated at the interface between the Real and different patterns of human consciousness.

These many different perceptions of the Real, both theistic and non-theistic, can only establish themselves as authentic by their soteriological efficacy. The great world traditions have in fact all proved to be realms within which or routes along which people are enabled to advance in the transition from self-centredness to Reality-centredness. And, since they reveal the Real in such different lights, we must conclude that they are independently valid. Accordingly, by attending to other traditions than one's own one may become aware of other aspects or dimensions of the Real, and of other possibilities of response to the Real, which had not been made effectively available by one's own tradition. Thus a mutual mission of the sharing of experiences and insights can proceed through the growing network of inter-faith dialogue and the interactions of the faith-communities. Such mutual mission does not aim at conversion – although occasionally individual conversions, in all directions, will continue to occur – but at mutual enrichment and at co-operation in face of the urgent problems of human survival in a just and sustainable world society.

Notes

1 See Michael Goulder and John Hick, *Why Believe in God?*, London: SCM Press, 1983.
2 David Hume, *An Enquiry Concerning Human Understanding*, x. ii. 95. Para. 95.

Source: John Hick, 1984, 'Religious Pluralism', in Frank Whaling (ed.), *The World's Religious Traditions: Essays in Honour of Wilfred Cantwell Smith*, Edinburgh: T&T Clark.

Outline for an Orthodox Pluralist Christology

ROGER HAIGHT

Many Christians today, even those whose sympathies may lie with a pluralist conception of Jesus Christ, do not understand how a pluralist christology can be considered orthodox. This chapter primarily addresses these Christians and aims at explaining, at least in the form of an extended outline or map, the reasons why a pluralist christology is orthodox. It does not attempt to prove the point, for such a task would require a full-length study. It is written for a group of people other than those who deny the possibility of an orthodox pluralist christology, namely, those who are open to the possibility and are looking for a rationale by which they can understand how it can be the case. It is possible that the logic deployed here may find analogies within other religious traditions. In other words, this essay, written in a religiously pluralistic context, tries to show how people can be absolutely committed to a religious tradition without competing with other religious traditions.

I begin by simply defining the terms as they are used in this discussion. By christology I mean a Christian theological understanding of Jesus of Nazareth with special attention to his status relative to God and to other human beings. A pluralist christology affirms Jesus as the Christ in a way that does not construe Christianity as the one and only true faith and way of salvation uniquely superior to all others. An orthodox christology meets the criteria of being faithful to the normative teaching of the New Testament and the classical christological councils of Nicaea and Chalcedon. It thus conforms to traditional doctrine and respects an intrinsically conservative impulse of Christians ...

Other Religions from a Christian Standpoint

The next discussion unfolds within the context of the classical doctrine of Jesus being a genuine human being but also embodying no less than God for our salvation. While remaining in that context what can a Christian say about other religions that both remains faithful to the classical doctrine and accommodates the new sensitivity to the value and vitality of other religious traditions? The extensive argument which follows is controversial within Christian theology, but it remains within the boundaries of accepted doctrine ...

In Jesus the Christian encounters a God who as creator is immanent and active in all of creation. The idea of creation developed after the period of the New Testament into the doctrine of creation out of nothing. That formula implies a direct or immediate presence and activity of God to all finite reality. No form of presence and activity can be closer, for the being itself of the creature depends on God sustaining it in being. Christian belief in God entails a God who is so immanent in and present to all reality that all things, even though they are other than God, may be said to exist in God because God exists within them. This presence takes the form of personal love in those creatures able to respond to it. This God is transcendent but not distant.

Jesus reveals the very nature of this creating God to be loving and bent on the salvation of all. This has already been affirmed as part of the logic of christology. The usual way this teaching from the New Testament is stated is that God wills the salvation of all human beings. But I also want to under-line that, when Christians affirm the revelation of God's universal will and character as benevolent and saving, this is applicable to all human beings. In the measure that such a proposition on the very character of God is true, it is relevant for all.[1] In other words, the subject matter aimed at here transcends the sphere of the socially and culturally relative. This is rather a matter that has bearing on the human as such. One can see the significance of the conception of the unity of the human race at this point. A true characterization of the nature and character of ultimate reality is valuable for all human beings. In short, truth and what is often referred to as normativity in substantive religious matters are synonymous.

To be effective in history, God's active saving presence to all requires mediation through historical symbols and religious institutions. Historical effectiveness in this statement really refers to the revelation of God's saving presence and 'action' relative to human consciousness. One can of course creatively imagine God at work within human beings apart from all human consciousness of it. But this would come very close to sheer projection. The issue in this discussion precisely revolves around human religious consciousness of the effectiveness of transcendent power immanent to the human condition. The discussion itself rests on the implicit premise that religious consciousness responds to and correlates with God's presence and power in history. Nothing less than this can explain the longevity and power of antique religious traditions.

From a Christian standpoint, therefore, a pluralism of religions is to be expected. That is to say, if one is convinced that God wills the salvation of all people, and that that salvation is not a sheerly eschatological reality but a presence and power in human life that is accompanied by some form of human consciousness of it, then it follows that the same consciousness will take the social form of a religion. This means that the multiplicity of religions from a Christian standpoint is not surprising, but entirely coherent with the Christian conception of God as transcendent but immanently present and operative in the lives of all human beings. Not to affirm an expectation of religious pluralism, or to be embarrassed by it, runs counter to the basic Christian conception of God. It would entail a view of God's saving will as not being universally effective in history. Positively, precisely because God as creator and savior relates to all of history, the articulation and experience of God's presence takes on multiple different forms.

The other side of the historicity of the experience of God's engagement with human beings is the limitation of any particular experience and expression of it. Given the limitation of all historical mediation, and given the transcendent character of ultimate reality, no single salvific mediation can encompass God's reality or human understanding of it. This represents the standard Christian view that God as transcendent should be characterized as infinite and incomprehensible. Ultimate reality, which in the Christian view is God, so transcends every and all finite mediations of it, that no single mediation of God can be said adequately to encompass or be equal to the infinite reality itself of God.

From the transcendence of ultimate reality, or God, it follows that no religion in the sense of a set of religious truths can adequately portray its object. Nor of course can multiple finite mediations. But from a Christian standpoint, the plurality of religions, with their symbolic variety and richness, mediates 'more' revelation of God than any single religion including Christianity itself. To view one religion as the fullness of revelation in any historical or categorical sense does not cohere with the object revealed: there can be no such thing as a historical representation of infinite reality that is adequate or comprehensive. The frequently cited Christian idea that Jesus Christ is the fullness of God's revelation has a bearing on the ontological reality of God that is truly revealed because present and at work in him, but this cannot be understood in concrete quantitative or qualitative terms.

In the measure in which other religions are historically distinct from Christianity, autonomous in their mediation of revelation of ultimate reality, and true, they are relevant for all human beings. This idea applies the principle considered earlier, namely, the universal relevance of Christian truth, insofar as it is really true, to all religions. Likewise, if the beliefs of other religions are true in matters concerning the stance of humanity itself before reality and the character of ultimate reality in relation to the human, they are in that measure universally relevant. This correlation of fundamental religious truth and the universally human provides the very ground for interreligious dialogue. To subvert this universal relevance or 'normativity' directly undermines the deep anthropological conviction that supports interreligious dialogue itself and the common interest in it.

But this means that Christianity should not be understood as absolute in the sense that it relates to no other religion while other religions are dependent upon it or relate to it as their fulfillment. The revelation of God found in any given religion possesses a historical autonomy that enters into a dialogical relationship with Christianity and other religions and not one of dependence. In the measure that the conceptions about ultimate reality are true, they are relevant to all and bear a normativity that makes a universal claim. This does not mean that all religions are equally revelatory of transcendent reality or the human; some may be more adequate and thus more universally applicable than others. But this is something that can only become apparent within a dialogical situation.

Thus the conviction that Christianity is not exhaustive, but that other religions contain salvific truth not formally contained in Christianity, can through inference be regarded as entailed in the teaching of Jesus. This formulation expresses the point of the argument that has been schematically outlined thus far. That point places the source and quality of the positive conviction about religious pluralism within the core of Christian faith and revelation. The positive view of other religions possesses its value in being drawn out of Christian revelation itself. That core consists in the nature of God revealed in Jesus as a savior God who wills the salvation of all whom God created, and the historical efficacy of that divine and salvific initiative. The conclusion, therefore, does not consist in a proposal that comes from outside Christian faith and threatens it, but lies implicit in the revealing message of Jesus himself. Surely the depths of Christian revelation are inexhaustible and always yield new convictions in new situations. Globalization and current religious dialogue and conflict have thus yielded new awareness of the implications of what has been revealed in Jesus Christ.

An Orthodox Christology

In this concluding section I will outline theological reasons that explain why the pluralist christology described thus far is orthodox. In this question we get closer to the narrow christological issue and the place it holds within Christian theology. The issue deals with the estimate Christians have of Jesus Christ in relation to God, and how this relationship of identity with God is explained. This is a complex discussion within a tradition which I hope will not be compromised by the following brief treatment in nontechnical terms. I will again resort to theses to ensure clarity and to measure the elements of the argument.

A christology is orthodox when it meets the three criteria of intelligibility, faithfulness to tradition, and empowerment of the Christian life.

An orthodox statement must first of all be intelligible within the context of the contemporary world. It would make little sense to proclaim a doctrine which people generally could not understand because it was alien to the worldview of a people. Transcendent mystery should not be confused with what is unintelligible. One must be more careful in stating this than the brief space allows, for Christianity stands against the sin of the world (in which it also participates) and contains what is in many respects a prophetic and countercultural message. But even prophecy has to be understood, to be effective. Unintelligible orthodoxy gives no glory to God.

Second, orthodox doctrine and theology conform to the data of Christian tradition. Here tradition is taken broadly to include Christian scriptures and classical doctrines. 'Conforming' in the context of historical interpretation does not mean literal repetition in new contexts, which inevitably betrays the very message that is repeated, but consists in an essential fidelity of interpretation in the present to the object of interpretation as that is given in and through the traditional witness. I have to assume here sensitivity to the dialectical character of Christian theological interpretation: the community always lives in a tension, which often breaks out in dispute, between fidelity to the past and a contemporary possibility of relevance and meaning. All movement into the future along this line of loyalty to the past entails contention, because orthodoxy demands interpretation, and all interpretation is contextual.

The third vital criterion for the adequacy of orthodox interpretation consists in the presentation of the soteriological character and empowerment of the traditional teachings. The soteriological structure of religious faith becomes practically real in the spiritual life it simultaneously reflects and generates. An orthodoxy irrelevant to the spiritual life becomes empty and therefore nonexistent. Let me now measure the pluralist christology presented here by each of these criteria.

A pluralist christology is surely intelligible in today's globalized world.

It is precisely the current world that has raised the question to which pluralist christology is the answer. The more common problem for Christian consciousness consists not in the applicability of pluralist christology to our current situation but in whether such an understanding conforms with scripture and classical doctrine and the manner in which it empowers.

A pluralist christology conforms to the data of Christian tradition insofar as it 'explains' how no less than true God is present and active in the life of Jesus.

Often the idea of orthodoxy has been reduced to whether or not a christology adequately portrays the agency of God at work in Jesus. Although orthodoxy entails more than that, the divinity of Jesus is a central issue. In the New Testament this agency of God is primarily expressed through the symbol of God's Spirit. Less frequently but dramatically it is also represented as an incarnation of the Word or Wisdom of God in the human individual Jesus. Other christologies imply or connote the presence and agency of God in less forceful metaphors. None of these images confuse Jesus with Yahweh or identify him with the one Jesus addressed as Father.[2]

Christology today also employs the symbols of God's Word and God's Spirit to formulate or express God's agency in Jesus. A pluralist christology can be formulated in a language that privileges either one of these symbols. A particular pluralist christology would have to be worked out in considerably more detail before a judgment could be made on its orthodoxy. The goal of such a christology is to present the idea of God acting in Jesus in a language of today's culture that is proportionate to the way the christologies of the tradition represented God acting in Jesus in the language of the cultures in which they were proposed. It is worth noting in passing that no Christology is ever without critics within Christian theology.

Regarding the construction of an orthodox christology, it is crucial that Christians understand that the issue a pluralist christology has to contend with is not how 'high' the christology is or how 'distinctly divine' it portrays Jesus. The issue rather is whether what is predicated of Jesus is so unique to him that it cannot be shared by others. If God's being present and active in him bears no parallel with our own relationship to God, then the whole topic of his relevance for us and our salvation is undermined. The point of incarnation language is that Jesus is one of us, that what occurred in Jesus is the destiny of human existence itself: *et homo factus est*. Jesus is a statement, God's statement, about humanity as such. To encourage discontinuity between Jesus and other human beings is to miss the basic point of incarnation and Jesus' being the Second Adam. The projecting upon Jesus of a divinity that radically sets him apart from other human beings does not correspond to the New Testament and undermines the very logic of Christian faith.

Analogously, if God's being present and active in Jesus has no comparable manifestation in other religions that mediate consciousness of God or ultimate reality at work for human salvation, then once again the content of the revelation of Jesus about God is undermined. The identification of Jesus with God's Word means that what Jesus says about God is true. God, and not less than God, is truly at work within humankind as such and thus within various religions. Therefore one must expect incarnations of God in other religious mediations analogous to what occurred in Jesus. This entails no diminishment of what occurred in Jesus, but a new recognition in the light of Jesus' revelation of what God does outside the Christian sphere.

A pluralist christology empowers the Christian life insofar as it proposes Jesus as representing a meaning and direction of human existence that leads to final salvation in the reality of God.

The New Testament contains a pluralism of understandings of how Jesus Christ is savior. There is no single answer to the question 'what did Jesus do for human salvation?' The many soteriological formulas all reach out toward the mystery of God's saving approach to human beings in Jesus without being able to encompass it. That salvation appeared in his public ministry. It is read in a crucial way in a life dedicated to the reign of God but leads through death to God's raising of Jesus into divine glory. Many other images and symbols across the New Testament characterize the way God acted in Jesus for human salvation. But all of these metaphors and conceptions are not equal; many depend upon the particular culture and tradition in which they were constructed. For example, a pluralist soteriology rules our conceptions of the salvation mediated by Jesus as limited and confined in principle to Christians. The teaching of the New Testament that God wills the salvation of all human beings has been brought into new focus in today's context as an essential element of the meaning of Jesus. This renewed emphasis has so relativized the exclusivist themes that are also found in the New Testament that, when they stand alone, they seem like cultural myopia.

Orthodoxy is not measured by any one of its three criteria, but in the balance of all three.

There are multiple ways of expressing a response to the narrow christological question of the status of Jesus Christ in relation to God and other human beings. This is true especially of the New Testament, before christological discussion became narrowed down to the terms of an incarnation of the Word of God. But in all the christologies of the New Testament, that which binds them together is the soteriological conviction that God has worked human salvation through the mediation of Jesus of Nazareth. That mediation of salvation is the point of christology in this sense: the experience of salvation is that out of which christological reasoning is generated, and that which it attempts to explain and express. In the New Testament and patristic periods that experience took the form of the culture, language, and problems that were raised at that time. The tradition was intelligible to those who formulated it in the terms of the historical moment.

That logic is not different today. A pluralist christology conforms to the data of the past in the measure that it preserves the existential point of the many christologies of the New Testament and the classical doctrines: namely that it is truly God who is operative in Jesus Christ for human salvation. In other words, the measure of orthodoxy cannot be reduced to the comparison of words today with words of the past as though the words had no historical basis and communitarian life. A pluralist christology conforms to tradition when it preserves the existential, soteriological, and spiritual point of past teachings. Therefore a christology is meaningful and orthodox in the measure in which it intelligibly expresses and 'explains' the salvation from God that Christians experience in and through Jesus of Nazareth. But to be intelligible today that explanation must include within God's reign the possibility of the effective salvation of all in history. And the concrete efficacy of that entails in its turn recognition and functional validation of the religions that make the religious question and the experience of ultimate reality available to people.

The new and distinctive character of pluralist christology lies in its noncompetitive premise and context.

I conclude this schematic map of a christology that is pluralist and orthodox with a statement of where its specific difference from earlier christologies lies. This does not consist in lowering a Christian estimate of Jesus, but in expanding its relevance. The difference lies in recognizing that what God has done in Jesus, God does generally. Pluralist christology does not differ from christologies of the past in what it affirms about Jesus Christ, but in the context in which christological doctrine is formulated and in the noncompetitive way in which Jesus Christ is understood. Pluralist christology recognizes that other religions and other religious symbols mediate the 'same' transcendent source and power of salvation. Put simply, pluralist christology is orthodox in affirming the basic experience and conviction of Christians regarding the true divinity of Jesus, but it does so in a non-competitive way. It simply recognizes that what God has done in Jesus, God can do in other religious mediations and does.

Notes

1 Often the term 'normative' is used for the word 'relevant.' But normativity has become an ambiguous and perhaps dysfunctional category at this point, and I use it sparingly.

2 It is often said today that Jesus did not preach his own person, but was theocentric in focusing his message on the reign of God. This contextual reflection is important and significant. This whole discussion aims at negotiating a shift from christocentrism to theocentrism. Christian faith is necessarily christomorphic because Jesus Christ is the central symbol focusing Christian faith on God. But Christian faith is not necessarily christocentric, but can be theocentric, in the way it construes all objective reality.

Source: Roger Haight, SJ, 2005, *The Future of Christology*, New York: Continuum, pp. 148, 156–64 (chapter: 'Outline for an Orthodox Pluralist Christology').

Section B: Other Approaches

4

Particularities

PAUL HEDGES

Introduction

These readings reflect approaches to other faiths often termed 'particularist', an approach that rejects and tries to move beyond the threefold schema of exclusivism, inclusivism and pluralism. Some classify its adherents as exclusivist or inclusivist, others suggest it may be a fourth category; however, such classifications would not please proponents of this view who see themselves as occupying a space beyond it. They see the classical typology (and its views) as 'modernist', while their own stance is 'post-modern',[1] and is explicitly anti-pluralist in seeking to base a discourse on other faith traditions from within one tradition alone, and to stress the utter difference of disparate religious worldviews.

Our selections come from two principal exponents of this viewpoint, Gavin D'Costa and Paul J. Griffiths. D'Costa is a significant Roman Catholic contributor to debates on the theology of religions; his Catholicism is central to his theology, with much of his work seeking to interpret and respond faithfully to Vatican II and subsequent documents from the *magisterium*. Originally a supporter and advocate of both inclusivism and the threefold typology, he has, in recent years, taken up the particularist stance.[2] Some have seen this as his moving to an exclusivist position, but I think this fails to do justice to his position, and perhaps also suggests why we may wish to see particularities as a fourth paradigm, for its proponents do not always clearly fit the categories in ways we would expect. Our extract encompasses two parts of a chapter on 'Trinitarian Theology and the Religions', from sections entitled 'The Trinity and Openness to Other Religions' and 'Whose "Openness", Which "Tolerance"'. These headings tell us something of his purpose: he suggests a Trinitarian stance allows Christians to be more open to truth than a pluralist, and questions what he sees as the totalizing tendency of pluralists to deny difference. He asserts his approach exhibits 'a greater "openness" than found within … pluralists …'.[3] Griffiths' academic speciality is in Buddhism, but he is also a Christian theologian. He has sought to reconcile what he finds to be the very different basis of Buddhist and Christian thought, and suggests that traditional pluralist or inclusivist thinking, which sees them as moving to similar ends, is simply naive. In our selection he expounds a view of religion as a total way of life, before suggesting that, if taken seriously, this view, which encompasses thought and practice, makes it impossible to combine a worldview which crosses the boundary between two faiths. To this end, he employs a linguistic comparison (something common in particularist writers) suggesting that, as with languages, we cannot be native speakers of two faith traditions. While the arguments of particularists are open to question, and even if we do not agree with their stance, we must certainly take seriously the challenges and issues they present.

Notes

1 A clear statement of particularity as a post-modern alternative is found in the writings of the notable evangelical scholar, Alistair McGrath, 1996, 'A Particularist View: A Post-Enlightenment Approach', in D. L. Okholm and T. R. Phillips (eds), *Four Views on Salvation in a Pluralistic World*, Grand Rapids, MI: Zondervan, pp. 151–80. Post-modernism is a notoriously tricky term to pin down, and is used in various ways; for an overview of how it commonly seems to be employed within particularist-style thinkers and in much academic discourse on religion and related fields (at least as interpreted by the present writer), see Paul Hedges, 2008, 'Particularities: Tradition-Specific Post-Modern Perspectives', in Paul Hedges and Alan Race (eds), *SCM Core Text Christian Approaches to Other Faiths*, London: SCM Press, pp. 112–35, pp. 113–15.

2 E.g., the earlier *Theology and Religious Pluralism* (Oxford: Blackwell, 1986) is very different in tone and character from the work from which our extract comes, *The Meeting of Religions and the Trinity* (Maryknoll, NY: Orbis, 2000).

3 D'Costa, *The Meeting of Religions*, p. 134. This quote immediately follows the section given here, and his reference to pluralists refers specifically to John Hick, Paul Knitter and Dan Cohn-Sherbok, whom he critiques at length.

Whose 'Openness', Which 'Tolerance'

GAVIN D'COSTA

To return to my question about the implications of affirming the presence of the Holy Spirit in the world, something that the church does see fit to do, without denying John's rightful caution,[1] we might well bring some of the threads together regarding the church and its Trinitarian self-understanding. One might even turn the question round and ask, what does it mean to the church to say that the Spirit is present outside itself within the world religions? There are at least seven important points that follow.

First, it is clear from our exegesis, that all talk of the Spirit is only properly related to the ecclesial set of events in which the church's discernment of the Spirit actually generates new forms of practice and articulation in its non-identical repetition and reception of Christ's gift of redeeming love. This means that we must be *extremely reticent* about any abstract talk of the

'Spirit in other religions,' for this bears little Johannine rhetorical sense. If it is to bear any Johannine sense, then it can only be generated in the context of *specific* Christian engagements with non-Christian cultures and practices, for the claim that the Spirit is at work in the world can only be part of the church's discernment (not ownership) of the hidden depths of God's trinitarian action of love, struggling to be born into creation and culture. Hence, any claim about the Spirit in other religions should be taken neither as a phenomenological socio-historical description of a religion, nor as a claim that will necessarily be well-received by a non-Christian (although such usage will always be meant positively). Rather it constitutes a theological evaluation that must spring from and lead to fresh practices *within the church* if the claim is to have any credence. The claims of the Holy Spirit's presence is therefore an *intra-Christian claim* and does not at all mitigate the challenges and questions that Christians might put to such alternative practices. It indicates that in such engagements with non-Christian cultures, the church is called to be a sign of judgment and forgiving redemption, like Christ. It may also receive the 'gift' of God from the Other, in a way that is only retrospectively discerned by the church, and might well be denied, or not so interpreted and understood, by that Other.

Second, John helps us to make clear from the outset that a bogus question has haunted much of the contemporary discussion on other religions regarding whether 'revelation' takes place within the religions of the world. For John, the resurrection means that the question of new, different, and alternative 'revelations' is a non-question, for it posits a false understanding of time and history. All creation, all time and history, all the irreducible particularities of each person, are now taken up into the new creation inaugurated by Jesus. This is why allegorical and typological readings of Israel's history and world history were permissible in the early and medieval church: for all history, especially Israel's, both prefigures and participates in this single new creation inaugurated in Jesus Christ. There can be no question of 'other revelations' in so much as this might be understood as other 'gods,' or a cancellation of how God has chosen to reveal God's-self in trinitarian form. However, by saying *a priori* that there is no new revelation apart from Christ, one is neither circumscribing nor restricting the reality of the Holy Spirit's universal and particular activity, or limiting it exclusively to previous practices and understandings within the living tradition. The statement that there is no new revelation is a claim that all truth, in whatever form, will serve to make Christ known more fully to Christians – (and to the world?), *without understanding* what this will mean in advance in practice and theory. Milbank puts the matter well regarding the corporate 'person' of Jesus as including reference to all other 'persons':

> Jesus is perfectly identified only as the source, goal and context of all our lives: the *esse* of his personality is, in Thomist terms, *esse ipsum*, or the

infinite totality of actualized being which is 'eminently' contained in God. If this is the case, then it cannot be true that we have a metaphysically 'initial' perfect vision of Jesus ... which we later approximate through our imitations. On the contrary, only through such imitations, and through observing the likeness of Jesus in others, will a full sense of Jesus's personality be approximated to.[2]

Third, this 'observing' the likeness of Jesus in others is precisely part of what it also means to say that the Holy Spirit is present in the world, in the 'Other,' and requires an ecclesial act of discernment, as it is here that the possible use of 'Christ' language takes shape. The Spirit in the church allows for the possible (and extremely complex and difficult) discernment of Christ-like practice in the Other, and in so much as Christ-like activity takes place, then this can also only be through the enabling power of the Spirit. It must be clear from this that other religions, in keeping with their own self-understanding, may generate profoundly Christ-like behavior. It may also be that such Christ-likeness is in resistance to elements within their own tradition. It may also be that the church fails entirely to recognize this Christ-likeness, as it has done in its own history (when persecuting those who are eventually declared saints, like Joan of Arc). Either way, this point facilitates an open and generous enjoyment of 'good lives' found within other religions; indeed, to such an extent that Christians might even colloquially use the word 'saint' of a non-Christian. However, I am extremely reticent about technically calling non-Christians saints, not because of any lack of holiness and sanctity within those who are not Christians, but because 'saints' is a public term of recognition by the church of its own mission being incarnate in the life of a person.[3] However, the experience of holy lives outside the church is extremely significant for the church. It is here that the distinction and relationship of Spirit and Son language takes on one possible meaning in the context of other religions. This never-ending process of non-identical repetition involves reading *all creation* in Christ through the guidance of the Holy Spirit, in each and every moment of the church's life, such that Milbank adds immediately to the statement just cited:

> To some extent, the observation of *every* human 'person' follows this pattern, but only in the case of Jesus does an accurate rendering of his personhood involve an ultimate attention to everyone, in so far as their 'truth' lies in Christ.[4]

Fourth, this brings out the dynamic of John's theology, for it properly means that in so much as the Spirit is present in the world, then the world can be challenged on account of the elements of truth it might already hold, and these elements, when incorporated into Christian articulations and practice, serve to once more give praise to the triune God – even though such incorporation may rightly involve radical discontinuity. This under-standing certainly precludes any triumphalist understanding of the Spirit's presence, for it does not elevate to an Archimedian point either the practices or articulations of the church, but shows the constant need to re-engage and re-present the gospel under the guidance of the Spirit.

Fifth, in the light of John, saying that the Spirit is present in the lives of non-Christians as do the Conciliar and post-Conciliar documents, is both a *judgment* upon the church and a sign of *promise* to the church. It is a judg-ment, for John has told us that the Spirit's presence in bringing to form a new Christ-like creation is always a condemnation on the powers of dark-ness, 'the ruler of the world is judged' (Jn 16:11). For the church, it may be that through the actions of non-Christians it comes to recognize how it is itself ensnared by the powers of darkness. Through the witness that non-Christians give through their lives and teachings, Christians have often been called into more faithful discipleship. The Spirit's presence in other religions is also the source of promise and great joy to the church, for in being open and attentive to the Holy Spirit, it grows in its own relationship to God and those from other religions. This first movement (relationship to God) will mean inculturation and transformation. Dom Henri Le Saux (Abhishiktananda), at least in his early days, experienced precisely this in his meeting and learning from Hindu gurus, as did Thomas Merton in his meetings with Buddhist monks. Both 'returned' to generate richer forms of Christian discipleship. There are countless other important testimonies, including one of the most famous: Jesus' exaltation of the Samaritan as an example of real love of neighbour (Lk 10:25–37).[5]

Sixth, despite the above, one should certainly not say that every event that prompts new practices of non-identical repetition is of the Spirit, for this would simply be an uncritical baptism with the Spirit of all creation and culture. Rather, it is to say that when the church's encounter with religions generates this type of Spirit language from the Christian (since it is language that belongs within the Christian context), then we must remain radically open to its implications which are deeply ecclesiological and trinitarian.

Seventh, John's theology of the Spirit drives us even further to explore any such affirmation of the Spirit's presence in other religions, for the new prac-tice enjoined of the church in the making of such statements requires also the issues of indigenization and mission to be further clarified and devel-oped for they are intrinsically interrelated. In the context of the present chapter, I would only like to make one general point. I would like to suggest that the often cited distinctions between mission, dialogue, and incultura-tion are fluid and unhelpful. This is because if the church must learn another language as its first language, if it is to engage in dialogue and mission, then both activities are intrinsically related. In any engagement, even the act of understanding, questions and criticism as well as affirmation will surface. In this sense, mission is impossible without dialogue, and vice versa.

Furthermore, in so much as learning this second language will eventually alter our first language, especially when the second language users convert to Christianity, then a process of inculturation will follow, which will both possibly enrich Christian self-understanding and practice (see GS 44)[6] or/ and transform it so that radical discontinuity sets in (how modernity determines Christian discourse in Hick, Knitter, and Cohn-Sherbok).

Proper and legitimate inculturation or indigenization is always an act of continuity within a greater discontinuity: a taking up of what disciples from different cultures and religions may bring to the church, but in this taking up, this being raised, the configuration of new life that emerges can never be predicted or even fully assessed except retrospectively. So while inculturation is always a process of transforming that which may have already been enlivened by the Spirit, it cannot but recreate and reconfigure elements within the church's new practice. Vatican II expresses this precisely and starkly concerning growth in indigenous churches:

> Whatever good is in the minds and hearts of men, whatever good lies latent in the religious practices and cultures of diverse peoples, is not only saved from destruction but is also healed, ennobled, and perfected unto the glory of God, the confusion of the devil, and the happiness of man. (LG 17)[7]

...

To conclude this chapter, I want to take the tenets so valued by pluralists and appropriate them but in so doing, transform them. This rhetorical strategy suggests that my trinitarian orientation may better attain the real goals of pluralists, 'openness,' 'tolerance,' and 'equality,' even if these goals are so changed as to be unrecognizable to pluralists. In this sense, they are not the same goals at all. However, since my dialectical arguments were deployed to show that the pluralist goals, as they themselves understood them, were unattainable, then this strategy allows us to see coherent and sustainable ways in which openness, tolerance, and equality might be displayed – and even be proposed as attractive to pluralists. There may be a clearer relationship between dialectics and rhetorics for my engagement with Christian pluralists, but obviously less so for those from other religions.

Regarding openness, I tried to show that a certain *a priorism* operated negatively regarding other religions within our Christian, Jewish, Hindu, and Buddhist thinkers. In varying ways, they all knew what they would find within other religions prior to any real historical engagement. In varying ways they also all knew what they would value and prize within other religions, prior to their meeting them. In varying ways they were all actually left untouched by the different engagements with others, with the exception of the Dalai Lama who felt, for example, that Christianity's social engagement helped him understand compassion more fully. In contrast, there are at least three important ways in which openness can be genuinely said to exist within my trinitarian orientation. First, I have been arguing above that since the trinitarian doctrine of God is only eschatologically 'closed,' and is always also a doctrine about the shape of the church, it means that the very doctrine of a trinitarian God within Christianity allows Christianity to maintain a real openness to God *in history*. Since God acts historically, as we have seen in the incarnation, and the doctrine of the church is such that we see this action continuing in history, although through a 'glass darkly,' and this very church acknowledges God's continuous activity outside its visible confines, we therefore have a strong theological basis for such an openness. Since we have seen that the Holy Spirit may be active within other religions, if the church is closed to other religions, then the church will be guilty of being inattentive to the promptings of God which may lead it into greater holiness, truth, and goodness. Being inattentive to other religions is a form of idolatry.

Second, there can be no *a priori* knowledge of what other religions may disclose: the surprises, beauty, terror, truth, holiness, deformity, cruelty, and goodness that they might display. The history of religions is still in the making and it is therefore necessary for the church to be attentive to the auto-interpretation of the religions if it is to be open to history. Of course, there is an *a priori* set of commitments within this process, that of commitment to the Roman Catholic church, but what I want to suggest is that this commitment cannot *a priori* negate or affirm other religions apart from the context of detailed historical engagement with those traditions. Any such positive or negative judgments are then *a posteriori* and must be accounted for.

Third, taking the reality of other religions seriously, either in their auto-interpretation or within Christianity's hetero-interpretation (which may or may not overlap in part), means that the church is laying itself open to genuine change, challenge, and questioning. I tried to show learning from other religions is not simply a matter of looking at the Other to see Christianity's already attained mirror image (as the undialectical notion of fulfillment tended to suggest), but in meeting the Other, there may be a real challenge to Christian identity in the radical manner expressed in *Gaudium et Spes* 44. Hence, Christian practice and reflection may change in ways that are not *a priori* predictable in the light of encountering other religions.

Notes

1 This refers to his previous discussion of John's Gospel, about the nature of the church, and problems in fulfilling its mission (ed.).

2 Milbank, 'Name', 325 [John Milbank, 1991, 'The Name of Jesus: Incarnation, Atonement, Ecclesiology', *Modern Theology* 7.4, pp. 311–33]. He uses 'imitation' here in contrast to the earlier citation (note 20 [sic – citation should be to note 30 of D'Costa's

chapter]) to mean non-identical repetition as the imitation of Christ.

3 See discussion of non-Christian saints in chapter 5, pp. 152–3, and see also David McCarthy Matzko, 'Christ's Body in Its Fullness: Resurrection and the Lives of Saints', in Gavin D'Costa, ed., *Resurrection Reconsidered*, Oneworld, Oxford, 1996, 102–17. See also Jean Daniélou's beautiful treatment of pre-Christian saints: *Holy Pagans of the Old Testament*, Longman, Green & Co., London, 1957. All easy talk about saintly lives avoids the complex question of identifying saintliness, which is still one good reason for the cumbersome process of canonization employed by the Roman Catholic church. Countless unsung saints are also praised in the Roman Missal.

4 Milbank, 'Name', 325, my emphasis.

5 The Samaritans were seen at best as heretical and schismatic Jews, and at worse, as 'pagans.' See Jospeh A, Fitzmyer, *The Gospel According to Luke: XXXIV*, The Anchor Bible, Doubleday, New York, 1985, 887. One should also recall the earlier rejection of Jesus by the Samaritans in Lk 9:51; and Jesus' exchange with the Samaritan woman at the well in Jn 4:1–42. These other passages make the story in Lk 10:25–37 even more remarkable.

6 The reference is to the Vatican document *Gaudium et Spes* (ed.).

7 The reference is to the Vatican document *Lumen Gentes* (ed.).

Source: Gavin D'Costa, 2000, *The Meeting of Religions and the Trinity*, Maryknoll, NY: Orbis, pp. 128–31, 132–3 (chapter 4).

Problems of Religious Diversity

PAUL J. GRIFFITHS

For a comprehensive form of life to seem to those who belong to it incapable of abandonment it must seem to them that living in it is sufficiently constitutive or definitive of who they are that leaving it is impossible without also leaving themselves. All of us, I expect, belong to forms of life that seem to us like this. The most obvious example is the form of life constituted by speaking and thinking in our native language. I live in the house of English in this way, and it seems to me that I can't cease to do so. This doesn't mean, of course, that I can't learn to read or speak another language; but it does mean that in so learning I will always and necessarily be a native speaker of English grafting another linguistic skill upon the trunk of my Englishness. Abandoning the form of life *speaking English natively* is certainly unimaginable to me, even if not strictly inconceivable.

A religious form of life will also be like this. It will seem to those who inhabit it not only to be comprehensive, but also to be incapable of abandonment. A Catholic Christian, for example, baptized as a baby, trained up in the faith, a regular and faithful attender at Mass, a reader of the Bible, a sayer of prayers – such a person is likely to be in the same case as a native speaker of English. She may be able to express in words the claim that she might cease to be a native speaker of English. But such expressions will be as imaginatively empty as the claim *I might run a mile in two minutes* or *I might be able to solve cube roots in my head with rapidity and ease*. They will bear no phenomenal content, which is to say that they will conjure nothing but a concept in the minds of those who use them.

Yet a third characteristic needs to be added to comprehensiveness and incapability of abandonment in order to make a form of life religious. It is *centrality*. To say of a form of life that it is central for those who belong to it is to say that it seems to them to address the questions of paramount importance to the ordering of their lives. Such a question might be: Should I think about and behave toward all humans as if they were in all important respects equal? A Catholic Christian form of life will provide an affirmative answer to this question (all humans have been created by God and bear God's image, and as a result should be so treated); a Brahminical Hindu one will provide a negative answer (your fundamental duties toward any particular human being are given by your respective places in the ordered hierarchy of caste; this will differ from case to case). Other such questions might be: How should I understand my fundamental purpose in life? Should I kill and eat sentient nonhuman creatures? Is beauty the primary value? And so on.

...

On this understanding of religion, what is to be said about religious diversity? The first and obvious point is that there are likely to be many religions, which is to say that there are likely to be many different forms of life that seem to those who belong to them to be comprehensive, incapable of abandonment, and of central importance. This can reasonably be said without knowledge of the particulars of any such forms of life. It is, after all, easily possible to imagine religions significantly different from one another in their particulars. A man excessively devoted to his wife might, for instance, live in his marriage as a form of life of the relevant sort; in such a case, *being married* would seem to him to comprehend all his other forms of life, to be constitutive of his very being, and to address all questions of central importance to his life. Another person, excessively committed politically, might belong to a form of life in which the party (whatever it happens to be) provides a comprehensive form of life that seems incapable of abandonment, and so forth. Perhaps such people are in important respects pathological or deluded; but there can be no doubt that the forms of life they belong to are religious in the sense in play here.

This imagination of religious diversity shows only that significantly different religions may exist. But even the most superficial investigation of particular forms of life that seem, on the face of things, to qualify as religious makes this possibility actual: not only can there be significantly different religions, but there actually are. The particulars of a Marxist form of life that seems to its inhabitants comprehensive, incapable of abandonment, and centrally important (and there are still Marxists who inhabit Marxism religiously) are deeply different from the particulars of a Christian form of life that bears the same characteristics for those who belong to it. And the same would have to be said, with appropriate changes of substance, for the particulars of a Buddhist form of life as compared with those of an Islamic form of life. And so on. This fact, the fact that there is deep religious diversity, raises two questions immediately. First, what makes one religion different from another? Second, how does the kind of difference among religions so far mentioned map on to the great complexes of thought and practice often called the *world religions* – Christianity, Buddhism, Islam, and so on?

It's relatively easy to answer the first question – What makes one religion different from another? – in a formal way. A religion ceases to be the religion it is just when one or more of the elements essential to it is lost by abandonment or transformation; and one religion is different from another just when it is not possible for the same person to inhabit a Buddhist form of life that loss of any contact with members of the Sangha, the monastic order, is also loss of something essential to their religion, and as a result amounts to abandonment of it. Or, it may seem to a Muslim who adds belief in the Trinity to his Islamic form of life that he has replaced it thereby with a new one because the theism that informed the old religion has been transformed. By contrast, it may seem to a Reform Jew who becomes Orthodox that she has not abandoned or replaced her earlier religious form of life, but only modified it as one might modify one's marriage by adding to it a severer and more demanding observance of the disciplines of love. And, finally, it seems reasonable to say that Greek Orthodox Christianity and Gelug Tibetan Buddhism are different religions in much the same way that it's performatively impossible to belong to both at once – to be a sumo wrestler and a balance-beam gymnast, or natively to live in the house of English and the house of Japanese.

Source: Paul J. Griffiths, 2001, *Problems of Religious Diversity*, Oxford: Blackwell, pp. 10–11, 12–13.

5

Feminisms

JEANNINE HILL-FLETCHER

Introduction

The major thrust of feminist thought has been to illuminate the distinctive experiences of women as they have been impacted by gendered constructions of social norms and expectations. Applied to the discourse on religious pluralism, a feminist lens illuminates the reality that what is often described as the encounter or experience of religious difference has been focused on male actors and male experiences. Thinking from the experiences of women, feminist writings are directed towards unearthing the masculinist bias and writing towards a theology that ensures the well-being of women. As such, feminist theological writings tend to include the following features: (1) a critical engagement with God-talk; (2) a new understanding of Christ; (3) a liberationist reading of salvation; (4) a theology beyond the Bible; and (5) the criterion of women's well-being.

The following essays exhibit some of these fundamental features as they argue that women's interreligious engagement is of a unique form, rooted not only in 'being other' to a male-centred tradition, but embracing one's own 'otherness within' through an understanding of hybrid identity. Kate McCarthy provides an overview of feminist methodology in religious pluralism, touching on many features of a feminist theological method and underscoring the 'plural identity' which shapes a feminist outlook. Chung Hyun Kyung extends this plurality to recognize the hybridity and syncretism of religious identities that shape her understanding of God, Christ and the value of religious differences. For this feminist theologian, religious pluralism is not a problem 'out there in the world' but a reality that shapes a single life in multiplicity. Together, these essays reflect the way that feminist theology aims at the well-being of women and positively draws on the many religious outlooks to achieve that aim. For contemporary feminist theologians, religious pluralism is a syncretistic dance for the healing of the world.

Seeking the Religious Roots of Pluralism

CHUNG HYUN KYUNG

I am a Christian theologian from South Korea. When I think about Christianity in human history, it has been one of the most exclusivistic religions, and we have this record of crusades, witch hunts, colonization in the name of God, and imperialistic Western expansion in the name of Christianity. So, I come with my historical burden, but here I want to talk about pluralism, specifically from the perspective of Korean Protestant women.

When I was a young feminist in my twenties, I saw a T-shirt that grabbed my attention. It read, 'Women who want to be equal to men lack ambition.' I felt how true that was. Throughout all my participation in various people's movements, such as the Anti-colonization Nationalist movement, the Democratization movement, and the Labor movement in Korea, I felt in my bones that, indeed, women are the last colony. Following Virginia Woolf s words, 'As a woman, I don't have a country,' I want to add that, as a woman, I do not want a country. As a woman, the whole world is my country.

When I heard about the topic for this occasion, the first thing that came up in my mind was that T-shirt I saw when I was twenty. Now, as a forty-year-old Asian, postmodern, eco-feminist, liberation-feminist theologian, I would like to say that people who want religious pluralism in church and society lack ambition. Following the debates on pluralism in academia, the church, and society, I have been disappointed, because calling for pluralism still seems to remain at the 'minimum level of tolerance for the differences.' Of course, that is important. After witnessing painful conflicts in Northern Ireland, Bosnia, and India and the burning of churches in the South here and the burning of temples in Korea, I know how important it is to have a minimum level of tolerance such as not to kill or violate other human beings in the name of God or in the name of the Holy.

I am, however, unsatisfied when I listen to the importance of pluralism, diversity, multiculturalism, and cross-cultural understanding of academia, church, and society in the U.S.A., because their emphasis on pluralism, diversity, and multiculturalism is establishing soft, not hard, pluralism, diversity, and multiculturalism. Soft pluralism or multiculturalism means we welcome ethnic food, ethnic clothing, ethnic music. You can have a Chinese breakfast, Italian lunch, and French dinner, but do not touch our political or economic power. You can also contribute in these soft areas, but we are for the capitalist globalization, Coca-colonization, CNN-ization of the world, so we do not have any willingness to share this kind of power. We do not want to have respect for differences in this area. Therefore, soft pluralism does not deal with serious economic and political power or differences. I call it lazy, selfish, immoral pluralism.

Without dealing with this lazy pluralism in politicoeconomic justice, I do not know whether we can have religious pluralism in religion or vice versa. Therefore, I do not like the common usage of 'pluralism.' I think that we have to go beyond pluralism. We need an interdependent, interpenetrating, power-sharing, mutual transformation for our common survival and liberation and for the sustainable earth community.

The organizers of this panel asked me to provide a justification of pluralism within my religious tradition. After being forced to justify my mere existence as an Asian intellectual woman for so many years, I do not want to use up my precious time for another sort of justification. Rather, I want to say, 'I am who I am, and religious pluralism is what it is.' It is a fact. Look at the world; there are thousands of different religions, thousands of different manifestations of Christianities in Asia, Africa, and the Latin Americas. Whether you like it or not, they are there. However, I want to pinpoint some theological foundations that are open to religious pluralism and move to my ambition of going beyond religious pluralism.

My Christian tradition has been one of the most exclusivistic religions of the world and one of the religions that has created the most wars in human history – claiming the uniqueness, finality, and centrality of Jesus Christ and claiming no salvation without Jesus Christ. We do have an alternative tradition that is more inclusive and open to other religious traditions. First, I will call it creation tradition. We believe that God is a creator. God created everything in the world and said, 'It is beautiful.' In this creation, the other world religions are included. Therefore, other religions are also beautiful in God's eyes. I also want to pinpoint the tradition of mysticism in Christianity. In Christian mysticism, God is beyond our naming, beyond our form and imagination. God is pure emptiness, as Meister Eckhardt said. Talking about God is always the speaking of the unspeakable in this tradition. We share the silence of this original emptiness. In this mystical union, silence and emptiness are the places for all other religions.

I also want to point to the tradition of Gnosticism in Christianity. In Christian Gnosticism, which was defined by our church as heretical, every one of us shares a divine spark, a divine wisdom, that will connect us to God. This divine wisdom and spark we share with everybody. This divine spark can be interpreted as Tao, Prajnaparamita, Brahman. Here we can meet with all other world religions. In Gnosticism, Jesus said, 'If you bring out what is within you, what is within you will save you. But, if you cannot bring out what is within you, then what is within you will destroy you.' In this 'what is within you,' we can meet all the people of all the other religions.

Why must we go beyond religious pluralism? When people ask what I am religiously, I say, 'My bowel is Shamanist. My heart is Buddhist. My right brain, which defines my mood, is Confucian and Taoist. My left brain, which defines my public language, is Protestant Christian, and, overall, my aura is eco-feminist.' I am proud to say that it took three Master's degrees and one Ph.D. in theology, five years in intense psychotherapy and Zen meditation, and my participation in various people's movements! As a Korean woman, I was raised in the 5,000-year-old Shamanist tradition and the 2,000-year-old Taoist-Confucian tradition, with 2,000 years of Buddhist tradition, 100 years of Protestant tradition, and twenty years of eco-feminist tradition. So, my body is like a religious pantheon. I am living with communities of Gods, a continuum of divinity, and a family of religions. Therefore, I need many years of archeological exploration of my religiosity within my body and within my community. Especially as a woman, it is necessary.

So-called, all higher world religions are patriarchal and are institutionalized under the patriarchal light. So we have patriarchal Buddhists and patriarchal Christians having interreligious dialogue, and we have a nice patriarchal conclusion there. This is not just my existential reality but the reality of many women's popular religiosity in Asia. Women are margins of the patriarchal, institutional churches, and, of course, the Korean Church embodied the nineteenth-century American imperialistic, triumphalistic, fundamentalist Protestantism that brought Christianity, with American political imperialism, to Korea. What we learned from Christianity was the ultimate missionary position! Western culture is always up, and our culture and experience are always down. In order to overcome this missionary position, we have to get back our primordial religious experience.

When I look at our women's religious experience very critically, it is not a religious pluralism. It is sometimes syncretism, sometimes symbiosis, and sometimes a synergetic dance of many religions in our daily lives. Therefore, when I see the debate of religious pluralism in the United States, I feel that it seems very academic, very Western, very male. By academic, I mean that, when I look at women's popular religiosity, each religion – Christianity, Buddhism, Taoism, Confucianism – is not a neatly separated, packaged, or sanitized religion. It is all blurry. They permeate each other. It is not like a packaged, sanitized Perdue chicken bleeding there. Also, when I think about this debate, it is very Western because many world religions in the West are still very young. So, communities are not intermingled, and religious values did not become mainline cultural values. However, when you come to Asia, our religious and our cultural values many times are intermingled.

I also think it is a very male-centered perspective, because, in our academic discipline, we say 'pluralism, yes' but 'syncretism, hell no,' because I think there is a fear of chaos, a fear of the body. In the Christian tradition, we mix and appreciate other religions in a kind of religious adultery. When I look at women's religiosity, I can see that it can be described with the metaphors of a medicine chest, a kaleidoscope, and alchemy, because women use the different drawers of this medicine chest to heal, to liberate, and to survive. They also intermingle some part of their religions for their life, for their survival, through multiple colors and shapes of the kaleidoscope. It is also alchemy, as women mix something and develop something new. So, there are many fusions of horizons, which I think is the future.

Of course, there are many dangers. There are many people who ask about this danger: 'Are you making stew, soup, or a salad bar?' No, it is not stew or soup or a salad bar. Rather, it is like a living organism. At the center, there is a center criterion, which is of course subjective, but it is based on women's survival and liberation. Sometimes it is very dangerous, because their survival and liberation are really at the expense of others; however, I think that, by our common dialogue, sharing, and participation in the common liberation praxis, we can expand our criteria. Our criteria should be justice and peace, the integrity of creation, and building of a sustainable, life-giving earth community.

What I am saying is that it is not a kind of intermingling where hegemonic power eats up all other differences. Rather, in this fusion of horizons, differences vivify, transform, and enhance each other – as Rabbi Marc Tanenbaum said, 'Our differences enhance our lives.' For me, as an Asian Christian woman, God is not one. God is not many. God is energy beyond one and many. God penetrates and permeates all of us. We are all children of God, and all religions are different-colored flowers in this magnificently beautiful and painful garden of God called Earth.

Source: Chung Hyun Kyung, 1997, 'Seeking the Religious Roots of Pluralism', *Journal of Ecumenical Studies* 34.3, pp. 399–401.

Women's Experience as a Hermeneutical Key to a Christian Theology of Religions

KATE MCCARTHY

The problem of a Christian theological interpretation of religious pluralism is an ancient one. Unfortunately, most contemporary proposals do little to improve on ancient solutions. Mainstream Roman Catholic and Protestant approaches by and large reject the exclusivism and absolutism of traditional orthodoxies, but their inclusivist and pluralist alternatives have similarly shaky foundations and equally troubling implications. The limited scope of the present discussion, it increasingly appears, is in large part due to the limited range of participants in the conversation: despite attempts to ground interreligious dialogue in the living faith of the world's religious communities, the effort to define a Christian theology of religions remains almost completely a Western, and masculine, academic enterprise.

My hypothesis that women theologians might turn the problem over in a new way, as they have in so many other branches of theology, is frustrated by the fact that, to date, women have done very little writing on this subject. As feminist theology moves into its second generation, it is demonstrating both breadth and depth in the issues it takes on and the methods it employs, but it does not seem especially interested in the problem of other religions, at least not in any systematic way. But while feminist theologians themselves may not be so interested in the perennial Christian theological problem of religious pluralism, I believe their work offers resources for a new approach to that issue that is both exciting and timely.

The present dilemma in Christian theologies of pluralism can be put like this: how do we move toward a de-absolutized, pluralism-endorsing understanding of Christianity's relation with non-Christian traditions without losing the distinctiveness of Christian identity and the solid foundation on which to base committed Christian praxis? Pluralist theologies like that of John Hick[1] have gone far in recovering a sense of Christian humility and openness to the diversity of divine *personae* manifested in the world's spiritual traditions, but they have been charged with divesting the Christian worldview of the power to define and sustain Christian commitment that traditionally resided in the tradition's claims to uniqueness. By the same token, theologies like those of Paul Griffiths, Schubert Ogden and, for different reasons, George Lindbeck, which would maintain the claim to Christian normativity, thus far have not demonstrated an alternative to the pluralist move that can meaningfully bridge Christian commitment with openness to real religious difference.

When women's experience, diverse and complex as it is, is made the point of departure for theological reflection on religious pluralism, new resources emerge for a theology of religions that can genuinely encounter the otherness of the non-Christian without either subsuming that otherness or sacrificing the specific content that enlivens Christian community. The diversity of women's religious experience is critical to this project. If we have learned anything in the past decades of feminist research and writing, it is that we must constantly check our tendencies to speak for each other, to flatten out our racial, class, cultural and sexual diversity in our celebration of our commonality as women. I am attuned to that risk here, as I draw general conclusions from the work of very different theologians writing in very different contexts: Carter Heyward of the United States, Ivone Gebara of Brazil, Mercy Oduyoye of Ghana, and Chung Hyun Kyung of Korea. Indeed, the risk of distortion is especially great here, in that I am hazarding to explicate positions on a matter most of these women have not themselves systematically addressed. But the resources for a viable theology of pluralism implicit in their work in other areas are great enough, I believe, to warrant that risk.

The task of articulating a distinctive women's contribution to a Christian theology of pluralism has two parts. First, those aspects of women's experience that are relevant to this problem must be named and explicated. What, if anything, about the sexual, social and religious experience of women can contribute to new ways of approaching the question of religious diversity? Second, the specific theological implications of those experiences for a Christian understanding of religious difference must be elucidated. What do women's theological method and their reflections on God and Christ, considered in light of these experiences, contribute to an understanding of the place of Christian faith in a religiously plural world?

Three aspects of women's experience across cultures seem particularly relevant to this task: the experience of otherness; a plurality of social location; and an embodied spirituality. One thing that can be said about women without fear of overgeneralizing is that they are not men. Living in a social world characterized by patriarchy and a religious tradition whose theological questions and answers have been provided almost exclusively by men, Christian women have a double experience of otherness that is critical to understanding their theological perspective. Women come at the theological act with a sense of disjunction, knowing that the realities of God and Christ, spirit and grace are central to their identities. Yet they are also aware that the language the tradition offers as an expression of these realities misses the mark, is not their own, and has excluded and distorted them. At the same time that it decries it, women's theology makes of this social and theological otherness a resource – one that is especially useful to a reckoning with religious difference. The challenge of religious pluralism is that of accounting for otherness without subsuming it or annihilating it, and without abandoning one's own distinctive religious identity. In a very real sense, women embody that challenge. Feminist theology of both the first and the third worlds celebrates and makes meaning of theological difference by speaking from its own particularity and resisting the totalizing impulse that is discernible in even the most generous mainstream interpretations of religious pluralism.

The gender-based experience of being other may contribute to the prominence in women's theology of a sense of multiple social location. Women theologians are inevitably 'something else' at the same time they are theologians. The very fact that we identify ourselves as women theologians indicates a consciously plural identity. For Carter Heyward, who defines herself as a 'white Anglo Christian lesbian priest and academic' (1989b, 8[2]), each of these identities calls up a different community of tradition and accountability, communities whose visions are often in tension with one another. But for Heyward, these particular and multiple social locations serve not only as limiting factors in her knowledge, but also as empowering in that they serve as 'a lens through which we may catch a glimpse of what is paradoxically, universally true – that all people are limited by the particularities of their life experiences' (1989b, 9–10).

This universal truth – about the unavailability of universal perspective

– has been a hard-learned lesson for the dominant theological tradition. It is a special challenge for that branch of theology that has tried to reconcile the religious diversity of the world with the normativity of Christian revelation, usually by constructing a universal system large (and vague) enough to encompass all human religiousness. The self-conscious particularity and multiplicity of women's location presents an experiential route to understanding and affirming difference that pluralists would do well to explore.

The ability to stand simultaneously in two or more social locations has been honed to an even greater degree by those women who do theology in postcolonial contexts. In Africa, Asia, and Latin America, Christian women speak out of a tradition that Ghanaian Methodist theologian Mercy Amba Oduyoye calls 'soul-snatching,' a theology that taught the radical disjunction of indigenous religious patterns and Christian revelation and required 'absolute conversion of heart and life' (1986, 37[3]). But of course such conversions are never possible. Indigenous African images and perspectives live on in Oduyoye's theology, giving it a second source of identity. She draws out the implication of her double identity for her theology:

'I cannot be anything else but African. And so, bringing my whole being and life experience to bear upon what I hear of God through Christ, I appropriate for myself a theory of knowledge that does not permit me to see truth as a given that I have to accept or reject. Rather I see myself, in community with others and in the enabling power of the Holy Spirit, called to participate in growing into a fuller understanding of what God is about. Neither the Bible nor the African corpus of sociocultural history can be treated as fossilized touchstones' (1986, 147–8).

This is more than a matter of 'inculturating' Christian truth in an African context; for Oduyoye it constitutes a new *concept* of truth.

Similarly, Korean theologian Chung Hyun Kyung writes of the multiple contexts of Asian Christian women's theology:

The specific historical experience of Asian women is manifested in their struggle as victims and agents of liberation as women. Asian women also use their religiocultural and socio-political traditions for theologizing. They claim their identity as both Asian and Christian. They take themselves seriously ... Recently Asian women theologians have started to look into Asian myth, folktales, songs, poems, proverbs, and religious teachings from Hinduism, Buddhism, Islam, Taoism, shamanism, tribal religions, Confucianism, and Christianity for their theological resources. (1990b, 108[4])

This plurality of sources does not seek to distil a universalized common humanity. As historical victims of that universalizing tendency, Asian women instead opt to hold together these different identities in dynamic and creative tension.

The otherness and multiple social locations of women's experience as represented by Heyward, Oduyoye and Chung are foundations, I believe, for a new kind of affirmation of religious difference. Women's theological work suggests that a life lived at the margins – pressed to the edges by dominant cultures, races and machistic traditions – affords a perspective not granted to those who stand at the center. From the outer edges where women stand, exclusive truth claims tend to ring false, both because women are sensitive to the distortions such claims have wrought on those who lack power and because women's own experience has attuned them to the complex multiplicity of human experience. Brazilian Catholic Sister Ivone Gebara makes this connection explicit:

> The theological work of women reflects an ability to view life as the locus of the simultaneous experience of oppression and liberation, of grace and lack of grace. Such perception encompasses what is plural, what is different, what is other. Although this way of looking is not the exclusive property of women, we must say that it is found to an extraordinary extent among women. In popular struggles, in which women have played a very important role, this ability to grasp in a more unified way the oppositions and contradictions, the contrasts and differences as inherent in human life, has been characteristic of the way in which women live and express their faith. Such behavior enables them to avoid taking dogmatic and exclusive stances, and to perceive or intuit the real complexity of what is human. (1988, 132[5])

If Gebara is correct the voices of women, all women, will be a vital resource for theologies of pluralism. Whether it is the Brazilian Catholic woman presiding over a Candomblé ceremony, the white North American woman making the audacious claim to be both lesbian and Christian, or simply the everyday experience of Christian women everywhere living the contradictions of sex and theological heritage, women's experience offers a history of living the riddles of difference that theologies of religious pluralism thus far have failed conceptually to solve.

A third feature of women's experience that bears on this issue is the pattern of embodied spirituality that also seems to be quite consistent across cultures. In different ways, the theologians I am considering here all draw deeply on the experience of life in woman's body as a theological source. Heyward is perhaps best known for her work in this area. She has identified God with the erotic power that draws us into passionate interrelatedness (1989b, 94), and argues that our most 'christic' experiences are 'our most fully embodied (sensual and erotic) connections in relation to one another, other creatures, and the earth' (1989a, 22[6]).

Gebara draws attention to the mystery that women's embodied experience calls forth when it is finally brought into theological discourse:

When women's experience is expressed in a church whose tradition is machistic, the other side of human experience returns to theological discourse: the side of the person who gives birth, nurses, nourishes, of the person who for centuries has remained silent with regard to anything having to do with theology. Now she begins to express her experience of God ... It is as though we were discovering, very powerfully and starting from our own situation, the mystery of the incarnation of the divine in the human. (1988, 128)

In the work of Gebara and others, this embodied, affective quality of women's experience leads to poetic, analogical theology, one that reaches beyond the limits of formal doctrine.

Chung describes a similarly embodied spirituality among the Asian women she studied. Their theologizing, she notes, begins with storytelling:

The power of storytelling lies in its *embodied truth*. Women talked about their concrete, historical life experiences and not about abstract, metaphysical concepts. Women's truth was generated by their *epistemology from the broken body*. Women's bodies are the most sensitive receiver for historical reality. Their bodies record what has happened in their lives. Their bodies remember what it is like to be a *no-body* and what it is like to be a *some-body*. (1990b, 104)

She relates the storytelling of older Korean women sexually abused by the Japanese, of young Philippine women telling of their guilt, shame and anger about their work as prostitutes in Manila's sex industry, and explains how this kind of embodied truth builds bridges across diverse experiences. For the task of developing a genuinely pluralist theology of religions, the affective – indeed passionately embodied – spirituality of women may draw forth unsuspected points of contact between traditions and open alternative meanings of the Christian claims that have long been stumbling blocks in the interreligious conversation.

With these two features of women's experience in mind, let me now offer a sketch of the specific theological implications that can be drawn from women's theological work for a better Christian theology of pluralism. The first contribution women's theology stands to make is methodological. There is, in the work of the women I am drawing upon, a *hermeneutical audacity* unparalleled in even the most radical of male liberation theologians. Women employ a vast set of theological resources and use the orthodox sources of the tradition in a highly selective and critical way. Oduyoye draws upon African understandings of the self-in-relation for her theological anthropology when she writes, 'In the Akan worldview that operates in the dark mysterious center of my being there sits a sense of my being mystically incorporated into an ever-expanding principle of human be-ing'

(1986, 148). Chung uses the Korean shamanist notion of Han to elucidate a Korean Christian women's theology of suffering and liberation (1990a, 135–46[7]).

For these women, the Bible is a valuable, but not the only source and is read very critically. Chung observes that among Asian women the Bible is used as 'a reference and insight' from which they draw wisdom for their lives but not, because of the great cultural and historical gap between the world of the Bible and their lives, as 'an unchangeable truth from God' (1990b, 106). The norm for her and other women's theology is much more fluid than that of traditional Christian doctrine:

> [T]he norm of Asian women's theology lies in its liberating power, which frees women from the many layers of oppression. Its transforming power heals Asian women to wholeness and enables them to celebrate their lives in fullness with other oppressed people in their communities. (1990b, 109)

Gebara offers a similar explanation of Latin American women's critical use of the tradition:

> [T]he theological tradition shared by different churches does not function as a legitimizing justification that we need only to go on repeating. If we do repeat, it is because that is what today's situation demands, because it does touch the roots of our existence, because to some extent it responds to the problems that ongoing history sets before us. In this sense, what is normative is primarily the present, what calls out today. (1988, 132)

Finally, consider Heyward's radical questioning of christological orthodoxy. Her feminist analysis leads her to 'think the unthinkable' in her diving into christological tradition to challenge the closed canon of christological doctrines by asking whether 'there is something fundamentally damaging to most of humankind in the Christian belief in, and commitment to, Jesus Christ as God's only begotten Son, God the Son himself, our only Lord and Savior' (1984, 213–14[8]).

This kind of method – grounded in lived, embodied experience, drawing on multicultural and multi-religious sources, and willing to challenge the sacrality of both scripture and the tradition's most venerable doctrines – is called for but thus far has not been employed in Christian efforts to come to terms with religious pluralism. Not only does this method facilitate an experientially grounded rather than conceptual interreligious exchange, it also allows for thoroughgoing reassessments and creative reinterpretations of such doctrines as the uniqueness of Christ, which have so long been stumbling blocks in the way of a full Christian endorsement of pluralism.

A second area in which women's theology promises to enrich the theology of pluralism is in its doctrine of God. Out of their experiences of otherness, multi-locatedness and embodiedness, these women articulate an understanding of God that breaks open the often reified categories of the tradition. Consistently across the cultural divides represented by these four theologians, God is understood in thoroughly relational terms. In a 1990 interview, Gebara acknowledges that she does not even have a consistent image of God: 'I'm more likely to speak of God as Vital Force, Greater Mystery, Love or Justice. I see God less as a being and more as a value, an energy that dwells in us that I can't limit to a theory' (1994, 208[9]). Chung explains that Asian Christian women view God not only as both male and female but also as a community, and 'in this image of God as the community in relationship, there is no place for only one, solitary, all-powerful God who sits on the top of the hierarchical power pyramid and dominates all other living beings. Where there is no mutual relationship, there is no human experience of God' (1990b, 49).

Similarly, Oduyoye calls for a relational view of God to help overcome the problems of gendered God language and imagery: 'Relational language about God may provide us with integrated models of community ... The Christian proclamation that God is not a nomad but rather a center of relations ... may provide us with a model of the integrity of persons within community and their interrelatedness' (1986, 136–7). In her glossary to Touching Our Strength, Heyward more radically defines God as 'our power in mutual relation ... both personal and transpersonal. God is the active source of our creative, liberating power ... We embody the sacred when we generate right relation, acting with one another as resources of the divine spirit' (188–9). She affirms the Trinitarian doctrine insofar as it recognizes 'the dynamic relationality in God as well as between God, Jesus, and the rest of us' but insists that this relational God cannot be boxed into any one image and that we 'need not be Christian to experience the dynamic relational movement of the Sacred' (1989b, 189).

The implications of these more fluid conceptions of God for a theology of pluralism are clear. If God, the Christian conception of ultimate reality, is understood as relational rather than monistic or dualistic, the Christian is afforded a new way of thinking about religious truth and about those who understand ultimate reality differently. While monism permits the condemnation of nothing; and dualism promotes the condemnation of anything one disagrees with; a relational understanding of God and truth can condemn as error that which isolates and breaks away from such relationality but endorse and indeed depend upon diverse manifestations of the divine relationship. The view of God that comes through these women's theologies illustrates concretely what pluralist theologian Raimundo Panikkar calls for theoretically: an understanding of pluralism as the factual structure of ultimate reality, not just as a tolerated feature of our human religious expressions (1984, 111[10]). If God is ultimately relational, and those relations are as pluriform as the human struggles for fullness of life, then God is in godself pluralistic, open-ended, future-leading but always embedded in relation and therefore irreducible to monistic abstractions. And because this inexhaustible God is experienced primarily in struggles with and for history's others, these theologies suggest, fuller relation with God requires not only general attention to non-Christian stories, but particular attentiveness to the stories of those on the underside – politically, sexually, economically – of all the world's religious traditions.

The third and last resource I want to draw from these women's theology for a Christian understanding of religious pluralism is their christology. Feminist theologians have struggled for decades with the problems of traditional christology: indeed many see the whole christological enterprise as suspect. While it stems largely from gender-related concerns, women's work in christology is equally significant to a theology of pluralism. The powerful experience of disjunction and exclusion from orthodox affirmations of Jesus as the unique God-man have led women to reconceive questions of christology in terms of soteriology.

In her earlier writings, as noted above, Heyward went so far as to challenge the doctrine of the divinity of Jesus, arguing that it 'grows out of and feeds into unjust social relations' (1984, 217) in that it closes off the ongoing dynamic interrelations of all people with the divine. More recently, she has recognized the danger that a 'fully and only human' Jesus can tend to leave God in the sky, to reject the possibility of incarnation (1989a, 16). Instead, she insists that we move christology from ontological categories to justice categories and seek out those experiences where, today, the christic 'praxis of relational particularity and cooperation' is occurring (1989a, 20).

Oduyoye, too, rejects metaphysical questions of christology and opts instead for soteriological terms. The salvation Jesus affords African Christian women is here and now, touching human needs at all levels (1986, 98–100). She also presses the possibility of multiple incarnations, multiple Christs:

> Does Christianity have room for the concept of many Christs, persons in whom the spirit of God dwells in all its fullness? Has history seen many 'Christs' and will such Christ-figures continue in perpetuity? These would be legitimate questions for a Christology that focuses on Jesus of Nazareth as our ancestor in religious obedience. (1988, 39[11])

Oduyoye's willingness to take seriously her locatedness in an African tradition of ancestor reverence and in the struggle of African women for full humanity leads her to a christological boldness that pluralists have yet to fully embrace.

Chung's assessment of the meaning of Jesus Christ for Asian women also reflects this soteriological orientation. Among Indian, Korean, Taiwanese, Indonesian and other Asian women, Jesus is understood as liberator,

mother, worker, political martyr, shaman, even as the grain of daily susten-
ance. Where traditional images are used, their soteriological dimension is
what is most prominent. For instance, the lordship of Jesus is understood as
that which frees Asian women to claim their own authority, free from all the
earthly lordships that dominate their lives (Chung, 1990a, 53–73). Chung
reflects the broad stream of women's theology when she characterizes Asian
women's emerging spirituality as a movement 'away from Christo-centrism
and toward life-centrism' (1990a, 114). Applied to the problem of religious
pluralism, this life-centered, soteriological perspective opens christology
to dialogue with other traditions and places emphasis on the movement
toward just community, or in Heyward's phrase, right relatedness, rather
than ecclesial affiliation as the mark of salvation.

A theology of pluralism that drew upon these three dimensions of wom-
en's theological reflection – their grounded and audacious method, their
relational understanding of God, and their humanity-based, open-ended,
soteriocentric Christology – would be well positioned to address the current
dilemma in Christian approaches to pluralism described above. Without
having explicitly addressed the issue, these women theologians suggest that
there is a way to maintain, indeed strengthen, the specific Christian praxis
that has nurtured Christian identity for centuries, while celebrating and
truly engaging non-Christian religious realities. These theologies that are
anchored in the real-world experiences of people (especially those who for
reasons of sex, race, culture, or class have been deemed other by their histories and their theological traditions), theologies that are alive to the presence
of God in non-Christian and – to many traditional Christians – non-sacred
experience, theologies that are willing to question even the most venerable
texts and creeds of the tradition, these offer a solid foundation for those
Christians who want to affirm both religious pluralism and the specificity
of God's engagements with the world.

An ancient fear lies unnamed behind much of the resistance to this kind
of theology, the fear that in saying yes to the other we will in some way say
no to ourselves and the God of our devotion or, more poignantly, that we
will simply lose our way. At some points in Christian history, this danger
has been called heresy, at others syncretism, and more recently, perhaps,
co-optation. These are real and permanent risks for authentic faith. But
the greatest risk facing Christian theology in this world is not that it will
become corrupted but that it will simply become irrelevant. And that threat
would seem to justify the risk of what Chung calls a 'survival-liberation
centered syncretism' (1990a, 113) that the intersection of feminist and pluralist theologies portend, because the promise such an encounter holds out
is even greater.

Notes

1 The most thorough expression of Hick's vision of interreligious relations is found in Hick, 1989 [John Hick, *An Interpretation of Religion: Human Responses to the Transcendent*, Basingstoke: Macmillan]. His position is summarized and defended in response to critics in Hick, 1995 [*A Christian Theology of Religions: The Rainbow of Faiths*, Louisville: John Knox Press].

2 Carter Heyward, 1989b, *Touching Our Strength: The Erotic as Power and the Love of God*, New York: Harper Collins (ed.).

3 Mercy Amba Oduyoye, 1986, *Hearing and Knowing: Theological Reflections on Christianity in Africa*, Maryknoll, NY: Orbis Books (ed.).

4 Chung Hyun Kyung, 1990b, *Struggle to Be the Sun Again: Introducing Asian Women's Theology*, Maryknoll, NY: Orbis Books (ed.).

5 This reference is to Ivone Gebara, 1988, 'Women Doing Theology in Latin America', in Virginia Fabella and Mercy Amba Oduyoye (eds), *With Passion and Compassion: Third World Women Doing Theology*, Maryknoll, NY: Orbis Books (ed.).

6 Carter Heyward, 1989a, *Speaking of Christ: A Lesbian Feminist Voice*, ed. Ellen C. Davis, New York: Pilgrim Press (ed.).

7 Chung Hyun Kyung, 1990a, '"Han-pu-ri": Doing Theology from Korean Women's Perspective', in Virginia Fabella and Sun Ai Lee Park (eds), *We Dare to Dream: Doing Theology as Asian Women*, Maryknoll, NY: Orbis Books (ed.).

8 Carter Heyward, 1984, *Our Passion for Justice: Images of Power, Sexuality, and Liberation*, Cleveland, OH: Pilgrim Press (ed.).

9 'Ivone Gebara', interview in Mev Puleo, 1994, *The Struggle Is One: Voices and Visions of Liberation*, Albany: SUNY Press (ed.).

10 Raimundo Panikkar, 1984, 'Religious Pluralism: The Metaphysical Challenge', in Leroy S. Rouner (ed.), 1999, *Religious Pluralism*, Notre Dame: University of Notre Dame Press (ed.).

11 Mercy Amba Oduyoye with Elizabeth Amoah, 1988, 'The Christ For African Women', in Fabella and Oduyoye (eds), *With Passion* (ed.).

Source: Kate McCarthy, 1996, 'Women's Experience as a Hermeneutical Key to a Christian Theology of Religions', *Studies in Interreligious Dialogue* 6.2, pp. 163–73.

6

Interfaith Dialogue

ALAN RACE

Introduction

Interfaith dialogue has become firmly established as a means for people from different traditions to share experiences and learn from differences. These contributions offer perspectives on both of these elements of dialogue. They originate from quite different contexts, which itself is an indication of how dialogue is beginning to make an impact in all areas of spirituality and theology.

The first piece is a narrative account of an experiment in dialogue that has received a great deal of attention since its occurrence in 1984. M. Darrol Bryant (Distinguished Professor Emeritus, Centre for Dialogue & Spirituality in the World's Religions, Renison University College/University of Waterloo, Waterloo, Ontario, Canada) outlines what is known as the 'Snowmass Dialogue', an encounter set in the context of a Benedictine monastery in Colorado, USA. Representatives from the Christian, Jewish, Muslim, Buddhist and Native American traditions responded to one another from the heart of religious commitment in spirituality. It was not simply a dialogue that interrogated participants on the level of beliefs, but endeavoured to penetrate to the core of spiritual endeavour, intuition, experience and understanding. The value of Bryant's account is that it charts the encounter as a 'whole' journey – involving the effects of the monastic round of prayer and silence, the recognition that dialogue takes place between human beings and not simply ideas, and the assumption that mystical awareness reaches deeper than words. The dialogue itself yielded a sense that the religions shared much common ground, at least in terms of the structure of basic religious awareness. Bryant then analyses this commonality, problematizes it, and draws out some unanswered questions and openings for further explorations.

The second piece is a correspondence between two celebrated commentators on the meaning and purpose of dialogue itself. Jonathan Sacks is Chief Rabbi of the United Hebrew Congregations of the Commonwealth and Leonard Swidler is Professor of Catholic Thought and Interreligious Dialogue at Temple University, USA. Sacks contrasts the western 'Platonic' tradition of universal values with the Hebrew tradition of God's preference for the 'dignity of difference' among individuals and, ultimately, religions. It is this divine affirmation of dignity that yields the impetus for dialogue. Swidler's permission for dialogue is necessitated both by the religious apprehension that the divine can never be exhausted by any one tradition's account of the mystery of life and by the western critical approach to reason, which observes that all knowledge is perspectival. How far these two approaches can be said to be complementary or compatible leads to an exercise in dialogue itself.

Meeting at Snowmass

M. DARROL BRYANT

Introduction

My primary purpose in this paper is to describe an event involving twelve people from Buddhist, Christian, Hindu, Jewish, Muslim, and Native American traditions. The event was held at St. Benedict's Monastery in Snowmass, Colorado, in October, 1984. I was present as an observer. Father Thomas Keating, a Trappist monk long interested in interfaith dialogue, initiated the meeting and presided over the gathering. It was jointly funded by St. Benedict's Monastery and the New Ecumenical Research Association. The purpose of the meeting was exploratory. What would happen when a group of spiritual leaders, drawn from a wide range of traditions, came together? Would they be able to discern elements of unity amidst the differences of traditions and practices that had nourished each of them? Would differences of practice, belief, and conviction hinder – or facilitate – a genuine encounter? And in what ways? Could ways be found to speak with, rather than at, one another? What might emerge from such an encounter? Could a genuine 'meeting' be achieved? ...

The Setting

The setting of the meeting is not irrelevant to what occurred. The participants met at St. Benedict's Monastery in Snowmass, Colorado. The explicitly religious character of the setting had an impact upon the meeting. Rather than gathering in an academic or secular setting, the participants came to a place dedicated to religious life and practice ...

One further element of the setting needs also to be mentioned, namely, that it was initiated by Father Keating. This means that the impetus for the meeting grew out of Father Keating's own religious life and efforts to discern the meaning of the many paths that characterize the religious life of humankind. In a paper entitled 'In Search of the Ultimate Mystery,' that was circulated to the participants, Father Keating offers his own proposal for appropriating religious diversity.[1] In his paper, Father Keating argues that 'many paths lead to the Source.' Though this source is named in varying ways 'depending upon our cultural or religious frame of reference,' he prefers the term 'Ultimate Mystery.' Further, he contends that 'all who seek to participate in the experience of the Ultimate Mystery... are united in the same search.' Here his emphasis falls on the *common search* that can be discerned across traditions, rather than on the varying ways in which that search is articulated in different traditions. It is the *aspirational* dimensions of the religious life that allow recognition across boundaries that are often conceived as separating one from another. Further, it is noteworthy that his emphasis falls on participation 'in the experience of the Ultimate Mystery' which again de-emphasizes the role of explicitly doctrinal elements of religious life. In this moving paper, Father Keating affirms the value of people remaining 'in their own chosen path or religious tradition,' while simultaneously calling for 'attention upon what unites rather than what divides.'[2] The extent to which the participants recalled what Father Keating had said in his paper is not clear, but it was these convictions that informed his sense of the exploration the participants were about to undertake ...

...

The Daily Structure

What is especially noteworthy of the daily structure of this gathering was the emphasis on the shared silence and practice of the religious life coupled with discussion that centred on the experience of the participants in regard to their own spiritual journeys. Rather than an academic model that emphasizes the dialectics of debate, or even a theological meeting that would focus on patterns of doctrine, this particular meeting focused on the religious and spiritual experience of the participants. In retrospect, such an orientation is consistent with Father Keating's stated conviction that 'the most fundamental contribution' people in the several religious traditions can make is 'to cultivate in their personal lives the experience of oneness with the Ultimate Mystery, with every other human being, and with the cosmos.'[3] Such an orientation encourages attention to one's own actual experience of the spiritual life as the foundation for relating to those whose experiences of the spiritual life may be different from one's own. When such experience is made fundamental to interfaith encounter and exchange, then the likelihood of becoming involved in more abstract discussions is undercut. Moreover, the emphasis on primal religious practice – the disciplines of prayer and meditation – certainly created a special ethos for the discussions that followed.

Sharing Spiritual Journeys

As I had already indicated, the discussion sessions focused on the sharing of the personal spiritual journey of each participant.[4] While it is not possible to either recall or represent each of those life stories, I do want to present some of the participants' stories in order to give you a taste of what occurred. One of the most moving accounts for me was that of Gerald Red Elk, a medicine man of the Sioux nation. I grew up in North Dakota near an Indian reservation and have always been fascinated by the Indian peoples while at the same time appalled at what they suffered at the hands of the European settlers of the American continent. Gerald Red Elk is now an elderly man who still recalls some of the stories of his people that were told to him by his grandfather. He began by indicating the 'need to give our account of our sacred life. Otherwise people will not know.' He said that in the past, the Sioux shared their stories with other tribes when they visited the Sioux. But there is, he indicated, some reluctance among the Sioux to share these stories outside the tribe. Nonetheless, his conviction is that it is now necessary. He recounted how devastated his people have been by their encounter with the white man, but simply as a matter of fact. Red Elk served in the U.S. Army during the Second World War and it was there that his interest in his own tradition was rekindled. During the war, he said, Indians often came together to pray. And he vowed that if he survived he would 'go into his People's way, into their tradition.' But after the War he became caught up in alcoholism. He eventually got very ill and prayed for another chance, vowing that he would love his fellowman or, in his words, 'have pity for one another, because we are pitiful.' He noted that like many Indians, he was part of two religions, going to white churches yet practicing the Indian ceremonies. He did recover from his illness and then some very moving things began to happen to him. He told of his visions of the 'Star people' who helped 'him to live and to understand.' He learned to pray to the Creator first and then to the Four Directions. From this experience, Red Elk began to realize his vocation and his need to live a 'humble life, be generous and charitable.' Other Sioux holy men came, unbidden, to visit Red Elk and told him that he was to be a holy man.

Red Elk believes that it is crucial for the Indian people to come to know 'who they are.' This is what he is striving to teach young people. Just as older people taught him that 'you must respect other people's ways, but not forget your own way,' so he strives to recover the traditions of his people. For example, he said that Indian people must recover the traditions of 'the Drum' since it is 'the heartbeat of Mother Earth.' They must learn to 'call people first by their relationship – Mother, Cousin, Aunt – and not by names, because this is the courteous way.' They must practice the 'sun dance' and remember the legends of their people. Later he told me that the teaching of the tradition falls to the grandparents rather than parents because parents are too close to their children and do not have the requisite distance. He also told us that the Indians think of God as Grandfather, saying that Jesus spoke of God as his father thus making God our grandfather. He also spoke of the Hopi legends of a coming time of catastrophe and his encounters with Tibetan Buddhists who, he believes, share ancient wisdom with the Indians of North America. And he indicated his conviction that meetings of the kind held at St. Benedict's were important and approved by the Great Spirit. According to Indian belief, 'the whole planet is sacred' and 'all people are God's children.' Following Red Elk's statement of his spiritual pilgrimage, Father Keating commented on the depth of forgiveness one finds in Red Elk towards white people, and others asked about Indian rituals and practices. Here, as with the other participants, the attempt was to 'walk in the other's moccasins.'

Another of the participants, Ane-la Pema Chodron, was an American convert to Buddhism. Ane-la spoke of her training under a Tibetan Buddhist, Chogyam Trungpa Rimpoche, who had left Tibet when the Chinese Communists came to power. He sought to immerse himself in Western culture and to 'transplant the essence of Buddhism to the West.' She sees her own teacher as one who does not begin with 'suffering,' but with 'goodness and the possibility of enlightenment.' She spoke of her own efforts 'to work wholeheartedly with existing things' in order to discover the 'unboundedness of the present.' The aim of her religious practice is, she said, 'the cultivation of human inquisitiveness.' Rather than 'perfecting a belief system' in order to 'give comfort,' she saw her own training as leading her to 'go beyond belief to an experience of Ultimate Reality.'

Ane-la emphasized her own conviction that 'traditions are ways to connect with the primordial.' But what she discovered in herself and noted in others was that people tend 'to confuse the vehicle with the end.' Thus much of her own spiritual practice is designed to 'let go of anything that limits.' For example, she noted that we find 'within ourselves a conflict between the desire to be open and bigotry.' Thus our path has to be designed in ways that 'overcome the tendency to hold on' to whatever blocks an encounter with what is. Ane-la emphasized the Buddhist virtue of mindfulness because, as she said, 'every moment and every time is open to enlightenment.' Thus we must take 'seriously whatever the situation is.' She noted that in Shambhala training – the name given to the practice encouraged by her teacher – the emphasis does not fall on 'sin' as the problem, but rather on 'materialism understood as the seeking of comfort.' This, she said, was what needed to be overcome in people in order that they might reach 'something beyond comfortable or uncomfortable.' She described her own life and the teaching she follows as one that distinguishes (1) the ground of the spiritual life, (2) the path, and (3) the fruition. The irony is, Ane-la observed, 'that the great traditions of the world are gates to take down gates.' The purpose of religious training is something beyond training itself. It is this paradox that often confuses people. The point, she insisted, is not to 'move away from traditions' but it is to 'overcome narrow-mindedness,' it is not to do away with vehicles, but to use 'vehicles to go beyond our limited perspectives.' She noted that this was often a problem within Buddhism itself where people become 'attached to what they think Buddhism is' rather than to the now, to the wonder of what is.

Her story generated a good deal of discussion about the role of religion, practice, and particular paths in the spiritual journey. Are paths ways to certain goals or are they themselves part of the goal? Is what we are seeking something that lies ahead, or must we overcome this way of thinking itself in order to realize that we are already related to the Ultimate Mystery? Is it the case, as Rabbi Shapiro exclaimed, that 'I am what I am becoming! This is it! Nothing happens later!' Is the problem that our lives are tangled in 'isms,' as the Zen Buddhist remarked, that we cannot see that 'the Path is the IS – both the relative and the absolute at the same time.' Is the problem as Father Hopko said, that 'all the idols have to go. No more clinging to them.' Or could it be that 'the Buddhas in our heads are idols.' Can we discern some clue to these questions in the story Imam Bilal told: 'Moses saw the bush and started to tread the path. Then he saw the fire and heard the words, "I am what I am" and took a leap into the fire to become part of it and he, the fire, and the path are all the fire of love.' Or is it as Gayatri Devi observed: 'The most important factor is not the tradition, or the form, or the structure, but we ourselves: how far do we want to go, can we live what needs to be lived?'

A third spiritual journey that was shared with the participants at Snowmass was that of Imam Bilal Hyde. He began by noting that he does not often speak with people of other religions. This is because of the history of conflict between Christianity and Islam and because, especially now, there is such a negative image of Islam among people in the United States. Nevertheless, he decided to accept the invitation to be part of this meeting because he 'felt it was crucial for world peace to have a Muslim voice in these discussions.' He then shared with the group his own Sufi vision. He also noted that in the late eighteenth century almost ninety percent of the Muslims had been initiated into a Sufi order, but now less than ten percent of the Muslims are also Sufis. According to Bilal, the Sufi imagination can be pictured 'as a wheel or circle. And at the centre is an absolute Mystery around which we all sit. And all existence cries out for a return to its divine source.' In this vision, 'each path, dharma, or tradition represents a way or a door to the Ultimate Mystery or garden' that lies at the heart of things. Contrary to the popular image, Islam holds, said Bilal, that 'a messenger has been given to every nation.' And the message is finally one message: a message of unity. While there is no ultimate difference between the Prophets, *we*, Bilal emphasized, can 'only travel on one pathway in our life.' He chose what seems to many the narrowest of doors – Islam. But he emphasized, again, that all seekers must enter some doorway. And though the outer rim of the circle is 'law,' it is the roadway that 'leads to an oasis.' Within Islam, Sufism, Bilal stated, is 'the inner path.' This path is not in conflict with the 'law' but it instead emphasizes 'the Pearl that everyone has: a heart.' In lovely, poetic images, then, Bilal talked of that inner path as a life of love and growth towards union with the Centre. Citing Rumi, the great Sufi poet, who said that 'men and women scream in agony from separation from the Beloved,' Bilal asserted that 'all are driven towards the mystery by love.' Bilal too noted the different ways that the spiritual pilgrimage appears from different vantage points when he said that 'from outside, the paths towards the centre may appear diverse, but the further people are along their chosen paths the closer they come to one another.' Or again, 'from the centre, looking back, the gates look more and more alike.'

Following his presentation, several noted their surprise and appreciation of what he said: surprise because this was not a familiar view of Islam and its spiritual practice, and appreciation because many found what he had said to be quite moving. Others raised questions concerning the seeming disparity between his account of the Muslim sensibility and, for example, the commitment of Islam to jihad. Imam Hyde responded by saying that jihad means 'struggle' and not 'holy war.' And, he continued, the Sufis felt that after the year 632, the struggle was to be understood in inward terms as the struggle to overcome the self in submission to Allah.

Each of the stories presented are deserving of attention, but for our purposes this short account will have to suffice.[5] I want to note the variety of response to each particular story. When Red Elk spoke, there was an inward reception of and meditation on what he had said; but when Ane-la described her journey, it provoked a lively discussion. Then, in response to Bilal came a sense of surprise and further questions about Islam. This unpredictable, wide-ranging, and free-moving discussion was, to me, quite pleasing, but I could imagine that others might like to see more detailed discussion on certain points. However, what happened partially reflected the orientation of the meeting, namely, towards a sharing of that fund of experience of the spiritual life that was present in the participants ...

Points of Common Agreement

After each of the participants had shared something of their own religious lives in the context of shared times of prayer and meditation, Father Keating raised the question of whether or not there were things that were shared across traditions. On the last evening of the meeting and the morning before departures, a number of possibilities were discussed and the following points of common agreement emerged. There was a great deal of modesty that surrounded what might be said in common and an equal amount of care that what was said be seen as speaking only for those who had participated in this event. At the same time, many felt that given the amount of hostility and suspicion there often is in relations between people of differing religious traditions, it would be highly appropriate to indicate that at least some people from different traditions felt there were points of convergence and agreement between traditions. It was, then, in the light of these considerations that there emerged the following:

Points of agreement

1 The potential for human wholeness or, in other frames of reference, liberation, nirvana, self transcendence, transforming union, enlightenment, salvation, is present in every human person.
2 The human mind cannot form any adequate idea of the Ultimate Mystery, but the Ultimate Mystery makes Itself 'known.'
3 The Ultimate Mystery, however understood or experienced, is the source of all existence.
4 Faith is opening, accepting, and responding to the Ultimate Mystery.
5 Confidence in one's self as rooted in the Ultimate Mystery is the necessary corollary to faith in the Ultimate Mystery.
6 As long as the human condition is experienced as separate from the Ultimate Mystery, it is subject to ignorance and illusion, weakness and affliction.
7 Disciplined practice is essential to the spiritual life; yet spiritual attainment is not the result of one's own efforts, but the result of the experience of oneness with the Ultimate Mystery.

Again, it was emphasized that each of these points require the commentary of the persons from the different traditions in order that their meaning and significance become more transparent. Read outside the context of the meeting and the sharing that took place at St. Benedict's, they could strike one as 'mere abstractions.' But seen as the fruit of the meeting itself – the shared silence and the shared journeys – these points of agreement then gain a more significant resonance and content.

As the meeting came to a close, then, there was a pervasive sense that something significant had been accomplished. At the same time, the way to name that significant something was difficult, perhaps impossible, to articulate. In listening to one another there were moments of insight and mutual recognition, other moments that invited further reflection, and still others that remained genuinely opaque, puzzling, and simply hidden. But what was evident throughout was a deep respect and regard for the experience of the spiritual life. Since the meeting unfolded as an intra-religious event rather than as an academic or explicitly theological encounter, the significance was to be found primarily in the impact of the meeting on one's personal, religious self-understanding rather than elsewhere. How does one articulate the significance of shared silence? Or of prayer and meditation in the presence of those whose ways and objects seem, at least on the surface, so different from one's own? How does one account for the significance of those moments of mutual recognition that transcend the outward difference of path and patterns of belief? How does one acknowledge that spirit that testifies within that we share a common aspiration to relate our lives to a ground and mystery that transcends each of us yet encounters us in the depths of our being? The questions remain open ...

Commentary and Critique

The meeting I have described above invites, I believe, comment on a wide range of matters. Here I would like to select three issues that are most interesting to me: (1) the universal and the particular, (2) silence, speech, and conceptualization, and (3) the implications of interfaith encounter. These three matters certainly do not exhaust the issues that arise from such a meeting, but they are three that bear further comment and critique. Let me, then, take them in order.

First, the universal and the particular. The tacit assumption evident in the 'points of agreement' is that there is a 'common' though variously named and experienced, reality that is encountered in the spiritual journey. Whether or nor what Father Keating called the 'Ultimate Mystery' could be articulated in ways that would gain the assent of all the participants remained untested. Indeed, one of the operating existential assumptions of the meeting was that it probably could not be articulated in ways that would be satisfying to all the participants. Nonetheless, one can still ask about the relationship between the universal and particular in this meeting. Clearly, it was affirmed that there were certain universal, or at least trans-religious, dimensions that are to be discerned in significant encounters between persons from different traditions. At the highest or deepest level, there is the reality of the Ultimate Mystery or divine life. But what is the relationship between this 'transcendent' and universal dimension of reality and the particular religious traditions that apprehend and are apprehended by that reality? Earlier I indicated that one formula used was that of Father Keating who affirmed in his paper, 'In Search of the Ultimate Mystery,' that 'many paths lead to the Source.' In this perspective, one finds a particular way of relating the universal and the particular, namely, as the aspirational ground of the particular religious paths. In that same paper, Father Keating elaborates his conviction in the following way:

> True unity is expressed in pluralism: unity in the experience of the ultimate values of human life: pluralism in one's unique response to these values in the concrete circumstances of one's life.[6]

Here, then, Keating affirms unity in what is encountered, but particularly in response to what is encountered. This model has some things to commend it, but what it leaves unresolved is the *way* of knowing the identity of what is encountered. How do we come to affirm that what others encounter is the same as what we encounter when our *responses* are so varied? That I have raised the question is not to suggest that I know the answer, but it does seem to me a troubling issue. Keating does, however, offer some hints when he goes on to discuss the relationship of faith and belief. Here is what he says on this point:

> Faith is deeper that one's belief system. Belief systems belong to the level of pluralism; faith to the level of unity. Faith is constitutive of human nature itself. It is openness to the Ultimate Mystery as such, before the Ultimate Mystery is broken down into various belief systems.[7]

Here again we see the dialectic of the universal and the particular at work: for Keating there is, as it were, a faithful encounter with the Ultimate that the moment one attempts to express in belief is involved in the realm of particularity, not the universal. Even if one were to accept this account, couldn't we ask if some belief systems are closer to that Ultimate Mystery than others? Or are they all at the same level? Again, these are perplexing and troubling issues that require considerable care and attention.

These questions are deepened and made more complex when we bring into the discussion the affirmation, found in more than one tradition, that we do not simply seek the Source, but that the Ultimate seeks us and discloses itself in particular self-disclosures or revelations. If, as many Christians affirm, God reveals Himself in a person, history, or text, then are we not claimed by something beyond our seeking which transforms our path and thus discloses the limitations of the path? Or, even more radically, discloses our path to have been either mistaken or fruitless? In other words while the Snowmass group affirmed that many paths lead to the Source, would they want to affirm that all paths do? How do we differentiate, or can we, those ways rooted in divine life from those rooted in self-deception? Is there any way to know in advance? And don't we recognize, even within our own traditions – ones we certainly affirm to be authentic – that there are ways or paths within one's own tradition that are less than life-giving? My guess is that many of the participants would speak here – and quite elegantly – about the self-correcting character of an authentic relationship to the Ultimate Mystery. That is, that in prayer and meditation, as one gives oneself to the transcendent ground of life itself, there is a transforming action within the self that leads to an authentic apprehension of the Ultimate and the self. Nonetheless, the question awaits clarification.

Perhaps it would not be unfair to the Snowmass group to suggest that they implicitly affirmed the distinction one finds in Frithjof Schuon's work on

The Transcendent Unity of Religions.[8] Here Schuon differentiates between *esoteric* and *exoteric* understandings of religion. In the esoteric approach to religion, religion is a window to the divine and what shines through the religion is that reality that transcends the particular while being apprehended through it, whereas in the exoteric approach it is the religion itself which is affirmed as one with its object. This distinction cuts across traditions, and one can find in each particular tradition those who understand their experience of the Ultimate in esoteric or exoteric terms. While such a distinction may be helpful in grasping what happened in the meeting described above, it remains a troubled distinction for those who see in it a loss of the content of religion in mystical consciousness. My point here, however, is not to solve the issue of the universal and particular but to raise it as a troubling question for inter-religious encounters.

In part, what I have discussed above is related to the second issue I wished to raise, namely, the issue of the relationship between silence, speech, and conceptualization. For the Snowmass group these three terms reflect a certain hierarchy of value that was implicit in the event, with silence being highly valued and conceptualization running a distant third. It struck me that it was commonly held among the participants that it is in silence that we most profoundly and most fully encounter the Ultimate Mystery. What is 'known and communicated' in silence is, really, beyond words. At best our words can inadequately point to and express that which we intuitively or inwardly grasp in the encounter with the Ultimate that precedes words. And at times I found myself wondering what was being said, especially when I could not immediately discover in myself analogies from my own experience. Perhaps this was due to the fact that I am not a spiritual master. But that certainty aside, it still strikes me that there is an important assumption being made in an encounter such as this that bears further consideration.

While I am generally persuaded that the encounter with the Ultimate always *exceeds* our capacity to fully express it in words since it is, finally, ineffable. However, I am not persuaded, as some here seemed to be, that the Ultimate is wholly inexpressible, or better, that some words are better pointers to that reality than other. Or, that we should not seek to give voice to our experience. Now let me be as clear as I can be: I am not affirming that what is encountered in silence is expressible in Cartesian 'clear and distinct ideas.' That is another issue. What I am pointing to here is the relationship of speech to silence and silence to speech. Do the words which emerge from silence *body forth* that which in silence awaits expression in order to fulfil or realize itself such that reality is itself constituted by the Word? Or must we instead affirm that words merely approach that which in silence is always beyond words? Of course this is a false antithesis since even in relation to other spheres of experience we know something of the truth-and- falsity of this antithesis. Nonetheless, it does strike me as an issue that bears further consideration for at least two reasons. First, if ultimate reality is so constituted as to be beyond articulation, then we ought not to waste our efforts in what is, no matter how carefully attended to, beyond the realm of possibility. But if this is true then how do we determine where our confidence should be placed? Are we left to await the self-authenticating inward testimony of the spirit that is beyond words? Secondly, such a view has important consequences for other areas of life – especially the social and public spheres. If words are never adequate to what is encountered in silence, then the significance of public debate and discussion as the way to make evident what is necessary and desirable is rendered silly. While silliness is often the mark of public discourse, there remains an issue of principle here, namely, that our social and public life (and significant dimensions of our personal life as well) are mediated through words. Even the encounter with other human beings is dependent upon our capacity to communicate, to find words adequate to creating a shared reality. Even in what happened in Snowmass we see not only the *consequent* significance of speech, but that it is through words that we have access, albeit limited and imperfect, to what the other has experienced and come to know. Thus there is a sense in which the words, or the speakability of what is, is constituent of silence itself. And if this is so, then the dialectical relationship of silence and words is reversed even though the adequacy of particular words remains at issue.

The debasement of speech, so common in our time and nowhere more so than in religion itself, should not lead us to further this trend, but rather do everything in our power to restore to the Word its rightful place in the order of being. My own Christian Trinitarian assumptions are evident here, I imagine, in that I want to affirm a relationship of *perichoresis* or 'dancing around' in the relationship of the Ultimate, the Word, and the Spirit. This affirmation is, nonetheless, sympathetic to the implicit critique of conceptual schemes found in the Snowmass group. While the word stands as a caution against the limits of silence, it also stands over against an abstract conceptualization that would render the living God captive to its demands. Hence I would agree to ranking conceptualization behind silence and words while simultaneously affirming the ontological priority of the word out of silence.

The third issue concerns the implications of interfaith encounter. There is a great deal of anxiety that surrounds interfaith dialogue and discussion. Stanley Samartha, former director of the World Council of Churches' Unit on Dialogue with People of Living Faiths and Ideologies, alludes often to these anxieties in his *Courage for Dialogue*,[9] but I do not wish to review them here. Rather I want simply to raise the question on the basis of the particular meeting described above. What are the implications, if any, of the meeting described above. Here it seems to me we must be rather cautious and not claim too much. The participants themselves emphasized this very point when they drew up their points of common agreement. They did not speak as 'representatives' of their respective traditions, but as persons who, out of their living dialogue with one another, were willing to say what they said. And, in my view, this was highly appropriate. Thus we should take care in the implications we draw from such a meeting since it is unclear what, if anything, can be said other than what was said. Earlier I alluded to the fact that we are, I believe, at the beginning of an era where the kind of meeting described above will become more and more commonplace. But the consequences of such meetings will be open-ended. I certainly do not see that such meetings will be other than *events* within the longer and larger patterns of the unfolding of religious traditions. It is highly unlikely that such affirmations as those found here will be embraced by the institutional representatives of major traditions. And yet such events will continue to occur. They will occur because, as Raimundo Panikkar observes, 'the meeting of religions is an inescapable fact today.'[10] But at this stage that will likely only involve small numbers of people in various traditions. Perhaps at this point I can do no better than to close with some words from Panikkar's important and provocative essay on 'The Rules of the Game in the Religious Encounter:'

If the encounter is to be an authentically religious one, it must be totally loyal to truth and open to reality. The genuinely religious spirit is not loyal only to the past, it also keeps faith with the present. A religious Man is neither a fanatic nor someone who already has all the answers. He also is a seeker, a pilgrim making his own uncharted way; the track ahead is yet virgin, inviolate. The religious Man finds each moment anew and is but the more pleased to see in this both the beauty of a personal discovery and the depth of a perennial treasure that his ancestors in the faith have handed down. And yet, to enter the new field of the religious encounter is a challenge and a risk. The religious person enters this arena without prejudices and preconceived solutions, knowing full well he may in fact have to lose a particular belief or particular religion altogether. He trusts in truth. He enters unarmed and ready to be converted himself. He may lose his life – he may also be born again.[11]

Notes

1 Thomas Keating, 'In Search of the Ultimate Mystery,' unpublished paper. I am grateful to Father Keating for his sharing this moving paper with me.

2 Keating, pp. 1–2.

3 Keating, p. 1.

4 Helpful introductions to the larger traditions in which the participants stand are Huston Smith, *Religions of Man* (New York: Harper & Row, 1964), W. C. Smith, *The Faith of Other Men* (Toronto: CBC Publications, 1962), and Ninian Smart, *The Religious Experience of Mankind* (New York: Scribner's, 1976).

5 These accounts are drawn from my notes. I have had them reviewed by the par-

ticipants themselves and they have graciously assented to the account of their stories and words that I have presented.

6 Keating, p. 2.

7 Keating, p. 2.

8 Frithjof Schuon, *The Transcendent Unity of Religions* (New York: Harper & Row, 1975).

9 See S. J. Samartha, *Courage for Dialogue: Ecumenical Issues in Inter-religious Relationships* (Geneva: World Council of Churches, 1991), especially pp. 1–14 and 49–62.

10 R. Panikkar, *The Intra-Religious Dialogue*, New York: Paulist Press, 1978, p. 26.

11 Panikkar, p. 27.

Source: M. Darrol Bryant, 1986, 'Meeting at Snowmass: Some Dynamics of an Interfaith Encounter', in John Miller (ed.), *Interfaith Dialogue: Four Approaches*, Waterloo, Ont.: University of Waterloo Press, pp. 1–28.

Dialogue and Difference

JONATHAN SACKS AND LEONARD SWIDLER

The Dignity of Difference: Avoiding the Clash of Civilizations

Jonathan Sacks

Religion has become a decisive force in the contemporary world, and it is crucial that it be a force for good – for conflict resolution, not conflict creation. If religion is not part of the solution, then it will surely be part of the problem. I would like therefore to put forward a simple but radical idea. I want to offer a new reading, or, more precisely, a new listening, to some very ancient texts. I do so because our situation in the 21st century, post-September 11, is new, in three ways.

First, religion has returned, counter intuitively, against all expectation, in many parts of the world, as a powerful, even shaping, force.

Second, the presence of religion has been particularly acute in conflict zones such as Bosnia, Kosovo, Chechnya, Kashmir and the rest of India and Pakistan, Northern Ireland, the Middle East, sub-Saharan Africa, and parts of Asia.

Third, religion is often at the heart of conflict. It has been said that in the Balkans, among Catholic Croats, Orthodox Serbs, and Muslims, all three speak the same language and share the same race; the only thing that divides them is religion.

Religion is often the fault-line along which the sides divide. The reason for this is simple. Whereas the 20th century was dominated by the politics of ideology, the 21st century will be dominated by the politics of identity.

The three great Western institutions of modernity – science, economics, and politics – are more procedural than substantive, answering questions of 'What?' and 'How?' but not 'Who?' and 'Why?' Therefore when politics turns from ideology to identity, people inevitably turn to religion, the great repository of human wisdom on the questions 'Who am I?' and 'Of what narrative am I a part?'

When any system gives precedence to identity, it does so by defining an 'us' in contradistinction to a 'them'. Identity divides, whether Catholics and Protestants in Northern Ireland, Jews and Muslims in the Middle East, or Muslims and Hindus in India. In the past, this was a less acute issue, because for most of history, most people lived in fairly constant proximity to people with whom they shared an identity, a faith, a way of life. Today, whether through travel, television, the Internet, or the sheer diversity of our multi-ethnic and multi-faith societies, we live in the conscious presence of difference. Societies that have lived with this difference for a long time have learned to cope with it, but for societies for whom this is new, it presents great difficulty.

This would not necessarily be problematic. After the great wars of religion that came in the wake of the Reformation, this was resolved in Europe in the 17th century by the fact that diverse religious populations were subject to overarching state governments with the power to contain conflict. It was then that nation-states arose, along with the somewhat different approaches of Britain and America: John Locke and the doctrine of toleration, and Thomas Jefferson and the separation of church and state. The British and American ways of resolving conflict were different but both effective at permitting a plurality of religious groups to live together within a state of civil peace. What has changed today is the sheer capacity of relatively small, subnational groups – through global communications, porous national borders, and the sheer power of weapons of mass destruction – to create havoc and disruption on a large scale. In the 21st century we obviously need physical defence against terror, but also a new religious paradigm equal to the challenge of living in the conscious presence of difference. What might that paradigm be? In the dawn of civilization, the first human response to difference was tribalism: my tribe against yours, my nation against yours, and my god against yours. In this premonotheistic world, gods were local. They belonged to a particular place and had 'local jurisdiction,' watching over the destinies of particular people. So the Mesopotamians had Marduk and the Moabites Chamosh, the Egyptians their pantheon and the ancient Greeks theirs. The tribal, polytheistic world was a world of conflict and war. In some respects that world lasted in Europe until 1914, under the name of nationalism.

In 1914 young men – Rupert Brooke and First World War poets throughout Europe – were actually eager to go to war, restless for it, before they saw carnage on a massive scale. It took two world wars and 100 million deaths to cure us of that temptation. However, for almost 2,500 years, in Western civilization, there was an alternative to tribalism, offered by one of the great philosophers of all time: Plato. I am going to call this universalism. My thesis will be that universalism is also inadequate to our human condition. What Plato argued in *The Republic* is that this world of the senses, of things we can see and hear and feel, the world of particular things, isn't the source of knowledge or truth or reality. How is one to understand what a tree is, if trees are always changing from day to day and there are so many different kinds of them? How can one define a table if tables come in all shapes and sizes – big, small, old, new, wood, other materials? How does one under-stand reality in this world of messy particulars? Plato said that all these particulars are just shadows on a wall. What is real is the world of forms and ideas: the idea of a table, the form of a tree. Those are the things that are universal. Truth is the move from particularity to universality. Truth is the same for everyone, everywhere, at all times. Whatever is local, particular, and unique is insubstantial, even illusory. This is a dangerous idea, because it suggests that all differences lead to tribalism and then to war, and that the best alternative therefore is to eliminate differences and impose on the world a single, universal truth. If this is true, then when you and I disagree, if I am right, you are wrong. If I care about truth, I must convert you from your error. If I can't convert you, maybe I can conquer you. And if I can't conquer you, then maybe I have to kill you, in the name of that truth. From this flows the blood of human sacrifice through the ages.

September 11 happened when two universal civilizations – global capital-ism and medieval Islam – met and clashed. When universal civilizations meet and clash, the world shakes and lives are lost. Is there an alternative, not only to tribalism, which we all know is a danger, but also to universalism?

Let us read the Bible again and hear in it a message that is both simple and profound and, I believe, an important one for our time. We will start with what the Bible is about: one man, Abraham, and one woman, Sarah, who have children and become a family and then in turn a tribe, a collection of tribes, a nation, a particular people, and a people of the covenant.

What is striking is that the Bible doesn't begin with that story. For the first eleven chapters, it tells the universal story of humanity: Adam and Eve, Cain and Abel, Noah and the flood, Babel and the builders, universal archetypes living in a global culture. In the opening words of Genesis 11, 'The whole world was of one language and shared speech.' Then in Genesis 12, God's call to Abraham, the Bible moves to the particular. This exactly inverts Plato's order. Plato begins with the particular and then aspires to the universal. The Bible begins with the universal and then aspires to the par-ticular. That is the opposite direction. It makes the Bible the great counter-Platonic narrative in Western civilization.

The Bible begins with two universal, fundamental statements. First, in Genesis 1, 'Let us make man in our image, in our likeness.' In the ancient world it was not unknown for human beings to be in the image of God: that's what Mesopotamian kings and the Egyptian pharaoh were. The Bible was revolutionary for saying that every human being is in the image of God. The second epic statement is in Genesis 9, the covenant with Noah, the first covenant with all mankind, the first statement that God asks all humanity to construct societies based on the rule of law, the sovereignty of justice and the non-negotiable dignity of human life.

It is surely those two passages that inspire the words 'We hold these truths to be self-evident, that all men are created equal, that they are endowed by their Creator with certain unalienable Rights ...' The irony is that these truths are anything but self-evident. Plato or Aristotle wouldn't know what the words meant. Plato believed profoundly that human beings are created unequal, and Aristotle believed that some people are born to be free, others to be slaves. These words are self-evident only in a culture saturated in the universal vision of the Bible. However, that vision is only the foundation. From then on, starting with Babel and the confusion of languages and God's call to Abraham, the Bible moves from the universal to the particular, from all humankind to one family. The Hebrew Bible is the first document in civilization to proclaim monotheism, that God is not only the God of this people and that place but of all people and every place. Why then does the Bible deliver an anti-Platonic, particularistic message from Genesis 12 onwards?

The paradox is that the God of Abraham is the God of all mankind, but the faith of Abraham is not the faith of all mankind. In the Bible you don't have to be Jewish to be a man or woman of God. Melchizedek, Abraham's contemporary, was not a member of the covenantal family, but the Bible calls him 'a priest of God Most High.' Moses' father-in-law, Jethro, a Midianite, gives Israel its first system of governance. And one of the most courageous heroines of the Exodus – the one who gives Moses his name and rescues him – is an Egyptian princess. We call her Batya or Bithiah, the Daughter of God. Melchizedek, Jethro, and Pharaoh's daughter are not part of the Abrahamic covenant, yet God is with them and they are with God. As the rabbis put it two thousand years ago, 'The righteous of every faith, of every nation, have a share in the world to come.' Why, if God is the God of all humanity, is there not one faith, one truth, one way for all humanity?

My reading is this: that after the collapse of Babel, the first global project, God calls on one person, Abraham, one woman, Sarah, and says 'Be different.' In fact, the word 'holy' in the Hebrew Bible, kadosh, actually means 'different, distinctive, set apart.' Why did God tell Abraham and Sarah to be different? To teach all of us the dignity of difference. That God is to be found in someone who is different from us. As the great rabbis observed some 1,800 years ago, when a human being makes many coins in the same mint, they all come out the same. God makes every human being in the same mint, in the same image, his own, and yet we all come out differently.

The religious challenge is to find God's image in someone who is not in our image, in someone whose colour is different, whose culture is different, who speaks a different language, tells a different story, and worships God in a different way.

This is a paradigm shift in understanding monotheism. And we are in a position to hear this message in a way that perhaps previous generations were not. Because we have now acquired a general understanding of the world that is significantly different from our ancestors'. I will give just two instances of this among many: one from the world of natural science and one from economics. The first is from biology. There was a time in the European Enlightenment when it was thought that all of nature was one giant machine with many interlocking parts, all harmonized in the service of mankind. We now know that nature is quite different, that its real miracle is its diversity. Nature is a complex ecology in which every animal, plant, bird, every single species has its own part to play and the whole has its own independent integrity.

We know even more than this thanks to the discovery of DNA and our decoding of the genome. Science writer Matt Ridley points out that the three-letter words of the genetic code are the same in every creature. 'CGA means arginine, GCG means alanine, in bats, in beetles, in bacteria. Wherever you go in the world, whatever animal, plant, bug, or blob you look at, if it is alive, it will use the same dictionary and know the same code. All life is one.' The genetic code, bar a few tiny local aberrations, is the same in every creature. We all use exactly the same language. This means that there was only one creation, one single event when life was born. This is what the Bible is hinting at. The real miracle of this created world is not the Platonic form of the leaf, it's the 250,000 different kinds of leaf there are. It's not the idea of a bird, but the 9,000 species that exist. It is not a universal language; it is the 6,000 languages actually spoken. The miracle is that unity creates diversity, that unity up there creates diversity down here.

One can look at the same phenomenon from the perspective of economics. We are all different, and each of us has certain skills and lacks others. What I lack, you have, and what you lack, I have. Because we are all different we specialize, we trade, and we all gain. The economist David Ricardo put forward a fascinating proposition, the Law of Comparative Advantage, in the early 19th century. This says that if you are better at making axe heads than fishing, and I am better at fishing than making axe heads, we gain by trade even if you're better than me at both fishing and making axe heads. You can be better than me at everything, and yet we still benefit if you specialize at what you're best at and I specialize at what I'm best at. The law of comparative advantage tells us that every one of us has something unique to contribute, and by contributing we benefit not only ourselves but other people as well.

In the market economy throughout all of history, differences between cultures and nations have led to one of two possible consequences. When different nations meet, they either make war or they trade. The difference is that from war at the very least one side loses, and in the long run, both sides lose. From trade, both sides gain. When we value difference the way the market values difference, we create a non-zero sum scenario of human interaction. We turn the narrative of tragedy, of war, into a script of hope.

So whether we look at biology or economics, difference is the precondition of the complex ecology in which we live. And by turning to the Bible we arrive at a new paradigm, one that is neither universalism nor tribalism, but a third option, which I call the dignity of difference. This option values our shared humanity as the image of God, and creates that shared humanity in terms like the American Declaration of Independence or the UN Universal Declaration of Human Rights. But it also values our differences, just as loving parents love all their children not for what makes them the same but for what makes each of them unique. That is what the Bible means when it calls God a parent.

This religious paradigm can be mapped onto the political map of the 21st century. With the end of the Cold War, there were two famous scenarios about where the world would go: Francis Fukuyama's *End of History* (1989) and Samuel Huntington's *Clash of Civilizations and the Remaking of World Order* (1996).

Fukuyama envisaged an eventual, gradual spread first of global capitalism, then of liberal democracy, with the result being a new universalism, a single culture that would embrace the world.

Huntington saw something quite different. He saw that modernization did not mean Westernization, that the spread of global capitalism would run up against countermovements, the resurgence of older and deeper loyalties, a clash of cultures, or what he called civilizations – in short, a new tribalism. And to a considerable extent, that is where we are. Even as the global economy binds us ever more closely together, spreading a universal culture across the world – what Benjamin Barber calls 'McWorld' – civilizations and religious differences are forcing us ever more angrily and dangerously apart. That is what you get when the only two scenarios you have are tribalism and universalism.

There is no instant solution, but there is a responsibility that rests with us all, particularly with religious leaders, to envision a different and more gracious future. As noted earlier, faced with intense religious conflict and persecution, John Locke and Thomas Jefferson devised their particular versions of how different religious groups might live together peaceably. These two leaps of the imagination provided, each in their own way, bridges over the abyss of confrontation across which future generations could walk to a better world.

I have gone rather further than Locke's doctrine of toleration or the American doctrine of separation of church and state because these no longer suffice for a situation of global conflict without global governance. I have made my case on secular grounds, but note that the secular terms of today – pluralism, liberalism – will never persuade a deeply passionate, indeed fanatically passionate religious believer to subscribe to them, because they are secular ideas. I have therefore given a religious idea, based on the story of Abraham, from which all three great monotheisms – Judaism, Christianity, and Islam – descend.

A message of the dignity of difference can be found that is religious and profoundly healing. That is the real miracle of monotheism: not that there is one God and therefore one truth, one faith, one way, but that unity above creates diversity here on earth. Nothing has proved harder in civilization than seeing God or good or dignity in those unlike ourselves. There are surely many ways of arriving at that generosity of spirit, and each faith may need to find its own way. I propose that the truth at the heart of monotheism is that God is greater than religion, that he is only partially comprehended by any one faith. He is my God, but he is also your God. That is not to say that there are many gods: that is polytheism. And it is not to say that God endorses every act done in his name: a God of yours and mine must be a God of justice standing above both of us, teaching us to make space for one another, to hear one another's claims, and to resolve them equitably. Only such a God would be truly transcendent. Only such a God could teach mankind to make peace other than by conquest or conversion and as something nobler than practical necessity.

What would such a faith be like? It would be like being secure in my own home and yet moved by the beauty of a foreign place knowing that while it is not my home, it is still part of the glory of the world that is ours. It would be knowing that we are sentences in the story of our people but that there are other stories, each written by God out of the letters of lives bound together in community.

Those who are confident of their faith are not threatened but enlarged by the different faiths of others. In the midst of our multiple insecurities, we need now the confidence to recognize the irreducible, glorious dignity of difference.

Toward a Dialogue of Civilizations: Deep-Dialogue/Critical-Thinking

Leonard Swidler

Rabbi Sacks, you have insightfully related the history of humanity to the basic biblical vision, bringing the contemporary world into sharp, creative focus. I find that I am in fundamental agreement with your interpretation, and have been for quite some time. I am grateful for your showing how the history of humanity can be helpfully seen in the light of the Hebrew Bible.

You have done this by relating the two terms: *Universalism* and *Particularism*. This approach sheds its own particular light on human history. I would like to offer my interpretation through two other terms: *Deep-Dialogue* and *Critical-Thinking*. This is not an 'instead of' approach, but an 'in addition to' one.

I have made an argument elsewhere that from the beginning of human history we humans have been in a monologic mode, that is, we have always talked in monologues, i.e., with ourselves: with other persons who thought as we did – or should! Fundamentally we never talked with persons who thought differently from us in the search for 'truth', for reality; we talked to other-thinking persons to teach them the truth we knew. We were convinced that we held the truth – we would not hold the position we did if we were not convinced that it was true, was the real. However, we are now moving – slowly, painfully, but ever more rapidly – out of this monologic mode into a dialogic mode.

One of the advantages of so-called 'Post-Modernism' is its lifting up the importance of difference. Its main disadvantage, in my judgment, is its tendency to claim that there is only difference. This of course is a strange position, since it would not be possible to talk with someone about differences were there not a commonality as a basis to communicate, as a starting point to compare with in order to discern the differences.

Remembering that 'dialogue' in contemporary usage *primarily* means a conversation with someone who thinks differently so we can *learn*, not so we can teach, the dialogic approach is fundamentally the classic 'catholic' both-and way. We are not limited to *either* the 'universalistic' or the 'particularistic' way of understanding human reality. In fact, though it was perhaps almost impossible to see in the past, we now see that it is not only *possible* to choose both the universal and the particular, but that it is *necessary* to embrace both!

We are increasingly aware that there is no knowledge except *interpreted* knowledge. The very act of knowing is basically a *relational* act. Knowing is the relating of the known to the knower. That means that the knower is part of the act. As Thomas Aquinas noted centuries ago, 'the known is present in the knower according to the mode of the knower.' For example, if the only way I can 'see' is by wearing rose-colored lenses, then everything I see will be rose-tinted, whereas if you do not wear rose-colored, but blue-colored (or any other kind of) lenses, things will not appear rose-tinted to you, but blue-tinted. Obviously there is something 'objective' out there that I see in a rose-tinted manner and you in a blue-tinted.

You and I will never be able to see 'reality' except through our lenses. However, the fact that you and I are able to communicate with each other about the 'reality' we each see through our own lenses, and perhaps even actually do things with/to that reality – which we both then see and can agree at least that something has been done to reality, and at least to some degree what has been done – convinces us that there is a reality existing outside our seeing, our perception of, it. The 'reality' out there is analogous to the 'universal' you speak of Rabbi Sacks, and my and your rose-tinted and blue-tinted sight of it is analogous to the 'particular.' Now, as said, we humans are more and more coming to realize that we need to dialogue with each other to gain an ever-expanding vision of reality. By the very nature of 'knowing' no one knower, no one group of knowers, can ever see reality except through its particular lenses. Therefore, we are all very much in need of dialogue with others who have different lenses so as to gain a never-ending greater sight of reality. To the extent that we grasp the very meaning of knowing, and draw its implications for how we should relate with those who have different lenses (different cultures, religions, classes, genders ...), we will realize that we *need* to be in dialogue with them so we can come ever closer (but never completely so!) to a full grasp of reality. This transforming understanding of ourselves and our relationship to 'reality' and to those who think differently from us is what I designate *Deep-Dialogue*.

In short, by *Deep-Dialogue* I mean to:

1 *Reach out in openness to the Other in the search for Truth and Goodness;*
2 *Be open to the Other primarily so we can learn, find Truth and Goodness;*
3 *Perceive that for us to learn, to find the good, the Others must teach and open themselves – and vice versa;*
4 *Recognize that because Dialogue is a two-way project, we then both learn – and share the good;*
5 *Learn there are Other ways of understanding, of embracing the world than our own;*
6 *Learn to recognize our commonalities and differences – and value both;*
7 *Learn to move between different worlds and integrate them in care;*
8 *Learn that Deep-Dialogue thus gradually transforms our inner selves – and our shared lives.*

However, the other side of the coin of *Deep-Dialogue* is *Critical-Thinking*, by which I mean:

1 *(a) Raise our un-conscious pre-suppositions to the conscious level, and (b) After reflection, make a reasoned judgment ('critical', Greek krinein to judge) about them;*
2 *Think analytically (Greek: ana up, lysis break), i.e., to break ideas into their component parts to see how they fit together;*
3 *Think synthetically (Greek: syn together, thesis to put), i.e., to put components of different ideas together in new ways;*
4 *Understand and use very precisely each word and phrase so that our*

deliberations and decisions are informed with clarity and grounded in reality;

5 *Understand all statements/texts in their con-texts; only then apply them to our contexts;*

6 *(a) Recognize that our view of reality is one view, shaped by our experience, becoming aware, thereby, of multiple worldviews, and (b) See that each worldview is a new meaning network; (c) Again, only then can we reasonably appreciate/critique them.*

In order even to understand the relational character of knowing, and thus what *Deep-Dialogue* is and its necessity for us to continue to grow as humans, we obviously need the skills of *Critical-Thinking*. Again, the 'unconscious pre-suppositions' that each of us have about everything is analogous to the 'particular' you speak of, Rabbi Sacks. We can never rid ourselves of all of them, for they are like the lenses through which we are able to see reality. They are all the things we are taught by every one and every thing around us from the moment of our birth and which we absorb without even being conscious of them. As we say colloquially, we drink them in with our mother's milk.

However, if we are going to dialogue effectively, we are going to have to constantly raise these un-conscious pre-suppositions to the conscious level (and in mutuality the best way to become conscious of an un-conscious pre-position is through a dialogue partner, who one day will ask us why we assume a certain position – and we then in perhaps startled fashion will for the first time become aware that we held this unexamined position). When we then become conscious of this un-consciously held position, we will then be able to examine it analytically, synthetically and eventually be able to make consciously rational (i.e., 'universal') decisions about it: to keep, modify, or reject it.

But to do this effectively we are also going to have to develop the skill of using our terms (including denotation, connotation, emotional and historical baggage, body language, etc.) as carefully and precisely as possible so we can communicate with our partners what is really in our mind. And the most important 'partner' we need to communicate clearly and accurately with in *Deep-Dialogue* is ourselves!

Thus, as said, *Deep-Dialogue* and *Critical-Thinking* are two sides of a single coin of humanity – and there is no such thing as a single-sided coin! Let me summarize as follows:

1 *Deep-Dialogue and Critical-Thinking are two sides of the one human reality.*

2 *Deep-Dialogue entails at its root clear, reflective, critical thought.*

3 *Critical-Thinking entails a dialogue within our own minds and lives – and hence, at its root, is dialogic.*

4 *Deep-Dialogue/Critical-Thinking eventually must become a habit of mind and spirit, traditionally known as a virtue – a new basic mentality, and consequent practice.*

A response to Professor Swidler from Rabbi Sacks

Dear Leonard (forgive the first name, but this is deep dialogue),

Thank you for entering into conversation with some of my ideas. I see they are also yours.

Yes: the very act of dialogue is a fugue built on the tension between universality and particularity. As I once put it: if we had nothing in common, we could not communicate. If we had everything in common, we would have nothing to say.

And yes, in the biblical tradition we share, knowledge is relational. The word *da'at* in biblical Hebrew refers not to a cognitive state but to an intense and morally charged relationship. Thus, 'And Adam knew Eve, his wife' (Gen. 4:1). 'And God saw the children of Israel, and God knew' (Ex. 2:25). 'I will betroth you to Me in faithfulness and you will know the Lord' (Hosea 2:20). In each of these cases – there are countless others – the Hebrew verb is *la-da'at* yet the meaning, depending on context, is 'to be intimate with, to be moved to compassion, to be linked in an indissoluble bond with' and so on. Knowledge for the Bible is not detached, but engaged; not impersonal but the essence of the personal. It is the redemption of solitude. The Babylonian Talmud (*Berakhot* 26b) contains four words of great beauty: *ein sichah ela tefillah*, which I translate as, 'Conversation is a form of prayer.' It is in and through the encounter with a human other that we rehearse our encounter with the Divine Other. Indeed I would define biblical spirituality as openness to otherness.

That is why the canonical texts of Judaism are anthologies of arguments. In the Hebrew Bible, Abraham, Moses, Jeremiah, Jonah and Job argue with God – and for His part, God argues with mankind. Rabbinic Midrash represents the idea that 'there are seventy faces of Torah' – each scriptural verse or phrase has multiple interpretations. Mishnah and Talmud consist of legal arguments between sages. Judaism is a conversation scored for many voices – and God is not in one of the voices but in the totality of the conversation.

And yes: openness to otherness means that my perspective is not the only one. In a circle, each point has a different perspective yet they are equidistant from the point around which the circle turns. Humanity is called on to be a circle at whose centre is God.

Source: Jonathan Sacks and Leonard Swidler, 2004, 'Toward a Dialogue of Civilizations: A Dialogue Between Jonathan Sacks (Jewish, UK) and Leonard Swidler (Christian, USA)', *Interreligious Insight: A Journal of Dialogue and Engagement* 2.3, pp. 35–46.

Part Two

CHRISTIAN RESPONSES TO INDIVIDUAL FAITHS

Section A: Abrahamic Traditions

7

Judaism

ALAN RACE

Introduction

In both the mainline Churches and the academy the view that Christianity was intended by God to supersede Judaism has been overturned. The reasons for this are many, not least the horrors of the Shoah (Holocaust) and its abiding challenge to any simplistic doctrine of moral or theological progress through history. If Christian discipleship was meant to be an improvement on Judaic faithfulness the Shoah demonstrates the 'hidden demonic' within such a view.

But if the Shoah has been the essential lever behind the Christian world's about-turn in relation to Jews and Judaism, then perhaps the main tool behind the re-evaluation of the doctrine of supersessionism has been a sharpened historical sense of the period before and after the impact of the figure of Jesus of Nazareth. It has become commonplace now to note how *both* Christianity *and* Rabbinic Judaism emerged from the ruptures within the Judaism of the first century of the common era, largely in reaction to the destruction of the second temple in 70 CE and to different readings of Hebrew texts in the construction of new communities.

Both James Parkes (Anglican) and Rosemary Radford Ruether (Catholic) have been pioneers in the re-education of Christian responses to Jews and Judaism. Parkes called attention to the skewing of standard interpretations of Jewish history by Christian biblical scholars as early as the 1950s. The book from which this extract is taken documents how Jewish and Christian scholars interpret the period immediately before and after Jesus very differently, with an already Christian bias towards later supersessionism and a Jewish emphasis on survival. The extract is entitled an 'Epilogue' on this historical work and opens the door to what later scholars would call a 'two covenant' theory. Ruether, in turn, deconstructs the whole edifice of Christian supersessionism by examining a host of theological mechanisms by which Judaism was declared historically redundant and Christianity triumphant. Much of this she claims has been Christologically driven and she calls for a reassessment of the person of Christ by the Christian world.

Not everyone in the Churches or Academy has taken up these suggestive leads from Parkes and Ruether, but we include them here for their strong scholarly suggestiveness and their ground-breaking quality. There are those

who think that if we can get the Jewish–Christian dialogue on a better foot-
ing then other relationships stand a better chance of also being set on sound
scholarship.

Two Religions: Two Chosen People

JAMES PARKES

It is the Christian claim that all that was spiritually valid in Judaism was
taken over by the Church. Early father and modern writer speak with the
same voice on at least this subject. Justin in the second century had written
concisely 'your Scriptures or rather not yours but ours'[1] and had claimed
with the Scripture all the spiritual gifts mentioned in their pages.[2] Almost
identical words are used by the Very Rev. S. C. Carpenter, D.D. in a Pelican
book published in 1953 entitled *Christianity*. For him, as for Justin, Judaism
is just its predecessor. In a chapter entitled 'The Antecedents of Christianity' phrases abound such as these (the italics in all the quotations are mine):
'The Christian disciples of the first generation *inherited*, unhesitatingly and
enthusiastically, *the great and splendid things for which Judaism had stood*'
(p. 18). The *had* marks Judaism as already outmoded. Quoting the magnifi-
cent passage of Isaiah 40 which begins: 'To whom then will ye liken God?',
he asserts that 'all this wealth of affirmation *became at once the property of
the Christians*' (p. 20). On the same page we find: 'Old Testament religion
was a historical religion ... depending on *what God had done* for [Israel]
as a nation. All this the Church took over'. On the following page we read:
'A third element of the Old Testament religion which *was taken over* by the
Christian Church was belief in a Messiah.' The ordinary reader for whom a
Penguin book is published would not gather from such passages that in no
case had Judaism surrendered or abandoned any of these ideas, or repudiated them as part of her possession. The word 'sharing' is never used: indeed
both Dr. Carpenter and Justin would find it inappropriate. For, like Justin,
he finds that the divine purpose 'had never been understood, had in fact
never been clearly disclosed, until it was realised in Christ' (p. 18).

Painful as such a conception of their history would be for loyal Jews, yet
it would be inevitable for Christians to make such a claim, *had they in fact
taken over the heritage of the Old Testament*. The astonishing thing about
this iterated claim is that not only has the Church not done so but, without
realising it, has constantly repudiated her intention of doing so. Every time
she makes a distinction between 'secular' and 'religious' she repudiates the
Old Testament. Every time she condemns 'religion mixing in politics' she
emphasizes that she does not accept the values of Judaism. No one could

imagine the religion described in the previous chapter to be the Christianity of the early Church. Whether it be right or wrong, the Christian conception of being a chosen people is completely different from the Jewish, and is a consequence only of the Incarnation, not of either the Law or the prophets. To both it would have been inappropriate and 'born out of due time'.

Both religions accept the belief that God has chosen from humanity certain men as vehicles of his universal purpose and design. Neither, at its best, considers the choice a privilege; both regard it as a responsibility. But,[3] since Christians are apt to think that the Jewish conception of being a chosen people sets Jews apart, and narrows their religion down to tribalism, it is perhaps well to emphasize that the original word for the Church, the Greek word *ecclesia*, means those who are called out from among others or chosen, and that the Latin word *electi*, the elect, a favourite title for a Christian community, means just the same thing. Christians as much as Jews believe themselves subjects of a divine choice.

Christianity, however, sees the divine choice enshrined in the biblical story narrowing down to the single figure of Jesus the Messiah, then, after his Incarnation, it sees this same choice widening out again to embrace mankind without distinction of Jew or Greek, bond or free, or, one may add, white or coloured. But within boundaries limited only by mankind, it still holds that only some are chosen, chosen as the elect from every nation, to receive the mystery of salvation, and to become, in the words beloved of Paul, 'new men in Christ', the new Israel, the new chosen people.

To Judaism it is the whole of one people which is chosen for a divine responsibility, chosen as it now is, in its present condition, with its imperfections and its good and bad members. This is not tribalism as opposed to universalism; for the choice is to responsibility not to privilege, and is related to the same assertion of the universal dominion of God, and of the ultimate responsibility of those he has chosen towards the whole of his creation.

Both religions, then, rest on the idea of choice. Both see that choice within a universal framework. But the result of these two different conceptions of the nature of the choice was to be naturally and logically to make the two religions differ in almost every conceivable emphasis and interest.

Both religions start with the acceptance of the divine authority of certain written Scriptures, but their differences began already in the two attitudes developed to these Scriptures. The Judaism which survived the destruction of Jerusalem, of the Temple and of the whole apparatus of sacrifice, drew its inspiration from the Pharisaic doctrine of interpretation – a doctrine most frequently misunderstood by New Testament scholars. The rabbis saw in the written Torah the focusing point through which the infinity of God's wisdom and design in creation reaches out to meet the infinity of men's needs as generation succeeds generation in a never static world. Each generation had the task of interpreting it anew, in terms of its own needs; and an interpretation once accepted by the scholars of a generation had the same divine authority as the original. In a sense it had more, for they regarded it as a greater sin to deny that God is continuously speaking to man, than to deny that he had once so spoken at Sinai.

Christianity made a sharp distinction between the Old and the New Testaments and interpreted the former only in terms of its 'fulfilment' in the latter. The main interest in the Old Testament of the Church fathers was as a quarry of proof texts that Jesus is the Christ foretold by the prophets. They had no conception of its unity comparable to the Jewish doctrine of Torah, and no doctrine of its interpretation. They used it in its literal sense, often with unhappy results, especially on the development of law and the justification of wars.[4] From a doctrinal point of view the only sphere in which they regarded it as a focusing point between two infinities is in the development of Christological doctrine. And here we must come back to the two conceptions of a chosen people.

The development of Judaism was determined by the belief that a divine way of life was set before a whole people, here and now; and that its primary mission, and its primary contribution to mankind, was to explore, understand and express in every aspect of its daily life that divine plan for a whole community. In the literature of rabbinic Judaism there is to be found practically no interest in theological speculation and nothing which could be called a systematic theology. Having accepted the existence and the unity of God without hesitation, the rabbis concentrated all their interest on his activities in creation as they were to be embodied in the living of the chosen people. A number of consequences flowed from this determination of interest.

In the first place it demanded a strong emphasis on education, for *understanding* occupies in Judaism the same key place as *faith* in Christianity. In the second place it put an end to the reasons for the existence of a clerical or priestly hierarchy. The priesthood disappeared with the Temple except for some trifling concessions to past prestige. The Judaism which grew in the second century was a religion of educated laymen. Moreover, it was a religion whose details were worked out by men following every occupation open to the community. The rabbis of the Talmudic period were not merely not priests; they were not even in the modern sense 'professionals'. If some gave almost the whole of their lives to study, they did it for love of Torah not because they were salaried or held official posts. Some were wealthy landowners, some were merchants, some were artisans taking only such time off from their studies as would ensure the most meagre and frugal existence.

Because they represented every aspect of the life of the community, they dealt freely with every aspect. Their discussions of education, of economics, of agriculture, of family life, of social relations, of communal responsibilities, in spite of the curious techniques which they employed, were infused with an astonishing realism just because they knew from experience what they were talking about. This realism reached its culmination in their conceptions of the functions of a law court, since it was an obligation of a scholar to be ready to judge in disputes. It is important to emphasize this point since Christian scholars are so apt to assume that 'Jewish' conceptions of justice are still based on the more primitive sections of the Pentateuch. I have again and again seen Christian and Jewish attitudes compared by contrasting 'the law of love of the Gospel' with 'the Jewish belief in an eye for an eye'. In fact, it is only in some parts of the Christian world, and in the nineteenth and twentieth centuries, that Christian justice has begun to approximate to the sensitivity and compassion of Jewish rabbinical courts fifteen hundred years earlier.

Finally the rabbis, in their perpetual concern with interpretation, were constantly conscious of the fact that it was a whole community, not a select body of saints, with which they were dealing. This concern is charmingly illustrated by a midrashic interpretation of the reason why, at the Feast of Tabernacles, Jews hold a sweet-smelling citron, and wave the *lulav*, a nosegay with twigs of palm, myrtle and willow.[5]

> The fruit of the hadar tree symbolizes Israel: just as the citron has taste as well as fragrance, so Israel have among them men who possess learning and good deeds. Branches of palm tree, too, applies to Israel; as the palm tree has taste but not fragrance, so Israel have among them such as possess learning but not good deeds. And boughs of thick trees likewise applies to Israel; just as the myrtle has fragrance but no taste, so Israel have among them such as possess good deeds but not learning. And willows of the brook also applies to Israel: just as the willow has no taste and no fragrance, so Israel have among them such as possess neither learning nor good deeds. What then does the Holy One, blessed be He, do to them? To destroy them is impossible. But, says the Holy One, blessed be He, let them all be tied together in one band, and they will atone, one for another. If you have done so [says God] then at that instant I am exalted.

This tenderness for 'the willow in the lulav' runs all through their activities. They were concerned with the attainable. They certainly did not make Judaism a soft religion, but they were concerned that men should not fail and fall away through despair of ever attaining a loyal conformity to the will of God for their lives; and to this end they made 'a fence about the Torah' by which men could be aided in their daily loyalty. Sometimes the fence may seem to us too high, or the bricks of which it is composed too small; but its provision was in modern terms good psychology and wise therapeutics. For Christendom and Islam saw to it that a Jew should have every temptation to be disloyal and to desert his ancestral faith. The fence was not the core of Judaism, but it kept the core inviolate through nearly two thousand years of unparalleled external pressures.

The Christian conception of a chosen people was no less profound than the Jewish, no less universal in its implied responsibilities, but it rested on the idea that men were chosen individually and personally to receive salvation in Christ without regard to their race or status – without regard indeed even for their family ties. As the Church soon discovered, once the apostles had begun their preaching, this conception could easily be abused. Men could and did arise, falsely proclaiming that they held the key by which the longed for salvation could be assured. Men could and did so fashion redeemer Christs that they fitted into the pattern of every eastern mysticism and occult cult. The insistence on the finality and fullness of the divine choice could lead to even darker consequences; and men could proclaim a rigid predestinarianism, and even that, once saved, there was no indulgence of the flesh which need be avoided, since to wallow in sin only exalted the divine mercy and the wonder of the choice. In such a situation Christianity emphasized the unattainable as rightly as Judaism was emphasizing the attainable. To human duty to love God and to love men, neither religion set any limits. But a religion calling on men to be 'saved' had always to remind them that salvation was a beginning not an end, lest they should believe that no further spiritual growth was required, or that faith had no further experience to offer.

This totally different picture was reinforced by the fact that, while Judaism was coping with the appallingly difficult problem of finding a new centre for the survival of a people whose every natural insignia – government, land, public religious centre – had been destroyed, Christianity, proclaiming that the saved were from every people and nation, had to struggle to maintain its proclamation in competition with the religions, philosophies, temptations and peculiarities of every people and nation. And so it became an intensely theological religion. It created and strictly determined its official interpreters in a clerical hierarchy geographically covering every Christian community. Above all, it built around the person of the Redeemer and Saviour a fence of Christology as high, and with bricks as small, as that of the rabbis about the Jewish way of living; and with the same justification, and the same vindication by history.

It is only as we contemplate the task which was set to the Christian Church by its chosenness that we can understand sympathetically the bitter heresy hunts, the condemnation of men of the most upright lives and sincere beliefs for false views on what may seem to us academic trifles, and the long story of schism and excommunication which mars Christian history. For, just as the rabbis knew that it was vital to safeguard their way of life, so the theologians knew that it was vital to safeguard the historic Jesus of the Gospels, the historic crucifixion and Resurrection, against interpretations which might deny the unity of God or the true humanity of Jesus, which might take Jesus out of actual history or God's activity out of the world he had created. Credal definition and credal conformity had as natural a place in Christianity as the sabbath and *kashruth* in Judaism. Christianity was as naturally a faith directed by educated clergy as Judaism a practice directed by educated laymen.

It is surely unnecessary to seek to substitute one conception for the other or to deny the validity, in the present world, of both. Christianity is not a substitute for Israel, nor is its mission made unnecessary by the survival of Judaism. But the reverse is true to a precisely equal degree. Judaism is not a substitute for Christianity, nor is its mission made unnecessary by the existence of the Christian Church.

Notes

1 Justin Martyr, *Dialogue with Trypho*, Ch. 29.

2 *Ibid.*, Ch. 82.

3 The text from here to the end of this chapter reproduces, with small alterations, pp. 6–11, of a lecture entitled *The Concept of a Chosen People in Judaism and Christianity* delivered at Chicago in 1954 and published by the Union of American Hebrew Congregations.

4 See p. 81.

5 Lev. 23.40 in *Midrash Rabba on Leviticus* 30.12. Ed. Soncino, pp. 392 f.

Source: James Parkes, 1960, *The Foundations of Judaism and Christianity*, London: Valentine Mitchell (extracts from 'Epilogue – Two Religions: Two Chosen People').

The Question of Jewish–Christian Relations

ROSEMARY RADFORD RUETHER

Many [such] Christians have developed a mode of ecumenism with Jews that does not force them to reexamine the roots of their faith. They have attributed anti-Semitism to more extraneous cultural factors. Their Jewish counterparts have not pressed them to go farther, partly, I suppose, because they did not feel empowered to challenge Christian theology. But also, I suspect, because they feared to awaken what they, from long experience, recognized to be a pathology that readily turned to violence on subjects such as Christology and messianism. Better to let sleeping dragons lie.

I have encountered very different responses to this work from Jews and from Christians. For Jews the critique is not surprising. It corresponds, to a large extent, with what they already know. But they are astonished that a Christian can say it, and, more so, that such a person remains a Christian. From Christians (with a few notable exceptions) I encounter incomprehension. First, the long history of Christian bigotry and violence toward Jews is unknown to them. They find it hard to believe that they could have studied history and have not been told about this. Second, they become openly hostile and fall into personal attacks when the link between Christology and anti-Semitism is raised. They find it unthinkable that there could be any connection between the two. Often, in the process of reaffirming their understanding of Christology, they verbally reiterate exactly the sort of anti-Judaic patterns of Christian thought which I have described as the 'left hand of Christology!'

Such experiences reinforce my impression that anti-Judaic patterns in Christian thought are very deep, woven into the fabric of Christian thought, as much unconscious as conscious, and not dependent on the existence of contemporary sociological friction with existing Jewish communities. This is discouraging, because it also suggests the near impossibility of eradicating these patterns. At most, perhaps, they can be modified sufficiently, while, at the same time, building solidarity with the Jewish community to prevent their being translated into new pogroms.

Christology and Anti-Judaism: Reconstruction of the Tradition

The anti-Semitic heritage of Christian civilization is neither an accidental nor a peripheral element. It cannot be dismissed as a legacy from paganism or as a product of purely sociological conflicts between the church and the synagogue. Anti-Semitism in Western civilization springs, at its root, from Christian theological anti-Judaism. It was Christian theology that developed the thesis of the reprobate status of the Jew in history and laid the foundations for the demonic view of the Jew that fanned the flames of popular hatred. This hatred was not only inculcated by Christian preaching and exegesis. It became incorporated into the structure of canon law and also into the civil law formed under the Christian Roman emperors, such as the codes of Theodosius (A.D. 428) and of Justinian (6th century). These anti-Judaic laws of the church and the Christian empire laid the basis in Christian society for the debasement of the civic and personal status of the Jew, which lasted until the emancipation in the nineteenth century. These laws were, in part, revived in the Nazi Nuremberg laws of 1933.

The understanding of Christology is, I believe, at the heart of the problem. Theologically, anti-Judaism developed as the left hand of Christology. Anti-Judaism was the negative side of the Christian affirmation that Jesus was the Christ. Christianity claimed that the Jewish tradition of messianic hope was fulfilled in Jesus. But since the Jewish religious teachers rejected this claim, the church developed a polemic against the Jews and Judaism to explain how the church could claim to be the fulfillment of a Jewish religious tradition when the Jewish religious teachers themselves denied it.

At the root of this dispute lies a fundamentally different understanding of the messianic idea that developed in Christianity, in contrast to the Hebrew scriptures and the Jewish teaching tradition. Judaism looked to the messianic coming as a public, world-historical event which would unequivocally overthrow the forces of evil in the world and establish the Reign of God. Originally Christianity also understood Jesus' messianic role in terms of an imminent occurrence of this coming Reign of God. But when this event failed to materialize, Christianity pushed it off into an indefinite future, i.e., the Second Coming, and reinterpreted Jesus' messianic role as inward and personal with little resemblance to what Jewish tradition meant by the coming of the Messiah. An impasse developed between Christianity and Judaism, rooted in Christian claims to messianic fulfillment and supersession of Judaism that were not only unacceptable, but incomprehensible, in the Jewish tradition. The real difference between these views has never really been discussed between Christians and Jews in any genuine fashion because, at an early stage of development, these growing differences of understanding of the messianic advent were covered over with communal alienation and mutual polemic.

Christian teachers sought to vindicate their belief in Jesus as the Christ by reinterpreting Hebrew prophecy to accord with the Christian view of Christ. This Christian exegesis also denied the ability of the Jewish teachers to interpret their own scriptures. The Jews, Christians said, had always been apostate from God and their teachers spiritually blind and hard of heart. In effect, Christian theology set out to demonstrate the rejected status of the Jewish people and the spiritual blindness of its exegesis and piety in order to vindicate the correctness of its own exegesis and its claim to be the rightful heir of Israel's election.

According to Christian teaching, it is the church that is the true heir to the promises to Abraham. It is the spiritual and universal Israel, foretold by the prophets, while the Jews are the heirs of an evil history of perfidy, apostasy, and murder. As a result the Jewish people have been cut off from their divine election. Divine wrath has been poured down on them in the destruction of the temple and the national capital city of Jerusalem. They have been driven into exile and will be under a divine curse as wanderers and reprobates until the end of history, when Jesus returns as the Christ, and the Jews finally have to acknowledge their error.

In effect, the church set up its polemic against the Jews as a historical task of Christians to maintain perpetually the despised status of the Jews as a proof of their divine reprobation. At the same time, the church taught that the Jews must be preserved to the end of history as 'witness' to the ultimate triumph of the church. This theological stance was expressed in the official policy of the church toward the Jews through the centuries, combining social denigration with pressure for conversion. It also unleashed waves of hatred and violence that were seldom controllable within the official church policy of minimal protection of Jewish survival. In Nazism the Christian demonization of the Jew's spiritual condition was converted into a demonization of their biological condition. Hence the Nazi final solution to the Jewish question was not religious conversion, but physical extermination, to make way for the millennium of the Third Reich.

For us, who live after the Holocaust, after the collapse of Christian eschatology into Nazi genocidal destruction, profound reassessment of this whole heritage becomes necessary. Although the Nazis hated Christians as well as Jews, the church nevertheless must take responsibility for the perpetuation of the demonic myth of the Jew that allowed the Nazis to make them the scapegoat of their project of racial purity. This Christian tradition also promoted an antipathy toward Jews, which generated little need to respond to the disappearance of their Jewish neighbors. We have to examine the roots of the theological patterns that fed this attitude toward the Jews and perpetuate it, even in liberal theologies, today.

Let us consider three basic theological patterns that promote anti-Judaism and see how these dualistic patterns of Christian faith and the negation of Judaism have operated historically. I will present critical reconstructions of these theses, hopefully freed from their anti-Jewish bias, and will focus on Christology as the center around which these dualisms cluster, and ask how Christology itself has to be reconstructed in the light of these criticisms.

The Schism of Judgment and Promise

The Christian *Adversus Judaeos* tradition was built on a two-sided exegesis of the Hebrew scriptures. On the one hand, Christian *midrash* of the psalms and prophets sought to show that the scriptures predicted Jesus as the Christ, and also that they demonstrated the perfidy of the Jews and predicted their final apostasy. This exegesis was developed by Christian teachers before the New Testament was written as a part of the oral tradition of catechetics. It was incorporated into the exegesis and theology of the New Testament. The argument continued as a proof-texting tradition into the patristic period. Writings against the Jews in the corpus of the church fathers continued to be built on a tradition of christological and anti-Judaic prooftexts. This exegetical tradition shows the close connection between Christology and anti-Judaism.

This type of exegesis distorted fundamentally the meaning of prophetic criticism. The dialectical structure of prophetic thought was split apart, so that its affirmative side, of forgiveness and promise, was assigned to the Christian church, while its negative side, of divine wrath and rejection, was read out against the Jews. This splitting of the left hand of prophetic criticism from the right hand of hope and promise creates an unrelieved caricature of evil, projected upon another people with whom the Christian no longer identifies. The church thereby divorces herself from the heritage of prophetic self-criticism and stands triumphant and perfect. The Hebrew scriptures, which actually contain the tradition of Jewish religious self-criticism and repentance, is [*sic*] turned into a remorseless denunciation. All the evils condemned by the prophets are seen as characteristic of this perfidious people. Anti-Judaism and ecclesiastical triumphalism arise as two distortions of a false polarization of the prophetic dialectic.

This ancient Christian tradition of exegesis has practically disappeared among Old Testament scholars. Most Christian scholars of Hebrew scripture interpret them historically, and not as predictions of Jesus as Christ. This leaves largely unexplained the theological claim that the New Testament 'fulfills' the Old (the term 'Old Testament' itself, of course, reflects a christological and anti-Judaic bias).

A more difficult problem occurs in the New Testament. Here anti-Judaic exegesis has been woven into the very patterns of theological interpretation and put into the mouth of Jesus himself. Consider, for example, denunciations of the scribes and Pharisees that occur in the Synoptic Gospels. I suggest that we have here two stages of development. In the first stage, in the ministry of Jesus, there is a denunciation of hypocritical religion that stands in the authentic line of Hebrew prophecy.

As the prophet Amos cried out against externalized ritual: 'I hate, I despise your feasts, and I take no delight in your solemn assemblies … take away from me the noise of your songs, to the melody of your harps I will not listen, but let justice roll down like waters and righteousness like an ever flowing stream' (5:21, 23–24). So the Jesus of the Synoptics cries out: 'Woe to you, scribes and Pharisees, hypocrites! for you tithe mint and cummin and have neglected the weightier matters of the law, justice and mercy and faith; these you ought to have done without neglecting the others' (Matt. 23:23).

Such denunciations are not rejections of Judaism, but are built upon Judaism itself. They presuppose Hebrew faith and existence within the covenant of Israel. The Matthew passage does not in any way reject the Torah. It stands within the debate of rabbinic schools of Jesus' time about the priorities for interpreting and following Torah.

A second stage occurs when the Christian church comes to perceive itself as a fundamentally new covenant founded on the new way of salvation, Christ, that supersedes the Torah and renders it obsolete and inferior. Then the prophetic critique of hypocritical ways of living the Law come to be read as a denunciation of the Law itself as *essentially* hypocritical. The criticism of bad scribes and Pharisees is taken to be a rejection of all Jewish scribes and Pharisees as essentially teachers of this bad religion rejected by Jesus.

The shift from one to the other may appear subtle, but, in fact, it is fundamental. In contemporary terms, it would be the difference between the person who denounces a patriarchal reading of Christology and the person who denounces Christology as essentially patriarchal and calls on all people who desire justice to leave the Christian church and found a new religion based on a different soteriological principle. The first person remains within the Christian tradition, though what is said to many may be unacceptable. The second person rejects the Christian community as a context of identity.

The Jesus who announced a coming Reign of God and preached to the poor in a manner critical of religious elites was undoubtedly a radical and controversial figure, but not one who stood in any way outside the Jewish tradition. Contemporary Jewish scholars have no difficulty affirming this Jesus as a part of the spectrum of controversy over the Law and the Kingdom in the first century. But the Christ of Christian faith, whose messianic identity has been translated into a supersessionary principle over against the Torah, is a figure that departs fundamentally from the ground of peoplehood in Israel. He has become the basis of an anti-Judaic gospel.

There is no way to retrace this historical path and assume literally the stance of Jesus as prophetic critic and messianic proclaimer in the Judaism of his day. If the 970 million Christians were suddenly to apply to reenter Judaism, the 14 million surviving Jews would certainly not know what to do with us. Rather we must reconstruct the stance of Jesus in a way appropriate to our own historical condition.

There are two elements needed to correct the anti-Jewish reading of Jesus' criticism of religion. On the one hand, we must recognize that prophetic criticism is always internal criticism, springing from loyalty and commitment to the true foundations of the people whom you criticize. It is fundamentally distorted when it becomes the repudiation of another people who are no longer your own. Therefore, whatever is valid in the denunciation of legalism and hypocrisy in the Gospels must be appropriated by Christians as self-criticism. We must translate 'scribes' and 'Pharisees' into such words as 'clerics' and 'theologians.' Since most of us who have that opportunity are ourselves clerics and/or theologians, it should be evident that what is being criticized is not Christianity, or even Christian leadership, but certain false ways of setting up leadership that crushes the message of the gospel. We might remember that Jesus himself was called rabbi by his apostles.

This kind of internalization of the gospel critique of religion is already quite common in Christian theology and preaching. Many liberal and liberation theologians, such as Hans Küng or Leonardo Boff, put particular emphasis on this denunciation of false religion precisely for the purpose of criticizing fossilized hierarchical religion within their own communities.

However, this internalization of the gospel criticism will not overcome the anti-Judaic stereotype unless we are willing to concede to the Judaism of Jesus' day the same religious validity that we attribute to our own Christian faith. Surely we expect our own religion, not only to survive, but to be purified through such criticisms. If Hans Küng does not think he becomes anti-Catholic because he denounces hypocritical hierarchicalism in the Roman Catholic Church, then he should not assume that Jesus fundamentally departs from the ground of Torah and Israel when he makes a similar denunciation of false teachers.

This second principle is seldom observed by Christian scholars. Again and again we find theologians, not just conservatives, but theologians on the left, who are happy to use the Gospel denunciations to critique legalistic tendencies in their own community. And yet they continue to write as though these bad traits, which are only distortions of their faith, are somehow generic to Judaism. Indeed, such anti-Judaism becomes reasserted and defended by liberal and liberation thinkers as though the purging of the shadow side of their own faith still demanded the Jewish scapegoat as its point of reference.

This negative projection of Christian self-criticism onto Judaism cannot be corrected without a positive appreciation of Judaism, of the rabbinic tradition, and of Jesus' place in the Judaism of his time. Christians must discover that leaders of the Pharisaic schools, such as Hillel, were making some of the same interpretations of the Law as did Jesus; i.e., that love of the neighbor is the essence of the Law. Christians must correct the stereotypic use of the word 'Pharisee.' Only then will Christian exegetes and preachers be prepared to translate the New Testament language into the same kind of nuanced appreciation of Jesus' Judaism that they would expect to convey about their own Christianity; namely, a religion that contains the possibilities both of prophetic vision and of institutional deformation.

The Schism of Particularism and Universalism

Christians have seen their faith as the universal religion, superseding the particularism of Judaism. Paul's 'neither Jew nor Greek' is seen as the great breakthrough from tribal religion to the religion of universal humanity. Christianity fulfills the messianic promise of the ingathering of all nations, as opposed to the particular identification of Israel with one people and one land. It is true that particularism, even in the Hebrew scriptures, sometimes becomes ingrown ethnocentricity and animosity to others. But what has been less apparent to Christians is the way universalism can become imperialism toward other peoples. Christianity has seen itself as the *only* valid, redemptive identity. All other religions are spurious, demonic, and lacking true relationship to God. To be saved, all must incorporate themselves into the one true human identity, the Christian faith. Even modern liberal theologians, such as Bultmann or Küng, speak of Christianity as 'authentic humanity' without asking whether this means that all other peoples have an inauthentic humanity. The missionary who viewed non-Christians as 'devil-worshipers' did not always avoid translating this theological judgment into a racial judgment on the inferior nature of non-Christian peoples. The zeal to conquer and subdue often went hand-in-hand with the command to convert all nations.

Such imperialist universalism fails to be authentically universalist. It actually amounts to absolutizing one particularism. In this respect Christianity can learn something from the very different way in which Judaism has understood universalism. Judaism has seen itself as having a universal mission to enlighten other nations about higher religion, expressed particularly in monotheism and their basic code of ethics; i.e., the Noachic code, as distinct from the Torah. Although Judaism is open to the true proselyte, it has not seen its mission primarily as conversion of others. This is both because Judaism sees its special characteristics as given to a particular people, and also because it believed that the 'righteous Gentile' could be saved in his or her own religion. Conversion to Judaism is not necessary for salvation. These views lay the basis for a self-limited particularism that, potentially, recognizes the rights of other peoples to define their own identity and relation to God in terms of their own religious culture.

True universalism must be able to embrace existing human pluralism, rather than try to fit every people into the mold of religion and culture generated from one historical experience. Only God is one and universal. Humanity is finally one because the one God created us all. But the historical mediators of the experience of God remain plural. There is no final perspective on salvation available through the identity of only one people, although each people's revelatory point of reference expresses the universal in different contexts. Just as each human language points more or less adequately to universal truths, and yet is itself the product of very particular peoples and their histories, so religions are equally bearers of universal truth, and yet are particular in form. To impose one religion on everyone flattens and impoverishes the wealth of human interaction with God, much as imposing one language on everyone steals other peoples' culture, and memories. If there is a messianic end-point of history that gathers up all these heritages into one, it can only happen through incorporating them all, not through suppressing them all in favor of the experience of one historical group. In order to be truly catholic, Christians must revise the imperialistic way they have defined their universality.

The Schisms of Law and Grace, Letter and Spirit, Old and New Adam

Classical Christian theology brought together two kinds of dualism, one inherited from apocalyptic Judaism and the other from hellenistic philosophy. The apocalyptic dualism divided the messianic people of the new age from a fallen and apostate history. The Qumran community, for example, saw themselves as the messianic Israel of the age to come, over against the apostate temple and unconverted Jewish nation.

In the hellenistic Jewish philosopher Philo we see an exegesis built on the dualism of letter and spirit, outwardness and inwardness, body and soul. Philo himself did not translate this into a sectarian type of Judaism. Rather he wished to give a sacramental understanding of Jewish laws and rites whereby the outward observances point to higher spiritual and universal truths. He did not negate the laws and rites themselves, but enjoined fellow Jews to observe them with a new understanding.

The apocalyptic dualism of the messianic community against the apostate Israel fostered polemical sectarianism. In the Dead Sea sect only the Qumran covenanters are regarded as the true Israel that will inherit the promises in the age to come. The apostate Israel will be cut off and thrown into the pit of fire. Yet the Qumran sect remained intra-Jewish. It sought to convert fellow Jews into its own community. Christianity originally probably shared this type of Jewish messianic sectarian perspective. But, as it became progressively Gentile and alienated from fellow Jews, it translated this intra-Jewish sectarianism into an anti-Jewish sectarianism. Judaism became the alien religion and nation that has been superseded and negated by God.

The absorption of the Platonic dualism of letter and spirit into the sectarian apocalyptic dualism allowed Christianity to define itself over against the old Law and covenant. The old covenant and Law is seen as only the 'fleshly foreshadowing' of a redemptive truth that is now fulfilled on a higher spiritual plane in Christianity. Christianity is seen as superseding Judaism, not only historically, but morally, and even metaphysically. Judaism becomes only letter, fleshliness, and carnality, compared with Christianity as spirit and grace.

The fallacy here lies in confusing the break between two historical peoples with the theological line between history and eschatology. The distinction between ambiguous historical existence and perfected messianic life is imported into history to define the line between two peoples and two historical eras. Israel as the harlot people (which, in the Old Testament, expressed critical historical realism) is used by Christianity to depict the Jews only in negative terms over against the perfectionist version of the church as the messianic bride of Christ. This results in a mystification of Christian reality. Christians project the shadow side of human life on to the Jews as the symbol of the fallen and unfulfilled side of existence. We find here a polarization of a dialectic, which makes sense when applied to one community but creates a completely distorted perspective, both for oneself and for the others, when split into two peoples and two 'eras.'

Judaism is not only letter, any more than Christianity is only spirit. All religions, indeed all human cultures, are a complex dialectic of letter and spirit, faith and law. Religious renewal always wishes to make the content, the inner experience, predominant. But this never takes place without mediating community structures, patterns of prayer, creed, liturgy, ethics, and community life. Christianity has certainly not been without all these embodiments. Indeed, ironically, its constant search for renewal of the inward experience means that it has proliferated far more 'embodiments' of itself than any other historical religion. But it has also mystified the relationship between the spirit and the institutional embodiments, either trying to deny historical embodiments, as in spiritualist, charismatic movements, or else idolizing its historical, institutional form as perfect and divinely given. Christians have yet to develop a realistic account of the relative, yet necessary, relationship between inner content and historical embodiment.

Christian churches have also tended to proliferate supersessionist views of historical relationships. Not only is Christianity seen as superseding Judaism, but each renewed church sees itself as superseding its parent church. The new church is the true church of spirit and faith, replacing the old church of dead letter and rote ritual. This same supersessionist pattern has also been projected into the secular doctrine of progress. Progressive peoples see themselves as superseding and rendering obsolete the unprogressive. We must criticize this supersessionist view of historical relationships.

We can indeed value and affirm those breakthrough experiences of human life that allow new groups to arise and to develop historical identities that are authentic and fulfilling. But this does not mean that the religion or nation from which the group has departed becomes superseded in some absolute way. The former group may be discovering, at that very same time, an equally authentic way of renewing themselves on the basis of their traditional symbols and forms. Thus Christianity, at the very period when it was shaking the dust of Judaism off its sandals, failed to notice that Judaism was undergoing a creative renewal. Indeed it was the Pharisees who refounded Judaism after the demise of the temple and laid the basis for rabbinic Judaism.

Christianity, as much as Judaism, continues to live in a dialectic of fulfillment and unfulfillment. Christianity, in the Resurrection, looks back to a foundational experience that expresses hope and conquest of defeat. Judaism, which did not participate in this particular experience, continues to renew itself out of the experience of the Exodus, which mediates much the same message. For each, the hope mediated by the breakthrough experiences of liberation is the basis for a continued struggle for the final resolution to the riddle of history, which is as much ahead of us Christians as it is ahead of the Jews.

The supersessionary pattern of Christian faith distorts both Jewish and Christian reality. We should think rather of Judaism and Christianity as parallel paths, flowing from common memories in Hebrew scripture, which are then reformulated into separate ways that lead two peoples to formulate the dialectic of past and future through different historical experiences. But the dilemma of foretaste and hope remains the same for both. For both live in the same reality of incompleted human existence itself.

The Key Issue: Christology

The anti-Judaic patterns of Christian theology were, and are still today, tied to a dogma of fulfilled messianism. So it is not possible to rethink these anti-Judaic patterns without questioning their christological basis. Two steps in this critique of Christology are necessary. First, Christians must formulate the faith in Jesus as the Christ in terms that are proleptic and anticipatory rather than final and fulfilled. Jesus should not be said to fulfill all the Jewish hopes for the coming Messiah, which indeed he did not. Rather, he must be seen as one who announced this messianic hope and who gave signs of its presence, but who also died in that hope, crucified on the cross of unredeemed human history.

In his name we continue to proclaim that hope, and also to begin to experience its presence. But, like Jesus, we also do that under the cross of unresolved human contradictions. The final point of reference for the messianic advent still remains in the future. Its unambiguous arrival still eludes us. Here and now we, as much as the Jews, struggle with unresolved history, holding on to the memory of Jesus' resurrection from the grave as the basis for *our* refusal to take evil as the last word and *our* hope that God will win in the end.

This proleptic understanding of Jesus' messianic identity is familiar to Christian exegetes. It has been particularly renewed in liberation theologies. It is the exegesis that best translates the New Testament experience. Jesus' message is falsified when it is translated into a final fulfillment that is spiritualized and institutionally lodged in the past.

Second, we must see Christology, not only as proleptic, but also as paradigmatic. We must accept its relativity to a particular people. This will be a more difficult principle for many Christians to accept, but it is equally inescapable. The Cross and the Resurrection are contextual to a particular historical community. These are breakthrough experiences that found *our* people, that mediate hope in the midst of adversity *for* us. But this does not mean these are the only ways this may happen, or that other people may not continue parallel struggles on different grounds; namely, the Jews, for whom the events of Jesus did not become paradigmatic events, and for whom the Exodus and the Torah serve as the memory and the way.

Some Christians will see such contextualizing of the Christian symbols as totally unacceptable. For them, Jesus as the only name that may be named on earth and in heaven is absolute. I can only say that our two thousand years of human experience do not allow that assertion to be taken literally. He may indeed be the only name *for us*. But other names continued to be named and do not fail to bear fruit. Nor does it seem to me that the power of Jesus' name will become less if we cease to use that name to deny the validity of other peoples' experience of God through other means. Indeed, only when we cease to use Jesus' name to negate other peoples' experiences of the victory of life over death, can the name of Jesus cease to be a name that creates alienation of Jew from Christian, Christian from non-Christian. Then we can begin to find in our differing ways of mediating hope in the midst of defeat new possibilities of human solidarity.

Source: Rosemary Radford Ruether, 1989, *Disputed Questions: On Being a Christian*, Maryknoll: Orbis Books, pp. 55–73.

8

Islam

PAUL HEDGES

Introduction

It is clear that the relationship with Islam is one of the most important ones facing Christianity today. In a world where many take seriously Samuel Huntington's 'Clash of Civilizations' thesis, we must surely agree with Hans Küng's dictum, 'No world peace without peace between the religions', for fault-lines of misunderstanding and tension exist between the broadly (though rather inaccurately) conceived Western-Christian and Islamic-Middle Eastern-and-beyond blocks.[1] I would suggest therefore that there is an onus on Christian theologians and churches to seek to build bridges, engage in dialogue, and engender mutual understanding and respect. For this reason, the two readings chosen both emphasize points of contact and point to positive aspects of encounter (though without ignoring the problems).[2]

The readings pick up on two important sources of relation and tension between these fellow Abrahamic faiths. These are the questions of religious founders and texts. The first text, which considers whether Christians can see Muhammad as a prophet, is from Hans Küng's *Christianity and the World Religions*, which may be considered a classic. Küng, as perhaps the world's most famous theologian, hardly needs an introduction, suffice it to say he is a Swiss Catholic theologian (though one who was deprived of his Catholic professorship for his outspoken views) who since the 1980s has been drawn into issues around interfaith dialogue and the Global Ethic.[3] While dated in part, Küng's masterful treatment of the Christian understanding of Islam's main prophet raises questions and issues that are still fresh and need to be considered again.[4] Certainly, as far as dialogue with Islam is concerned, many Muslims find it a point of vexation that while they give respect to Jesus as a religious leader many Christians find it hard to give a comparable status to Muhammad, so Küng's theological exploration of how Christians may legitimately and faithfully see Muhammad as a prophet is a critical issue. Similar issues arise in relation to the Qur'an, with many Muslims respecting the Bible, but Christians not knowing what to make of the Islamic sacred text. These and other themes are raised by our second piece, which considers the use and relationship of the Bible and Qur'an in dialogue. The author, Kenneth Thomas, who has worked in mission and dialogue, considers some of the common heritage and context of the two traditions, and hence their texts, while also dealing with the differences and the misunderstandings this can lead to. His experience in dialogue and encounter shows through in the skilful exploration of these issues.

Notes

1 Quote from Hans Küng, 1991, *Global Responsibility: In Search of a New World Ethic*, London: SCM Press, first published 1990 in German, p. xv; for Huntington's thesis, see Samuel P. Huntington, 'The Clash of Civilizations?', *Foreign Affairs*, summer 1993.

2 For those wishing to find some of the negative views Christians have expounded about Islam see references in the chapter on Islam in the accompanying textbook, Martin Bauschke, 2008, 'Islam', in Paul Hedges and Alan Race (eds), *SCM Core Text Christian Approaches to Other Faiths*, London: SCM Press.

3 For Küng on the Global Ethic, as well as the work cited in note 1, see Hans Küng, 1993, 'Declaration Toward a Global Ethic', in Hans Küng and Karl-Josef Kuschel (eds), *A Global Ethic: The Declaration of the Parliament of the World's Religions*, London: SCM Press. For a commentary around this notion see Paul Hedges, 2008, 'Concerns about the Global Ethic: A Sympathetic Critique and Suggestions for a New Direction', *Studies in Interreligious Dialogue* 18.1 (Fall), pp. 1–16, and 'Are Interfaith Dialogue and a Global Ethic Compatible? A Call for an Ethic to the Globe', *Journal for Faith, Spirituality and Social Change* 1.2 (May), pp. 109–32 (these both offer critical views), and Alan Race, 2008, 'Interfaith Dialogue', in Hedges and Race (eds), *Christian Approaches*, 155–72, pp. 163–6 (which offers a positive view, and offers a response to the criticisms found in Hedges).

4 Bauschke, 'Islam', offers more thought on this topic.

Muhammad: A Prophet?

HANS KÜNG

The figure of Muhammad and his message have to be seen in their historical context, a current amid the tremendous stream of the religious history of all humanity. This is the point of departure for modern day scholarship. And the eminent expert on Islam Wilfred Cantwell Smith bids us understand this tremendous stream as a historical continuum in which we can observe at all points a pattern of crossovers and overlaps, interdependence and interaction, give-and-take between religions that are unquestionably different but by no means disparate. Muhammad stands at an intersection in world history where the ancient Arabian tribal religion encountered Judaism and Christianity. In this way, there was from the outset a confluence of certain elements of a common religious heritage (from the idea of God to forms of piety).

And yet the case of Muhammad makes it clear that this historical continuum of the religious history of humanity must be understood – dialectically – as a continuum in *discontinuity*. Naturally a 'Big Bang theory,' to use Smith's ironic term, is not what we want for interpreting the history of religion: Neither for Muhammad and Islam nor for Buddha and Buddhism nor, finally, for Jesus and Christianity was there in the beginning any *creatio ex nihilo*, a sudden creation out of nothing, but a quite specific historical context that frames everything spoken and done and that guarantees a connection with all of the past and contemporary life.

On the other hand, neither would it seem right, as Smith argues, to talk about a continual creation, a single mighty stream of religion. Organic images, such as a river or a tree, tend to make us overlook the fact that the religious history of the human race is not a natural 'flow' or organic 'growth.' That history simply cannot be explained if we reject outright 'dialectics' (Hegel) or 'the category Novum (novelty)' (Ernst Bloch) and 'leading individuals' (Karl Jaspers). History is always a process of unfolding and entangling, with not just quantitative but qualitative leaps, with changes and breaks, extinction and new life. And Muhammad – to be more precise, the Qur'an – obviously constitutes an epochal turning point in the history of the Arab peoples: Muhammad is discontinuity in person, an ultimately irreducible figure, who cannot be simply derived from what preceded him, but stands radically apart from it as he, with the Qur'an, establishes permanent new standards. In that respect, Muhammad and the Qur'an represent a decisive break, a departure from the past, a shift toward a new future. It was fitting to make the Hegira the start of a new era: Without Muhammad as a source, there would be no stream; without this sprig, there would be no tree.

Hence we can't say that in the religious history of mankind everything runs in cycles, as, for example, with the custom of saying the rosary, which was originally Hindu-Buddhist, then Islamic, and finally Christian; or the legend of the Christian saint 'Josaphat,' who proves to be none other than the 'Bodhisattva,' the Buddha. At certain specific moments in time, the figure of the prophet emerges and breaks clear from the continual flow or, better, the prophet wades into the sluggish stream of religious history and tries with all his might to change its course. If he succeeds, he joins the company of those 'leading individuals' who have set the standard for their religion by which the centuries to come will all be measured. Karl Jaspers, of course, pays no attention to Muhammad, ostensibly because the Prophet lacked originality, but this is a serious misunderstanding. Muhammad has functioned as a religious archetype for a large part of the human race; down through the ages, people have repeatedly, consciously fallen back on him, on the earliest Islamic community, on the Qur'an.

Many religions, as we know, are unacquainted with prophets in the strict sense: The Hindus have their gurus and sadhus, the Chinese their sages, the Buddhists their masters; unlike *Jews*, *Christians*, and *Muslims*, none of these groups have prophets. Meanwhile, when the history of religion speaks of 'the Prophet,' *tout court*, of a man who claimed to be *that* but absolutely nothing *more*, then there can be no doubt that this is Muhammad. But was he one? Even orthodox Christians (or Jews), provided they confront the facts with an open mind, cannot deny certain parallels:

- Like the *prophets of Israel*, Muhammad based his work not on any office given him by the community (or its authorities) but on a special, personal relationship with God.
- Like the prophets of Israel, Muhammad was a strong-willed character who saw himself as wholly penetrated by his divine vocation, totally taken up by God's claim on him, exclusively absorbed by his mission.
- Like the prophets of Israel, Muhammad spoke out amid a religious and social crisis. With his passionate piety and his revolutionary preaching, he stood up against the wealthy ruling class and the tradition of which it was the guardian.
- Like the prophets of Israel, Muhammad, who usually calls himself a 'warner,' wished to be nothing but God's mouthpiece and to proclaim God's word, not his own.
- Like the prophets of Israel, Muhammad tirelessly glorified the one God, who tolerates no other gods before him and who is, at the same time, the kindly Creator and merciful Judge.
- Like the prophets of Israel, Muhammad insisted upon unconditional obedience, devotion, and 'submission' (the literal meaning of 'Islam') to this one God. He called for every kind of gratitude toward God and of generosity toward human beings.
- Like the prophets of Israel, Muhammad linked his monotheism to a humanism, connecting faith in the one God and his judgment to the demand for social justice: judgment and redemption, threats against the unjust, who go to hell, and promises to the just, who are gathered into God's Paradise.

Anyone who places the Bible, especially the Old Testament, alongside the Qur'an, and reads both together, inevitably wonders: Don't the three Semitic *religions of revelation* – Judaism, Christianity, and Islam – have *the same basis*? And isn't this particularly true of the Old Testament and the Qur'an? Doesn't one and the same God speak loudly and clearly in both? Doesn't the Old Testament's 'Thus says the Lord' correspond to the Qur'an's 'Say,' as the Old Testament's 'Go and tell' matches the Qur'an's 'Take your stand and warn'? As a matter of fact, the millions of Arabic-speaking Christians have only one word for God: 'Allah.'

Perhaps, therefore, it is only dogmatic prejudice when we recognize Amos and Hosea, Isaiah and Jeremiah, as prophets, but not Muhammad. Whatever objections one may have against Muhammad from the standpoint of Western-Christian morality (armed violence, polygamy, sensuality), there is no way to deny the following facts:

- To this day nearly 800 million men and women living in the vast expanses from Morocco in the West to Bangladesh in the East, from the steppes of Central Asia in the North to the islands of Indonesia in the South, are all marked by the exacting power of a faith that, more than practically any other, has shaped its followers into a uniform type.
- All these people are bound together by a simple profession of faith ('There is no God but God, and Muhammad is his prophet'), by five basic duties (professing the faith, prayer, almsgiving, a month of fasting, pilgrimage to Mecca), by an all-pervasive resignation to the will of God (suffering, too, is to be accepted as an immutable, divine decision).
- Among all these peoples there continues to be a live feeling for the fundamental equality of all human beings before God, and an international brotherhood that has managed to overcome barriers between the races (Arabs and non-Arabs).

In the Christian world today the conviction is surely growing that, faced with the world-historical reality of Muhammad, we have no choice but to make some corrections. The 'plague of exclusivity' stemming from dogmatic intolerance, which Arnold Toynbee so castigated, must be abandoned; and with regard to the Prophet the following points must be conceded:

- The people of seventh-century Arabia were justified in listening to Muhammad's voice.
- They were lifted to the heights of monotheism from the very this-worldly polytheism of the old Arabian tribal religion.
- Taken as a whole, they received from Muhammad, or rather from the Qur'an, a boundless supply of inspiration, courage, and strength to make a new departure in religion, toward greater truth and deeper knowledge, a breakthrough that vitalized and renewed their traditional religion. Islam, in short, was a great help in their life.

For the men and women of Arabia and, in the end, far beyond, Muhammad truly was and is *the* religious reformer, lawgiver, and leader: *the* prophet, pure and simple. Actually, Muhammad, who always insisted he was only a human being, is more than a prophet in our sense for those who follow in his footsteps (*Imitatio Mahumetis*): He is the model for the kind of life that Islam wishes to be. And if, according to Vatican II's Declaration on the Non-Christian Religions, the Catholic Church 'also looks upon the Muslims with great respect: They worship the one, true God ..., who has spoken to man.' Then, in my opinion, that Church – and all the Christian Churches – must also 'look with great respect' upon the man whose name is omitted from the declaration out of embarrassment, although he alone led the Muslims to the worship of the one God, who spoke *through* him: Muhammad, the Prophet.

The fact is often overlooked that even in Old Testament times there were very different sorts of prophets, not all of whom were necessarily great saints. And according to the New Testament there were authentic prophets who came *after* Jesus: men and women who attested to him and his message, who interpreted and translated it for a new age and a new situation. Thus, as we see in I Corinthians, the 'prophets' occupied the second rank in Pauline communities after the apostles. Nevertheless prophecy, whose origins were primarily Judeo-Christian, disappeared soon after the end of the Pauline mission as Jewish Christianity faded from the picture of most Christian communities. After the Montanist crisis, in the second and third centuries (the teachings of Montanus, inspired by the primitive Church and apocalyptic visions, were presented as 'the new prophecy'), prophets largely fell into discredit. But the New Testament doesn't bid us reject in advance Muhammad's claim to be a true prophet *after* Jesus and in basic agreement with him. Naturally, the relationship between Jesus the Messiah and Muhammad the Prophet has yet to be explained in detail. Still, the simple recognition of Muhammad's title of 'prophet' would have momentous consequences, especially for the message he proclaimed, which is written down in the Qur'an.

Source: Hans Küng, 1987, *Christianity and the World Religions: Paths of Dialogue with Islam, Hinduism, and Buddhism*, London: Collins, pp. 24–8 (section 'Muhammad: A Prophet?').

The Qur'an and the Bible

KENNETH J. THOMAS

We might begin by asking why should we be concerned with the place of the Bible in Muslim–Christian relations. That question, though, takes us to a prior question: 'Why are we concerned with Muslim–Christian relations?'

We live in a society with people of several faiths, including Hindus and Muslims. As Christians who live and work, worship and witness, serve and share in this society, it is important that we understand and relate to those who form major parts of the population. As fellow citizens and human beings we obviously share many of the same concerns: the provision of sufficient food, and maintenance of health, the need for education, the opportunity for employment, the establishment of just and equitable government institutions, and many others. The meeting of these concerns is not the work of any one segment of society but requires the cooperation of all groups in the country based on good mutual understandings and relationships. As Christians – and the other religious groups have similar mandates – we have divine directives to love our neighbours, serve their needs, and witness to the grace of God offered to all people. To fulfil these directives we must relate to the lives of other people: we need to learn of their needs, meet those needs in love, and show the significance of God's love and grace through our words and deeds. In a society where there is religious suspicion, competition and conflict, it is impossible to cooperate in meeting our common concerns and needs and thus fulfil the commission of our Lord. Therefore, Muslim–Christian dialogue or discussion or relations is basic to our task.

Good Muslim–Christian relations are necessary for there to be an open and free interchange of ideas about faith, religious practices, and ethical values. Basic to such discussion is the sharing of the sacred texts, which form the basis of our views: the Qur'ân and the Bible. There are some among us, perhaps, who think that such relationships should not involve the discussion of the Bible as that will only lead to disagreements and conflict. We need to be aware of the dangers in using the Bible in our interfaith relations. To use the Christian scriptures in an authoritarian way to impose our views on others, to assert what they say in a one-way form of communication which allows neither an answer nor a negative response, or to insist blindly and dogmatically on our interpretation of them will close the door to any meaningful discussion and block the establishment of the very kind of relationship we are hoping to engender. What then is the place of the Bible in Muslim–Christian relations? Let us consider this question in terms of a number of commonalities which exist between Christians and Muslims while realistically keeping in mind the differences which exist within those very things which we have in common.

Common Respect for Scriptures

The fact that both Muslims and Christians have a high regard for Scripture is basic to any consideration of Muslim–Christian relations. In fact, we have a common respect for what the Muslims call the 'previous scriptures': the Tawrât, the Zabûr, and the Injîl.[1] This respect is evident in the fact that the Jews and the Christians are called 'People of the Book' and the Scriptures are referred to many times in the Qur'ân. This commonality is acknowledged in the Qur'ân:

> Say: "People of the Book! Come now to a word common between us and you, that we serve none but God, and that we associate not aught with Him; and do not some of us take others as Lords, apart from God." (3:64 [57])

Because of the supreme place which Muslims give to the 'Book', they expect Christians to have the same high regard for and knowledge of their Scriptures. The Qur'ân is viewed as confirming what God has already revealed in the 'previous scriptures':

> So let the People of the Gospel judge according to what God has sent down therein. Whosoever judges not according to what God has sent down – they are the ungodly. And we have sent down to thee the Book with the truth, confirming the Book that was before it, and assuring it. (5:52–53 [41–48])

Even Muhammad is instructed in the Qur'ân to confirm what God has said to him from those who know the previous scriptures:

> So, if thou are in doubt regarding what We have sent down to thee, ask those who recite the Book before thee. (10:93)

The Scriptures are understood by Muslims to be the actual words of God revealed verbatim to the prophets. For this reason Muslims have much greater interest in the Bible than in any Christian literature as a basis for discussion: they want to read or hear what God has directly revealed.

While this high regard for Scripture provides an immediate basis for Muslim–Christian discussion, the particular Islamic views of Scripture also create problems in making a common approach to the Bible. Generally, Muslims have very little direct knowledge about the Bible and expect that it will be like the Qur'ân – a record of the direct revelation of God to Moses, David and Jesus. They are very surprised that the Bible includes history, letters, biography, and many writings obviously by human beings. A Muslim once asked a Christian to show him in the Gospel the words of God – a kind of red-letter edition of God's oracles. On the basis of this experience that the Bible does not contain just the words of God, the second reaction of Muslims is that the Bible does not contain the actual books revealed to the prophets and therefore the Bible is 'corrupt' or incomplete. More specifically, it is expected that all that is revealed in the Qur'ân will be found in the Bible since the Qur'ân is considered to be a summary and confirmation of what had been previously revealed to the prophets. Finally, since Muslims have a high regard for the previous scriptures, they expect Christians also to accept the Qur'ân as a divine revelation and respect it as holy Scripture.

Given these difficulties it may be questioned whether the Bible has any place in Muslim–Christian relations. It is important in our relations that we not gloss over our differences. The fact that we both have Scriptures, that we both accept the Tawrât, Zabûr, and Injîl as Scriptures, and that we can believe there are historical written records of God's revelations can provide a sufficient basis to share our understandings of Scripture and to discuss our differing views. This means that we must also be ready to read the Qur'ân and listen to Muslims' understandings of it, even though we might not be ready to accept it as divine revelation. I suggest that any discussion of the Bible with a Muslim should begin with those passages and writings which are most like the Qur'ân in giving the direct oracles of God. Then we can explain that those revelations were given in a historical context which is also included in the Bible. We consider the understandings of God's revelations – both in words and works – to be Scripture as we believe they came through divine guidance.

Common Cultural Background

It is natural to use the Bible in Muslim–Christian relations since the origin of our two faiths are from the same part of the world and our Scriptures reflect a common cultural background. I once flew over Saudi Arabia passing by Medina where Muhammad established the first Islamic community, over the Sinai Peninsula passing by Mount Sinai where Moses and the children of Israel entered into a covenant relationship with God, and over Palestine where Jesus lived and taught and established with his disciples the new covenant community. I was impressed that in that part of the world, in oases fairly close together in a vast desert area, three great relations of the Book erupted with great energy and conviction and spread throughout the world.

The Bible, containing the Jewish and Christian sacred writings, reflects a cultural situation and milieu familiar to Muslims. The forms of family life, society, economy, nomadic life, government, agriculture, animal-husbandry and societal customs described in the Bible are Middle Eastern and are known to all three religious traditions. Particularly the moral codes, legal forms, and stern ethics of desert societies reflect the context within which all three religions originated. There is far more similarity and commonality between these three religions with their common cultural background than any of them have with Far Eastern cultures and religions. So the Bible provides a basis for immediate communication between Muslims and Christians, even in non-Middle Eastern situations.

It needs to be recognized, though, that each of the three faiths provides differing views and critiques of that Middle Eastern culture. The Hebrew prophets called their contemporaries to reject unethical cultural standards and practices and to follow the Law of God. Jesus condemned the Pharisees and others who used the Law to justify their immorality and cultural ways. Muhammad led his people in a reform of societal and family relationships. While the Bible and the Qur'ân reveal Middle Eastern culture, they also stand over against many of the cultural customs and values. The Bible has a place in Muslim–Christian relations as a means of approach to and critique of the non-Christian and non-Islamic aspects of any culture in which they both live.

Common Knowledge of Historical Figures

The three religions of the Book have historical Middle Eastern connections. The history of the children of Israel and the life of Jesus are referred to and summarized in the Qur'ân. The major biblical characters of the Bible are familiar to Muslims: the patriarchs, the early kings of Israel, certain prophets, Jesus and Mary. These are all accorded respect in the Qur'ân and portrayed as examples to be followed. In addition, the events of the life of Abraham are the basis of the hajj ritual in Mecca. This common knowledge of particular figures in the history of our faiths provides a basis of contact and discussion. The Bible has an important place in this relationship as a resource of information about these persons, information presupposed in the Qur'ânic accounts.

Again it must be recognized that the Bible and the Qur'ân have some very different traditions and views about these persons. A Muslim reading the biblical accounts for the first time is shocked at the realism in the portrayal of sins committed by 'prophets', and a Christian reading the Qur'ân is amazed at the purity and ideal qualities imputed to these same 'prophets'. An important aspect of the use of the Bible in Christian–Muslim relations is an exploration of the difference in these portrayals; this can be the basis for important discussions about our views of sin, faith, prophets, Scripture, life, and the way God works with people.

This difficulty does not arise in relation to the life of Jesus who is represented as sinless in both the Bible and the Qur'ân. The Bible has an important place in Muslim–Christian relations as a resource to provide much more information about the life, teaching, and activities of Jesus than is found in the Qur'ân. There is, however, a basic and irreducible difference between the biblical and Qur'ânic views of Jesus, but the full background about him as presented in the Gospels can provide a basis for discussion of this difference of view which ultimately divides the Christian faith from the Jewish and Islamic faiths.

Common Theological Language

In languages predominantly spoken by Muslims there is a significant amount of Arabic vocabulary, particularly for religious terms and theological concepts. This provides Muslims and Christians with a common vocabulary for certain basic terms which facilitate communication and understanding. Where the Bible has been translated into the common language of the culture using these terms, the Bible is helpful and important in Muslim–Christian relations. The Bible is immediately intelligible to Muslims who do not have to struggle with strange and unfamiliar words. Likewise Christians are used to the same terms used by Muslims and can converse with them about theological concepts with a common vocabulary.

Obviously there are some differences between Muslims and Christians in the understanding of some of the religious terms (even as there are between Christians). For example, *injîl* is a pre-Islamic word used by Christians derived from the Greek language through Syriac, the language of Eastern Christians during the time of Muhammad. The word would have been familiar to Muhammad as his Christian acquaintances read and accepted the *injîl* as the authoritative, divine message of Jesus the Messiah. He believed that it had been revealed by God directly to Jesus. Given the historical connection between the use of the word by Muhammad and Christians and the common semantic elements, the use of the word *injîl* provides a basis for communication, discussion, and clarification between Christians and Muslims.

The concept of *jannah*[2] also differs for Muslims and Christians. For the Muslim it refers to a realm in the next life where the faithful will be able to enjoy various physical and intellectual pleasures. Christians generally believe that it refers to a spiritual realm in which the relationship of the believers to God to give praise and glory to God will be perfected and a new life of peace and happiness is to be enjoyed. But for both, the common, and most important, element is the concept of *jannah* as the realm of the life to come for believers in God.

We could continue this contrast of concepts for almost every term: *iman*, *mahabbah*, *nabî*, etc.[3] But it is sufficient to say that the use same words [*sic*] by both Muslims and Christians has a historical continuity with pre-Islamic Jewish and Christian usage. There are basic components of meaning and significance which are the same and are the basis for understanding particular aspects of basic concepts as one reads the Bible and the Qur'ân. The Bible is very important in this regard as it is through the reading of these words in the context of their use in the biblical passages that their particular biblical meaning can be apprehended.

Common Religious Concerns

The Bible also has an important place in Muslim–Christian relations because Muslims and Christians have many common religious concerns which are addressed in the Bible. For example, both believe in the one God and both are concerned to do God's will as it has been revealed. The Bible contains the accounts of God's revelations in history through the children of Israel, the prophets, Jesus the Messiah, and the Church. Through these revelations

God's will has been proclaimed with God. The Qur'ân also indicates that God's will has been revealed through the prophets in the history of the children of Israel and through the life of Jesus the Messiah.

Both Muslims and Christians are concerned about the failure of people to keep God's will for there is an ultimate judgement in the life to come for those who reject the revealed way of God. For both, the nature of sin and its eschatological consequences are serious matters of faith. Much Islamic thinking on these matters is related to that found in the Bible; and the Bible is an important source of background information about these concepts.

There are some fundamental differences in the views of Muslims and Christians about these matters. The place of law in revealing God's will and the nature of human sin are two areas in which there is a difference of belief, even as there is between Jews and Christians. The discussion of the differences in the Jewish and Christian views of law and sin in the New Testament (e.g., in Paul's 'Letter to the Galatians') is an important resource for illuminating the different approaches and provides a thought-provoking means of initiating discussion and consideration of these basic concerns between Muslims and Christians.

Common Human Concerns

Finally, both Muslims and Christians understanding [sic] themselves to have a responsibility to live as God's creatures in God's world and thus have many common human concerns: how to order and preserve family life in a way which is constructive and beneficial to human society; how to use and conserve the natural resources of the world in a way which will not upset the ecological balance but enable the natural environment to continue to be a place contributing to our health and providing for our physical needs; how to order and maintain social, economic, and political institutions which will provide justice, fairness, and peace in society and human relationship.

We are familiar with Roman Catholic, Protestant, and Orthodox statements about these concerns, but we also need to acquaint ourselves with Muslim statements about them. For example, the Universal Islamic Declaration of Human Rights states:

> Whereas the age-old human aspiration for a just world order wherein people could live, develop and prosper in an environment free from fear, oppression, exploitation and deprivation, remains largely unfulfilled;
>
> Whereas the Divine Mercy unto mankind reflected in its having been endowed with super-abundant economic sustenance is being wasted, or unfairly or unjustly withheld from the inhabitants of the earth; ...
>
> Therefore we, as Muslims, believe in our obligation to establish an Islamic order wherein all human beings shall be equal and none shall

enjoy a privilege or suffer a disadvantage or discrimination by reason of race, colour, sex, origin or language ...

All persons are equal before the Law and are entitled to equal opportunities and protection of the Law;

All persons shall be entitled to equal wage for equal work;

No person shall be denied the opportunity to work or be discriminated against in any manner or exposed to greater physical risk by reason of religious belief, colour, race, origin, sex or language.[4]

Muslims joined Christians in a joint statement issued at the conclusion of the Independent Commission on Christian–Muslim Relations in Amman, Jordan, 1 October, 1985:

Because so many Christians know little about Islam and so many Muslims lack understanding of Christianity – and indeed so many on each side lack comprehension of their own traditions – it may be helpful to summarize our major common affirmations. We may phrase these matters in different ways and interpret them variously but, essentially, we share these basic beliefs:

1. We live in a universe and a planet ruled by God.
2. This God is one, the universal, all-wise, all-powerful and merciful creator of us all.
3. God has revealed to mankind the essential law by which individual behavior and the conduct of society should be governed.
4. We are all called to submit ourselves to the will of God.
5. We are all accountable to God and subject to divine judgement.
6. We are all equal before God, who is a God of justice.
7. We are all the beneficiaries of the mercy of God, the Compassionate one.
8. We affirm the divine ordination of marriage and the central role of the family in transmitting essential moral and spiritual values and in building effective communities and a healthy Society.
9. We hold that God has willed the family to be a covenant of mutual love and support, to be the proper environment for the begetting and rearing of God-fearing and decent children.

On the basis of these shared beliefs, we acknowledge our individual and group responsibilities to combat those forces, influences, and changes which produce family instability and disintegration.

These are concerns which are addressed in the Bible. The Bible provides an abundance of material on these matters which is relevant to Muslim–Christian relations in the pursuit of social justice, human rights and family stability.

The great difference between Muslims and Christians on these matters is on the type of political institutions and power needed in society to assure the existence and protection of these rights. Christians are not united in their views on this point, but the various Christian views all derive from the Bible. The study of the Bible can provide a means for a consideration of the ways in which the will of God for human society can be instituted.

Conclusion

Muslims read the Bible for many reasons. Recently I met a Muslim in Australia who in his youth in Egypt had never read the Qur'ân or practised his faith. While he was studying in Germany, he met some Christians who gave him a Bible, and he started to study it. After reading the Bible he became interested in reading the Qur'ân. He said it was because Christians introduced him to the Bible that he studied the Qur'ân. In the light of his study of the Bible he had many insights into the Qur'an which are not found in commentaries on the Qur'ân. He is now a writer of books on the Qur'an interpreting it in the light of the Bible. In the process he is introducing the Bible to many Muslims. We had some fascinating discussions together on his interpretations of the Bible and the Qur'an.

The Bible is one of most valuable [sic] resources we have as Christians in our relationships with Muslims. The other most valuable resource is our own interest in relating to Muslims in a spirit of love and service. This combination of personal relationships and study of the Bible provides the basis of common understanding, approach to social concerns, and appreciation of faith. We should recognize the value of the Bible in this situation and be ready to discuss it with our Muslim friends. Only one warning: we may find that in encouraging these friends to read the Bible we will need to spend hours discussing emerging matters of common concern.

Notes

1 The Torah, Psalms and Gospels respectively (ed.).

2 Heaven (ed.).

3 Faith, love and prophet(s) (ed.).

4 This is quoted from the Preamble of this document which may be found online, e.g.: http://www.alhewar.com/ISLAMDECL.html (accessed 12 January 2009) (ed.).

Source: Kenneth J. Thomas, 2001, 'The Place of the Bible in Muslim–Christian Relations', in David Emmanuel Singh and Robert Edwin Schink (eds), *Approaches, Foundations, Issues and Models of Interfaith Relations*, New Delhi: ISPCK, pp. 337–46.

Section B: Indic Traditions

9

Hinduism

K. P. ALEAZ AND PAUL HEDGES

Introduction

This section includes a classic text responding to Hinduism, from a famous Indian convert in the nineteenth century, which deals with the relationship of Christianity to the classical traditions of Hinduism, as well as a specially commissioned piece that draws one of India's oppressed groups, the Dalits, into discussions of religious pluralism and dialogue.

Krishna Mohun Banerjea was born in Calcutta on 24 May 1813. He came under the influence of the famous missionary Alexander Duff in 1831, receiving baptism in 1832, before moving on, studying at Bishop's College, Calcutta in 1836, and receiving Anglican ordination in 1839. Renowned for his learning, he was from 1852 to 1867 Professor of Oriental Studies at Bishop's College, became a Fellow of the University of Calcutta in 1860, and from 1867 to 1869 was President of the Faculty of Arts there. He was actively involved in all the progressive social movements of the day. He died on 11 May 1885. Banerjea's theological works are *Dialogues on the Hindu Philosophy* (1861), *The Arian Witness* (1865), *Supplements to the Arian Witness* (1880) and *The Relation Between Christianity and Hinduism* (1881), the text cited here. These works represent the theological struggles of Banerjea in actualizing a transition from exclusivism to inclusivism in the theology of religions. If *Dialogues on the Hindu Philosophy* mostly represents an exclusivist position, the other writings present a clear inclusivism in terms of an interpretation of Jesus Christ as the true Prajapati. This interpretation was an attempt to establish the fact that Christianity is not an alien religion, but rather the fulfilment of the Vedas. Banerjea here becomes the first Indian Christian to suggest the 'fulfilment theory', at a time when it was still theologically innovative, if not radical. For him the cardinal teaching of Christian faith is connected with the great sacrifice of Jesus. In the Vedas we read about Prajapati (elsewhere termed Purusha), the creator God, who sacrificed himself for the Devas, i.e., emancipated mortals. The priests solemnized the Asvamedha (horse sacrifice) as an offering of Prajapati himself and also Prajapati is elsewhere spoken of as Atmada (giver of self) whose death is immortality (Rig Veda 10.121.2). The self-sacrifice of Christ is thus seen to be prefigured in the Vedas. None other than Jesus has appeared in the world claiming the character and position of Prajapati.

The second piece moves us into the twenty-first century and pushes the boundaries of the conventional modes of dialogue. One criticism of much Christian reflection on Hinduism is that it idealizes Hinduism, being concerned with 'spiritual' realities alone, and relies upon the texts of the religious and social elite, and thereby excludes those who are subordinated in this encounter. Therefore, Sara Singha's paper on Dalit theology and pluralism is an important and exciting contribution to this debate. Singha is a doctoral student at Georgetown University, USA, whose work is exploring the way that the Dalit experience, and their liberation perspective, may play out in relation to discourses on religious pluralism and dialogue, especially within the Indian context.

The Relation Between Christianity and Hinduism

KRISHNA MOHUN BANERJEA

To do justice to Hinduism, therefore, we must look at its original form as disclosed in the Vedas both in doctrine and in ritual; the doctrine as laid down dogmatically, and the ritual as perpetuated practically in illustration of the doctrine. In this respect it must be admitted that inconsistencies will often be discovered; we shall meet with conflicting doctrines and self-contradictory precepts. But we shall endeavour to present as fair a view as truth and justice can allow. We shall eschew pessimism and avoid undue optimism.

... In all communities theology commences with cosmogony. It is on the dependence of the creature upon his Creator that the religious sentiment in human nature is founded ... It is, however, difficult to say that the Vedic doctrine was pure monotheism, untainted by polytheism. At the same time, I must confess that those, who delight in charging those most ancient records with the gross corruptions of a later period, forget three important points clearly indicated in the Veda. These three points are the following:

1stly. The Rig Veda (i. 164, 6. ii. 27, 10 x. 82)[1] declares in several places the existence of one unborn or eternal Being as different from and superior to *Devas* and *Asuras*, and far above heaven and earth.

2ndly. The same Veda declares that the *Devas* were originally and by birth mortal like men, and that they got to Heaven by virtue of Sacrifice.

3rdly. The Rig Veda, again, (i. 164, 46.) as if to apologize for an incipient polytheism that was growing up, declared dogmatically that the sages designate the One Eternal Being in manifold ways. They call Him *Indra, Mitra, Varuna, Agni, Yama, Matariswa* etc.

It is not necessary for the purposes of this discourse to dilate on this point.
...

Now, the first and foremost rites of religion, which they regularly celebrated, and on which they most firmly relied as the great cure for all the
evils of life, and the secret of all success in the world, were *sacrificial* rites.
Not idolatrous worship, not observances of caste, not any popular ceremony of our days, but *yajna* (sacrifice) and its connectives were the religious
rites cherished by them.

The rites of Sacrifice were called 'the first primary rites,' and this was
because the first man after the deluge, whom the Hindus called Manu, and
the Hebrews Noah or *Nuh*, had offered a burnt-offering, which was held
by all his successors as the first and most important ceremony of religion.
The high estimation in which the rite of Sacrifice is held in the Vedas will
appear (1) from the date and authorship assigned for its institution, (2) the
great virtues attributed to its performance, both for spiritual and temporal
purposes, (3) the benefits it is said to have conferred on the gods themselves.
We shall briefly review it under these different aspects.

(1) The authorship of the institution is attributed to 'Creation's Lord'
himself, and its date is reckoned as coeval with the creation. 'Creation's
Lord instituted the Sacrifice.' 'He uttered the *Nivid* (sacrificial formula), all
things were created after it.' In the post-diluvian world, the first act of the
surviving patriarch, whom the Indo-Arvans called *Manu* (a name not very
dissimilar to the Semitic *Nu*), was a sacrificial offering. This latter tradition is confirmed as well by the Bible as also by the account found in the
Assyrian Inscriptions. It will not be regarded as an extreme act of credulity
if we declare that much consideration is due to the concurrence of so many
curious traditions. With reference to the legend of the institution of sacrifice
being coeval with the creation, we can only interpret the writer's meaning
in the sense of that institution having existed from time immemorial. The
Vedas knew of no time when it was not practised.

(2) With reference to the great virtues attributed to the celebration of
sacrifices, it was considered as the potent remedy for all evils – the pana-
cea for all distempers. Even the briny ocean and the dust of the earth distil
sweets for the regular performer of the sacrificial ritual.

The world was called into being by virtue of sacrifice and is still upheld
by its force, being indeed its 'navel'.

In it lay all strength against enemies. The *Zendavesta* too concurred with
the Vedas here. The evil spirit had asked Zarathustra: 'By whose word wilt
thou smite, by whose word wilt thou annihilate, by what well-made arms
smite my creatures?' *Zarathustra* answered boldly: 'Mortar, Cup, Haoma,
and the words which *Ahura-Mazda* has spoken – these are my best weapons.' And these were the implements of Sacrifice.

Nor was the virtue of sacrifice less conspicuous from a spiritual point of
view. It was the great means of escape from the pernicious effects of sin.

'Give us, O Indra, multitudes of good horses with which we may offer our oblations, and thereby escape all sins.'

'Do thou lead us safe through all sins by the way of Sacrifice.'

'Do Thou, (O Sacrificial Soma), who knowest all things, make us to pass over sin, as a navigator ferries men over the sea.'

Varuna, whose name appears the same as the Greek word for Heaven (*Ouranos*), and who, as we have seen, was regarded as the supreme Being under the title of *Asuraprachetas*, is thus invoked for such knowledge as may make us wise unto salvation: 'O illustrious Varuna, do thou quicken our understanding, while we are practising this ceremony, that we may embark on the good ferrying boat by which we may escape all sin.' On this passage the *Aitareya Brahmanana* of the Rig Veda says: 'Sacrifice is the good ferrying boat. The black sink is the good ferrying boat. The word is the good ferrying boat. Having embarked on the word, one crosses over to the heavenly world.'

Sacrifice offered according to the true way – the right path – has been held in the Rig, Yajur, and Sama to be the good ferrying boat or raft by which we may escape from sin. It was expressly declared to be the authorised means both for remission and annulment of sin. 'The animal he offers to *Agnishoma* is his own ransom.'

The following formula gives the words which were uttered by the sacrificer as he offered each limb to the Fire on slaughtering and cutting up the victim. 'O thou animal limb now being consigned to the fire, thou art the annulment of sins committed by the Devas, thou art the annulment of sins committed by the (departed) fathers. Thou art the annulment of sins committed by men. Thou art the annulment of sins committed by ourselves. Whatever sins we have committed by day or by night, thou art the annulment thereof. Whatever sins we have committed, knowing or unknowing, thou art the annulment thereof. Thou art the annulment of sin – of sin.'

But our ancestors seem to have understood, or at least suspected, that 'it is not possible that the blood of bulls and of goats should take away sins.' The conception of the principles which underlay the institution of the ceremony had been, perhaps, well nigh forgotten. The ritual was performed as an *opus operatum*. Its true meaning had fallen into oblivion. They therefore called it a *maya* or mystery, thus: 'O death; the thousand myriads of thy bands for the destruction of mortals, we annul them all by the *maya* or mysterious power of sacrifice.'

(3)   They had the same conception of this mysterious power in the case of the *Devas* who were 'originally mortals,' who were 'in the beginning like men,' but had been 'translated to heaven by the virtue of sacrifice.' *Indra* himself was no better at first. He was 'our man', and as such the 'best of men'. But like other gods, though more excellently than any other, he had performed numberless sacrifices, and been thereby promoted to heaven, free from 'want, misery and death.' Again: 'by this sacrificial hymn the gods had

overcome the *Asuras*. By the same does the sacrificer, whoever he be, still overcome the most wicked enemy (sin).'

And it has been expressly declared that as sacrifice was the way by which the *Devas* got to heaven, the same is still the way open for mankind. 'Whosoever desires the felicity of heaven, let him perform sacrifices in the right way.' And such performances were reckoned as the first acts of religion, the first and primitive *dharma*. The *Devas* performed a sacrifice by means of a sacrifice. Those were the first acts of religion. 'They became glorified and attained to heaven, where the pristine *Sadyas* live.'

Now the secret of this extreme importance attached to sacrifice, and the key to the proper understanding of the whole subject was the self-sacrifice of *Prajápati*, the Lord or supporter of the Creation, the 'Purusha begotten before the world,' 'the *Viswakarma*, the Author of the universe.' The idea is found in all the three great Vedas – Rig, Yajur, and Sama – in Sanhitas, Brahmanas, Aranyakas and Upanishads. The Divine *Purusha* who gave himself up as a sacrifice for the *Devas*, i.e., *emancipated mortals*, had, it is said, desired and got a mortal body fit for *sacrifice*, and himself became *half mortal* and *half immortal*. It is added that he made sacrifice a reflection or figure of himself; that the *equine* body was found fit for sacrifice, and that whenever a horse-offering (*Asvamedha*) was solemnized, it became no other than an offering of *himself*.

This idea of the sacrifice of a Divine Person is not found merely in a single isolated passage, in which case it might have been explained away; but in various passages in the different Vedas it finds expression in different ways, sometimes clearly, sometimes obscurely; and, taken as a whole, it appears a prominent doctrine, which gives signification to the frequent exhortations to the performance of sacrificial rites and ceremonies. The same idea throws light on the texts which declare the celebration of Sacrifice to be the only way of attaining heaven, after the example of those quondam mortals, the *Devas*; and the only good vessel for getting over the waves of sin, which would otherwise overwhelm mankind. Both the Rig and the Yajur tell us that 'when the Devas celebrated the sacrifice, and bound Purusha as the victim, they immolated Him, the Sacrifice, on the grass, even him, the *Purusha* begotten in the beginning.'

There is again an obscure passage in the Rig Veda, which *Yaska* the author of the *Nirukta* thus expounds: '*Viswakarma* had in a universal sacrifice offered all creatures, and then eventually offered Himself also.'

The Yajur summarises the same passage by putting into the mouth of the Divine Self-sacrificer the words: 'Let me offer myself in all creatures and all creatures in myself.'

The obscurity is not removed by these different readings. The idea is nevertheless somewhat cleared up by the light of other passages, and by the assistance of the Bible. The world was condemned, and offered for sacrifice, that is to say, was devoted to destruction, for sin; and the Divine Saviour then offered himself for its deliverance. The Bible says, 'If one died for all then were all dead.' The Veda says, conversely, *Because all were devoted to destruction, therefore one died for all*. The one reasoned from the consequent to the antecedent; the other from the antecedent to the consequent; but both appeared to concur in the nature of the antecedent and the consequent.

The *Brihadaranyaka*, itself an Upanishad, says, '*Prajápati* desired to offer a great Sacrifice. He desired: – may I have a body proper for sacrifice (*medham*), and may I become embodied by it.'

The same Upanishad adds: 'Priests solemnize the sacrifice (*Asvamedha*) as if it were an offering of *Prajápati* himself, or the, universal Godhead.'

Again, 'it (the sacrifice) becomes an only *Devata*, even Death,' which, to borrow for the moment a Biblical phrase *reigns over all*. And then the same sacrifice eventually 'conquers death, nor can death get to it again.'

The *Satapatha* says with reference to *Prajápati* that 'half of himself was mortal and half immortal.' Again, 'when he had given himself up for them he made a figure or image of himself, which is sacrifice. Therefore they say, *Prajápati* is the sacrifice Himself.'

Prajápati or *Purusha* is elsewhere spoken of as *Atmada* (giver of self) whose shadow, whose death is immortality. And this immortality, again, regarded not only the soul but the body also. Thus in Rig Veda x. 14. 7. 8 the son of a righteous man was instructed to use the following formula in his last address to his dead father: 'Depart, depart, (O Father!) where our fore-fathers have already gone by the old paths (of the primitive *Rishis*). See there both the Kings, Yama and the divine Varuna, enjoying their immortal repast. Unite there in the highest heaven with Yama and the Fathers, having your good works following you. Giving up your vile (body) get to your abode and be again united with a body of great splendour!' So the overthrow of death was complete.

Without going further with these quotations and citations ... I may now undertake to declare that the first of the two propositions with which I commenced this discourse, is proved, viz.:

> That the fundamental principles of Christian doctrine in relation to the salvation of the world, find a remarkable counterpart in the Vedic principles of primitive Hinduism in relation to the destruction of sin and the redemption of the sinner by the efficacy of sacrifice, itself a figure of *Prajápati*, the Lord and Saviour of the Creation, who had offered himself a sacrifice for that purpose.

All that has just been shown appertaining to the self-sacrifice of *Prajápati* curiously resembles the Biblical description of Christ as God and man, our very Emmanuel, mortal and immortal, who 'hath given Himself for us, an offering and a sacrifice to God for a sweet-smelling savour', of whom all previous sacrifices were but figures and reflections, who by His sacrifice or death hath 'vanquished death, and brought life and immortality to light through the Gospel.'

The Vedic ideal of *Prajápati*, as we have seen, singularly approximates to the above description of our Lord, and therefore remarkably confirms the saving mysteries of Christianity.

Christian evangelists when they draw our attention to the claims of Gospel truth do not utter things which can be called *strange* to Indian ears. Salvation from sin by the death of a Saviour, who was God and man himself, was a conception which had administered consolation to our ancient *Rishis*, and may yet, in a higher form, and to a greater degree, do the same to all India.

I proceed now to discuss the second proposition: 'That the meaning of *Prajápati* – an appellative, variously described as a *Purusha* begotten in the beginning, as *Viswakarma* the Creator of all – coincides with the meaning of the name and office of the historical reality Jesus Christ; and that no other person than Jesus of Nazareth has ever appeared in the world claiming the character and position of the self-sacrificing *Prajápati*, half mortal and half immortal.' The name *Prajápati* not only means 'the Lord of Creatures', but also 'the supporter, feeder and deliverer of his creatures.' The great Vedic commentator Sayana interprets it in that wider sense. The Lord and Master has to feed and maintain his servants and subjects. The name Jesus, in the Hebrew, means the same. The radical term stands for *help, deliverance, salvation*. And that name was given Him because He would save His people from their sins. In the prophecy cited by St. Matthew, He is described as *Heigoumenos*, a leader or ruler, who 'shall *feed* (*poimanei*) my people Israel'. He is therefore to His people what a shepherd is to his flock – both leader, ruler, and feeder. The same is the import of *pati*; the name *Prajápati*, therefore, singularly corresponds to the name Jesus.

Now in order to clear our way to the proper appreciation of this second proposition, it is necessary to consider that the doctrine of Sacrifice, as a figure of *Prajápati* (who had offered himself as a sacrifice for the benefit of the world), did not long continue in its integrity among our forefathers; but had fallen into oblivion even before the age of Buddha. The practice of sacrifice continued indeed, but its origin and object, its chief characteristic as the good vessel which carries us over the waves of sin, as a figure or type of a self-sacrificing Saviour, had long vanished from the conceptions of our countrymen; so much so, that to some of us, both Hindus, and Christians, it sounds, on first hearing it, as strange in our ears, as the Gospel, when first preached, must have sounded in the ears of the people of Athens. But the *litera scripta* of the Vedas, in the providence of God, still remains, and tells us that the practice of sacrifice, however lifeless and therefore irksome it might have appeared in the age of Buddha, had nevertheless the stamp of universal truth at its commencement. We must therefore inquire what has become of that precious Truth; what was the personality of *Prajápati*, half mortal and half immortal; and how, and by what means, at the present time, we are to respond to the invitation of the Rig Veda; and embark on the good vessel which will carry us in safety over the waves of sin. To you, my Hindu countrymen, these questions are of the utmost importance. Your religion, though now scoffed at by both friends and foes, at one time taught doctrines and practices that approached to the Gospel. What has become of those doctrines and practices now? We shall first consider the personality of *Prajápati*. The appellative has been applied in the Hindu *Sástras* to several characters. But none of these corresponds to the ideal of a *self-sacrificing Saviour of the world*, as a sacrifice for the benefit of humanity. There is, as all educated persons must know, only one historical person, Jesus of Nazareth, whose name and position correspond to that of the Vedic ideal – one mortal and immortal, who sacrificed himself for mankind. By the process of exhaustion you may conclude that Jesus is the true *Prajápati*, the true Saviour of the world, 'the only Name given among men whereby we must be saved.' No other character, no other historical personage can satisfy the lineaments of the Vedic ideal. None else has even come forward to claim that identity.

I am now in a position to say that the precious truth we have been investigating, though lost in India, is not lost to the world. It was in fact a fragment of a great scheme of salvation which was at first partially revealed and has since appeared in its integrity in the Person of Jesus Christ – the true *Prajápati* of the world, and in His Church – the true Ark of salvation, by which we may escape from the waves of this sinful world. Do you wish to join in the prayer to Varuna, the most ancient personality of God in the Rig Veda: 'O illustrious Varuna, do thou quicken our understanding, we that are celebrating this sacrifice, that may embark on the good navigating vessel, by which we may escape all sin?' Do you wish to embark on that good navigating vessel? Hear the Veda then: 'Sacrifice is that good navigating vessel.' Sacrifice, the image of *Prajápati* the self-sacrificing deliverer of the world. And if *Prajápati*, be found only in the Person of the historical Christ, it will follow that the gospel navigating vessel or ark, is no other than the Church of Christ.

I think I may therefore declare our second proposition to be also demonstrated. Christ is the true *Prajápati* – the true Purusha begotten in the beginning before all worlds, and Himself both God and man. The doctrines of saving sacrifice the 'primary religious rites' of the Rig Veda – of the double character priest and victim, variously called *Prajápati*, *Purusha*, and *Viswakarma* – of the Ark by which we escape the waves of this sinful world – these doctrines, I say, which had appeared in our Vedas amid much rubbish, and things worse than rubbish, may be viewed as fragments of diamonds sparkling amid dust and mud, testifying to some invisible fabric of which they were component parts, and bearing witness like planets over a dark horizon to the absent sun of whom their refulgence was but a feeble reflection.

All this may seem a strange saying to some, and a hard saying to others. But to the Hindu who reveres his Vedas, and the Christian who loves his Bible, to all who are friends of truth, it cannot be an unwelcome saying ...

The Christian, with the wide sympathy which incites him to invite all nations to the faith of Christ can only rejoice that the Jesus of the Gospels responds to the self-sacrificing *Prajapati* of the Vedas, and that the evangelist's chief work will be to exhibit, before his neighbours and fellow subjects, the true Ark of salvation – that true 'vessel of sacrifice by which we may escape all sin.' He will only have to exhibit, for the faith of the Hindus, the real personality of the true *Purusha* 'begotten before all worlds,' mortal and yet divine, 'whose shadow, whose death is immortality itself.'
...

One word more in conclusion. Do not think what I have said is my voice only, or only the voice of the learned Missionaries who have so ably lectured in this place, or even the voice of Christian England only, which spends millions annually, proclaiming the glad tidings of salvation throughout the world; it is the voice also of your primitive ancestors calling upon you in the words of their Vedas to embark on the good ferrying boat for passing safely over the waves of sin. That Ark of Salvation can only mean the Church of Christ. If it were possible for those hoary *Rishis* to reappear in the world, they themselves would exhort you, nay, beseech you, implore you, perhaps also constrain you not to neglect so great a salvation; not to waver in your duty to acknowledge and embrace the true *Prajápati*, the true *Purusha* begotten before the worlds, who died that you might live, who by death hath vanquished death, and brought life and immortality to light through the Gospel ...

Note

1 Notes are omitted from this source as they give the Vedic references in Sanskrit.

Source: Krishna Mohun Banerjea, 1998, 'The Relation Between Christianity and Hinduism', in K. P. Aleaz (ed. and intro.), *From Exclusivism to Inclusivism: The Theological Writings of Krishna Mohun Banerjea (1813–1885)*, Indian Contextual Theological Education Series 18, Delhi: ISPCK, pp. 594–611.

Dalit Theology: An Indian Christian Response to Religious Pluralism

SARA SINGHA

> We are the broken, torn, rent, burst and split.
> We are the opened and expanded.
> We are the bisected, the driven asunder, dispelled and scattered.
> The down trodden; the destroyed.
> We are the Crushed.
> Therefore, we will be the Manifested and Displayed.[1]
>
> *Arvind P. Nirmal*, Dalit Theologian

Christianity, with its doctrinal and theological promise of equality, has not managed to redeem millions of Dalit Christians from social oppression; rather, in some cases it has increased Dalit difficulties. Conversion from Hinduism disqualifies Dalit Christians from many constitutional privileges and protections and, therefore, offers no respite from discrimination in society or in the church. This paper explores the social and religious oppression facing Christian Dalits in modern India to include Dalit Theology in the current conversation on Religious Pluralism.

First, by examining a particular Hindu creation myth, I briefly trace the concept of 'untouchability' to locate the Dalits historically and contextually in Indian society. Second, I accentuate some possible reasons why Christian Dalits are considered 'untouchables' though they no longer theologically participate in the Hindu caste system. Third, I explore the potential implication of Dalit Theology for religious pluralism and suggest that recognizing Jesus as a Dalit is a viable symbol through which Christianity can engage other religious traditions trans-historically, ethically and theologically. I argue, Dalit Theology enables non-Christians to connect with the 'untouchable' Christ of the past through the common experience of human suffering thereby transforming him into the 'touchable' Christ of the present. This is an important addition to religious pluralism because it maintains the particularity of Christ while inviting non-Christians to access him in a manner appropriate to their own ethical and theological commitments.

Intrinsic Creation in the Hindu Brahmanic Tradition

The Laws of Manu, a text composed by Brahmin priests sometime between 200 BCE and 200 CE, contains several thousands of rules concerning purity and impurity in the Brahmanic system. In addition, the creation myth in this text also reveals that God issues humanity intrinsically from within God's body. The narrative asserts that God issues divine matter through a mitotic process 'by mingling with the minute particles of his own self',[2] constructing all living things from within his physical body. The result of this creative process is a sinuous relationship between God, universe and self, where '[God] divided his own body into two and became a man with one half, a woman with the other half.'[3]

Although this divine engendering is embodied, it is not egalitarian as is evident during the creation of the four *varnas* (castes). *Manu* states, 'from his mouth he created the priest [*Brahmin*], from his arms the ruler [*Kshatria*], from his thighs the commoner [*Vaishya*] and from his feet the servant [*Shudra*]'.[4] However, what is omitted from this divine ordering, are the '*Panchamas*' or the 'fifth group', commonly known as the *avarnas*, or the 'no-caste'. The *Panchamas* lie outside this divine mitotic process and outside of God's body. Therefore, according to traditional interpretation of *Manu*, the *Panchamas* are 'non-human' because they are not engendered intrinsically from within God's body.

Anthropologist Mary Douglas argues, 'the body is a model which can stand for any bounded system. Its boundaries can represent any boundaries which are threatened or precarious.'[5] Positioning the hierarchical bodies in this creation myth reveals that caste categories are maintained because of their function within the Hindu social structure. In this system, 'the lowest castes are the most impure and it is they whose humble services enable higher castes to be free of bodily impurities'.[6] Moreover, Douglas argues, 'The whole system represents a body in which by the division of labor the head does the thinking and praying and the most despised parts carry away the waste matter.'[7] Therefore, the higher caste groups in this religious system depend on the lower castes in order to preserve their social position and maintain their theological purity.

Because Hindu Dalits are religiously and socially bound by the pollution of the 'untouchable' caste category, contemporary Christian Dalits are still conscious about their *Panchama* past. Although they are now Christian, their past *avarna* status is still a social stigma in a culture sensitive to caste. Therefore, even though Christian Dalits theologically severed their ties to caste when they converted to Christianity, they are still not socially free from these bonds. Moreover, because their current social conditions are controlled by rules of 'touchability' and 'untouchability' their particular Christian theology is imbued with past Hindu theological structures. To explicate the nature of this complex Christian Dalit environment, I will briefly sketch some *Panchama* struggles in recent Indian history.

The 'Scheduled Castes' in Modern India

The exact date Christian Dalits emerged is unknown. Many Hindus converted to Christianity as early as the first century and can trace their lineage to the Apostle Thomas. In addition, many Hindu *Panchamas* were attracted to Christianity because of its lack of hierarchy and a God that was sensitive to the needs of the poor and the oppressed. Thus, when Mohandas K. Gandhi denounced the Hindu caste system and resulting Dalit oppression, it is more than likely that both Hindu and Christian Dalits existed. Today, there are roughly 160 million *Panchamas* living in India and almost 85 per cent of Indian Christians are Dalits.[8] Although Gandhi renamed the *Panchamas*, the *Harijans* or 'beloved children of God', in an attempt to elevate their social standing, this did not have the far-reaching effects he desired. According to contemporary Christian Dalits neither Gandhi nor other 'high caste' Hindus did enough to liberate the *Panchamas* before or after the caste system was officially abolished.

During India's independence from colonial powers, one of Gandhi's loudest critics was B. R. Ambedkar, a jurist, and one of the architects of the Indian Constitution. Ambedkar was a *Panchama* and a witness to the social oppression that kept his friends and family impoverished and destitute.[9] In 1920, Ambedkar argued for separate electorates for the Depressed Classes[10] and led a march to fight for *Panchamas* to draw water from a public well in Mahad, a town primarily occupied by high caste Hindus.[11] After his rise to power, Ambedkar told the *Panchamas*, 'We must shape our course ourselves and only by ourselves.'[12] He also argued with Gandhi contending the only hope for the Depressed Classes was through social elevation, education and conversion to a more accommodating religion.[13] Meanwhile, Gandhi maintained that Hinduism could, and would, liberate all those politically, religiously or economically oppressed in India.

In June 1936, Gandhi addressed the Indian Congress and spoke with bitterness about the indifference of his fellow high caste Hindus to *Harijan* work, stating, 'The tragedy is that those who should have especially devoted themselves to the work of [caste] reform did not put their hearts into it.'[14] After India's Independence from the British on 15 August 1947, the New Congress appointed multi-religious pundits to the Constitution Drafting Committee with Ambedkar as the Chairman. Ambedkar finally won support for an Affirmative Action system for members of 'Scheduled Castes'. However, almost 60 years after the official abolishment of caste and the accommodating Indian Constitution, Hindu and Christian *Panchama* oppression remains pervasive and rampant in Indian society.

As Christians, the *Panchamas* are ineligible for any of the 'Scheduled Caste' benefits that Ambedkar so carefully drafted in the Constitution. The Indian government maintains that caste is a Hindu religious construction; therefore Christians need no special protections or privileges under the law. However,

Panchamas are oppressed and discriminated against in many villages in contemporary India: they are raped, murdered, and drowned because they are still considered excluded members of a strict religious system. Therefore, in response to their suffering and lack of legal protection, the *Panchamas* rejected their Gandhian title of *Harijan*, and officially changed their name to Dalit, which means, 'The Crushed, broken, torn, rent, burst and split'.[15] In addition, because the upper castes (*Brahmin*, *Kshatria* and *Vaishya*) are called the 'twice-born,'[16] in Vedic texts, the Dalits call themselves the 'twice-dead'.

In 1985, Christian Dalits living in Tamil Nadu formed an association called 'Ambedkar Mandrum' to educate themselves on their legal rights and memorized this particular part of the Indian Constitution:

> No citizen shall, by grounds of religion, caste, race, sex, place of birth, be subject to disability, liability, restriction with regard to: (a) access to shops, restaurants, hotels, and places of public entertainment or (b) the use of wells, tanks, bathing *ghats*, roads and places of public resort maintained wholly or partly out of State funds or dedicated to the use of the general public.[17]

Because of this grass roots movement, in 1989, Christian Dalits in local villages participated in India's Independence Day celebration; an uncommon event in high caste neighborhoods. The results were devastating. In describing the violence that ensued, Christian Dalit Theologian M. R. Arulraja writes, 'Not even pregnant women were spared. They were stamped upon with booted legs. The police thrust cudgels into their vaginas. People were dragged and beaten black and blue. Even the children were beaten.'[18] In response to these atrocities, a contemporary Dalit theologian, Arvind P. Nirmal, writes,

> When my Dalit ancestors walked the dusty roads of their village, the *sa varnas* [those with caste] tied a branch of a tree around their waist so that they did not leave any unclean footprints and pollute the roads.[19]

Implicit in Nirmal's response is a sense of resignation: Dalits have always been treated as sub-human in Indian society. Why would a few words in the Constitution change their fate? Arulraja argues that although they are considered 'untouchable' by high caste members of the community, on average three Dalit women are raped every day.[20] 'Non-Dalits have been treating Dalits as untouchables for centuries but enjoy the food produced by Dalit sweat, the water from wells dug by the Dalits, and the houses built by the Dalits.'[21] In addition, Nirmal responds, 'This goes beyond ideas of purity and pollution. The *sa varnas* [with caste] tie an earthen pot around our necks to serve as a spittle. If my Dalit brothers try to learn Sanskrit or some other sophisticated language, it is not uncommon that the oppressors gag them permanently by pouring molten lead down their throat.'[22] Unfortunately, these are not hyperbolic examples to create foreign sympathy but common experiences for many Dalits.

The most pervasive oppression facing the Dalit Christians does not come from Hindus but from 'high caste' Christians in their own community. Dalits are not allowed to draw water from the same wells as high caste Christians. They have separate cemeteries, separate drinking glasses at restaurants and must remove their shoes when they meet a high caste Christian person.[23] Yet, it is within churches that the oppression is truly staggering. Dalit theologian Z. Devasagayaraj writes,

> After the Dalit has entered the church, the high caste members will sprinkle 'holy' water to purify all that has been touched by them. They do not share the communion cup because they fear becoming polluted. They cannot even sit on the pews, for the high caste Christians will not sit beside them.[24]

Dalit priests are also not allowed to serve communion or perform marriage rites for non-Dalits because of the fear that they may pollute the marriage or taint the unborn children. The magnitude and frequency of this oppression and abuse prompted the Dalit community to articulate their own 'countertheology'[25] that represents a 'radical discontinuity with classical Indian Christian theology of the Brahmanic [and Western Colonial] tradition'.[26] Furthermore, because dominant traditions, both cultural and theological, tend to 'accommodate, assimilate, and finally conquer others', Dalit theology is a form of 'methodological exclusivism'.[27] Moreover, because this theology is not *for* the Depressed Classes but rather *from* the Depressed Classes[28] Dalits contend that the dominant Brahmanical and Western Christian theological traditions be excluded from Dalit consciousness. This emerging theology, then, is exclusively Dalit and uniquely Indian.

Emerging Dalit Theology

Many non-Dalit theologians like John C. B. Webster,[29] Sathianathan Clarke[30] and M. M. Thomas[31] argue that Dalit theology is just an Indian form of Liberation Theology. However, while Liberation Theology calls God the liberator *of* the oppressed,[32] Dalit Theology argues, God *is* the oppressed. While Liberation Theology emphasizes the *praxis* of the historical Jesus, Dalits contend that the *sva dharma* (eternal nature) of Jesus is Dalit. Because the New Testament reveals that, 'Jesus the Son of Man had to encounter rejection, mockery, contempt, suffering, and death – all these from the dominant religious tradition and established religion',[33] Dalits argue that Jesus is the 'prototype of all Dalits'.[34] In addition, Jesus' genealogy proves that he shares a 'low caste' birth because Jesus' ancestors include prostitutes like Tamar,[35] Rahab,[36] and King Solomon 'the illegitimate child of David'.[37] Through this hermeneutical process, *Panchamas* are able to extend Jesus' body to include their own intrinsic creation and legitimize their position within Indian society. Therefore, Dalit theology merges the historical Jesus with the *sva dharma* of Christ to reclaim a part of God's mitotic engendering of humanity.

Dalits also create a paradigmatic shift within existing caste structures by reinterpreting their function and importance in society. By examining passages in *Manu* that claim the *Shudra* was created for servile work, Dalits argue, 'We are *avarnas* [no-caste] below the *shudras*, and yet our claim is this: The God of the Dalits, the self-existent, does not create others to do servile work but does servile work himself.'[38] By making these theological claims within a society conscious about caste and divine ordering, Dalits radicalize the *dharmic* nature of humanity by claiming that 'servitude is the *sva-dharma*, [eternal nature] of our God'[39] not of humans. Servitude, then, becomes a contact point for Dalits to engage God intrinsically with their own bodies. Their servitude and God's become divinely entwined and their *sva-dharma* becomes imbued with theological awareness.

Dalit theology does not solely focus on 'brokenness' but also on the transformation into the 'manifested and displayed'[40] people of God. Dalit consciousness affirms, 'brokenness belongs to the very being of God',[41] and during the crucifixion Jesus was 'the crushed, the split, the torn, the driven-asunder man; the Dalit in the fullest possible meaning of the term'.[42] However, he does not remain broken, rather, during the resurrection Jesus is 'manifest' and 'displays' the *sva dharma* of Christ. Therefore, 'brokenness' becomes a symbol of hope: all that is 'crushed' will eventually manifest its intrinsic divinity like the resurrected Christ. Dalitness then, becomes part of the *sva dharma* between humanity and God where the brokenness of the crucifixion leads to the wholeness of the resurrection. As all humanity, regardless of religious affiliation, experiences some form of oppression in life, the symbol of Jesus the Dalit provides a method to encounter religious pluralism and creates theological space for multi-religious healing.

Dalit Theology and Religious Pluralism

The theology of religions is touted as an emergent need in the 'spiritual marketplace'[43] of contemporary society and can take many methodological forms: dialogical, social, ethical and theological. The traditional theological categories are often defined as inclusivism, exclusivism and pluralism,[44] or ecclesiocentrism, Christocentrism, and theocentrism or Realitycentrism.[45] Most of this terminology is part of the Western pluralism project and tries to reconcile the uniqueness of Christian incarnational theology with other religious traditions. Because of the 'scandal of particularity'[46] of incarnation and salvation, it is exceedingly easy for Christianity to enjoy a position of hierarchy among world religions: what other religion can claim that Godself became human and died for the salvific freedom of the world? However, while some maintain the supremacy of Christ others downplay the unique aspects of the Christian tradition to accommodate religious pluralism. For this reason, some pluralists like John Hick[47] and Paul F. Knitter[48] are criticized for their efforts because pluralism can eradicate the particularities with which, and in which many adherents find comfort.

Dalit Theology is a unique form of engaging religious pluralism because it maintains the particularities of incarnational theology while inviting other religious traditions to participate with this symbol. The *sva dharma* of the 'Primordial Dalit' stretches beyond Dalit consciousness and experience to enter the sphere of human consciousness and experience. Not all human beings are physically Dalits. However, all human beings will or have experienced Dalitness in some aspect of their lives. One has only to open a newspaper to find the unfortunate truth that caste categories are not just part of Indian society. On the contrary, millions all over the world are 'down trodden, destroyed and crushed'[49] on a daily basis.

Many people experience physical and psychological abuse through war, rape, incest, assault, societal exclusion, racism, and/or discrimination. People are marginalized because of gender – namely, women, gays, lesbians, bisexuals and members of the transgender community that do not enjoy equal rights and legal protection. There are those that are crushed by the weight of disease, such as HIV/AIDS or cancer, and others with severe mental and physical disabilities that are relegated to a life of exclusion. The economically poor are cast aside to suffer the whims of incompetent welfare systems and pay the egregious cost of medical care. People are negatively judged because of alcohol and narcotic addictions, and still others are cast into categories of uselessness because of old age. All these examples of modern 'caste categories' traverse the bounds of Dalit experience and become shared human experience. Therefore, the Primordial Dalit becomes a 'touchable' necessity for those suffering an 'untouchable' existence. Dalit Theology, then, becomes a significant addition to religious pluralism because Jesus the Dalit maintains the particular while incorporating the universal.

The *sva dharma* of the Dalit Jesus is to be 'crushed' on the cross as a testament to human suffering – not just Christian suffering. Furthermore, Dalit consciousness incorporates a sense of cyclical time so the divine principle is not just the 'crushed' Dalit on the cross accessible through the *praxis* of pain but also the 'displayed and manifested'[50] reality of the resurrection. Therefore, humans suffer and are then healed; crushed and then made manifest; downtrodden and then displayed. The Primordial Dalit understands every form of human 'untouchability' and touches all peoples that suffer the caste oppressions of their environment. Therefore, the particular cross of Jesus relates to universal human suffering and enables the emotional, psychological and ethical resurrection of all humanity.

In conclusion, Dalit Theology can engage religious pluralism while incorporating others into an inter-faith relationship in an egalitarian manner. With human suffering as the common bond between religious traditions, the Dalit Jesus becomes the Son of Man for all peoples that experience 'rejection, mockery, contempt and suffering'.[51] Therefore, reinterpreting the historical Jesus into the Primordial Dalit allows people across traditions to engage in fruitful dialogue. First, the divine principle enters the human sphere and enables discussion about suffering, oppression, hierarchy and power. Second, it lifts humanity into the divine realm because Jesus' Dalitness becomes a sacred method to encounter the profane caste categories of our world. Therefore, the relationship between humanity and the divine principle is actively engaged trans-historically and pan-theologically: the untouchable Dalit is a touchable necessity for a suffering world.

Notes

1 Arvind P. Nirmal, 'A Dialogue With Dalit Literature', in *Towards a Dalit Theology*, ed. M. E. Prabhakar (Delhi: Delhi Press, 1990), 63.

2 Wendy Doniger (trans.), *The Laws of Manu* (London: Penguin Books, 1991), 4.

3 Doniger, *Laws of Manu*, 4.

4 Doniger, *Laws of Manu*, 7.

5 Mary Douglas, *Purity and Danger* (New York: Routledge & Kegan Paul, 2005), 142.

6 Douglas, *Purity and Danger*, 142.

7 Douglas, *Purity and Danger*, 153.

8 National Campaign on Dalit Human Rights (NCDHR), June 2007 population statistics http://www.dalits.org/CasteRaceandWCAR.html.

9 Christophe Jaffrelot, *Dr. Ambedkar and Untouchability: Fighting the Indian Caste System* (New York: Columbia University Press, 2002), 22.

10 Depressed Class or Scheduled Class are both synonymous with the term Dalit in modern India and are used interchangeably.

11 Jaffrelot, *Dr. Ambedkar and Untouchability*, 25.

12 *Thus Spoke Ambedkar*, vol. I (Selected Speeches of Dr B. R. Ambedkar), compiled and edited by Bhagwan Das, published by Dalit Today Parkashan, 18/455, Indira Nagar, Lucknow (UP) India-226016, 56.

13 *Thus Spoke Ambedkar*, 67.

14 *Thus Spoke Ambedkar*, 67.

15 Nirmal, 'A Dialogue with Dalit Literature', 63.

16 Doniger, *Laws of Manu*, 3.

17 M. R. Arulraja, *Jesus: The Dalit Liberation Theology by Victims of Untouchability* (Secunderabad: India Jeevan Institute of Printing, Sikh Village, 1998), 6.

18 Arulraja, *Jesus*, 7.

19 Arvind P. Nirmal, 'Towards a Christian Dalit Theology', in *Frontiers in Asian Christian Theology: Emerging Trends*, ed. R. S. Sugirtharajah (Maryknoll, NY: Orbis Books, 1999), 33.

20 Arulraja, *Jesus*, 9.

21 Arulraja, *Jesus*, 11.

22 Nirmal, 'Towards a Christian Dalit Theology', 33.

23 Revd Fr Z. Devasagayaraj, *Towards a Dalit Theology*, ed. M. E. Prabhakar (Dehli: ISPCK Press, 1996), 89.

24 Devasagayaraj, *Towards a Dalit Theology*, 89.

25 Nirmal, 'Towards a Christian Dalit Theology', 31.

26 Nirmal, 'Towards a Christian Dalit Theology', 31.

27 Nirmal, 'Towards a Christian Dalit Theology', 32.

28 Nirmal, 'Towards a Christian Dalit Theology', 31.

29 For examples of his work see *Religion and Dalit Liberation: An Examination of Perspectives* (New Delhi: Manohar Publications, 1999); *Journal of Asian Studies* 61.1.

30 For examples of his work see *Dalits and Christianity* (New Delhi and Oxford: Oxford University Press, 1998).

31 For examples of his work see M. M. Thomas and P. T. Thomas, *Towards an Indian Christian Theology* (Tiruvalla: Christava Sahitya Samithi, 1998).

32 For further explanation of how the biblical God stands with the oppressed and the poor see James H. Cone, *God of the Oppressed* (New York: Orbis Books, 1997).

33 Nirmal, 'Towards a Christian Dalit Theology', 37.

34 Nirmal, 'Towards a Christian Dalit Theology', 37.

35 Tamar is the daughter-in-law of Judah who tricked her father-in-law into sleeping with her and conceived a child. Genesis 38.1–30 NRSV.

36 Rahab is the prostitute who helped Israelite spies. Joshua 2.1–21.

37 Nirmal, 'Towards a Christian Dalit Theology', 37.

38 Nirmal, 'Towards a Christian Dalit Theology', 35.

39 Nirmal, 'Towards a Christian Dalit Theology', 35.

40 See Nirmal for his explanation about the groups of meanings associated with the word Dalit, including 'manifested' and 'displayed' in Nirmal, 'Towards a Christian Dalit Theology', 39.

41 Nirmal, 'Towards a Christian Dalit Theology', 39.

42 Nirmal, 'Towards a Christian Dalit Theology', 40.

43 See Stephen Prothero, *American Jesus: How the Son of God Became a National Icon* (New York: Farrar, Straus & Giroux, 2003), 6.

44 For further explanation of these categories see John Hick, *An Interpretation of Religion: Human Responses to the Transcendent*, 2nd edn (New Haven, Conn.: Yale University Press, 2004).

45 For further explanation of this terminology see Veli-Matti Kärkkäinen, *An Introduction to the Theology of Religions: Biblical, Historical and Contemporary Perspectives* (Downers Grove, Ill: Inter Varsity Press, 2003), 165.

46 Theologian Karl Barth's terminology to describe the incarnation of Jesus Christ in *Dogmatics in Outline* (New York: Harper & Row, 1959).

47 For examples of his work on religious pluralism see Hick, *An Interpretation of Religion*.

48 For examples of his work on religious pluralism see Paul F. Knitter (ed.), *The Myth of Christian Superiority: A Multifaith Exploration* (Maryknoll, NY: Orbis, 2005).

49 Nirmal, 'A Dialogue with Dalit Literature', 63.

50 Nirmal, 'Towards a Christian Dalit Theology', 39.

51 Nirmal, 'Towards a Christian Dalit Theology', 37.

Source: Sara Singha, original piece, an earlier version of which was presented at the Annual AAR Conference in Chicago on 1 November 2008, entitled 'Dalit Theology: An Indian Christian Response to Pluralism'.

10

Buddhism

ELIZABETH HARRIS

Introduction

The writers of the two following extracts on Buddhist–Christian encounter differ. One is a woman and the other a man. One comes from the West and the other from Asia. One is a Disciples of Christ minister and the other a member of a Roman Catholic Order, the Jesuits. One is a New Testament scholar and the other a liberation theologian. Both, however, are Christian academics who have been so deeply touched by Buddhism that they have been able to draw on Buddhist insights in their personal religious journeys.

The first extract is taken from a paper that was originally part of a conversation initiated by the American-based Society for Buddhist–Christian Studies, in which a group of Buddhists and Christians were asked to reflect on, respectively, Jesus or the Buddha. The Revd Dr Bonnie Thurston was one of the Christians who were asked to reflect on what the Buddha meant to them. On her own admission, it is, 'an embarrassingly personal reflection' in which she claims that the Buddha has helped her see the Christ more clearly, encouraged her to open further the doors of her own heart and impressed upon her the need for a detachment that is about living in the present moment.

Dr Aloysius Pieris SJ is a Sri Lankan Jesuit, Director of Tulana Research Centre near Colombo. Born in 1934, he joined the Jesuits as a young man and focused on indological research. He was the first Christian, let alone priest, to gain a doctorate in Buddhism from a Sri Lankan university. His interest in Buddhism, however, was not restricted to the academic. In his youth, under the guidance of a Buddhist monk, he stayed in a Buddhist *vihāra* (monastery) anonymously. Throughout his life he has worked with Buddhists and encouraged Buddhists to help Christians see their faith in a new light, for instance through works of art. All the pieces of art on Christian themes at Tulana Research Centre are the work of Buddhists. Pieris has published over a hundred articles and several books, three of which are collections of his articles. The extract in this Reader is not an easy piece to fathom but it is worth the struggle. Pieris begins with the nineteenth century, when the encounter between Buddhism and Christian missionaries in Asia, under British colonialism, led to the emerging of 'Protestant' Buddhism, a form of Buddhism that both protested against Christianity and drew into itself some Protestant Christian practices. His hope is that the polarization of this period will give way to each religion being challenged in a positive way by the other. For instance, the Buddhist emphasis on knowledge or wisdom can help Christians realize that Christianity too emphasized this in the past. The language of self-giving love in Christianity can help Buddhists realize just how important compassion is in Buddhism. Each emphasis, Pieris argues, needs the other. Christ hanging on the cross in self-giving love and the Buddha sitting under a tree in silent meditative wisdom are complementary to each other.

The Buddha Offered Me a Raft

BONNIE THURSTON

Es gibt, so glaube ich, in der Tat jenes Ding nicht, das wir 'Lernen' nennen.

Hermann Hesse, *Siddhartha*

I must warn you at the beginning that what follows is an embarrassingly personal reflection – a confession even – and not a scholarly essay. I cannot be dispassionate about the Buddha, to whom in a roundabout way I owe both my status as an ordained Christian minister and perhaps the greatest joy of my life, the study and practice of the Christian scripture. How? In February 1970 I was given a copy of Hesse's novel *Siddhartha*, a fictionalized account of the Buddha's life. Already an active Christian, it was this gift, received [in] my senior year in high school, that introduced me to Buddhism and to the reality of spiritual journey and the possibility of enlightenment. While I know the Buddhist meaning of that term, it serves for Christians as well, because our God could not leave us in darkness but made light the first creature (Gen. 1:1–5) and came among us as light (John 1:1–5).[1] When in the fall of 1970 my brother travelled to Japan, the memento I requested was a small statue of the Buddha. It is beside me as I write. In 1983 when we moved to Germany, the second book I bought in German was *Siddhartha*: the first was the New Testament.

Over the years I have had the opportunity to continue to study the life of the Buddha and the spread and development of his teachings. By the Buddha, of course, I mean Sakyamuni ('sage of the Sakyas') Buddha ('enlightened one'), son of Suddhodana and Maya, whom they called Siddhartha ('wish fulfilled' or 'goal realized') and whom we also know as Gotama or Gautama (literally 'superior cow'), whose dates are given variously as 560–480 B.C. or 460–380 B.C.[2] I am appreciative of what I have learned – applying the root meaning of that word, *appretiare*: 'to see' or 'to appraise.' The Buddha has helped me to see and to appraise or evaluate many aspects of life. The appreciation that follows, then, is both a grateful recognition as of benefits received and a sensitive awareness or an estimate. I have tried both to view the Buddha clearly and to appraise what he has meant in my life. In essence, Buddhism and the Buddha have been for me the means of establishing a personal, internal religious clarity about what I do believe, passionately. In a deeply Buddhist sense, the Buddha has been my raft. But he has not been my Savior.

There is, as Tillich noted in *Christianity and the Encounter with World Religions*, a point 'in the depth of every living religion ... at which the religion itself loses its importance, and that to which it points breaks through its particularity.'[3] It has helped me to understand religions as fingers and the Divine Reality as the moon to which they point. And I am convinced that Tillich's breakthrough point is usually reached by means of deep penetration into one religious tradition. Jacques-Albert Cuttat was exactly correct: 'The more deeply a person probes into his own religious faith, the more he is able to understand the religious faith of others from the inside; conversely, the more a person explores religious connections other than his own, the more he deepens his understanding of his own religion.'[4] This has been my experience. Dialogue with the Buddha has given me great clarity about the Christ. And the study and practice of Christianity has afforded me my glimpses of the moon.

What, then, do I appreciate about the Buddha? What have I learned from him? To help focus my answer, I read or reread a number of different accounts of his life[5] and noted six specific aspects of his life and teaching (his quest itself; his powers of analysis; his pragmatism; his moral vision; his compassion; and the outcome of living, his 'way') that have attracted and taught me.

First, I am appreciative of the Buddha's quest itself. To put it simply, according to the accounts of his early life he had it all but realized he had nothing. Many a lesser person has been content with a life of pleasure, safety, and satiety. I stand in awe of the Buddha's devotion to Truth and the hunger for transcendence that led to his Great Renunciation. Second, I appreciate his amazing powers of analysis that made the quest possible. He saw deeply into the nature of things. As Carrithers points out, 'the Buddha's laboratory was himself, and he generalized his findings to cover all human beings;' he 'depended wholly upon ... direct personal knowledge, direct personal experience, direct witnessing in the here and now.'[6] In light of my own propensity for self-deception, I find the Buddha's self-awareness (I use the term knowing, if not fully understanding, the doctrine of *anatta*) and ability to analyze what he found astonishing.

Third, the Buddha seems fully to have penetrated the realm of human realities. And his pragmatism in facing them has taught me a great deal. The Buddha faced facts. When he experienced the Four Signs, he did not turn away or retreat into the life of luxury offered by his father and his social status; he looked clearly and saw the Signs for what they were, metaphors for the human condition. Quoting Thich Nhat Hanh, Thomas Merton notes: 'The basic aim of Buddhism ... arises out of human experience itself – the experience of suffering – and it seeks to provide a realistic answer to man's most urgent question: how to cope with suffering. The problem of human suffering is insoluble as long as men are prevented by their collective and individual illusions from getting directly to grips with suffering in its very root within themselves.'[7]

The Buddha shed illusions and got 'directly to grips' with the human reality and described it in the Four Noble Truths. Then he proposed a pragmatic solution to the problem he saw (the Eightfold Path) that avoided the extremes of either asceticism or self-indulgence. The 'Via Media,' the Middle Way of the Eightfold Path, is a practical prescription for his particular diagnosis of the human condition. The Buddha not only saw the disease clearly; he proposed a cure that most people can undertake.

While the Physician basically prescribed 'heal thyself,' he never lost sight of the fact that human action has inescapable moral consequences that are both personal and corporate. What I do affects not only me, but others. The Buddha understood that the universe has a fundamental moral order. As one seeks to cure one's own disease, she or he must never lose sight of the effects of a person's actions on others. One's skill in doing so (*kusala*) is also a moral good. 'For the Buddha skillfulness cut two ways: its consequences were good for oneself but good for others as well.' For the Buddha 'to do good was precisely to act both in one's own and in someone else's interest.'[8] Again, this is a very practical test of 'the good.' The high morality of the Buddha's Way overcomes the selfish focus of much that calls itself 'contemplative spirituality' in our day. And that leads to my fifth point of appreciation of the Buddha – his great compassion.

Schumann is exactly correct when he writes that 'loving-kindness was the essential trait in the Buddha's character.'[9] While Buddhist literature contains many examples of it, I especially delight in the story that the little ringlets one sees on the head of the meditating Buddha are not hair, but snails he was too compassionate to disturb. This compassion of the Buddha, which His Holiness the Dalai Lama describes as 'undiscriminating, spontaneous, and unlimited compassion for all sentient beings,'[10] springs, I think, from his essential selflessness, his refusal to grasp at a 'self'. His was the kenotic impulse I find in my own Lord Jesus, who, in the words of St. Paul, 'emptied himself' and 'humbled himself' (Phil. 2:7, 8).[11] The Buddha and the Christ are both characterized by generous self-giving[12] and the willingness to share the fruits of their personal enlightenments with all comers. The Buddha's compassion for all beings is heard in his invitation, 'Let the doors to Deathlessness be opened to all who are able to hear!'[13] The example of the Buddha's compassion has stretched me and encouraged me to throw open the doors of my own heart to widen the circle of my concern and caring to all of life.

Before noting the final aspect of the Buddha's life and teaching of which I am especially appreciative, let me mention two aspects of his practice that have been enormously helpful, which I have taken home as gifts to be shared in the household of Christianity: meditation and detachment, both of which engender focus and 'presence.' I am not the only Christian for whom meditation (and the form I have in mind is zazen or 'sitting') has been an important discipline and practice. For example, William Johnston's book *Christian Zen* examines how 'Zen can teach [Christians] a methodology in prayer.'[14]

And sitting has impressed on me a fundamental truth that is expressed this way by Walpola Rahula: 'As long as you are conscious of yourself you can never concentrate on anything.'[15] Self-forgetfulness is a wonderful liberation that allows us to be fully present to others and to life itself. It partakes of something of the selflessness of the Buddha and of the Christ. (Tillich, in fact, noted that what is particular in Jesus 'is that he crucified the particular in himself for the sake of the universal.'[16]) Sitting meditation has helped me move beyond my particularity toward Being itself, and, paradoxically, I have found I am most myself when I am least self-conscious.

Shunryu Suzuki has said, 'What we call "I" is just a swinging door which moves when we inhale and when we exhale.' He continues, 'when we become truly ourselves, we just become a swinging door, and we are purely independent of, and at the same time, dependent upon everything.'[17] I think the same idea is expressed from the Christian viewpoint by Thomas Merton, who wrote that 'Zen is the very awareness of the dynamism of life living itself in us – aware of itself, in us, as being the one life that lives in all.'[18] Sitting has brought me to this awareness and is, itself, a wonderful corrective to the Christian compulsion to 'do.' It helps me simply to 'be' and simply to appreciate being. And it has introduced many of us Christians to similar forms of prayer that are deeply rooted but, alas, often choked out by historical weeds of various kinds in Christian soil. Sitting meditation has brought with it the gift of focus – a wonderful gift indeed.

The second aspect of practice that I lift up – detachment – is really intrinsically related to the second and third of the Buddha's Noble Truths, the truth of the arising of *dukkha* (Pali 'suffering,' 'pain,' 'sorrow,' or 'misery'[19] but perhaps most helpfully rendered in English by 'unsatisfactoriness') and of its cessation. If I understand him correctly, the Buddha teaches that because we are ignorant of the nature of reality, we 'crave' or 'thirst for' or 'desire.' This is a kind of grasping that ties us to a material world that is illusory. To be liberated from *dukkha*, one must cease craving. Put most simply, we must learn to be detached from things, persons, even our sense of self. As I observe it in myself, desire usually projects me into the future, where the things I do not have now and desire exist. Desire prevents me from living in the present moment, the only moment that is and the only one in which I can welcome and receive God. Desire prevents my being at peace with what is.

Understanding detachment as a means of living in the present is an especially helpful point for me as a Christian because, in what is perhaps the most dramatic self-revelation of God in scripture before the Incarnation of Jesus, the call story of Moses in Exod. 3—4, God reveals the divine self as 'I AM, YHWH.' While I understand that the Hebrew term is variously translated 'I AM the one Who IS,' emphasizing God's eternal Being, 'I AM the One Who causes to Be,' emphasizing God's creativity; and, less frequently, 'I WILL BE,' emphasizing the promise of God's presence, the I-AM-NESS of God suggests that if God is not received or welcomed or found in the now, God is unlikely to be experienced at all. (Perhaps this is why St. Paul tells the Corinthians, 'See, now is the acceptable time; see, now is the day of salvation' [2 Cor. 6:2] and, in speaking to the Colossians of the mystery of God, says it 'has now been revealed' [Col. 1:26]). The Buddha's teachings on detachment have led me as a Christian not only to freedom in the present moment, but into the Presence of God.

Finally, then, those who have heard of and responded to and lived out the Buddha's path have found a focus and equanimity that is impressive. Again admiring his pragmatism, the coarse (and very un-Buddhist) way to express this appreciation is to say that following the Buddha's path leads to positive results. Seeking the goals of the Buddhist path to liberation, 'to act without desire for success, with goodwill toward all, and clearly aware'[20] and to create 'an entirely new consciousness which is free to deal with life bare-handed and without pretenses,'[21] produces marvellous personal and social outcomes. I am deeply attracted to the Buddhist goal of 'living radiantly in the present'[22] and to the Buddha who both did it and demonstrated how to do it. And this is precisely where my problem lies, and what keeps me firmly Christian. I admire and am attracted to the Buddha, but he pushes me away.

This is to say that I personally have not been able to achieve the radical self-sufficiency upon which the Buddha insists. 'Be lamps unto yourselves,' he says. According to the *Digha Nikaya*, one of the last teachings of the Buddha to Ananda was: 'You should live as islands unto yourselves, being your own refuge, seeking no other refuge; with the Dhamma as an island, with the Dhamma as your refuge, seeking no other refuge ... Those monks who in my time or afterwards live thus, seeking an island and a refuge in themselves and in the Dhamma and nowhere else, these zealous ones are truly *my* monks and will overcome the darkness (of rebirth).'[23]

While I admire the confidence in the human being that asserts that everyone who strives for emancipation and enlightenment can find it by personal effort, that, alas, does not square with my experience. I strive to be selfless and am, in fact, often full of myself, selfish, and self-deceived. In the words of a famous Christian prayer by Thomas Merton, 'The fact that I think that

I am following [God's] will does not mean that I am actually doing so.'[24]

My experience is less that of the Dhammapada, which notes: 'By one-self indeed is evil done and by oneself is one defiled. By oneself is evil left undone and by oneself indeed one is purified. Purity and impurity depend on oneself,'[25] and more that of St. Paul, who lamented, 'I do not understand my own actions. For I do not do what I want but I do the very thing I hate' (Rom. 7:15) and 'For I do not do the good I want but the evil I do not want is what I do' (Rom. 7:19). The darkness is so great. My candle is so small. Strive as I may, I can't illuminate myself. Again, with Paul I cry out, 'Wretched [woman] that I am! Who will rescue me from this body of death? Thanks be to God through Jesus Christ our Lord!' (Rom. 7:24–25)

In the struggle to be a lamp to myself, I am brought face to face with Jesus Christ. There are many points of comparison between the Buddha and the Christ, and many helpful comparisons have been drawn.[26] I want to focus on one that I have not seen: the attitude of each toward his followers. The Buddha says, 'Be lamps unto yourselves' and 'one is one's own refuge.'[27] (At this point it may be clear to the Buddhist reader that I need more instruction in what it means 'to take refuge.' My understanding is that it means to rely on the example but not the person of the Buddha. But I stand ready to be corrected.) The Christ says, 'Come to me, all you that are weary and are carrying heavy burdens, and I will give you rest' (Matt. 11:28) and 'I am the light of the world. Whoever follows me will never walk in darkness but will have the light of life' (John 8:12) and 'I am the way, and the truth, and the life' (John 14:6). The Buddha directs me away from himself. The Christ invites me to himself. In the Four Reliances, the Buddha teaches, 'Rely on the teaching not the teacher.' In Christianity, the teaching is the Teacher.

The attitude of Jesus toward potential followers is clearly exemplified in a little scene in John's Gospel (John 1:35–42). John the Baptist commends Jesus to two of his own followers. They go to him and ask, 'where are you staying?' That is, 'will you remain with us if we follow you?' Jesus responds, 'Come and see.' That is, he invites them to himself and invites them to 'see,' the great, controlling metaphor of John's Gospel, which means to perceive physically with the eyes, to understand with the mind and heart, and to be enlightened. The point for us is that Jesus invites people to himself for enlightenment.

I know from bitter experience my own inability to be my own lamp. Perhaps it is a lack of right effort on my part, and certainly my ignorance enters into the problem. But something else has always seemed to be at work, something that encouraged me toward 'doing what I didn't want to do.' In classical, Christian terms, 'it' might be described as 'original sin' inherent in my own flawed nature. Thus, the argument continues, I need the atonement effected by Jesus on the cross to redeem that 'fallen nature.' I am not sure that I entirely agree intellectually with this formulation, but I do know, practically, that I need help from outside myself. In the language of the spiritual child I am, 'I need a God with skin on.' To put the matter practically, I know what I should do (for example to sit or to practice detachment), but I need empowerment to achieve what I know. My hope for this is not in the human realm. This is a fundamental difference between Christianity and Buddhism. The Buddha teaches me to remain fully in the realm of human experience, but the Christ offers me a hope outside myself. 'The hope of the Christian is ... a hope *for* man, but it places its confidence in God, and not *in* man'[28] (italics mine).

Jesus Christ has not only 'put skin on' and thereby redeemed and ennobled my flesh, but he invites me to profound identification with him, even participation in his very life. As Merton says, 'God Himself lives in us, by His Holy Spirit.'[29] Or as Brother David Steindl-Rast notes, 'Christ lives in those who follow his path, and they live in him ... They are alive with his life.'[30] Because he first invites me, not only can I come to him, but I can share and be empowered by his life to 'do' what I 'know.' We Christians believe that Christ comes to us and dwells within us. We even make the outrageous and unlikely claim that we receive Christ's body into our physical and spiritual bodies in our eucharistic celebrations! In John's Gospel Jesus says, 'those who eat my flesh and drink my blood abide in me, and I in them' (John 6:56). This is as shocking and audacious a claim today as it was when it was made in the first century of our era, and it means that 'Christ is not simply an object of love and contemplation whom the Christian considers with devout attention: He is also "the way, the truth and the life" so that for the Christian to be "on the way" is to be "in Christ."'[31]

I believe that God 'put skin on,' among other reasons, to enable the human longing for and journey toward God. I, personally, have not been able to make that journey under my own steam. I need the empowerment of what the Apostle Paul calls 'Christ in [us], the hope of glory' (Col. 1:27). I greatly appreciate and have learned much from the Buddha and his view of reality and his means of liberation, but the fullness of my being has responded to and been empowered by a personal invitation from Jesus to 'come to me,' 'come and see.' More precisely, I have had the experience that Brother David calls the 'experience of being grasped or occupied'[32] by what the evangelical hymn of my youth calls the 'Love that will not let me go.' Note that Love 'grasps' me. I respond to that glorious and terrible embrace, but I do not initiate it, and when I 'grasp' at the one who offers it, I lose both the embrace and the Love that bestows it because real love cannot be based on human grasping or attachment. And this, I think, is very Buddhist.

Don't misunderstand me. I am not suggesting that my experience is, abstractly, either good or bad (although for me it has been very good, indeed) or even that it must needs be true for all. But this is my deepest reality. And in this 'confession,' I follow the example of the Buddha, who in effect says, 'Be true to your own experience.' So perhaps, in this very limited way, I am my own lamp. But the oil and the flame are Jesus Christ.

Shunryu Suzuki reminds us that true understanding comes out of emptiness: 'When you study Buddhism, you should have a general house cleaning of your mind. You must take everything out of your room and clean it
thoroughly. If it is necessary, you may bring everything back in again. You
may want many things, so one by one you can bring them back. But if they
are not necessary, there is no need to keep them.'³³ More than once in my
life the Buddha initiated an enormous spring cleaning. It was always good
for me. I threw out a lot of useless stuff. I found some things I thought I'd
lost and learned to treasure some things that had been there all along. I have
immense gratitude to the Buddha and his Way. To change the metaphor, the
Buddha offered me a raft. The raft, itself, was Jesus Christ. Or again, the
Buddha pointed out a path that led me home. Jesus Christ was waiting for
me on that road with arms outstretched and a feast waiting. Perhaps in this
way the Buddha continues to bestow his enigmatic smile on me.

Notes

1 And Fr. Hugo Enomiya-Lassalle, S.J. (1898–1990), one of the first Western Christians seriously to study and practice Buddhism, thought Christians could experience
satori or enlightenment and integrate it into a Christian system of beliefs.

2 The matter of establishing the 'historical Buddha' is nicely treated in Nagao Gadjin's 'The Life of the Buddha' (*The Eastern Buddhist* 20 no. 2, 1987, pp. 2–7), from
which I have taken the etymologies, and is critically examined in Whalen Lai's 'The
Search for the Historical Sakyamuni in Light of the Historical Jesus,' *Buddhist–Christian
Studies* 2 (1982), pp. 77–91.

3 Paul Tillich, *Christianity and the Encounter with World Religions* (New York:
Columbia University Press, 1965), p. 97.

4 Jacques-Albert Cuttat, 'Christian Experience and Oriental Spirituality,' in *Concil-
ium* 49 (New York: Paulist Press, 1969), p. 131. (Note: I prefer and use inclusive language in my own remarks but feel it a matter of accuracy to preserve the exact quotations
of others.)

5 Michael Carrithers, *The Buddha* (New York: Oxford University Press, 1983);
Nagao Gadjin, 'The Life of the Buddha: An Interpretation,' *Eastern Buddhist* 20 no.
2 (1987), pp. 1–31; David and Indrani Kalupahana, *The Way of Siddhartha* (Boulder:
Shambala, 1982); F. W. Rawling, *The Buddha* (Cambridge: Cambridge University Press,
1975); H. W. Schumann, *The Historical Buddha* (London: Arkana, 1989).

6 Carrithers, *The Buddha*, pp. 11, 38.

7 Thomas Merton, 'Buddhism and the Modern World,' in *Mystics and Zen Masters*
(New York: Delta, 1967), p. 286.

8 Carrithers, *The Buddha*, pp. 76–7.

9 Schumann, *The Historical Buddha*, p. 203.

10 His Holiness Tenzin Gyatso the Fourteenth Dalai Lama, *A Human Approach to
World Peace* (London: Wisdom, 1988), p. 11.

11 Unless otherwise noted, all quotations of Christian scripture are from the New
Revised Standard Version.

12 This, of course, assumes a fully actualized self to give. Many feminist writers have
noted the problems of commending 'self-giving' or 'kenosis' or 'service' as positive goals

for women who may not have fully developed the self or who have been forced into service rather than being liberated and thus able to choose it. See, for example, Anne E. Carr, *Transforming Grace: Christian Tradition and Women's Experience* (San Francisco: HarperSanFrancisco, 1990).

13 Quoted in Schumann, *The Historical Buddha*, p. 62.

14 William Johnston, *Christian Zen: A Way of Meditation* (San Francisco: HarperSanFrancisco, 1979), p. 15.

15 Walpola Rahula, *What the Buddha Taught* (New York: Grove Press, 1974), p. 70.

16 Tillich, *Christianity and the Encounter*, p. 81.

17 Shunryu Suzuki, *Zen Mind, Beginners Mind* (New York: Weatherhill, 1976), pp. 29, 31.

18 Thomas Merton, 'Mystics and Zen Masters,' in *Mystics and Zen Masters* (New York: Delta Books, 1967), pp. 21–2.

19 Rahula, *What the Buddha Taught*, p. 17.

20 Schumann, *The Historical Buddha*, p. 138.

21 Merton, 'Buddhism and the Modern World,' pp. 286–7.

22 The phrase is Carrithers' and is found on p. 67 of *The Buddha*.

23 Quoted in Schumann, *The Historical Buddha*, p. 246.

24 See Thomas Merton, *Thoughts in Solitude* (New York: Farrar, Straus & Giroux, 1977), p. 83.

25 Quoted in Rahula, *What the Buddha Taught*, p. 130.

26 See, for example, Roy C. Amore, *Two Masters, One Message* (Nashville: Abingdon, 1978); Richard H. Drummond, *A Broader Vision: Perspectives on the Buddha and the Christ* (Virginia Beach, Va: A.R.E. Press, 1995); B. H. Streeter, *The Buddha and the Christ* (London: Macmillan, 1932); Steven C. Rockefeller and Donald Lopez Jr., eds., *The Christ and the Bodhisattva* (Albany: State University of New York Press, 1987).

27 Quoted in Rahula, *What the Buddha Taught*, p. 1.

28 Thomas Merton, preface to the Korean edition of *Life and Holiness* in *Introductions East and West*, Robert E. Daggy, ed. (Greensboro: Unicorn Press, 1981), p. 77.

29 *Ibid.*

30 Robert Aitken and David Steindl-Rast, *The Ground We Share: Everyday Practice Buddhist and Christian* (Liguori: Triumph Books, 1994), pp. 48–9.

31 Thomas Merton, preface to the Japanese edition of *Seeds of Contemplation* in *Introductions East and West*, p. 71.

32 Aitken and Steindl-Rast, *The Ground We Share*, p. 31.

33 Suzuki, *Zen Mind*, pp. 111–12.

Source: Bonnie Thurston, 2000, 'The Buddha Offered Me a Raft', in Rita Gross and Terry Muck (eds), *Buddhists Talk about Jesus, Christians Talk about the Buddha*, London: Continuum, pp. 118–28 (first published in *Buddhist–Christian Studies* 19, 1999).

Buddhism as a Challenge for Christians

ALOYSIUS PIERIS, SJ

Buddhist Challenge Neutralized

Many had hoped with Arnold Toynbee that an in-depth encounter between Buddhism and Christianity would usher in a new era in human history. Like no other two religions of the world, these two are a formidable challenge to each other, and their encounter, one hoped, would result in a *coincidentia oppositorum* that would give birth to a richer and nobler synthesis in each.

Subsequent events, however, have belied these expectations mainly because these two religions have never really met each other in their *authentic* forms, except perhaps in the hearts of a few individuals. For the most part, the Buddhist–Christian encounter has been a matter of a deformed Christianity colliding with a misapprehended Buddhism. The ideology of 'Euro-ecclesiastic expansionism,' which masqueraded as the religion of Christ, was not good news but a serious threat to Buddhism. In fact, it was this initial Christian offensive that compelled Buddhists to wear a *defensive mask* when facing Christians. This mask is still on.

A hardening of positions took place in the nineteenth century when a bitter controversy broke out between English Christianity and Sinhalese Buddhism: a Christianity occupying a politically advantageous position in a Buddhist culture in Asia but insecure in Europe in the prevailing climate of scientific rationalism and secular ideologies; and a Buddhism trying to retrieve its rightful place in a colonized nation and vindicate its intellectual respectability in Europe by presenting itself as a *'religion-less' philosophy having a scientific and rationalist basis.*[1]

This was the beginning of what one Buddhist sociologist has described as 'Protestant Buddhism' – a Buddhism originating as a protest against an un-christian Christianity aggressive toward and contemptuous of the doctrine and the person of Buddha.[2] This reaction continued up to the middle of our own century in the guise of a 'modernist Buddhism' apologetical in style and content. This form of Buddhism did not hesitate to employ such philosophical labels as 'rationalism,' 'empiricism,' and even 'logical positivism' for the purpose of interpreting the Buddha's spiritual message to the West.[3]

This kind of 'export Buddhism' (to borrow a phrase from Edward Conze), though widespread now, failed to be what it was meant to be: a challenge to Christians. Rather, it was just a dry doctrinal system with no religious sap to make it live, with no monastic nucleus to nourish it spiritually and with no Buddha cultus to draw out its essentially soteriological character. This nineteenth-century legacy still continues to hinder Christians from detecting what is truly challenging in Buddhism.

Though the polemical climate has yielded to a friendly atmosphere of dialogue, the nineteenth-century doctrinaire approach to Buddhism still persists in the works of many contemporary theologians. David Snellgrove's sophisticated tract on the 'theology of Buddhahood' is an example.[4] John Cobb and George Rupp have been hailed as two Christians who have allowed their theology to be revolutionized by the Buddhist challenge to Christian thought.[5] Though an intellectually fascinating exercise, a confrontation of Whitehead's process philosophy with the subtleties of ancient Buddhist dialecticians like Nagarjuna (Cobb does it brilliantly) is a far cry from an encounter between the gospel and the dharma!

Asian theologians have been even less enterprising. Mahayana Buddhism has received a fair degree of serious attention from Japanese theologians. But the overall impression is – that they *neutralize* the Buddhist challenge by filtering it through Western (often German) theological models.

In Asia, it was Lynn de Silva who pushed the doctrinal confrontation to its ultimate limit. His investigation into the Buddhist theory of reincarnation led him to revise his Protestant views on eschatology.[6] But his most daring achievement was the theological appropriation of the Theravada doctrine of *anatta* – the nonexistence of a human or any soul.[7] In the course of a much publicized dialogue between 'modernist Buddhists' and Christian theologians on the problem of God, the Buddhist argument, 'no soul, therefore no God,' made an about-turn in de Silva's theological response: 'no soul, therefore God.'[8] The Christian concept of *pneuma* was thus elucidated in terms of the Buddhist doctrine of *anatta*.

The Christian use of non-Christian doctrines is an apologetical method begun by the Greek fathers, and is hardly fruitful in the Asia of today, as I have argued elsewhere.[9] Yet in this instance, de Silva freed himself of the nineteenth-century approach by not treating the *anatta* doctrine as a mere philosophical tenet (on a par with, say, that of David Hume who is quoted approvingly in the writings of 'modernist' Buddhists). Rather, de Silva saw in it the Buddhist equivalent of the principle and foundation of Christian spirituality: the acknowledgement of one's *creatureliness*. For de Silva always worked within the soteriological parameter of the two religions, though, perhaps he did not give due recognition to the *gnostic idiom* of the Buddhists.

Challenge of the Gnostic Idiom

There are two irreducibly distinct languages of the Spirit, each incapable without the other of adequately mediating and expressing one's experience of God and of the world. Gnosis or *the language of liberative knowledge* is one; agape or *the language of redemptive love* is the other.

In Buddhism, *karuna* or love is an indispensable prelude to and an inevitable consequence of *prajna* or wisdom, which alone is considered intrinsically salvific. All affective currents of spirituality must at one point or other flow into the sapiential stream – notwithstanding the pietistic schools of Mahayana Buddhism. The dialectics of wisdom and love – that is, of gnostic detachment and agapeic involvement – constitutes a universally accepted dogma in the mainstream schools of Buddhism. Yet when Buddhism speaks of love, it normally does so in the language of gnosis.

Contemporary Christianity, which is almost exclusively agapeic, has not only lost its earlier familiarity with the gnostic idiom, but has also inherited an antignostic bias, though historians insist that there used to be an orthodox line of Christian gnosis and that the heretical gnoses were only 'embroidery' along this legitimate line.[10] A glance at the socio-political history of Buddhist cultures should convince any Christian that gnosticism is not necessarily ahistorical or apolitical. It is the antignostic bias that accounts for the Weberian sociologists' caricature of Buddhism as a 'world-denying asceticism' when in reality it is only a world-*relativizing* affirmation of the Absolute.

Because language is not just a way of speaking about reality, but a way of seeing and experiencing it, the Buddhist challenge consists primarily in reminding the Christian that there exists another legitimate way of seeing and interpreting reality, as the following observations will illustrate. Theresa of Avila, whose God-*experience* is expressed in the idiom of agape, refers to the mystical grace of 'suspension' (of senses and understanding) as being such an extraordinary and gratuitous gift of the divine Spirit that it would be presumptuous to make any human effort at acquiring it.[11] But whoever meditates under the guidance of a Theravadan master is soon made to believe that this 'suspension' (*nirodha samāpatti* or 'cessation trance' as Buddhists call it) is a natural, predictable, and humanly inducible, albeit rarely attained, psychic phenomenon not to be confused with nirvana, which defies human manipulation.

We are dealing here with two language games, each having its own set of rules. One game should not be judged/played according to the rules of the other. Thus, the Christian mystic speaks in terms of 'sin and grace,' but the gnostic vocabulary of the Buddhist arahant knows only of 'ignorance and knowledge.' The gnostic process of realizing an 'Impersonal I' and the agapeic encounter with a 'personal Thou' imply two modes of religious discourse, each having its own logic and its own grammar and syntax.

As with God-experience, so also with regard to the *external world*, we can adopt *two postures*; that of the Christian who delights in it and that of the Buddhist who keeps a critical distance from it. Each attitude has its own danger: stark consumerism and stoic indifferentism, respectively. Yet today more than ever, we Christians should be made aware that gnosis and agape are the two eyes of the soul and that our partial one-eyed vision of the world has led us to the brink of cosmic disaster.

Not inclined to *revere or adore the Absolute*, because it is a nonpersonal reality to be realized through gnosis, Buddhists tend, by contrast, to attribute a *quasi-personalist character to all that is not the Absolute*. Hence cosmic forces are personified in the process of being relativized. In other words, the elements of nature evoke a reverential attitude from humans. The cosmos makes *one ecological community* with humanity. Inasmuch as nature is humanity's cosmic extension, it cannot be mishandled without the whole human–cosmic continuum being disrupted. Buddhism knows a way of relativizing the world vis-à-vis the Absolute without in any way 'instrumentalizing' it.

Contrast this with Christian theism. The Absolute is adored and loved as a person; all else (human persons not excluded) shrinks to the level of an instrument to be used in the human quest for God. Ignatius of Loyola makes it the foundational principle of Christian asceticism.[12] Cosmic forces are thus regarded as impersonal things to be manipulated in the service of God and humanity rather than as quasi-personal beings to be treated with reverence or as silent companions in our pilgrimage toward the Absolute. It is this 'instrumental theory of creatures' – not yet challenged by the gnostic vision of the world – that has paved the way for the current impasse of technocracy, while biospheric pollution grows into an imminent nuclear holocaust.

There was at least one Christian who was endowed with a two-eyed vision: Francis of Assisi. But he seems to have been a freak in Christendom!

Challenge to Christology

The Indian sage seated in serene contemplation under the Tree of Knowledge, and the Hebrew prophet hanging painfully on the Tree of Love in a gesture of protest – here are two contrasting images that clearly situate the Buddha (the Enlightened one) and the Christ (the Anointed one) in their respective paradigmatic contexts of gnosis and agape. In no other gnostic religion (Jainism, Taoism, or Vedantic Hinduism) and in no other agapeic religion (Judaism or Islam) is *the person of the Founder* (if there is one) accorded so central a place in his own kerygma as certainly is the case with Buddhism and Christianity.

The parallel processes by which Gautama came to be revered as *the* Buddha and Jesus came to be proclaimed as *the* Christ indicate that any encounter between the dhamma (the message of Buddha) and the gospel has to reckon with an eventual kerygmatic conflict between the two 'personality cults.'

The nineteenth-century revival of Hinduism in India and of Buddhism in Sri Lanka bear testimony to this fact. The great Hindu reformers despite their critical stance regarding Christianity were willing to absorb the figure of the 'god-man' Jesus into their soteriological scheme,[13] sometimes giving the impression that they were trying to rescue the founder of Christianity from Christian distortions! Buddhist revivalists, such as Anagarika Dharmapala, on the contrary, were known to have been not only critical of Christianity but also spiteful toward the person of Jesus who, in their writings, contracts into a spiritual dwarf before the gigantic personality of the Buddha.[14]

In this connection we can note that the Pauline missiology of the Letters to Ephesians and Colossians, which installed Jesus Christ as the one cosmic mediator and also as the metacosmic Lord over all visible and invisible forces of the universe, had already been anticipated in Asia by Buddhist missionaries who had enthroned the Buddha over all elements of nature and all gods, spirits, and personified cosmic forces. This makes Buddhism the greatest challenge that the Christian kerygma has ever met in history – and vice versa.

Moreover, both the 'ontological' approach of traditional christology and the 'soteriological and functional' approach of contemporary theologians find their vague analogies in the history of buddhology.[15] Christians living in a Buddhist culture are therefore challenged to *revise* their *christological formulas*. Perhaps a new 'liberational' approach that would complement rather than cancel past achievements might best meet this Buddhist challenge. Because this suggestion has received sustained argumentation and careful formulation elsewhere,[16] I shall content myself here with merely making a few brief statements.

1. The only meeting point of the gnostic and the agapeic models of spirituality is the belief that *voluntary poverty* constitutes a salvific experience. Hence Jesus, as God's own kenosis and as the proof and sign of God's eternal enmity with mammon, is an endorsement of the Buddhist ascesis of renunciation. *The struggle to be poor* is one of the two dimensions of Christian discipleship, and it coincides with the Buddha's path of *interior* liberation – namely, liberation from possessions as well as from greed for possessions.

2. This same Jesus, according to the agapeic formula, is also the new covenant – that is, a defense pact between God and the poor against the prevailing order of mammon. It is precisely when the poor struggle for their freedom and human dignity that God glorifies the Son as God's covenant before the nations, thus breaking through the language barrier between gnosis and agape, turning *human love* into the supreme art of *knowing God* (1 John 4:7–8).

3. Christ, at once human victim and divine judge of *forced poverty*, lives in the oppressed in whom he announces himself to be unmistakably available as the recipient of our ministry (Matt. 25:31–46). *The struggle for the*

poor is, therefore, the second constitutive dimension of Christian disciple-ship and is also the means by which Jesus is proclaimed the Lord of history. All christological speculations that flow from this liberational praxis do not compete with buddhological theories.

4. A rich church that serves Christ who is in the poor now (Matt. 25:31–46), without following Jesus who was poor then (Matt. 19:21), is a neo-colonialist threat to Buddhists because it attributes to Christ a false political messianism. Conversely, Christian ashrams that follow *Jesus* by their 'strug-gle to be poor,' but do not serve *Christ* through a 'struggle for the poor,' fail to proclaim Jesus of Nazareth as the Christ and the Lord of history.[17]

Notes

1 For a brief outline of these events and relevant bibliographic references, see chap. 3 [of Pieris' book], pp. 28–31.

2 See Kitsiri Malalgoda, *Buddhism in Sinhalese Society* (Berkeley: University of California Press, 1976), p. 192.

3 See Gottfried Rothermundt, *Buddhismus für die moderne Welt. Die Religionsphilos-ophie K. N. Jayatillekes* (Stuttgart: Calwer Verlag, 1979), pp. 31–3, 115–16, 125ff.

4 D. Snellgrove, 'Traditional and Doctrinal Interpretation of Buddhahood: An Outline for a Theology of Buddhahood,' *Bulletin of the Vatican Secretariat for Non-Christians*, 5 (1970) 3–24.

5 See *Buddhist–Christian Studies*, 3 (1983) 3–60.

6 Lynn A. de Silva, *Reincarnation in Buddhist and Christian Thought* (Colombo: Christian Literature Society of Ceylon, 1968), pp. 161–3; idem, 'Reflections on Life in the Midst of Death,' *Dialogue*, 10 (1985) 4–17.

7 Lynn A. de Silva, *The Problem of Self in Buddhism and Christianity* (Colombo: Study Centre for Religion and Society, 1975).

8 Lynn A. de Silva, '*Anatta* and God,' *Dialogue*, 2 (1975) 106–15.

9 Aloysius Pieris, 'L'Asie non sémitique face aux modèles occidentaux d'inculturation,' *Lumière et Vie*, 33 (1984) 50ff. See *An Asian Theology of Liberation*, chap. 5 [Aloysius Pieris, Maryknoll, NY: Orbis, 1988].

10 L. Bouyer, *La Spiritualité du Nouveau Testament et des Pères* (Paris: Aubier-Mon-taigne, 1960), p. 34.

11 See David Knowles, *What is Mysticism?* (London: Burns & Oates, 1967), p. 86.

12 *Spiritual Exercises*, 23.

13 See M. M. Thomas, *The Acknowledged Christ of the Indian Renaissance* (London: SCM Press, 1969).

14 See Ananda Guruge, *Return to Righteousness: A Collection of Speeches, Essays and Letters of Anagarika Dharmapala* (Colombo: Anagarika Dharmapala Birth Centenary Committee, Ministry of Education and Cultural Affairs, 1965), passim.

15 I developed this theme in my Teape Westcott Lectures delivered at Cambridge Uni-versity (England) in October 1982.

16 Ibid.

17 See A. Pieris, *An Asian Theology of Liberation*, chap. 2.

Source: Aloysius Pieris SJ, 1988, *Love Meets Wisdom: A Christian Experience of Buddhism*, New York: Orbis, pp. 83–8 (chapter 7, 'Buddhism as a Challenge for Christians').

11

Sikhism

ALAN RACE

Introduction

Dr John Parry has been befriending Sikhs and studying Sikhism for most of his academic career and it is this which makes him uniquely qualified to contribute to this Reader. This essay is a hitherto unpublished work and adds to his theological entry in the original Core Text book.

Sikhism is often thought of as an ethnically based religion with minimal interest in missionary outreach, other than a desire to be appreciated as a tradition in its own right and not as an off-shoot of Hinduism. Concentrated in the Panjab region of the south Asia sub-continent and being relatively recent in historical origins, it has not received the same attention as the major traditions of Islam and Hinduism. Yet there is a history of encounter that is slowly being recovered and Parry is part of that scholarly endeavour.

This contribution traces the different views of three Christian missionaries in the Panjab, beginning in the mid-nineteenth century and extending into the second half of the twentieth. Taken together, the approaches demonstrate a clear path of development from seeking conversion to engaging in dialogue, a path not unknown in relation to Christian responses to other traditions. In this sense, these three profiles show how the modern dialogue movement has roots in the missionary movements of the last two and more centuries. They also show how a negative Christian theological assessment is challenged through the light of personal encounter and better-informed study. However, once Sikhism is allowed its own voice what shape the theological encounter might take is the next step for Christian–Sikh relations.

On the Rounding of Square Pegs

JOHN PARRY

There have always been missionaries who have bucked the system, that is nothing new. However, I want to explore three such people who were involved in witness to the Sikh community, who were all convinced of their role as witnesses to their Christian faith but who were also determined that Christians should understand and begin to appreciate the faith of Sikhs.

Background

First, by way of background we need to explore the early days of the encounter of Sikhs and Christians when Captain Wade, the British Political Agent in Ludhiana, invited Presbyterians from America to work in the Panjab. John Lowrie and William Reed, having arrived in Calcutta, wrote in November 1833 of their plans to Dr Elijah P. Swift, the secretary of their sending society:

> This territory is under the protection of the British government, though its chiefs enjoy a kind of independent authority. The people north of the Sutledge, in the territory of Lahore, are under the influence of Runjeet Singh, long the most formidable enemy of the British, but in friendship at present. They are all one people on both sides of the Sutledge, called Seiks or Sikhs; speaking the same language, the Punjabee; having the same religion and the same customs; so that we may hope our influence will not be confined to this side of that river. Their number is between one and two millions, among whom no efforts have yet been made to introduce the gospel; while they are described as more free from prejudice, from the influence of Brahmins, and from caste, than any other people in India. Indeed the Seik religion is quite distinct, the founder of the sect having rejected many of the doctrines and practices both of the Hindoo and Mohammedan systems, and having endeavoured to form a more perfect system out of them. We are informed that they are in a good degree more teachable, and that there is, at present, among their chiefs and better classes, a great desire to become acquainted with English, in consequence of a recent order of the English authorities of this country abolishing Persian, and substituting English, as the Court language. The desire, it is believed, may be turned to good account, and become a passport to other kinds of instruction, and more direct efforts for their good.[1]

They had high hopes of conversions from among the Sikhs – notice in the letter that they refer to their rejection of Muslim and Hindu doctrines and practices. If such seeds of doubt were already sown would it not be likely that they would respond positively to the truths of the gospel? Thus the missionaries reasoned. That John Lowrie should have made a good impression on Maharajah Ranjit Singh, to the extent that he was invited to found an English-medium school in Lahore, was also seen as a good omen. However, sadly that was not taken further because of Lowrie's ill-health and his consequent return to the USA and the fact that teaching the gospel along with literature and science was unacceptable to the Maharajah.

However, the Americans were not the only missionaries in the Panjab. The British Church Missionary Society had been invited by John Newton, one of Lowrie's successors, acting on behalf of an anonymous officer of the East India Company's army, who also gave a donation of some Rs10,000. Of the administrators in the Panjab Robert Clark in his history of the work of the CMS in the Panjab writes:

> Those were days ... in which both the Bible and the Prayer Book were believed in; when magistrates thought it not only their duty to execute justice, but were diligent also to maintain *truth* [his italics]; and were not ashamed to pray for grace to do it; when Rulers 'inclined to *God's* will and walked in His ways' ...[2]

And what motivated the missionaries and administrators alike?

> We believe, that when converted to Christ, they (the Sikhs) will become soldiers of the Cross, as brave and true and faithful to Christ, as they have been to Muslim invaders, or Delhi Emperors, or to their own Maharajahs, or to our English Queen. Our object is to enlist these races in Christ's service, so that they may as Christians join with us, and seek to win countries for Christ, even as they have joined us as soldiers in Burmah, in China, in Delhi, in Abyssinia, in Cabul, in Cyprus, and in Egypt, and have aided us in conquering many countries and taking possession of their capitals for our Queen.[3]

Having established the presence of both American Presbyterians and British Anglicans let us consider three missionaries who challenged the assumptions and methodologies of their peers.

The Revd William Keene

We start with the Revd William Keene, one of CMS's early recruits who worked in Amritsar between 1854 and 1871. Reading between the lines of various reports written during his time in Amritsar one gathers the impression of someone who did not always get on well with his colleagues, who was dissatisfied with his sphere of service and his lack of success with regard to conversions. The order of importance of the mission's work was given in terms of, first, preaching to the 'heathen', including writing and the translation of books, second, teaching the Christian converts, and third, educational work, especially schools. Bazaar preaching was out of the question. This was particularly the case after 1857. Keene visited villages but had to seek the advice of a local magistrate after coming under a barrage of bricks. So he finds himself working as a schoolmaster and in his annual letter in 1856 he bemoans the fact that ...

I have not been privileged to witness any fruit of my labours. No conversion has take place from either masters or scholars. Some are undoubtedly fully persuaded of the truth of the Bible and the falsity of their own systems, but yet there they remain, love of carnal pleasures of the world and the fear of men keep them away from Christ who alone can save them.

A question must have been forming in his mind for many years in the light of a debate at a CMS mission conference held in 1855 at which emphasis was made regarding the self-evident nature of the Christian faith:

Will not God own His own ... when put forth with the simple authority of 'Thus saith the Lord whether men allow it or not to be from God?' ... The word of God is undoubtedly 'the sword of the Spirit' and we may not use carnal weapons. We ought to rely much on the authentic declarations of inspired truth and show our hearers that we do so ...[4]

In 1858 he asked whether a study of other faiths should be made so as to understand the faith of one's hearers and so better present the Christian faith. The response was that that was fine but such study must be done in one's own time. The outcome was a presentation made by him at the mission conference in Lahore at the turn of the year, December/January 1862/3.[5] The title of his essay, 'The Sikhs: All that can be said about them from a missionary point of view', illustrates Keene's conviction of the need to present the Christian faith in the light of the beliefs of his hearers. He acknowledged the deep desire of Guru Nanak to find freedom 'from every earth-born trammel' but maintained that it is 'the Son (who) makes you free'. Like Cunningham,[6] he portrayed Guru Nanak as one who rejected the current practices of Hinduism and followed that by a relatively positive presentation of the Sikh understanding of the Godhead; their rejection of 'idolatry' and caste; liberation through grace; God's forgiveness and the futility of an outward show of religiosity through ceremonial ablutions. He carefully drew a distinction between iconoclastic Sikhism as a reforming faith and 'the gross errors of the popular Hindu belief' in which people 'prostrate (themselves) before senseless stone, and believe the Divine Being to be in such idols'.

Years before Farquhar and his colleagues were to suggest Christianity as the fulfilment of other faiths, Keene suggested that Sikh teaching is 'all in favour of the Christian missionary'.[7] Further he pointed out that the *Guru Granth Sahib* abounded in passages that struck common accord with Christian belief and asked if, like the teaching of Moses and the prophets, which was designed by God to prepare the Jewish people, the teaching of Nanak might prepare Sikhs 'for the reception of Christianity'. In effect he was proposing the *Guru Granth Sahib* as the Sikh's 'Old Testament' and thus implying the preparation of the Sikhs *by God* for the gospel. Thus God was at work among them before and outside the missionaries' activities.

He spoke further that some would argue that Sikhism had done nothing to prepare for the reception of Christianity, judging by the behaviour of certain people, and 'thereby fallaciously drawing a universal conclusion from a particular premise'.[8] Others, he claimed, would suggest that the very purity of Sikh teaching might have an adverse effect because 'it is more difficult for a moral, upright man to come to Christ than one who is openly profligate'.

Keene drew to the end of his paper by making a number of suggestions:

1 Missionaries should take up 'a particular line of study' and, further, that there should be distinct evangelists for Muslims, Hindus and Sikhs.
2 Itinerating missions should be established, and those missionaries dedicated to work among the Sikhs should work in the villages of the Manjha and the Malwa – the Sikh strongholds.
3 Such evangelists should have a thorough knowledge of Sikhism, the lives of the Gurus and the Vedanta system of philosophy, which he considered to be of influence on Sikhism.
4 The substance of preaching must be the person and work of Jesus Christ through the distinctive doctrines of Christianity, otherwise Sikhs and Hindus will claim that they have just as good teaching in their own systems.
5 '... the most effectual preaching to the heathen is the power of a holy, loving, Christ-like life.'[9]

The text of Keene's paper draws out the tension between his evangelical fervour and his appreciation of certain elements of the Sikh faith. His obvious frustration at the lack of converts as understood through his annual letters indicates his belief that that was his primary task, but unlike other missionaries of his day he does not reject Sikhism outright. Judging from borrowed phrases, it is possible that he derived such a view from reading Cunningham's book. Cunningham's work, still appreciated by Sikhs today, is sympathetic towards their faith and may have contributed to the tension within Keene's mind.

Even so, evangelism was still his major task, and his belief was that in Christ alone was salvation finally possible. What he proposed may not have been acceptable to his listeners at the conference since he did not set one religious system, Christianity, against another, Sikhism; rather he suggested that the latter be used as the foundation for the teaching of the former. Perhaps he realized that such a novel methodology would not be readily acceptable, since he attempted to steal his objectors' thunder by posing possible objections himself. The nature of the response is unknown since questions were ruled out of order even before Keene gave his paper. Could it be that his methodology was already known and rejected?

The Revd Edward Guilford

In fact, at Keene's suggestion or not, one who was to become a specialist in Sikh studies was appointed, and that was the Revd Edward Guilford, ordained by the Bishop of Lahore on Trinity Sunday 1882, some eleven years after Keene left Amritsar. One of his first decisions was to move away from Amritsar, as his letter to CMS subscribers indicates:

> Tarn Taran ranks second amongst the sacred places of the Sikhs. It has a population of about 6,000 souls, with over 300 villages surrounding it, containing 261,676 people. As a centre for missionary work it stands second to none in the Punjab; every month there is a *mela* (fair) held there, to which thousands of people flock from all parts. It is obvious, then, that the head-quarters of the mission should be fixed among the people themselves. To carry on the work from Amritsar is impossible, with any great hope of success. To do so would involve the loss of 7 months in the year, besides incalculable advantages derived from daily contact with the people. Having made two tours through the district in the last cold season, I can myself testify to the hearty desire of the people for Christian teachers. Everywhere we have been received most warmly, listened to most attentively, and pressed to come again soon.

> The cost of establishing our headquarters at Tarn Taran, and of erecting a small bungalow there, cannot be less than Rs 5000. We earnestly appeal to our friends to assist us in this great work. We believe that it is a work which lies very near the heart of our Divine Master. Nothing was so prominent in His life upon earth as his tender solicitude for the poor and the ignorant amongst men. We believe that he still has the same love now for the people in the villages of the Punjab, that He had, when He was on earth for the villages of the Holy land. We believe that Christian work in the villages will strengthen our work in the towns, and that the work in the towns will again react with the work in the villages. We believe that it is more for the interests of Christianity to occupy thoroughly one whole neighbourhood, than to scatter our efforts abroad at great distances from one another.

> At the present time there is not, we believe, any other English Missionary of our Society in the Punjab who is able to devote himself specially to the villages. Our Church Missionary Society have now made over this special

work to my hands, and I ask for your kind assistance to enable me, in dependence of the Divine help to seek to do it well.[10]

Guilford's task was mainly among villagers and farmers, the backbone of the Sikh community. As such it was a significant movement away from the attempts to convert the higher castes through work in the towns. It shows Guilford's willingness to challenge the accepted methodology of his mission society peers. He won the confidence of many people within the town through regular contact with them, and it is probably this that forced him not to make an outright rejection of the faith of others.

I discovered a copy of Guilford's original request in the CMS archives and found myself some six weeks later standing on the verandah of that same bungalow. This was the scene of a prayer meeting that demonstrates something of Guilford's temperament. In the same archives is a copy of a report sent by Guilford, above which a CMS secretary, possibly in high dudgeon, wrote in red ink, 'a strange prayer meeting for rain'.

We had some heavy showers of rain here last week amounting in all to some 2.32 inches of rain. Thirty-six hours before the rain fell, we had a remarkable prayer meeting for rain on the open place in front of the C.M.S. house. We numbered 500 in all comprising Christians, Hindus, Sikhs, Moslims and Chuhras, and a representative from each of the first four mentioned religions offered prayer, all being extempore prayer, except the Sikh's which had been written for the occasion.

The whole crowd listened very attentively to the address which I gave at the beginning of the meeting, and then repeated after me the first six verses of Psalm 130 and the first eight verses of Psalm 143.

It was a remarkable meeting and the people were much astonished at the speedy answer which we have received to our united prayer for at the time the heavens were as brass and they had been for many weary months.[11]

The fact that Guilford uses the term 'united prayer' would seem to indicate that although he obviously led the occasion it was not a trial of spiritual strength, as it were, nor were people of other faith considered by him to be mere observers. This was an *act* of interreligious dialogue, of cooperation in life issues.[12] In the light of his experience among Sikhs, Guilford was asked to write about them, and while he had intended to write at length – 'giving more in detail the results of his studies in the Granth and of his intimate experience and knowledge of religious and social life among the Sikhs' – he was able only to complete a short introduction. Weitbrecht indicates in his Preface to the introduction that 'this is no mere academic essay' but something that arises out of the fact that '[h]is whole life ... has been spent in intercourse with the Sikh peasantry, gentry and priesthood, and his great and beneficial influence over them' had been honoured by the government but ... '[b]etter still, a Christian church has been gathered in the town and villages of Tarn Taran, which includes a number of Sikhs who have become soldiers of Christ'.[13]

Guilford wrote his short book on Sikhism after Edinburgh 1910 and was influenced by that conference. However, in certain issues he retains his own interpretation, which was at odds with his peers at Edinburgh, perhaps reflecting the fact that he lived and worked among the Sikhs in their own heartland.

His account opens with a short history of the Sikhs much of which is appreciative of their fighting qualities and of the 'wonderful man, Maharaja Ranjit Singh', pointing out that it was the Sikhs who 'took up arms on behalf of England in the Mutiny of 1857'. Relevant to the period of writing (1914/15) was his appreciation of the Sikh regiments fighting on the side of the Allies in France.

He was critical but not dismissive of Sikhism and appreciative of many Sikhs. While some fell short of Nanak's ideals, in his opinion, 'yet the influence of his teaching has been such to mark the Sikhs, as a nation, as being far in advance of any other people of India in spiritual conceptions, and in moral ideals and aspirations'.[14]

Unlike many of his colleagues, both at Edinburgh and elsewhere, he regarded Sikhism as a distinct religion but also recognized the presence and practices of popular Hinduism among the Sikhs of his day, 'for they are still bound by the grave-clothes of Hindu superstition, and by the iron rules of caste ...'.[15] Like Keene he realized the need for a thorough-going study of the religion of the people among whom he worked and recommended that as being vital in the presentation of the gospel.

> There are many gems to be found in the *Japji*, but they need to be diligently dug out and searched for amidst a mass of unedifying matter. The labour is, however, well worth the best efforts of the Christian missionary, for it will yield not only a few points of contact with the great truths revealed in Jesus Christ. The *Shabd* of the Granth is in truth no other than the Eternal Logos.[16]

The same quoted sentence further reveals Guilford's conviction of the centrality of Jesus Christ in the gospel message and likewise indicates his taking seriously the question which was asked of delegates to the Edinburgh conference: 'What are the elements in the said religion or religions (i.e. that of the people amongst whom one works) which present points of contact with Christianity and may be regarded as a preparation for it?'[17] Guilford answered this in terms of the 'gems which may be got from Guru Nanak's teaching' and lists them as:

1 The Fatherhood, the love, the mercy, and the justice of God.
2 The brotherhood of man.
3 The necessity of obedience to the inward divine voice.
4 The unerring working of divine justice.
5 The necessity of a divine Teacher.
6 The existence of One who can put away sin, under the name of Hari. (Interpreted by him to mean the 'One Who puts away'.)
7 The folly and sin of idolatry.

Many of these suggestions for an apologetic to the Sikhs indeed take their origin from Guru Nanak's teaching, but it would be advisable to add a note of caution with regard to the matter of 'Hari', since Guilford may be placing an overly Christian interpretation on the meaning of this word.[18] Nonetheless, Guilford certainly lays the foundations for an apologetic to the Sikhs.

Such was Guilford's experience that he recognized the difference between the beliefs of Sikhism as outlined by the Singh Sabha movement and the claims made by the 'common people' who considered the Gurus to be 'ten different incarnations of the One all-pervading Spirit' which claim he indicates cannot be substantiated by the sacred books. This reflects the attitude of such people generations later when Clarence O. McMullen conducted his interviews, which showed that 79.4 per cent of the people asked believed that Guru Nanak was an incarnation of God.[19]

Guilford arrived in India five years after the publication of Trumpp's translation of the Sikh scriptures, and partly influenced by the translator's low opinion of Sikhs and Sikhism – they both had worked for the same mission society – he described the legends of the birth and childhood of Guru Nanak to be 'of a very puerile nature' and went on to quote Trumpp's opinion that Nanak was 'by no means an independent thinker'.[20] For Guilford, '... the religion of Nanak seems to be a serious attempt at ... establishing a religion that could embrace both Hindus and Mohammedans', which he describes as a 'compromise', 'which shares the weakness common to all compromises'.[21]

Rejecting the 'dreary round of transmigration', he bemoans the loss of identity involved in the Sikh concept of *moksha* (liberation), which he felt 'held out no more hope of future personal bliss than is afforded by Hinduism'.[22] Here one finds the inevitable conflict between the Christian search for personal salvation and the Sikh rejection of such individualism, since it reflects the egocentricity of *haumai* (self-centredness).

In common with many Christians who seem to claim a monopoly of spiritual truth, he suggested that the only explanation of the presence of such truths is through Guru Nanak's having come into contact with Christianity, 'for there are many things in his writings which have a Christian colouring, and which seem inexplicable, except on the hypothesis that Nanak had some personal knowledge of the faith', a hypothesis which he felt was strengthened by the existence of a sect of descendants of people converted to Christianity by the preaching of St Thomas. 'These men have in their possession both the Gospel of St Matthew and the writings of Nanak, and they render equal honour to both.'[23]

In a gentle manner Guilford rejected the thesis of Pandit Walji that Nanak was 'a convinced Christian who taught, but in obscure language the whole doctrine of the Life of Christ'. That said, Guilford's affirmation that Guru Nanak was a seeker after truth and his high opinion of the Guru's lifestyle are high praise indeed for one who sought the conversion of the Sikhs.

Nanak, in Guilford's eyes, provided a *praeparatio evangelica* for the Christian missionary, for although he 'laboured with many grand truths he was unable to give form to any. He was a great and saintly soul, and one who stood out beyond all others of his time in India.'[24] Guilford encouraged his fellow missionaries to search the Sikh scriptures, 'for it will yield not a few points of contact with the great truths revealed in Jesus Christ'.[25] Perhaps most surprising is his claim that the *Shabd* of the Granth 'is in truth no other than the Eternal Logos – "The true light that lighteth every man coming into the world"'.

Guilford showed that he was familiar with the work of the Singh Sabha movement in that he writes of the variety of sects to be found within Sikhism as then practised in the Panjab. He was well aware, as were many of his generation, of the danger of Sikhism being lost amidst an all-embracing Hindu environment.

Finally he acknowledged that 'the Sikhs are a noble race and ... their religion compared with the religions of some other peoples of India, is of a high order, and one worthy of study.' But to what end? It is so that Sikhs may be persuaded to 'accept the Christ of God as the Guru "sent from God" who "lighteth every man coming into the world"'. Using his recognition of the similarities of *Shabd* and *Logos*, Guilford encouraged his readers that Christ alone is the 'One Mediator', confessed by Guru Amar Das when he told his followers, 'Seek such a one for your Guru who is able to reconcile you to God.'[26]

Like his older colleague Keene, Guilford was convinced that the goal of his ministry must be conversion. Even the headed notepaper later used by him and his wife declares their address to be the *Gurdwara* or 'The Door of the True Light' – *Sat Gur Ka Dwara*; and using vocabulary familiar to those who read the Sikh scriptures they indicated by the heading on the opposite side of the page their belief in the 'Sinless, Eternal Being – Praise be to the Lord Jesus'.

However, a clearly perceptible development had taken place from the time of Keene with regard to the attitude taken to Sikhism. Keene was inclined to the belief that the theological ideas embraced by Guru Nanak, even though at best inadequate, and at worst false, could be used as a foundation for reception of the gospel message. Meanwhile, thanks to the climate of opinion developed after the publication of Darwin's *On the Origin of Species by means of Natural Selection*, Guilford was able to make use of its theological corollary, that Christianity could be presented as the fulfilment of Sikhism. Guilford's book was published at a time when the Fulfilment School normally associated with J. N. Farquhar[27] was popular among missionaries. Max Mueller's work also helped in the development of this understanding of the role of other faiths, for although he did not make any claim for the supremacy of Christianity he maintained that the non-Christian religions could be considered as 'part of the divine education of the human race'.[28] However, the idea of Christian superiority, benevolent or not, was considered by him to be inappropriate.[29] Perhaps the greater influence on Guilford was that of Monier Williams, who had suggested it may be the case that some of Christianity's 'grandest and most essential dogmas ... and its root ideas, do indeed lie at the root of all religions'. He asked, 'Is it not a fact that all gropings after truth, all the religious instincts ... find their only true expression and fulfilment – their only complete satisfaction – in Christianity?'[30] True that Monier Williams rescinded his view in a well received address at the 1887 CMS anniversary meeting, but Guilford was by then in the Panjab and had possibly experienced at first hand elements of Sikh spirituality which may have given him a more positive view. In keeping with the fulfilment theologians of his day, Guilford's attitude to Sikhism emphasizes sympathy while at the same time declaring its inadequacy. Thus Guilford conceived of the Sikhs' faith as a *praeparatio evangelica*,[31] as is illustrated by the final words of his book in which he states that the 'Christ of God' is the true 'Inward Light' for whom they search, the true 'Shabad' (Word) by which all things were created.[32] Guilford also had the benefit of the growth of knowledge in the West of the scriptures of India, thanks to the work of Monier Williams, Mueller and, in the case of Sikhism, Trumpp's translation of the *Guru Granth Sahib*, for all its deficiencies. Further, the reforming movements within Hinduism such as the Arya and Brahmo Samajes and the growth of the influence of the Singh Sabha within Sikhism enabled a new climate of opinion which was less inclined to reject all that was seen of Indian religions as satanic and crude. That being the case he was not opposed to contact with the Sikh community, rather he contributed to possible bridge-building by the weekly series of lectures on the New Testament which he gave at one of the Sikh 'theological colleges' in Tarn Taran, given, it must be stated, at the request of the college authorities.[33]

So, thus far we have two CMS missionaries who are prepared to challenge their colleagues, both in terms of their mission methodology and with regard to attitudes towards Sikhism. Keene was challenged to respond to the genuine spiritual searching of his Sikh interlocutors and Guilford quite obviously established good relationships with the people of Tarn Taran, to the extent, as we have seen, of being invited to lecture on the New Testament at the local training college for Sikh *granthis*. In 1910 that was not without significance.

The Revd Dr Clinton Loehlin

Just over a decade later there arrives in the Panjab an American Presbyterian whose work has remained in obscurity but who deserves to be better known. He was Clinton Loehlin, whose ability to befriend Sikhs and Sikh scholars established a firm rapport between the leaders of both the Sikh and Christian communities. Clinton Loehlin was an American Presbyterian missionary who must be regarded as playing a most significant role in bringing about an atmosphere of mutual understanding and an appreciation of dialogue between people of the two faiths. He went to the Panjab in 1923 as a Princeton graduate, and from then until his retirement 44 years later worked in Lahore, Moga, Ludhiana, Jullundar, Tarn Taran, Amritsar and Batala. Much of his time in the early years was spent in itinerant village mission work in areas that were the Sikh heartland, and it was then that he recognized the paucity of written material about the Sikhs which would enable the Christian missionary to understand their faith.

He wrote in the *International Review of Missions* of the difficulties faced by those who read the scriptures, such as the lack of divisions between words in copies of the *Guru Granth Sahib* and the reluctance of Sikh Granthis to separate the words of the text since it was 'cutting into pieces the body of our Guru';[34] the multiplicity of languages used in the Granth's poetry; its largely obsolescent language; the lack of a dictionary of the *Guru Granth Sahib* and suitable commentaries. Quoting Macauliffe's opinion that the 'Granth Sahib thus becomes probably the most difficult work, sacred or profane, that exists', he indicated this was 'probably the reason why there are among missionaries almost no authorities on Sikhism such as we have on Islam and Hinduism'.[35] Thereafter describing the nature of the Sikh scriptures, Loehlin briefly outlined Sikh theology, emphasizing the doctrine of grace, asked significant questions relating to Sikhism's nature and the lack of knowledge of the faith outside the Panjab, the effects of modern textual and historico-grammatical criticism on the faith and finally asked: 'Is Christianity in any sense the crown or fulfilment of Sikhism, or are the two mutually incompatible? Does Sikhism contain the truth and spiritual power essential to eternal salvation? What teachings of Jesus would appeal directly to Sikhs?' He provided no answer at that stage in his career, rather he called for 'contemporary contributions to the solution of the living and vital problem of Sikhism and the Sikhs'.[36]

As with Keene's similar suggestion, the request fell on fairly deaf ears since from the specific perspectives of church- or mission-related sources little material regarding Sikhism was published. Even the exception of the work of Loehlin's friend, the Yale scholar John Clark Archer, must be seen as coming from an academic rather than an ecclesial background and was more an exercise in comparative religion taking Sikhism as a model. He described Sikhism as an attempt to reconcile the Hindu and Muslim religions which eventually developed into 'an independent and conspicuous order of its own'[37] and in so doing confirmed Loehlin in his recognition of the distinctiveness of Sikhism, which faith he continued to study.

Loehlin was also engaged in a translation of the Bible into Panjabi published in 1959. He reflected on this work in a paper presented to the Punjab History Conference in March 1968. In it he rehearsed the many difficulties inherent in cross-cultural communication and indicated the need for translation work to be always done by a committee. Two Sikhs are said to have sat on one such working group to enable translators to express themselves in a Panjabi cultural idiom.[38] The resulting translations, like those into other Eastern languages, Loehlin claimed, became more vivid and meaningful than is the case in western languages. Similarly because many Panjabis are farmers they would have well understood the Hebrew Bible with its closeness to daily pastoral life.[39]

Loehlin's later working life coincided with that of many who contributed to the SCM 'Christian Presence' series, and much of his nature reflects their philosophy.[40] While his work in the Panjab started in the 1920s, from our perspective his most significant contributions were made after Indian Independence in 1947 when the Church recognized that it existed in a new situation in which the Christian faith was to be distinguished from its past with its association with western political, economic and cultural aggression. Likewise, in deep humility, many Christians were able to recognize that God had not left 'himself without witness' so that one could approach other faiths in the expectation that the love of God could be discovered in and through others. Though one may disagree with one's partners in dialogue one has to respect his/her integrity. In his editorial Introduction to William Stewart's *India's Religious Frontier*, Max Warren writes: 'We have to try to sit where they sit, to enter sympathetically into the pains and griefs and joys of their history and see how (they) have determined the premises of their argument. We have, in a word, to be "present" with them.'[41] Loehlin's manner was a fine example of this approach, to the extent that he won many friends among, and was trusted by, the Sikh community.

His period of work covered the time of Independence when millions of people were displaced. But the very evils which were inherent in Partition also brought a new impetus for reconciliation. Since the 1880s when the mass movements of 'outcastes' were searching for a more meaningful place in society, both Sikhs and Christians had tried to attract them into their respective folds. The year 1947 saw many Christians actively supporting Sikh refugees from Pakistan through the work of the mission hospitals. There were, of course, some Christians who continued to maintain old rivalries, but Loehlin was convinced that hostility could not be the attitude Christians should take. He rejected aloofness or separation and wrote of the discontinuity inherent in some of the attitudes of the Tambaram Conference of 1938 that this 'attitude breeds communalism, which is rampant in India. Its dangers were dramatized in the Partition rioting of 1947. Enough of it.'[42]

In Loehlin one sees a missionary who has taken a step beyond the 'fulfilment' theory to an attitude of cooperation. He recognized that some may see Christ as the 'True Guru', the 'Sinless Incarnation' but also had to acknowledge the failure of the Church: 'Where is the Sermon on the Mount fulfilled in the Christian Church? With the Sikhs, at any rate, who judge by the fruit of the tree, and who even might claim that Sikhism is the fulfilment of Christianity, being later in time, we might as well abandon fulfilment as an immediate approach, however much we may believe in it as the culmination of all history.'[43] Taking his lead from Archer,[44] Loehlin was convinced of the need to venture into the field of cooperation, not knowing what the future would be but leaving that 'in the hands of him whose Will both faiths acknowledge to be the supreme guide in life'.[45] Given that both faiths emphasize the working out of God's purpose within history, Loehlin suggested that the Christian's emphasis must be on a kingdom-centred theology. 'Surely a realm,' he wrote, 'where brotherhood, justice and love predominate will appeal to those who daily pray, "Help us to meet those beloved in whose fellowship Thy Name may come to mind ... By Thy favour may there be welfare for all."'[46]

As one of few people whose experience enabled him to write about the Sikhs for readers of English, Loehlin produced three books significant for this study. *The Christian Approach to the Sikh*[47] was based on, and is better presented than his earlier *The Sikhs and Their Scriptures*.[48] The latter book was well received by the Sikh academics Ganda Singh and Pritam Singh, who wrote in their Foreword: 'It is an objective study and an admirable introduction to the subject ... The author has dealt with his thesis with just appraisal and sympathetic understanding.'[49] However, it is a short introduction and by its very nature cannot include detail or depth. Loehlin deals with the geographical setting of the Gurus, the racial roots of the Sikhs, Sikh characteristics, the history of the development of Sikhism after the death of Guru Gobind Singh, the Sikh scriptures, both the *Adi Granth* and the *Dasam Granth*, and the official book on worship and discipline. A short chapter on Sikh theology was contributed by Dr Jodh Singh and an addition on Christianity and Sikhism as 'religions of grace' was made by Loehlin. The final chapters deal with the development of devotional religion (*bhakti*); Sufism and Sikhism; the Sikh orders; notes on some Sikh holy places; some translations from the two Granths and appendices of tables of the dates of the Gurus; other contributors to the scriptures and similarities and differences between Sikhism and Christianity.

Loehlin's Ph.D. gave rise to his third book: *The Granth of Guru Gobind Singh and the Khalsa Brotherhood*.[50] His purpose was to question the perception of many that Guru Gobind Singh, while a warrior, was not militaristic. The book essentially deals with issues relating to the study of the Tenth Guru and his writings and, therefore, while adding to the western appreciation and understanding of the Guru, is not primarily concerned with relations between the two faiths. Two issues are, however, significant. He gave notice of the founding, in 1967, of the Department of Comparative Religion at Punjabi University, Patiala, and the development of the 'Christian Institute of Sikh Studies' at Baring Christian College in Batala. Second, he made a very strong plea for careful textual critical study of the *Kartarpuri Granth*, widely believed to be the manuscript dictated by Guru Arjan. Likewise he supported calls from Sikh scholars such as G. S. Grewel and S. S. Bal for research on historical as well as textual problems within the Sikh tradition.

Shortly before he retired, Loehlin's acceptability within the Panjabi Sikh community was such that in December 1965 he was invited to speak at a meeting held to celebrate the birthday of Guru Gobind Singh at the 'Golden Temple' and attended by 8,000 people. He spoke on Guru Gobind Singh and the Emperor Aurangzeb and was appreciated by the congregation. Moved by the experience, he wrote: 'I felt I had been through a unique experience, which indeed it was, for they told me that this was the first time a Christian missionary had been asked to speak in the Golden Temple. I was pleased that I was introduced to the audience as a Christian missionary, for this was another evidence that Sikhs and Christians are coming closer to each other.'[51]

Loehlin's contribution does not, however, remain at this point. He and his wife, Eunice, chose to move to California in retirement, to live in Yuba County. This is in the light of the significant numbers of Sikhs who had settled in the Punjab-like Central Valley of California. He was invited to help in the foundation of Sikh *Gurdwaras* and regularly contributed to a Panjabi language programme on KUBY Radio and also spoke about Sikhism to the American audience.[52]

Loehlin left as his heritage a number of valuable resources. First was the goodwill he established with Sikhs, including leading scholars who recognized his sincere attempt to understand the Sikh faith as far as anyone of another faith is able to do. Second, his explorations into the comparative field established a number of areas of theology in which Sikhs and Christians would be able to find common ground for dialogue and further exploration. These were: the nature of God; the place of grace in salvation/liberation; the quest for religious reconciliation; missionary service; and the future life.[53] Third, he was closely involved in the establishment of the Christian Institute of Sikh Studies at Baring College in Batala. Within Loehlin's own working lifetime relationships between many people of the two faiths moved from suspicion and competition to cooperation.

Some Concluding Remarks

Let me be honest about my own perceptions of these three people. I started my studies as one interested in Comparative Religion as it was then called. It was under the supervision of Eric Sharpe, who introduced me to the encounter of faiths and from that to mission studies. Thus, these missionaries, from my perspective, move from the square-peggedness of the exclusive rejection of the 'other' to the more roundedness of, first of all, the simple understanding that enables the clearer presentation of the Christian faith, in the case of Keene, to the position of mutual understanding of cooperation and fellowship as was demonstrated by Clinton Loehlin. Guilford I see as an all-important and valuable transition stage.

Sadly few have taken up this encounter of Sikhs and Christians any further. I say 'sadly' because my experience is that with the Sikh community there is so much to which we can relate, and not simply in terms of academic study but in the theological and pastoral terms concerned with the outworking of faith in God's purposes.

Notes

1 See John C. B. Webster, 1976, *The Christian Community and Change in Nineteenth Century North India*, New Delhi: Macmillan, p. 13. The complete letter is found in 'American Presbyterians in India/Pakistan – 150 years', *Journal of Presbyterian History* 62.3 (Fall 1984).

2 Robert Clark, 1883, *A Brief Account of Thirty Years of Missionary Work of the Church Missionary Society in the Punjab and Sindh. 1852–1882*, Lahore: Albert Press, p. 5.

3 Clark, 1883, p. 24.

4 Report of Mission Conference 3–6 January 1855, CMS archives. C I 1 0/7/1.

5 See: *An account of the Panjab Missionary Conference held in Lahore in December/January 1862/63*, Lodhiana: American Presbyterian Mission Press, 1873, pp. 261–8.

6 J. D. Cunningham, 1994, *A History of the Sikhs* (1849), Delhi: Low Price, p. 41. Cunningham was an officer in the Indian army who took it upon himself to write about the Sikhs, against whom he had fought but whom he was later to command. Keene cribbed much of his pamphlet from Cunningham's book, the latest introduction to the faith published a short time before Keene left for India.

7 *An Account of the Panjab Missionary Conference*, pp. 261–8.

8 *An Account of the Panjab Missionary Conference*, p. 265.

9 *An Account of the Panjab Missionary Conference*, pp. 267f.

10 Quoted by Clark, 1883, p. 66. H. Oberoi, *The Construction of Religious Boundaries*, Delhi: Oxford University Press, 1994, p. 321, describes the nature of the monthly fairs to be such that they were detested by the Singh Sabha, who were determined to clean up the place, said to be full of drunken gangs of 'ne'erdowells and prostitutes freely (dancing) and (singing) vulgar songs' at the main gateway of the *Gurdwara*. Given the nature of the evangelical Christianity of the day, this was probably an added incentive for the establishment of a mission.

11 Letter from Guilford to the Revd Ireland Jones, 21 July 1900, G214/0/1900/281.

12 Cf. the third principle of Dialogue outlined in *In Good Faith*, London: CCBI, 2nd edn, 1991: 'Dialogue makes it possible to share in service to the community.'

13 E. Guilford, 1915, *Sikhism*, London, 'Preface'.

14 Guilford, 1915, p. 29.

15 Guilford, 1915, p. 29.

16 Guilford, 1915, p. 28.

17 The question list is given as an appendix in J. J. E. van Lin, 1974, *Protestante Theologie der Godsdiensten van Edinburgh naar Tambaram*, Assen: van Gorcum.

18 Here Guilford utilizes the questionable hermeneutic suggested in Pandit Walji's *Hari Charitra*, Lodhiana: Mission Press, 1893, p. 73, where the meaning of 'Hari' is said to be 'the one who takes away sin, sickness, pain and everyday calamity and saves'. However, 'hari' is also the third person singular of the verb *hiri*, meaning to 'snatch', 'take away by force', and thus is probably too strong an action to uphold Walji's suggestion.

19 See Clarence O. McMullen, 1989, *Religious Beliefs and Practices of the Sikhs in Rural Panjab*, London: Jaya Books, p. 83, Table 4.13.

20 Guilford 1915, p. 7.

21 Guilford 1915, p. 7.

22 Guilford 1915, p. 8.

23 Guilford 1915, p. 9.

24 Guilford 1915, p. 28.

25 Guilford 1915, p. 28.

26 Guilford 1915, p. 12.

27 Notably *The Crown of Hinduism*, 1913.

28 *Introduction to the Science of Religion*, 1909, p. 151.

29 *Chips from a German Workshop*, I, 1867, p. xxi.

30 Monier Williams, *Modern India*, 1887, p. 234, quoted in Sharpe, 1965, *Not to Destroy but to Fulfil*, Uppsala: Gleerup.

31 A similar attitude is struck by a Panjab lady missionary (unnamed) quoted by F. W. Youngson in his *Forty Years in the Panjab of the Presbyterian Missions of the Church of Scotland*, Edinburgh: R. & R. Clark, 1896, p. 50. Of the Sikhs she writes: 'Their religion is most interesting and touching to those who study it: it has so many strange insights and foreshadowings of the Great Revelation – as yet to come to them ... Surely they are a chosen people, meant to inherit the gift of eternal life, with many other nations who shall at that day be found saved, and walking in the light of the Lord.'

32 Guilford, 1915, p. 39.

33 CMS *Gazetteer* for July 1910.

34 The fact that critical methods demand an almost letter-by-letter analysis of the text of scripture means that if the same technique is used on the Sikh scripture, revered as it is as Guru, one is in effect dissecting that which is the Word, as much to be avoided as dismembering not simply a live human being, but a saviour-figure.

35 C. H. Loehlin, 1938, 'The Riddle of Sikhism', *International Review of Mission* 27, p. 227.

36 Loehlin, 1938, p. 232.

37 J. C. Archer, 1946, *The Sikhs in Relation to Hindus, Moslems, Christians and Ahmmadiyyas: A Study in Comparative Religion*, Princeton: Princeton University Press, p. v. This statement is not as clear-cut as what he had heard in an interview with Bhai Vir Singh at his house in Amritsar on 1 June 1937. In his diary entry he quotes the Bhai: 'Sikhism is not an eclecticism, as the Western books all say, not an attempt by Nanak to combine Islam and Hinduism. Its mission is and was purification ...'. Cathaline Alford

Archer: *John Clark Archer – A Chronicle*, Hamden, Connecticut, private publication of three diaries of visits to India in 1917/18, 1937 & 1946/7, 246 typed pages, Dec, 1959, p. 79.

38 Conversation with the Revd Rashid Choudhury in Batala, April 1994.

39 C. H. Loehlin, 1968, 'The History of the Gurmukhi Punjabi Bible', *Proceedings of the Punjab History Conference* 3 (March), pp. 187–90.

40 E.g. William Stewart; Kenneth Cragg; George Appleton; Raymond Hammer; Peter Schneider.

41 William Stewart, 1964, *India's Religious Frontier*, London: SCM Press, p. 15.

42 C. H. Loehlin, 1966, *The Christian Approach to the Sikh*, London: Edinburgh House Press, p. 71.

43 Loehlin, 1966, p. 72.

44 In July 1918 Archer had written in his diary: 'I am very excited over the big idea that came through last night, *Inter-Religious Cooperation* as a field of Christian activity ... it (the idea) has now broken on me with tremendous power.' [Cathaline Alford Archer, 1959, p. 96.] Further Archer wrote: 'This cooperation recognizes as sincere the best claims made by the best non-Christians regarding their systems, lets them evaluate and recognises their evaluation. Yet argumentation is not ruled out, it is, in fact made way for in friendly spirit ... By this method I no longer fear to speak good of other faiths ... I am not theorizing in a closet. And I am systematically re-reading the New Testament for light on the subject. My whole thought is directed towards the problems of Christian missions', p. 97.

45 Loehlin, 1966, p. 73.

46 Loehlin, 1966, p. 74.

47 London: Edinburgh House Press, 1966.

48 Delhi: ISPCK/LPH, 1958, 2nd edn 1974.

49 Loehlin, 1958, Foreword to the 1958 edition.

50 Lucknow: Lucknow Publishing House, 1971.

51 Unpublished 'Letter from Batala', February 1966.

52 Data sourced through a copy of a diary written by Loehlin's widow Eunice and kindly sent by Dr John Loehlin and his sister, Margaret Shafer.

53 C. H. Loehlin, 1982, 'Guru Nanak's Religion with Special Reference to Christianity', *Studies in Sikhism and Comparative Religion*, 1.1 (October). Also published in Gurmukh Nihal Singh (ed.), 1969, *Guru Nanak – His Life, Time and Teachings*, Delhi: Guru Nanak Foundation/National Publishing House.

Source: John Parry, previously unpublished paper.

Section C: Chinese Traditions

12

Chinese Religions

PAN CHIU LAI

Introduction

John C. H. Wu (1899–1986), a famous lawyer trained in the USA and having a very successful career in the legal profession in China, converted to Catholicism in 1937. Other than authoring books about law, he translated the New Testament as well as the Psalms into classical Chinese and wrote concerning Chinese literature, religions, philosophy and spirituality, including *Chinese Humanism and Christian Spirituality*.[1] In his *Beyond East and West*,[2] which is his intellectual and spiritual autobiography, he gave an account of the influence of Chinese religions on him and his attitudes towards the Chinese religions. The selections are from chapter 12 of this work, where he addresses 'The Religions of China'.

Wu's attitudes towards the Chinese religions indicated that for him the Christian identity should not be in contradiction with his identity as a Chinese. The question of dual identity or multiple religious identities has been raised by many contemporary Chinese Christians, including Julia Ching (1934–2001), a famous scholar of Chinese religions and former Catholic nun. In *Christianity and Chinese Religions*,[3] a book co-authored by her and Hans Küng, the issue was addressed by Küng (pp. 272–283) instead of Ching. In the text below, Ching gives her own account of her way of dealing with the issue of multiple identities. Different from Küng's mainly Catholic attitude towards the issue, Ching's personal approach is notably not only Christian, but also Chinese.

Notes

1 Jamaica, NY: St John's University Press, 1965.
2 New York: Sheed & Ward, 1951.
3 Hans Küng and Julia Ching, 1988, *Christianity and Chinese Religions*, London: SCM Press.

Religions of China

JOHN C. H. WU

Now that I am approaching the end of my spiritual wanderings, I must speak in some detail of the religions of China.

They constitute my moral and religious background, and hence they form an integral part of the development of my spiritual life. They are an important portion of the natural dowry with which God had endowed me in preparation for my marriage with Christ. I often think of myself as a Magus from China who lays before the Divine Infant in the arms of the Blessed Virgin the gold of Confucianism, the musk of Taoism, and the frankincense of Buddhism. At a single touch by His hands, whatever is false in them is purified, and whatever is genuine is transmuted into supernatural values. In this connection, Monsignor Fulton Sheen has written something about me which is as kind as it is keen:

> Although in his generosity he was ready to give up his pagan cultural heritage, he found out that none of it that was good was lost to him now that he was a Catholic. On the contrary, it was uplifted and complemented. Indebtedness to life became indebtedness to God for His graces, filial piety was made stronger because it had its source in filial piety to God and His Mother. Confucian moralism and Taoist contemplativeness were marvelously balanced and he could be even more Chinese because he was a Catholic. His thirst for Love was satisfied and he realized that true spirituality has its basis in moral life, which in turn is based on contemplation; and that the Love of God transformed action into prayer and made the latter overflow into action. He also realized that all the great minds he had followed were as nothing before God, Who alone is; and his intuition that love and not science is supreme became a joyous certitude.

What a wonderful privilege it is to have been born in China in my generation! I was brought up as a child entirely in the atmosphere of the old tradition. To be steeped in the old tradition and later to come into contact with the spirit of Christianity makes one feel like a contemporary of the first Disciples of Christ, who had more or less fully lived their lives under the dominion of Law and were suddenly introduced into the Reign of Grace. Far be it from me to assert that my cultural and spiritual heritage was on a par with the Old Testament. What I do assert is that, in an analogical way, the three religions of China served as my tutors, bringing me to Christ, so that I might find justification in faith (Gal. 3.24). Of course, every conversion is due to the grace of God; but there is no denying that in my case God used parts of the teachings of Confucius, Lao Tzu and Buddha as instruments to open my eyes to the Light of the world.

To begin with, to have lived under the moral tradition of old China has proved to me the absolute necessity of sanctifying and actual grace in order to live up, even imperfectly, to the lofty ideals of life. Speaking of the Mosaic Law, St. Paul said, 'Is the Law sin? By no means! Yet I did not know sin save through the Law. For I had not known lust unless the Law had said, "Thou shalt not lust." But sin, having found an occasion, worked in me by means of the commandment all manner of lust, for without the Law sin was dead' (Rom. 7.7–8). Now this was exactly what happened to me when I had read some of the moral books current in my childhood. They warned young folks against doing this and doing that. I do not know how they worked on others; as for me, they only served to stir up my curiosity and my passions, with the result that the more resolutions I made the more often I broke them. I honestly believe that few persons are as bad as I am by nature; but speaking for myself, the Confessional has proved to me the only effective channel of medicinal grace, so effective as many a time to surprise myself. I am no longer surprised, knowing as I do the absolute veracity and power of the Divine Physician Who said, 'It is not the healthy who need a physician, but they who are sick' (Matt. 9.13).

With this preface, I want to proceed to give a sketch of the three religions, paying particular attention to those aspects which in one way or another prepared my mind to recognize the True Lord and the Holy Trinity. The reader may skip the rest of this chapter if he chooses; but I hope he will not. For it bears not only on my own conversion, but on the whole relation of China to Christ.

Confucianism

Confucius has been called an agnostic. This seems to me hardly fair ... These passages which I have chosen from the *Analects* should suffice to show what Confucius conceived of Heaven. To his mind, Heaven has will, intelligence, creative power, and protective love. In fact, his attitude toward Heaven is that of a docile child toward its parent ... I cannot help thinking that Confucius was a theist. His childlike attitude towards Heaven, which was for him but another name for God, was the source of his greatness. It was only in the hands of his disciple Tseng Tzu that Confucianism became almost purely humanistic, laying exclusive emphasis on the moral duties involved in the ethical relations of man, especially the duty of filial piety.

...

During the Sung Dynasty (A.D. 960–1279) there arose a group of Neo-Confucianists, who broadened the idea of filial piety by transporting it to our relations with the Heaven-and-Earth, which is the Chinese expression for the Cosmos. I can only give here a specimen of their philosophy, which as the reader will see, is pantheistic rather than theistic. When Confucius used the word 'Heaven' he meant God; but when the Neo-Confucianists used 'Heaven-and-Earth' they meant the Cosmos.

...

The idea of filial piety is so deep-rooted in the Chinese mind that when a Chinese becomes a Christian he naturally would apply it to his relations with God. To him the imitation of Christ means the imitation of His supreme filial piety toward His Father Who is also our Father. It is significant that the great Chinese Benedictine Dom Lou Tseng-Tsiang should have written:

> If Providence permits me, I hope one day, in the light of filial piety, to approach with very profound reverence the most considerable fact in the history of mankind. I shall attempt to describe to my compatriots and my friends how the revelation and the redemption of Jesus Christ have seemed to me. That redemption is the great meeting-place of the ways, the unique point where the filial piety of children and men is opened upon a divine filial piety which Jesus Christ has shown us, and to which He gives us the right, and which reunites the human creatures with our Father who is in Heaven.[1]

The idea is not new, but the feeling-tone is typically Chinese. I regard Dom Lou's philosophy as the logical development of the original idea of Confucius that the virtuous man serves Heaven as his parent. Jesus has redeemed us from the slavish bondage to 'Heaven-and-Earth' which is but the creation, and has empowered us to become filial children of the Creator Himself. Thus Dom Lou has contributed a great deal toward the realization of the ideal set forth by Monsignor Celso Constantini: To conserve and deepen the ancient national Chinese culture, by giving it the rejuvenation of Christianity.

Taoism

So long as we are dealing with Confucianism, we feel our feet on solid ground. Everything appears so neat and distinct. All virtues have their appropriate names and proper scopes of application. Confucianism is essentially a science of ethical relations. But as soon as we pass beyond Confucianism to Taoism, we are plunged into the sea of mystery. By the word 'Tao' is meant Ultimate Reality which cannot be expressed in words. Tao is the undifferentiated, indefinable Source of all things and virtues. It is the Simple, the One. If we embrace the One, we embrace all. On the other hand, if we ignore the

One, we are lost in the many. In short, Confucianism deals with moral life, while Taoism is chiefly interested in contemplative life.

...

The Taoists never wearied of extolling purposelessness, uselessness, and complete detachment from the world. At the first sight, therefore, their theories and speculations might seem to be utterly impractical in the sense that they have nothing to do with life, being merely transcendental roamings in the clouds. And yet, if they talk about purposelessness, they have in mind a higher purpose; if they talk about uselessness, they have in mind a higher usefulness; and if they talk about a complete detachment from the world, it is only because they want to show how one should conduct oneself in the world. In the last analysis, Tao is nothing but a way of life. In this sense, the Taoists are eminently practical.

...

I have summed up the practical lessons in Taoism in these words: 'The significance of time is to evoke Eternity; that of voyaging is to evoke the Home; that of knowledge is to evoke Ignorance; that of science and art is to evoke Mystery; that of longevity is to evoke the Evanescence of life; that of all human greatness is to evoke Humility; that of complexities and subtleties is to evoke Simplicity; that of the many is to evoke the One; that of war is to evoke Peace; that of the cosmos is to evoke the Beyond. It is not the voyage that causes harm; but to lose oneself in the voyage so as to forget one's destination is a tragedy indeed.' Father John Monsterleet, SJ, writing on the influence of Confucianism and Taoism on my spiritual life, says: 'A disciple of Confucius for moral truth, he turns more to Lao Tzu for mystic truth, and the mystic in him surpasses the moralist.' This seems to me a keen insight into my soul. Not that I do not practise moral virtues, but that I do not want to be entangled in them. I agree entirely with Reverend Edward Leen that even one's own holiness 'is not to be pursued as an end', but 'must remain simply as a means to God.'[2]

Buddhism

Every Chinese, up to my generation, was an implicit Buddhist. So widespread and deep-rooted was its influence in China! In social relations, the Chinese acted according to the canons of Confucianism, as balanced by the Taoistic philosophy of detachment, but in their interior life they followed Buddhism. In my own case, its influence has sunk so deep in my mind that it is not easy to render an account of it.

...

From the above quotations it is as clear as daylight that Buddha was really more a moral teacher than a religious teacher. He had a most sensitive and generous heart; perceiving as he did the misery of life, he made heroic efforts to achieve an emancipation for himself and for others. But he had no knowledge whatever of divine grace, with the result that the contemplation and concentration he preached moved entirely in the natural and physical sphere. He attempted to achieve recollection, quiet and self-unconscious ness by means of reflection and self-hypnosis. Thus, he was a quietist like Molinos, because the means he used for the attainment of quiet were really active. What I admire about Buddha is his personality. Born a prince, he had the magnanimity to sacrifice all the luxuries and comforts that life could furnish to a human being in order to search for the Truth which would set himself and others free. Whether he actually found the Truth is quite another question. To my mind, he did not. But his was a glorious failure. A prince willingly becoming a beggar for the sake of finding the right path to lead all sentient beings to freedom! I often think of him as a foreshadowing of Christ, the eternal Son of God, Who 'descended from the kingdom of imperishable glory to our earth, in order here amid brambles and stones to seek the lost, weary, wounded sheep and lead them back to eternal bliss.'[3] I cannot dismiss Buddhism without mentioning the tremendous influence that its later development exercised upon my mind when I was a child through the popular Sutra called 'The Prajna-Paramita-Hridaya Sutra' (The Sutra of the Kernel of Transcendental Wisdom).

...

In my thirties, I was deeply influenced by a particular school of Buddhism, called the school of Zen (Dhyana). The mystical tendencies that I had imbibed from Taoism were reinforced tremendously by the study of the Zen masters ... C. G. Jung says, 'Zen is one of the most wonderful blossoms of the Chinese spirit, which was readily impregnated by the immense thought-world of Buddhism.'[4] Now, what is the most fundamental characteristic of the Chinese spirit? To my mind, it is the union of the abstract with the concrete, of the universal with the particular, of utmost unearthliness with complete earthliness, of transcendental idealism with a matter-of-fact prac-ticalness. This union is not a matter of theoretical synthesis, but a matter of personal experience. As Confucius put it, 'All people eat and drink, but few know the taste.' Wisdom is something to be relished, and no one can do it for you; you have to relish it for yourself. In the parlance of Zen, only he who drinks the water knows how warm or how cold it tastes ... It is the innermost personal experience of Wisdom, which you find within you, but which you cannot share with others, that the Zen masters set their hearts upon. They have not the slightest care for external things.

...

The idea that the ordinary duties of one's daily life are charged with spiritual significance is typically Chinese ... No doubt the idea was great-ly enforced by the characteristic industry and practicalness of the Chinese people by whom Zen was mainly elaborated. The fact is that if there is any one thing that is most emphatically insisted upon by the Zen masters as the practical expression of their faith, it is serving others, doing work for others, not ostentatiously indeed but secretly, without making others know of it. Says Eckhart, 'What a man takes in by contemplation he must pour out in love.' Zen would say, 'pour it out in work,' meaning by work the active and concrete realization of love. Tauler made spinning and shoe-making and other homely duties gifts of the Holy Ghost; Brother Lawrence made cooking sacramental; George Herbert wrote;

> Who sweeps a room as for thy laws
> Makes that and the action fine.

These are all expressions of the spirit of Zen, as far as its practical side is concerned. Mystics are thus all practical men, they are far from being visionaries whose souls are too absorbed in things unearthly or of the other world to be concerned with this life.[5]

Now that I think of it, I have inherited from Buddhism an intense longing for the 'Other Shore', which is but another name and a faint foreshadowing of the Kingdom of God which is within us. Furthermore, Buddhism had disposed my mind for the appreciation of such Biblical passages as:

> Vanity of vanities, said Ecclesiastes, vanity of vanities, and all is vanity. What has a man more of his labor, that he taketh under the sun?

> Make known to me, O Lord, my end, and what is
> the measure of my days,
> That I may know how frail I am.
> Behold Thou hast made my days but a short span,
> And my life as nothing before Thee:
> Every man is nothing but a breath.

It has also taught me the importance of direct personal experience in the matters of spiritual life. As Frank Sheed puts it, 'If you want to know how wet the rain is, do not judge by someone who went out into it with an umbrella.' He advises us to go stripped into the shower of truth and life. The spirit of Zen is nothing else than this. Since I became a Catholic, all the wisdom of the East is grist to my mill. The Psalmist put it very well, 'In Thy light shall we see light.' I suppose it primarily means that in the light of the Father we shall recognize the Son, Light of the World. But in a secondary sense, it may also be taken to mean that in the light of God, we can perceive all lights, whether natural or moral. To illustrate, when I read in a Buddhist Classic: 'Avoid all evil, cherish all good, and keep the mind pure. This is the teaching of all the Buddhas'; I said to myself, 'How similar this is to three ways of the Christian spiritual life: the purgative, illuminative and unitive!' When I read Confucius' program of education of his pupils: 'First arouse their interest in wisdom by means of poetry; then establish their character by making them practise the moral rules; finally, harmonize their personality by means of music'; it reminded me of the Psalm of the Good Shepherd. The spheres are wide apart as heaven and earth, but the stages of progress are quite similar, for the simple reason that even grace has to work upon the natural and psychological apparatus of man. With regard to the wisdom of the East and Christian wisdom, God has given to my mind an organic unity of transparent differences. Vis-à-vis the three religions of China and, for that matter, all other religions, I am in full accord with the sentiments expressed by Evelyn Underhill in the following passage:

> The greatest mystics have not been heretics but Catholic saints. In them 'natural mysticism' which, like 'natural religion,' is latent in humanity, and at the certain point of development breaks out in every race, came to itself; and attributing for the first time true and distinct personality to its Object, brought into focus the confused and unconditioned God which Neoplatonism had constructed from the abstract concepts of philosophy blended with the intuitions of Indian ecstatics, and made the basis of its meditations on the Real. It is a truism that the chief claim of Christian philosophy on our respect does not lie in its exclusiveness but in its Catholicity: in the fact that it finds truth in a hundred different systems, accepts and elucidates Greek, Jewish, and Indian thought, fuses them in a coherent theology, and says to speculative thinkers of every time and place, 'Whom therefore ye ignorantly worship, Him declare I unto you.'[6]

While the three religions were distinct from one another, the syncretic disposition of the Chinese mind fused them into a unity of diversities. While Confucius, Lao Tzu and Buddha were worshipped by the Chinese people, they were never regarded as more than sages and deified men. In the Chinese mind, they never took the place of Shang Ti, that is, God the Supreme Sovereign of Heaven and the Ruler over all the universe. When a Chinese worshipped the deities, whether Confucian, Taoist, or Buddhist, he worshipped them only as the representatives and favored children of God, but never as God himself.[7] But the question naturally arises: Why did not the Chinese worship God directly? The answer is that they regarded God as too high for them, and that, just as an ordinary subject did not deal with the Emperor directly but had to obey the orders of his immediate superiors, so the ordinary man, in his religious life, had just to pay his homage to the minor deities who were appointed by the Supreme Deity to supervise his daily life. As a child I used to worship the kitchen god, the deities of the village shrines and the city temples. But on the back of my mind was always God, whose ministers the minor deities were. In doing homage to them, I felt as natural as in honoring the tutors to whose hands my father had entrusted me. God was so high and heaven so far away that it would take the minor deities some days to go to report to Him their duties. For instance, we used to burn the paper image of the kitchen god on the 23rd of the twelfth month, and wait for his return from heaven on the New Year's Eve, when a brand new image of the same deity was installed. The mission of his trip to heaven was to report to God all our doings and sayings throughout the year. But we were not too anxious, because we knew that he was our friend.

Our conception of the Court of Heaven was really an idealized version of feudalistic officialdom. W. E. Soothill, in his interesting book *The Three Religions of China*, gives a very accurate picture of the popular religion, which constituted an amalgamation of the three:

> What, then, is, or was, the official religion? Its centre was the worship of Shang Ti, the Ruler over all, the Supreme Being. Its circumference was the worship and control of demons. Between center and circumference were concentric circles of nature deities, sages, ancestors, and deified men.

> The highest act of national worship was the imperial sacrifice to Shang Ti. Only the emperor, the High Priest of 'the world,' the Son of Heaven, might perform this great sacrifice, which existed from all antiquity until the fall of the empire.[8]

When I became a Christian in 1917, I felt as though I had become an emperor overnight, because now I could worship God directly, having been empowered to be a son of God. My embracement of Christianity was a tremendous spiritual revolution on a par with the political revolution which had changed an absolute monarchy into a republic.

Notes

1 Lou Tseng-Tsiang, 1948, *The Ways of Confucius and of Christ*, London: Burns, Oates & Washbourne, p. 114.

2 Edward Leen, 1937, *Progress Through Mental Prayer*, New York: Sheed & Ward, p. 89.

3 Nikolaus Gihr, 1902, *The Holy Sacrifice of the Mass*, St. Louis: Herder, p. 63.

4 Foreword, in D. T. Suzuki, *Introduction to Zen Buddhism*, London: Rider & Company, 1969, p. 12.

5 D. T. Suzuki, 1949, *Essays in Zen Buddhism* (First Series), New York: Harper & Brothers, I, p. 305.

6 Evelyn Underhill, 1911, *Mysticism*, New York: E. P. Dutton & Company, pp. 105–6.

7 It was in this homogeneous atmosphere of the Religion of the unknown God that both my wife and I were brought up. This is the ocean we swam in, while the 'three religions' were but waves on the ocean.

8 W. E. Soothill, 1929, *The Three Religions of China*, London: Oxford University Press, p. 229.

Source: John C. H. Wu, 1951, *Beyond East and West*, New York: Sheed & Ward, pp. 149–88 (chapter 12, 'Religions of China').

Living in Two Worlds: A Personal Appraisal

JULIA CHING

Having Multiple Identities

I do not find the values and cultures of either East or West entirely satis-fying, but I find enough in each culture that is worth appreciating, and also worth criticizing. I find that such an alternative – to be both Eastern and Western – is possible, because, in spite of the differences, and even the contradictions, there is sufficient common ground between East and West. And this common ground is that which makes all of us human. The values to which I am attached are, after all, human values, with all their potential for conflict. The community in which I live and work is, after all, a human community, with all its latent and manifest tensions.

Besides, if we all reflect more deeply on the subject, we would realize that, in a sense, it is our common lot, no matter who we are and where we are – to belong to, and to live in, different worlds. I am, of course, speaking of various levels of *duality* within the one identity. The levels include the outer, sociological, as well as the inner, psychological. We are all conscious of ourselves as selves, and of others as nonselves. In our behavior, we usually have to take into account the feelings and expectations of others, whether we like these or not.

When we turn inward, we become conscious of the actual/potential split within: what we are as opposed to what we would like to be. As in the case of Chuang Tzu, we might also muse over the choice of a butterfly in a dream as his *alter ego*: 'a butterfly flitting and fluttering around, happy with him-self and doing as he pleased.'

The image of the butterfly is here one of freedom and happiness, even if we recognize in the butterfly itself a creature whose very appearance bespeaks a hold on life that is evanescent. This is a contrast with the 'solid and unmistak-able Chuang Chou,' a recluse who meditated on the sufferings around him, whether they be disease or death, or war, poverty, and injustice. There are many ways of interpreting him. One way is to regard him as having much to say in protest against the society of his own times, while longing for greater happiness and freedom. Here, as someone imbued with the moral principles of both Christianity and Confucianism, I might add: this is a man with a personal as well as a social identity, with all the cares and responsibilities these bring him, even if he was living in semiretirement. In that sense, many of us could identify with Chuang Tzu, wishing perhaps that he was the butterfly, even if that means embracing the insecurity of evanescence.

The Threats to Identity

Is life but a dream? Even if we do not wish to accept this, we cannot but feel at times the fragility of it all. And, a person's identity is as fragile as the person who claims it. There are many potential threats to identity, of which the worst is the threat to life and health.

...

We have to live with the awareness of such threats to the very ground of our identity. Most recently, it has led to a whole society's quest to exclude from its conscious mind everything that may represent death. But long before that, it might also have launched some people into inquiries concerning what follows this life. And we know some of the answers that have been proposed.

There are those who assert this life is just one ring in a chain of many lives or existences of what is called samsara. Those believers in this theory who are not Buddhists have the consolation that personal survival is assured, although the form of existence may change. There are others who assert that this life will be followed by a qualitatively better life, in a change of state called resurrection, when one is taken into the embrace of the Godhead. The believers in this theory include today Jews, Christians, and Muslims. They can take consolation in the thought that the survival of their identity is assured, albeit in a transformed state. Such theories serve to give meaning to life, and with it, to one's identity. They are answers to the question, 'What for? Why am I what I am? Is there a purpose behind all this?'

Several times in my life, I have been seriously sick. Metaphorically speaking, I know what it means to look down into the abyss that may mean nothingness. Of course I realize that we are all mortal. And, with this realization, I cannot help but wonder sometimes what it all means – this identity, this unity with oneself, this belonging to a network of relationships with other identities, together with all that accompanied the building of this unity, when one day, it will all be taken away.

Chuang Tzu speaks often of dreams, and of the difficulty of distinguishing a dream state from a state of awakened consciousness:

> While [a man] ... is dreaming he does not know it is a dream, and in his dream he may even try to interpret a dream. Only after he wakes does he know it was a dream.[1]

I am, indeed, very conscious of the rhythm and contrast of day and night, of awaking and of sleeping, perhaps dreaming. In the daytime, I seek to affirm and assert my various identities, struggling to give them an overall unity. I have an active temperament. I live and work as a Westerner, even if my subject happens to be Eastern religion. My reason is usually in control.

At night, the situation is different. My reason is much less in control, as memories of the past, accompanied by repressed emotions, dominate my subconsciousness. When I do sleep, I often have difficult and intense dreams, in which I find myself in roles very different from those of the daytime. It is as if the conflicts of my multiple identities are coming back to haunt me. And I long for silence and contemplation, even in my dream state.

Without doubt, the dream often indicates a suppressed desire or an unresolved conflict, either of which might be related to certain threats to our personal identity. It takes wisdom to learn how to interpret and respond to one's dreams, since this is part and parcel of the whole of reality. There are, however, other threats to personal identity which regard free will and choice. The deeper ones usually involve our very survival, as we ponder the options of transcending self-attachment in the name of a greater good. In the words of the Chinese sage Mencius, who uses the analogy of food choices:

> Fish is what I want; bear's paw is also what I want. If I cannot have both, I would rather have bear's paw than fish. Life is what I want; virtue is also what I want. If I cannot have both, I would rather have virtue than life. For while I want life, I also want something more than life ... And while I loathe death, I also loathe something worse than death.[2]

Presumably, if life was not dear, giving it up would not only be easy, it would also be less costly. So we should not be surprised that the very brave are often those who feel themselves the most cowardly, as they confront their finitude. The Protestant theologian Dietrich Bonhoeffer (1906–45), while a prisoner in Nazi Germany, has given expression of his own inner struggle in a poem:

> Who am I? This or the Other?
> Am I one person today and tomorrow another?
> Am I both at once? A hypocrite before others,
> and before myself a contemptible woebegone weakling?
> Or is something within me still like a beaten army
> fleeing in disorder from victory already achieved?
> Who am I? They mock me, these lonely questions of mine.[3]

A Common Identity

Few of us may be called to make a voluntary self-sacrifice as was Dietrich Bonhoeffer. Safely removed now from the naive idealism of my youth, I am happy today that I did not have to be a Chinese Joan of Arc. Besides, with all my admiration for Bonhoeffer, I find it difficult to accept with childlike simplicity his final line:

> Whoever I am, Thou knowest, 'O God, I am thine!'[4]

To me, the word *God* is much more complicated than it is to him. I think of it first in English, and then in Chinese ... and I get a little confused. What does the word God mean? Is it the same as the Chinese word for spirit, *shen* (Japanese: *kami*), or is it rather the ever old and ever new Lord-on-high (*Shang-ti*), as the Chinese Protestants still call him, or perhaps we should only call him, as do Chinese Catholics, Lord of Heaven (*T'ien-chu*)?[5] Is this God strictly personal, or a God 'beyond theism', to use the words of Paul Tillich?[6]

Once more, I derive some consolation from Chuang Tzu's playful imagination:

> How do I know that loving life is not a delusion? How do I know that in hating death I am not like a man who, having left home in his youth, has forgotten the way back?[7]

The confusion, however, is only on the intellectual plane. Existentially, I live and pray as a believer in a God whom I presume to be good and loving. But even my manner of praying is an 'East–West' encounter. Since a recent illness, I have returned to regular meditation, which I do somewhat in a Taoist or Zen fashion. I don't meditate long enough or seriously enough. But I do try to meditate every day. At the beginning of each session, I am very conscious of the fears and anxieties that accompany my self-consciousness; I am also somewhat conscious of those others with whom I share my small world. But as I direct my intention to a higher presence, while forgetting my self and its ordinary anxieties, I derive a greater sense of inner peace.

Nevertheless, fears and anxieties usually return with self-consciousness, as the sense of peace subsides. The inner life has its own demons, sometimes worse than those of the outer life. And it has been said that the 'mystical courage to be lasts as long as the mystical situation'[8]:

> Its limit is the state of emptiness of being and meaning, with its horror and despair, which the mystics have described ... To experience this and to endure it is the courage to be of the mystic in the state of emptiness ... Since everything that is participates in the power of being, the element

of identity on which mysticism is based cannot be absent in any religious experience.[9]

So what is identity after all? It is so much part of our very self, and yet, it is only in forgetting this very self, that we may find oneness with the self. In those moments of silence, I lose my identity crisis, because I find my deeper identity. I forget who I am. And yet, I am very much at one with those others who may rub against me, or be rubbed against by me. In spite of all differences, we share a common identity in the human community.

I know that I shall have to live with many of my conflicts and uncertainties, rather than expect to resolve them. For years, I thought that a wise guide could help. With maturity, I realize that there is no other who can resolve them for me. In fact, I think that living with conflicts, and seeking to go beyond them, is itself a manner of resolving them, perhaps the only way, of resolving them.

> The courage to take the anxiety of meaninglessness upon oneself is the boundary line up to which the courage to be can go. Beyond it is mere non-being. Within it all forms of courage are re-established in the power of the God above the God of theism. The courage to be is rooted in the God who appears when God has disappeared in the anxiety of doubt.[10]

Life is more than a dream, because in life, we experience both the dream state and the state of awakening. But if the dream can be a symbol for the ambiguity of life, so the awakening can be a symbol for the clarity that we hope lies beyond. As Chuang Tzu has mused, at the end of his story about the dream in which he was the butterfly: 'And someday there will be a great awakening when we know that this is all a great dream.'[11]

Notes

1 English translation in Burton Watson, 1968, *The Complete Works of Chuang Tzu*, New York: Columbia University Press, p. 47.

2 Mencius VIA: 10. The English translation is my own. Bear's paw remains a delicacy served in certain restaurants in the Orient, to the dismay of many lovers of wildlife.

3 This is quoted in Gerhard Leibholz's memoir, in Dietrich Bonhoeffer, 1959, *The Cost of Discipleship*, rev. edn, New York: Macmillan, p.15. The English translation of the poem is by J. B. Leishman.

4 Bonhoeffer, *The Cost of ...*, p. 15.

5 I am referring here to the common practice today for Chinese Catholics and Protestants to address God in different terms, either as Lord of Heaven, or as Lord-on-High. This goes back to the controversy over translation of terms which occurred in the seventeenth and eighteenth centuries. But the practice continues to make Catholic and Protestants appear as if they belong to different religions.

6 Our problem for regarding God as personal is linguistics. The Chinese term for personal includes the words *jen-ko*, which basically implies anthropomorphic character.

7 Watson, *The Complete Works* ... , p. 47.

8 Paul Tillich, 1952, *The Courage to Be*, New Haven: Yale University Press, p. 159.

9 Tillich, *The Courage* ... , pp. 159–60.

10 Tillich, *The Courage* ... , p. 190.

11 Watson, *The Complete Works* ... , p. 47.

Source: Julia Ching, 1999, 'Living in Two Worlds: A Personal Appraisal', in Arvind Sharma and Kathleen M. Dugan (eds), *A Dome of Many Colors: Studies in Religious Pluralism, Identity and Unity*, Harrisburg, PA: Trinity Press International, pp. 15–22.

Section D: Other Traditions

Section D: Other Mushrooms

13

Indigenous Traditions

FRIEDEGARD TOMASETTI

Introduction

Remembered as the doyen of Protestant missiology, Gustav Warneck (1834–1910) and his work are introduced here to mark a turning-point in the Christian reflection on indigenous religions. Although a child of his time, he rises above the social-scientific attitudes governed by evolutionism, which accentuate 'savagery' and delineate the 'lowest races'. With theological reasons in mind he evokes both the concept of a primal monotheism (suggested by the biblical outlook) and the idea of a religious decline from it. As a missiologist he believes that the small-fry among the religions yearn for something higher, and thus for what the gospel offers – and he holds this to be true of all humanity. Strands of his thought lead back to Max Müller, the discipline of Comparative Religion and to current theories that the knowledge of languages is the key of understanding humanity's spiritual quest. As evident from the translation (given here), Warneck's reasonings open possibilities for a dialogue between Christian and indigenous people.

From 1896 until 1908 Warneck held the foundation Chair of Mission Studies of the University of Halle, where he began his studies and where he had been awarded an honorary doctorate in 1883. Warneck was a prolific writer. His bibliographer P[astor?] Strümpfel (*Allgemeine Missions-Zeitschrift* 38 (1911), pp. 231–6, 275–87) lists more than 400 titles of his own and works he edited. By co-founding the journal *Allgemeine Missions-Zeitschrift* for mission theory and history in 1874 and editing it until his death, Warneck set one of the cornerstones of his work. Apart from his magnum opus *Evangelische Missionslehre* (three parts in five volumes, 1892–1905), he produced another major study, *Die gegenseitigen Beziehungen zwischen der modernen Mission und Cultur*, translated into English as *Modern Mission and Culture: Their Mutual Relations* (1883), which attempted to estimate the complexity of value systems the evangelization process has to encounter in general.

The translation here is from volume 1 of *Evangelische Missionslehre*. It was the first systematic survey of existing missiological treatises and issues. Volume 1 covers basic historical, theological and anthropological perspectives on mission. Anthropology, although still in its infancy and carried by diverse academic disciplines, had already gathered an astounding volume of data on 'the other'. The second volume is concerned with mission agencies, notably the existence of mission societies because of the lack of engagement of the churches. The last part, divided into three, deals in general with issues of the mission fields. Warneck's core concept is 'the Christianization of entire peoples' (as expressed by Hans Kasdorf, 'The Legacy of Gustav Warneck', *Missionary Research* 4.3 (1980), p. 106).

A Turning Point: on the Anthropological Foundation of Mission

GUSTAV WARNECK

What the Old and New Testament Scriptures tell us of the unity of mankind also holds true from an anthropological point of view. Reflective members of the anthropological discipline now agree that the nature of man [is] the same everywhere, [and that] there is a highly gradual variability of peoples' mental (*geistig*) development that justifies seeing even the largest cultural differences that exist as only gradual ones; and that all human tribes hold equal dispositions for developing their mental faculties, so that from this point of view no sufficient reason could be found to assume species distinctions within mankind.[1] Not gulfs but gradual differences separate the parts of mankind, races, peoples, etc. from each other. Mankind is a unity but of a multifarious forming.[2] The most isolated peoples and the races which are least similar in appearance meet each other in their mental stirrings in such an astounding way that at least by their capability to think the unity and uniformity of mankind is beyond questioning.[3]

Of consequence for our enquiry are two eminent possessions that humans of all times, zones, colours and cultures share: language and religion. There are no people, and never have been any, without language. 'All those reports of tribes without languages, or of people with a language closer to the twittering of birds than to the articulate sounds of human beings, have been sent forth for all times to the realm of anthropological myth-making.'[4] Further, the more the languages of so-called savages have been researched, the more they astounded scholars because of their artful grammars and the wealth of their vocabularies.[5] Although often lacking expressions for abstract concepts, and as incomplete as they may be in this respect, they all are masterpieces of the mind, and in fact so grand 'that the art of all philosophers would fail to bring forth something similar'. People in general are capable of learning the language of other people; this competence is not restricted to sophisticated (*gebildete*) nations. All coloured races have their geniuses who master three, four or even more foreign languages ... but apart from them entire sections of the native populations in European colonial areas have acquired a foreign language, though often distorted. We will leave unsaid all the conclusions that essentially derive from these facts for the mental unity of the species Man and for the unbridgeability of the gulf between Animal and Man. However, we want to notice another fact which is conclusive for our line of reasoning – as Max Müller so succinctly expresses it: 'until now no language has been found that made impossible to render a translation of the Lord's Prayer'.[6]

If we found a language into which the Good News could not be rendered ... then the evidence of the universality of language for Christianity and its Mission would be untenable, since it would mean that these people would lack the ability to comprehend the gospel. However, as far as facts are at hand no such language could be found, keeping in mind that the Christian mission with its long history already had to deal with hundreds of languages. Leaving aside the situation of the Jews, the language that carries the gospel to any people is at first foreign to them, and experience has to determine whether or not the truth that is expressed in this foreign language can be conveyed into other languages without suffering loss of spirit. Herewith the Christian mission had been given an immense task; but already the first attempt succeeded famously. Though so profoundly dissimilar to Hebrew, the joyful gospel was preached and penned down in Greek as if it were its mother tongue. Although entirely new religious and ethical concepts were introduced into the Greek language by this ... translation process, the Greek verbiage itself provided appropriate phrases for these new beliefs and the spirit of the language made the process of trans- and new formations feasible. Hence, by these links, an intrinsic understanding of the deepest mysteries of Christian faith was mediated to the Greek-speaking world.

In its essence this first translation process in world history has been repeated for hundreds of times. The languages of all peoples to whom the messengers of Jesus came proved qualified to convey the mysteries of heaven in a way that their intrinsic meanings could be expressed; and again Christianity proved capable of exerting its language-transforming powers by remodelling existing language elements, as it did with connected concepts, so that these languages became vessels suited for the spirit of Christ. Not only the languages of the cultures of antiquity but also those of mediaeval barbarians became such vessels ...

And the mission of our days, which has to deal with a more multifarious language situation than did the apostolic and mediaeval missions when taken together, is placed with the very same processes of translation and by now can already talk of much experience.[7] In 1890 already 309 missionary translations of the Bible existed: 146 for Asian and 78 for African areas, 42 went to Oceania and 43 to America. Many of these translations comprise only parts of the Bible, and only a few are in languages of modern civilizations (*Kulturvölker*); most translations are into languages of so-called primitive peoples (*Naturvölker*) who did not have a script in their own right and hence no literature. Even further, many of these translations appertain to languages of tribes on the lowest gradation of civilization, referred to by an aberration of materialist anthropologists' philosophy as a kind of in-between of animal and human – for instance, the Hottentots and Bushmen, the Papuans,[8] the Fuegians. It should be freely admitted that many of these translations are pieces of poor work with inadequate phrasings; however, the blame should be laid not on to the respective language but on the trans-lator who had not yet been properly in command of the language. Besides particular difficulties each translation might give to an outsider, which can only be accounted for when native speakers work as translators, one has to consider that one language compared with another might prove more inflexible for genuinely rendering Christian thought. However, it is a gener-al missionary experience that the deeper one's knowledge of a language and the better one's understanding of its spirit, the more the verbiage will lend points of connection for the correct translation of the new tenets of truth, and the aforementioned capability of transformation be generated ... Even in our days, any language having been used for preaching and penning the gospel will become qualified for the message of the Holy Spirit by gradual development and refinement.

Having in language the means of expressing Christian thoughts will enable people to think these thoughts – as thinking is the prerequisite for speaking as well as its consequences. Two things are equally impossible: thinking without speaking[9] and speaking without thinking, although there are many people around who in the strict sense speak without proper think-ing. Here, however, we are only concerned with proving the human capabil-ity. We believe the following conclusion is fully justified: if people have a language in which Christian truth can be expressed, then they are mentally capable of acquiring Christian thought expressed in their mother tongue. It might be a slow process until the transformation of thinking, initiated by language transformation, is accomplished throughout the social strata; but psychologically it is a natural law (*Naturgesetz*) that eventually it will be accomplished. Of course, the process will not lead to an equal profundity with all, and for some the understanding will remain a faint hunch rather than become lucid knowledge. Well, we will even go a step further: as there are variously talented individuals of one and the same people so there are peoples with different gifts. Not all peoples and tribes are equally capable to achieve a high level of Christian insights, and this is by no means necessary for being a Christian. Christianity is neither law nor theology nor even philo-sophy. We do not claim that each tribe could be able to acquire the scholar-ship of Christian doctrine or even develop it further, but would be capable of making its own the principles of Christian truth as they are laid down in the common confession of faith of the Christian Church. It is an erroneous idea *iliacos muros intra et extra* to see the Christian religion as a system of dogma; and the claim that uncivilized peoples are not sufficiently mature for the acceptance of Christianity is to a larger degree based on the under-standing of Christianity as dogmatic.[10] But Christianity is not dogmatic; it is history, trust in historical events, above all it is faith in the person of Jesus Christ, devotion to Christ, and in the full force of this devotion it is obedi-ence, discipleship in Christ, New Life. For ... the essentials of Christianity are the simple belief in the Saviour and obedience in faith – like a child, so that the most simple minds can believe in it. The Gospel of Christ is so easy to comprehend that the most uneducated person can believe in it, and it is so difficult to fathom that the most sophisticated person has to expound that it passes all perception; a brook in which the child can bathe and a stream in which the elephant has to swim. The Moravian Protestant Church (*evan-gelische Brüdergemeine*)[11] has addressed with its mission especially the most wretched and lowest of the uncivilized peoples – the Eskimos, the West-Indian Negro slaves, the bush Negroes, the Papuans – and the experience of 150 years has established that even these tribes hold the capability for the Word of the Cross. Today there are around 16,000 schools in the entire area of the Protestant mission, institutions from the simplest elementary to university-like schools, about two-thirds of which are in the regions of uncivilized peoples. It is the general experience not only that the 800,000-odd pupils of both genders attending these schools are educable but also that they comprehend as well as schoolchildren of European nations the fundamental evangelical principles.

As there are no people without speech so there are no people without reli-gion. Religion is as old as mankind we know of, and it is as widely spread as mankind is. While several decades ago the fable of peoples without religion still held good as 'scholarship',

> these days we have learnt to judge otherwise, owing to missionaries who have spent their entire lives with savages, learnt their languages, gained their trust and in the whole have done full justice to the positive feature of their characters. We now can assert that despite much searching no human beings were found anywhere who did not have something that meant religion to them – to say it as general as possible: who did not have a belief in something that transcended their sensory perceptions.[12]

'We have now', to say it with Tiele,[13] 'the right to call religion a universal phenomenon' without fear of being banished by scholars, since almost all noted representatives of anthropology and religious studies admit to it as reality.[14] Without enquiring further about the origin of religion, or what has been its primal shape, etc.,[15] we will keep ourselves to the fact that religion exists, and it exists wherever we find humans.

Complete irreligiosity or genuine atheism is perhaps the answer to an undermining and mind-deadening *Überkultur* but never the impression of a primal culture. With the latter, even in the lowest [condition of] depravity, the want for religion remains though manifesting in practice in very deficient and confused ways.[16]

In view of these accounts one has to label as impudence the anti-religious bias of certain scholars who call transcendence 'an aberration of the human mind'. The situation is just the reverse: *denying* transcendence is an aberration of the human mind. The latter might have taken many wrong turns in search for religion, but at all times and in all places it brought forth the conviction that beyond the realm of our senses exists something invisible, infinite, superhuman, divine, the essential trait of the religious, that could hardly be an aberration, because one could say in the same mould of thought that language or logic is an aberration. In any case, no sufficient explanation has ever been given 'how it happens that all humans from the beginning of the world to our days had slipped into insanity in this one point only while in all other respects were doubtless of a healthy mind'.[17] Any impartial person will understand universal religiosity as a psychological necessity, as a universal human disposition – irrespective of the objectivity of the infinite that presupposes it. Even those who think that religion began with the most apathetic fetishism cannot tell us why a lump of wood, a stone, or even the sky, the sun, lightning and thunder, etc., were revered as divine if there had not existed at least a dark and profoundly veiled concept of God, which was brought in contact with noticeable items. This means the existence of a concept of God is the presupposition of religion even on its lowest grade. The concept of God could, of course, not have originated in the human disposition for religion. The human capacity for religion made the mind only more or less aware of it; the concept has to be rather an original and intrinsic presence of God in Man himself, something of God woven into the human being, as already the mightiest philosopher of religion of all times has explained to the learned Athenians (Acts 17.22ff.).

Analogous to language, natural religion is a vessel for Christianity to take root. However, the point of contact for communicating the gospel would be wanting for people without religion; but as far as we know no such people exist. There are, of course, tribes one has to research intensively to detect at least meagre remains of religiosity but they were found everywhere where a profound search was undertaken. A further twist is given by the assertion of 'scholarship', so rich in axioms, that the very tribes showing the [allegedly] lowest level of religion also represent its original state, an assumption connected with another anthropological dogma, that the so-called primitive people (*Naturvölker*) once and for all times remained stereotyped so that they could be studied as Primal Man (*Urmenschen*) by the scholarship of our century. But history provides irrefutable data that civilization as well as religion passed through depravation processes. Any known people's religion, the sacred books of which we could verify, deteriorated, degraded and ever further degenerated if no reformation took place. Should one not expect even more such depravation among religions without sacred writings by which reformation efforts could be established? Religiously the lowliest people do not represent the primeval religious human type but religiously degenerated people who can never rise again by their own efforts. However depraved they may be, their natural religious capacity has nowhere been completely destroyed.

All peoples have a name for the godhead; often it needed time to discover it, and it is no proof that the name does not exist, much less that it never existed, if it has not yet been found among certain tribes. In many instances missionaries discovered the name for god among older, almost forgotten, verbiages after having lived with a population for decades. The names for God of uncivilized tribes as well as the Chinese and Hindus[18] often refer to concepts which are hardly adequate for the Christian concept of God; but they always qualify for mediation to speak of the Father of Our Lord Jesus Christ, who is the Father of us All; however long the transformation of God-concepts needs to be accomplished, the process itself is definitely possible. In reality mainly deities and spirits dominate heathen religions instead of the divinity being driven into the background; but there are always to be found presentiments, necessities for and links to the divine that can be given the direction to the one living God. Wherever a belief in the supernatural exists, even in an aberrated superstition, bridges can be built to the Christian faith. Everywhere in the world we find people praying, and wherever a human turns to praying before invisible forces we will find threads into the Lord's Prayer. In brief: *mutatis mutandis* this applies to the barbarians as to the Hellenes, 'that God is not removed from any of them', 'that they live in Him, stir and exist', that they pay homage 'to an unknown God' whom they do not know, that they are of the kind 'to search for Him so that they might perceive and find Him'. For these reasons we find everywhere a point of connection and a vessel for the revelation of God in Christ, but it needs much love, understanding, perspicacity, patience and time to discover both of them everywhere.

Christianity does not only teach about God but also about conciliation, and the comprehension of both is preceded not only by a general awareness of God but also by that of guilt. There can be no doubts that the entire modern world is under the law ($\upsilon\pi o\delta\iota\kappa o\varsigma\ \tau\omega\ \theta\epsilon\omega$) as the entire world of antiquity has been. Sinning is a common human condition shared by everyone from the rudest to the most educated peoples without distinction, however multifarious its manifestations and shadings may be. Chinese and Negroes, Hindus and servants of fetishes, all come under the sin and justification of God. The philosophically educated Brahmins as much as the illiterate 'savages' (*Wilde*), the proud Mandarins as the despised Coolies, the subtle protectors of all animal life as base cannibals – they all need deliverance from sin. And as common as the guilt is, is also the need of redemption. Nothing can be said against this objective reality. However, one question remains: Is there a subjective want of redemption, a sense of guilt?

It almost seems that we have to deny this question. The most immoral matters occur within the tribes on the lowest gradation of civilization as well as in civilized heathen nations, and nobody seems to be aware of their abomination. Leaving aside cannibalism, we should be reminded of infanticide, common sexual excesses, the many gruesome acts of vengeance and inhuman cruelties, falsehood and similar things. More surprisingly, many of the social ills that are literally breeding grounds of injustice, such as polygamy, wife buying, child marriage, slavery, or caste system, are not seen as abuse or hardship even by those suffering from them ...

The 'Apostle of the Heathens' [Paul] had been faced with a similar situation in his times. What gave him the courage ... to believe in the possible comprehension of atonement that he offered to Jews and heathens? It was the law that both knew; with the Jews the revealed law, and the natural law that the heathens had buried in their hearts (Rom. 2.12–15). Both were transgressors of law but had a conscience that agreed with the demands of law, a profound moral judgement that made them aware of the evil in its meaning of guilt. The objective adherence to God for judgement is based on this constellation, the submission to the Last Judgement (Rom. 2.12, 16), but also the possibility of a personal conviction of sin. The λογισμοι [conceptual constituents] of conscience agree with the law by an inner dialogue, in its accusing or defending thoughts. Conscience does not create the law, it is only testimony of that which is laid down in the heart, as the witness of whether we have done right or wrong. But even where, as with the heathens, no revealed law exists, and Man is only dependent on φυσις [Nature], he does not escape accountability and punishment. However, with religious darkening a moral decline set in (Rom. 1.21ff.), and this led by psychological necessity to the clouding of conscience. Paul is not of the opinion that all the abominable things by which he characterizes the moral condition of the educated heathen world of his days (Rom. 1.24ff.) had everywhere been vices of a conscious mind; in the muddled and sleepy conscience an authority existed for recognizing them as sin and judging them as guilt-worthy. Even if the letter of the law engraved in the heart was almost wiped out, the heathen learnt the positive [form of] law; hence it was feasible to convict him as perpetrator since it is the nature of conscience to agree with the law of God. Further, if one takes the words 'they are a law to themselves' in the meaning of civil laws – that they bestowed on themselves and from which the public moral judgement derived – there, too, is a point of contact for the awareness of what is right and wrong.

One question now arises: Do all peoples have what one calls a conscience? Again, materialistic scholarship will immediately give a negative answer. Up until now it seems that not all languages have a term for conscience; but it would be absurd to say that the ancient Indians did not have a conscience or did not know what conscience meant just because, for example, Sanskrit has no term for συνειδησις.[19] Max Müller established that the Sanskrit word root *hri* = to glow, to blush, to be ashamed, had been the expression for awareness of right and wrong, and that originally with the Germanic tribes the word root *skam* or *kam* = to cover, to cover the face to hide blushing or to hide from the penetrating glance of the judge, had the same meaning before our term *Gewissen* (conscience) rendered the Latin *conscientia*. He also claims that in any language with terms for blushing, or to be ashamed, the notion of conscience is present.[20] At any rate the concept of conscience is universal. Since in modern India by and large the caste system moulds judgements of morals, casteless people claim to be outside of its moral ambience. Nevertheless, according to their feeling they live in a world of moral consequences; for them good or bad is a direct continuation of good and bad deeds, meaning that they actually have an awareness of good and bad and also know whether they have done right or wrong.

Peoples have different ideas of what is right and wrong, but in general the idea of moral right and wrong exists, and the awareness that somebody does one or the other is a common property of humankind. Not only the Chinese have a comparatively high morality; as Negroes and [American] Indians said, when explained to them, they already had known the five moral Commandments of the 'Second Table' (*Zweite Tafel*) of the Law for a long time. Lying is said to be a habit incarnate of the Hindus, but they are ashamed when detected in a lie since they are aware of doing something wrong. Many so-called savages think deceit, theft, even murder are wrong-doings between friends and tribal partners and admit that punishment is justified for those deeds of violence, which are, however, not wrong when committed against enemies and hence the European.[21] 'Our hearts tell us that we are wicked and not on the right path' – many missionaries have heard this confession in all variations from the most degenerate heathens. There are no doubts that the moral awareness of many a heathen people of today has sunk low and has become quite dull but it is nowhere obliterated, and it is possible to awaken it everywhere, to revive the faded engraving of the natural law that is written into their hearts. Being a genuine aspect of conscience to agree with the positive laws of God when held up to him, it will be possible everywhere, as slowly as it may proceed, to convince Man: you are under the judgement of God and you need your Redeemer.

Notes

1 T. Waitz, 1859, *Anthropologie der Naturvölker*, Leipzig, vol. 1, p. 477.

2 F. Ratzel, 1885, *Völkerkunde*, Leipzig, vol. 1, p. 4.

3 O. Peschel, 1874, *Völkerkunde*, Leipzig, p. 22.

4 F. M. Müller, 1880, *Vorlesungen über den Ursprung und die Entwicklung der Religion* (German trans.), Straßburg, p. 78. Ratzel, *Völkerkunde*, p. 22: 'Not only Haeckel's Alali fell into oblivion, a long time ago, so did all those of wanting speech or babbling who followed him. The differences of the organizational level of modern languages are

small.' [Note: *Alalus* (cf. Greek. *a-laleô*) was used by Haeckel to conceptualize almost speechless, prehistoric 'ape-like man', cf., e.g., his *The Evolution of Man* (English trans.), London, 1883, vol. 2, pp. 181–2; 189. – trans.]

5 Just to mention in passing, it is wrong to assume that the most educated people also have the most developed language. For instance, Chinese comprises only 450 monosyllables, increasing to 1,203 by different 'tones' and remaining unchanged, and it is astonishing that one can express everything by the means of word combinations, etc. But the fact remains that the ancient Chinese culture has a comparatively poor language while, for instance, the language of the Fuegians has a vocabulary of some 32,430 words (G. Bové, 1883, *Patagonia, Terra del Fuoco: mari Australi*, Genoa, pt. 1; Müller, 1890, *Natürliche Religion* (German trans.), Leipzig, p. 80). [It seems that Warneck displays a lack of understanding of the Chinese language, as despite the limited 'sound system' of the language, many words (distinguished in the written script) are conveyed by the same sound in a particular tone – generally distinguished by context in spoken Chinese – ed.]

6 *Natürliche Religion*, p. 80.

7 [Warneck, ed.,] *Allgemeine Missions-Zeitschrift* 18 (1891), pp. 322ff.: 'Was hat die gegenwärtige Mission für die Sprachwissenschaft geleistet? I. Die Bibelübersetzungen seitens der Missionare'; 8 (1881), p. 185: 'Aus der Studierstube eines Bibelübersetzers'; and 15 (1888), p. 353: 'Einige Gedanken über missionarische Bibelübersetzung'.

8 [This does not refer to Melanesia, but to Australian Aboriginals in Queeensland and Victoria; cf. C. Buchner, 'Der gegenwärtige Stand der Mission der evangelischen Brüdergemeine', *Allgemeine Missions-Zeitschrift* 23 (1896), p. 216; – trans.]

9 Müller, *Natürliche Religion*, lect. 14: 'Sprache und Denken'.

10 There might be some missioners who should be reproached for being to some extent dogmatic preachers; however, by and large, the reproach is unfounded. After all, their usage of vernacular languages ensures that they do not lose their way into dogmatic abstractions.

11 [Warneck refers here to the oldest German mission (founded in 1732), which quickly internationalized – trans.]

12 Müller, *Ursprung und Entwicklung der Religion*, p. 88; idem, *Natürliche Religion*, p. 78. The acknowledgement of the missionaries' merits for the study of religion by this scholar, which is repeated in various of his writings, is sufficient refutation of the contempt with which G. G. Roskoff likes to speak of missionaries in his *Religionswesen der rohesten Naturvölker*, Leipzig, 1880. It should be admitted that the earlier, especially Catholic, missionaries who he particularly mentions have given unfounded information of the religious, respectively non-religious, state of heathen tribes, because of their dogmatic bias. But it would have been his duty to adjust his opinion with reference to the missionaries of our days. Although we cannot accept his principal theological views, the cited book is, however, a valuable monograph which refutes the old prejudice of the existence of peoples without religion by such a large body of data that the old bias can be considered as buried.

13 C. P. Tiele, 1880, *Kompendium der Religionsgeschichte*, Berlin, p. 8.

14 Peschel, *Völkerkunde*, pp. 137, 273. Ratzel, *Völkerkunde*, p. 31. Comprehensive documentation in *Allgemeine Missions-Zeitschrift* 7 (1880), p. 339: 'Gibt es religionslose Völker?' O. Zöckler, 1875, *Das Kreuz Christi*, Gütersloh, Beilage V, p. 417, and idem, 1880, *Die Lehre vom Urstand*, Gütersloh, p. 191. On the biased opinions that are important in deciding this question, see Müller, *Natürliche Religion*, p. 83.

15 As in our opinion proven by Max Müller (*Ursprung und Entwicklung*, 58), it could not have been fetishism. *Allgemeine Missions-Zeitschrift* 6 (1879), p. 219: 'Ist Fetischismus eine ursprüngliche Form der Religion?'; and 7 (1880), p. 337: 'Die Urgestalt der

Religion'. There is no doubt in my mind that the more thorough the research of religions done in connection with linguistics, the more reliable the undivided God-knowledge that will emerge as result of scholarly expertise.

16 V. von Strauß, 1879, *Essays zur allgemeinen Religionswissenschaft*, Heidelberg, p. 15. This scholar also intercedes with good reasons and based on solid documents against the theory, persisting contrary to facts, of upward development of religion, yet for its primal monotheistic character, see pp. 20ff., 215ff.

17 Müller, *Ursprung und Entwicklung*, p. 194.

18 *Allgemeine Missions-Zeitschrift* 11 (1884): 106: 'Die Termquestion in China'; ibid. 18 (1891): 269: 'Der Gottesbegriff bei den Tamulen'.

19 The Tamil language does not have such a term either. Missionary G. Stosch (*Allgemeine Missions-Zeitschrift* 18 (1891), p. 343) noted that the Tamil language for the learned adopted the Sanskrit word *anuseidanniam* which means 'being privy to' but in the pure intellectual rather than a moral sense, hence it is not equivalent to our term 'conscience' ...

20 *Natürliche Religion*, p. 172. When he was well acquainted with people and language, missionary W. Gill found on the Hervey Islands (Hawai'i) that the term turning yellow (because of shame) was used to express conscience. I do not doubt that further research among most morally debased peoples will detect similar terms for conscience.

21 Europeans, by their own abominable behaviour, often enough blurred the moral stance of 'savages', and then scholars took their distorted conscience as natural when in fact it was a native behaviour arising from bad contact situations.

Source: Original translation by Friedegard Tomasetti from Gustav Warneck, 1897, *Evangelische Missionslehre: Ein missionstheoretischer Versuch*, vol. 1: *Die Begründung der Sendung*, Gotha: Friedrich Andreas Perthes, 2nd edn, extracts from chapter 15, pp. 285–99.

14

New Religious Movements

PAUL HEDGES

Introduction

Often ignored or side-lined (if not excluded outright) in discussions of the theology of religion and interfaith dialogue meetings, the various New Religious Movements (NRMs) are nevertheless an important element in many contexts. For instance, representatives of NRMs make up, quite often, the second or third largest religious community on many western university campuses and hold a significant appeal to many young people, especially in westernized societies. However, dialogue with them is complicated by many factors, including: (1) what is classed as an NRM is liable to considerable (mis)interpretation, for instance (in the West) many Eastern faiths are classed as NRMS, e.g. the International Society of Krishna Consciousness (ISKCON) and Sokka Gakkai International (SGI), despite both belonging to medieval lineages with ancient roots; (2) many NRMs are seen as belonging to superstitious, or even diabolical, sectors of belief and practice, and have frequently been branded by the term 'cult' (used in the pejorative sense), including mainstream Eastern faiths (e.g. ISKCON), and such traditions as Wicca; (3) many faiths will often not dialogue with groups they consider schismatic or heretical to their own – the Jehovah's Witnesses and Unification Church being key cases for Christians.[1] However, in recent years, a more constructive approach to NRMs can be found in various churches.[2]

Avoiding the first problem, at least, our two papers look at the New Age. While the term 'New Age' is now somewhat passé[3] the issues and questions raised, and the approach taken, raise many issues pertinent to other NRMs, especially what may be termed 'alternative spiritualities'. The first takes a very positive, though not uncritical, view of the movement. The author, Bruce Epperly, a Protestant minister, and alternative medicine practitioner, has taught at seminaries and universities, where he found students' encounter with the New Age striking and something from which Christians could learn. However, David Millikan, author of our second piece, a Protestant minister and broadcaster, takes a less positive approach, though he is not outright dismissive of the New Age. In the article from which our extract comes he seeks to sum up what the New Age is, and where it comes from, which he sees as a quest for meaning and spiritual values in life. Our extract is the final part of this, where he contemplates the notion of reincarnation and the

Christian response, and suggests that there is something of value in the New Age though he is quite polemical and dismissive of much of its ideology. Both approaches have much in common, they both find the New Age flawed, and the Christian approach the way to truth; however, they express this in somewhat different ways.

Notes

1 The Bahais and Ahmadiyya Muslims being key cases for Islam.

2 This includes the Roman Catholic Church as well as various Protestant groups; the Orthodox have been, on the whole, less open (for a good overview of the variations between denominations in this respect, see John Saliba, 1999, *Christian Responses to the New Age Movement: A Critical Assessment*, London: Geoffrey Chapman). It is perhaps the Roman Catholic Church that has released the most significant documents on dialogue with NRMs, and the justification for the exclusive use of Protestant works here is that these are readily available online: see, for instance, Cardinal Arinze's 'The Challenge of the Sects or New Religious Movements: A Pastoral Approach' (1991), posted at: http://www.cesnur.org/2004/arinze_en.htm; and from the Pontifical Council for Interreligious Dialogue, 2003, '*Jesus Christ the Bearer of the Water of Life: A Christian Reflection on the 'New Age'*, Vatican City: Vatican, posted at: http://www.vatican.va/roman_curia/pontifical_councils/interelg/documents/rc_pc_interelg_doc_20030203_new-age_en.html'.

3 There are fewer people these days who align themselves to what would be termed the 'New Age' movement, and, indeed, there has been something of a backlash against what is seen as its idealized spirituality; however, it is closely linked into what would be more broadly termed 'alternative spiritualities', which would include the growing pagan movements among other things.

Crystal and Cross

BRUCE EPPERLY

Primary Symbols

A primary symbol of the new age is the crystal. In its various shapes and colors, the crystal symbolizes for many new agers the intensified energy of spiritual transformation being released in our time.

For Christians, the cross has also been the symbol of the new age, the age of salvation initiated by the life, death, and resurrection of Jesus Christ. To Christians, the cross has been the primary symbol of God's transforming power in the midst of human sin and brokenness. By sharing in the power of the cross, we become citizens of a new world in which the alienation of humans with each other, the nonhuman world, and God has been overcome.

As I look across my own university congregation as well as the wider Christian community, I find many persons joining the crystal and the cross in their jewellery as well as in their personal spirituality. But, for the most part, the marriage of the cross and the crystal has been superficial and problematic. Few Christians have been able to integrate the insights of their faith with the new energies they have found through their participation in the new age movement. They have received little help from their pastors, who often evidence a shocking ignorance, if not antipathy, toward one of the most significant spiritual revolutions of our time. Their new age teachers have revealed an equally naive understanding of Christianity or have implied, in contrast to biblical spirituality, that authentic Christianity is more akin to Hindu mysticism than Hebraic world affirmation.

Thoughtful Christians and new agers alike ask, 'Must we choose between the crystal and the cross, between the insights of the new age movement and good news of Christian faith?' Throughout this book, I have contended that mainstream Christianity and the new age movement will both benefit from creative and honest dialogue. In contrast to fundamentalists who see the new age movement as a diabolical threat to orthodox Christianity, I believe that the new age movement is a reminder – like the influx of Asian religions in the 1960s and 1970s – that Christians must reclaim and revive their own spiritual and metaphysical roots. Beneath its varied forms, the new age movement points to the hope of a new world of spiritual transformation and personal healing in contrast to our current world of polarization, ecological destruction, and spiritual disease.

Ultimately, the Christian response to the new age movement is grounded in our understanding of Christ and salvation. On the one hand, Christians must not limit God's grace and revelation solely to the historical Jesus and the sacraments of the church. The light of the world enlightens and inspires every person and is present, in its many disguises, in every quest for truth. While Christians must affirm that Christ is of universal significance and is responsive to each person's need, we must equally remember that Christianity as a religious tradition is only one of many religious options within our global village. God may have sheep in other pastures (John 10:16).

On the other hand, Christians must not succumb to a relativism that suggests that Christ is only meaningful to those persons born within the sphere of the Christian tradition or Western culture. Further, Christians must avoid creating a Christian ghetto from which we as 'resident aliens' view a world of unbelief.[1] Today, as in every century in Christian history, we must avoid the pitfalls of absolutism and relativism in order to be faithful to Christ and sensitive to the needs of God's children. While our 'treasure' is in 'earthen vessels' and is imperfect and relative, the reality behind this treasure is universal and ultimate. The Christ, incarnate in Jesus of Nazareth, is the animating principle of all things and the source of all truths, even when the name of Jesus is unspoken or unknown. While Christians must proclaim that Jesus of Nazareth is the ultimate embodiment of God in the world, Christians must equally affirm that Christ is present in every quest for salvation and healing, including the authentic streams of spirituality of the new age movement.

Faithfulness to Christ involves embracing new and unexpected experiences of God as well as fidelity to the ancient expressions of faith. As the followers of Martin Luther and Ignatius of Loyola discovered, obedience to God involves the willingness to be transformed and go beyond the insights of the reformers themselves; the reformation must always continue even when it challenges old certainties. Just as Christianity was transformed by its encounters with Greek thought, the renaissance, modern science, biblical criticism, and, more recently, feminism, multiculturalism, and religious pluralism, so it now must allow itself to grow and be renewed by its encounter with the new age movement. Its openness to growth is not a witness to compromise or doubt but to the depth of its faith in the Christ who 'makes all things new.' When Christians critically and prayerfully embrace the insights of the new age movement, it is out of faithfulness to Christ and our commitment to the Christian vision of reality and human existence.

As Christians encounter the new age movement, they must be willing to explore their faith experientially as well as doctrinally. The truths of the faith must become living words rather than dead letters. Through the use of guided imaging, body prayer, meditation, and Ignatian spirituality, mainstream Christians are challenged to rediscover the Bible as a living word, addressed to the contemporary spiritual, political, and social situation in which they live. The inner journey of spiritual illumination must accompany the outer journey of liberating action. In so doing, they will experience the meaning of divine revelation and insight in every aspect of life: in worship, prayer, political action, and Scripture study as well as in family life, employment, and recreation. Christians must be willing to allow the gospel to become their own personal story and not a tired witness to a faith long dead.

As mainstream Christians seek to understand their faith in the context of pluralistic culture and the global village, they are challenged to retrace the steps of the first Christians. In the spirit of the Acts of the Apostles, the church is called upon to be a beacon of light, a place where healing, spirituality, justice, and personal transformation are sought, expected, and experienced. Today's church will reveal its unique mission not by isolating itself in a spiritual ghetto or condemning all who differ from it, but by its willingness to see the movements of the one Spirit within the diversity of human experience. Today's new age movement is a breath of the Spirit calling a fatigued and fearful church to remember its vital past, imagine its glorious future, and launch out into the strong winds of the Spirit.

However, in this age of pluralism, mainstream Christians must not shrink from sharing their faith with persons within the new age movement even as they listen to new age accounts of spiritual transformation. Mainstream

Christianity has much to offer the new age movement. Most important, mainstream Christianity offers the positive and life-affirming vision of the Christian faith. From my participation in many new age groups and conversation with many persons in the new age movement, I have discovered that most new agers are exiles and refugees from some form of rigid, lifeless, or doctrinally exclusive Christianity. Many complain of Sunday School and catechism classes that emphasized guilt rather than grace, and obedience rather than experience. Others found no room for their questions and struggles within the cramped confines of fundamentalist churches. Still others found the mainstream church unable to deal with issues of healing, death, and spirituality.

Tragically, the only god many persons have found in Christianity is a god they can neither love nor believe in. Yet, they still seek after God. Today, Christians must clearly proclaim that the tribal god of vengeance is not our God, but a perversion of deeper truths of divine love and justice. We must invite persons to look at Christian faith as if for the first time.

The church, along with the political and economic institutions of the northern hemisphere and western world, has midwifed destruction as well as creation, and now it must be transformed. Like General Motors, IBM, and other industrial giants, the church has often failed to respond to the novel movements and vital energies emerging in our time. It, like many established institutions, has forgotten the ultimate source of its spiritual energy and lost the vision of its true mission. The energies of transformation are moving – through crystal, computer chip, quality circle, and the human spirit. But they are also moving through the way of the cross. The church of today and tomorrow must be reborn – and its rebirth will come from its embrace and transformation of these new and challenging energies.

Today's church has the opportunity of becoming both the womb and the midwife for the great spiritual changes of our time. Apart from the guidance, structure, and historical tradition of the church, these ungrounded creative energies may collapse into chaos. Just as the new age is a breath of the Spirit, the church is also a revelation of the Spirit of God in our time. Today, the church cannot travel alone. It must open its doors to the winds of the spirit in all its varied forms and open its arms, heart, and mind to all those who seek to travel by the spirit embodied in Christ.

During a recent visit to Southern California, I had the opportunity to tour the Crystal Cathedral in Garden Grove. As I jogged at sunrise through the grounds of this monument to 'possibility thinking,' I was fascinated by a crystal cross that stands in the shadow of the Cathedral. Although its pastor, Robert Schuller, is hardly an adherent of new age theology and probably is unaware of the purported power of crystals, the image of a cathedral and a cross in crystal form represents the challenge Christians face today. It represents my own quest for a vital Christianity for this new age. We must embrace and affirm the vital energies of the new age as we discover the beauty of the crystal in all its many facets. But, as we embrace these energies, we must also transform them and mold them into the shape of a cross. In faithfulness to the one who promises a 'new heaven and a new earth,' we must lift high the cross and treasure the crystal as we journey together toward God's new-age.

Note

1 Stanley Hauerwas and William Willimon, *Resident Aliens* (Nashville: Abingdon, 1990).

Source: Bruce Epperly, 1996, *Crystal and Cross: Christians and New Age in Creative Dialogue,* Mystic, CT: Twenty-Third Publications, pp. 183–4, 185–7, 189–90.

Christians and Reincarnation

DAVID MILLIKAN

Finally, there is an almost universal commitment to reincarnation in the New Age. In fact it is difficult to find anyone writing on the New Age who does not believe in this. It is one of the philosophical success stories of the last 100 years. The idea of reincarnation has gone from a minority and somewhat quirky idea to one that can be said to be mainstream. A recent survey in the United States showed that more than 40 per cent of Americans now believe in reincarnation in some form or other. But we need to ask what is actually being said here.

In its broadest sense, reincarnation is the belief that this life is not the only time we have been on earth. It normally asserts that there is a vast number of lives which run into an eternal progression into the future. But there is not an entire agreement about what is meant by this. Most of the references I have seen in New Age literature have a very literal view of the relationship of past and future lives to the person we are now. Past lives therapy, which is popular at the moment, is based on the belief that the essence which defines our personality exists separate from the body we have now. 'Same'[1] tells us: 'Each of us is a spirit, choosing to come to Earth and manifest here to experience all that life can gives us ... .' If we are a spirit then we can come and go in this life according to the character of the life we have lived. According to this literal view of reincarnation the process is centred on the individual and is part of some sort of evolution into a higher form of realisation. For example, Barry Long:[2] 'The whole point of the living, dying and reincarnating process is to imbue man with an ever deepening sense of life. Through many, many lives of pain and pleasure each man grows in understanding and ability to convert his natural deep red (plane) emotional life into lighter and lighter shades or frequencies approaching the finest pinks – love in the world.'

The points of disagreement are over whether reincarnation ever ends, and the extent to which we continue as self-conscious entities through the vast number of other lives. Many people today take comfort from knowing that they were someone in a past life. There seems to be a competition to see who can find the most colourful past self, with American Indian chiefs and Egyptian princesses featuring well. People claim to be able to remember who they were and even come to some understanding of the legacy that the former life has passed on to them. That is a very specific contact from one life to another. It is certainly very different from the Buddhist concept.

Barry Long: 'The unbearable truth, which few are allowed to realise without going mad, is that every man is fighting or trying to live through his nature in order to make a better or more meaningful life for himself and the rest of humanity next time on earth ... each life is lived solely for the next life on earth.'

I have also noted a strong commitment [among New Agers] to the idea that Christianity is compatible with the belief in reincarnation. It is common to hear people say, 'reincarnation was part of early Christian belief but the church did away with it'. I have also heard the fanciful view that there are documents hidden in the Vatican which support the belief in reincarnation. Baghwan Rajneesh sums up the view of many about the relationship between Christianity and reincarnation: 'Jesus knew perfectly well about reincarnation. There are indirect hints spread all over the gospels. Just the other day I was quoting Jesus: "I am before Abraham was." And Jesus says, "I will be coming back." And there are a thousand and one indirect references to reincarnation. He knew perfectly well, but there is some other reason he did not talk about it, why he did not preach it.'

But this is not the case. The actual words of Jesus quoted in the New Testament are 'Before Abraham was I am'. It is not a statement by Jesus concerning any former life on this earth. It was a remark made in the midst of a controversy with Jewish theologians who wanted to know what right he had to gather the crowds around him and teach them things that were in conflict with orthodox religion.

As far as they are concerned, he was a nobody of dubious birth, who came from an obscure town in the country. They were asking him about his authority to teach. They were able to point to their own line of thinking, going back unbroken to Abraham. But Jesus went beyond that by saying, 'Before Abraham was I am'. They responded to his answer as a blasphemy, because it implied that he was in some sense on the same level as God. In fact they attempted to stone him.

It was not a statement that supports reincarnation. It says nothing about any former lives on this earth nor does it suggest anything about lives in the future, and nowhere in the New Testament, or any of the early church records is there any interest in the controversy over reincarnation. In fact there are significant philosophical differences between the belief in reincarnation and the teachings of Christianity.[3]

What is attractive about the idea of reincarnation is that it explains the difficulties and frustrations we experience in this life as an inheritance from a former life. It also relieves us of the harshness of the Christian view that we have only one life and what we do with that life has eternal consequences. That is a hard vision and the idea that we come back and have another go is appealing. But it does have a downside, which the Baghwan recognised. 'Why do you think we Indians have been so passive and accepting of suffering? Why do you think we Indians can walk past when they see someone in pain? It is because of the reincarnation ... it teaches that the urgency to do something about this world is put off by the possibility that there will be other worlds that follow.'

Reincarnation also provides a temptation for New Age people to look at the suffering of other people – the victims of famine in Africa, for example – and say it is the product of Karma. Indeed, I have heard it argued that we should not do anything to interfere with their situation, because we would be disturbing the requirements put upon them from a former life. This amounts to abandoning the moral judgements we make about ourselves and the world to the point that we judge nothing at all. 'Same', for example, tells us, 'Man does not need to be forgiven for sins, for those things called sins come from the sleeping souls.' At one level it would be nice to be relieved from the burden that this vision offers. But I believe that we lose an essential part of our glory as human beings when we relinquish the right to moral indignation.

Notes

1 I have no details of who (what?) 'Same' is, but Millikan uses this source on a number of occasions (ed.).

2 Barry Long (1926–2003) was a noted New Age teacher/guru/spiritual guide, and information on him can be found on a dedicated website: http://www.barrylong.org/, though some consider him a money-making charlatan (ed.).

3 Millikan here ignores the fact that we know reincarnation was part of at least North African Christianity for several centuries before being suppressed by church councils, and was famously discussed by the influential church father Origen, who many believe accepted the notion. The belief persisted in various minority Christian movements such as the Albigenses and Cathars until at least the Middle Ages, when they were violently suppressed (ed.).

Source: David Millikan, 1991, 'Religion and the New Age', St Mark's Review 144 (Summer), pp. 6–9, extracts cited from pp. 8–9 (the article also forms part of his book, with Nevill Drury, 1991, Worlds Apart: Christianity and the New Age, Sydney: ABC Enterprises).

Part Three

OTHER FAITH TRADITIONS RESPOND TO CHRISTIANITY

15

Abrahamic Faith Traditions Respond to Christianity

ALAN RACE

Introduction

Much serious interreligious dialogue spends a great deal of time on images of the other that come to us from history, especially when these images contain misrepresentation and stereotyping. Given the historic 'sibling rivalry' between people of the Abrahamic traditions it may be that the misrepresentation and stereotyping is hardest to overcome. The following two contributions demonstrate how historical legacies require not only painstaking truth-telling but also new approaches to the authenticity and identity of the sibling.

Dr Mahmut Aydin is Professor in the History of Religions and Interreligious Dialogue at the University of Ondokuz Mayis in Turkey. His intellectual work has concentrated on relations between Christianity and Islam and his book, *Modern Western Christian Theological Understandings of Muslims Since the Second Vatican Council*, brings the theological discussion of Christian wrestling with Islamic identity and faithfulness very much into the present. His essay for this Reader is a new contribution and builds on his earlier work. He considers how Christian thought is struggling to come to terms with recognizing both the authentic prophethood of Muhammad and the divine origins of the Qur'an, and he does this through the eyes of a number of well-known western scholars who are sympathetic to Islam. The task is of course unfinished but Aydin's essay provides a window onto ways forward.

Dr Marc Saperstein is principal of Leo Baeck College, London. Formerly he held prestigious positions at three American Universities: as Charles E. Smith Professor of Jewish History and Director of the Program in Judaic Studies at the George Washington University in Washington DC (1997–2006), Gloria M. Goldstein Professor of Jewish History and Thought at Washington University in St Louis (1986–97), and Lecturer, Assistant and Associate Professor of Jewish Studies at Harvard Divinity School (1977–86). He is a scholar of Jewish history, literature and preaching. The book from which this extract has been produced examines four significant moments in the history of Christian–Jewish relations, moments that have yielded a legacy of skewed negativity. Saperstein argues that attending to these negativities can pave the way for greater mutual responsibility in the future.

Western Christian Views of Islam: a Muslim Response

MAHMUT AYDIN

Introduction

When we examine deeply western perceptions of Islam and Muslims we can say that there are two main attitudes among westerners. The first view is of clash and confrontation. Its roots go back to the Christian rejection of Islam as a religion in the eighth century, when Islam first arose and was quickly perceived to be a theological and political threat to the Christian world. Supporters of this view have seen Islam as a major challenge to Christianity from the outset. The second view is that of coexistence and accommodation which has become a major alternative only after the second half of the twentieth century, although it has significant historical precedents in the examples of Nicolas of Cusa, Thomas Carlyle, Goethe, Emmanuel Swedenborg, Louis Massignon and other like-minded intellectuals. Advocates of this view consider Islam to be a sister religion and a part of Abrahamic tradition. These views demonstrate the possibility of coexistence with Muslims without giving away any concessions from the spirit of Christianity.

This chapter examines the status of the Qur'an and the Prophet Muhammad in the light of recent Christian Islamicists and renowned theologians who have contributed to the rapprochement between Christians and Muslims by adopting the view of coexistence and accommodation with Muslims.

The Status of the Qur'an

As is well known, the Qur'an stands at the centre of Muslim faith and religious experience and has shaped Muslim civilization from its advent to our modern day. For a committed Muslim it represents the Word of God as revealed or 'sent down' to the Prophet Muhammad. Until recently this important element of Muslim faith had been perceived by Christians as the product of the events of the life of the Prophet Muhammad in response to particular needs within his own community and not as God's revelation to him. After the second half of the twentieth century, this negative and prejudiced attitude towards the Qur'an started to change to a more positive and scholarly understanding. There were a number of reasons for this, such as the increasing number of scholarly and comprehensive studies on Islam, and specifically on the Qur'an in the light of new scientific developments and the increasing Muslim presence among Christians.

My first scholar, Montgomery Watt, as an historian of Islamic history and prolific modern biographer of the Prophet Muhammad, elucidates his views on the status of the Qur'an by maintaining that, as a result of new positive developments in Christian–Muslim dialogue, Christians should cease to think about the Qur'anic revelation either as the product of the Prophet Muhammad's own experience,[1] or as 'a mere hotch-potch of biblical material brought together by Muhammad himself',[2] or by discarding its originality.

Watt regards the Qur'an 'as a product of divine initiative and therefore revelation'.[3] Further, in his *Islam and Christianity Today*, he reaches the conclusion that the Qur'an is true and from God, since on the basis of the Qur'anic message 'a religious community developed, claiming to serve God, numbering some thousands in Muhammad's lifetime, and now having several hundred million members. The quality of life in this community has been on the whole satisfactory for the members. Many men and women in this community have attained to saintliness of life, and countless ordinary people have been enabled to live decent and moderately happy lives in difficult circumstances. These points lead to the conclusion that the view of reality presented in the Qur'an is true and from God.'[4]

In *Islamic Fundamentalism and Modernity*, Watt underlines that he has no objection to the Muslim belief that the Qur'an came to the Prophet Muhammad from God. What he objects to is the belief that there is no human element in the Qur'an.[5] In one of his recent essays he clarifies his position by indicating that 'I always took the view contrary to most previous scholars of Islam – that the Qur'an was not something Muhammad had consciously produced.'[6]

My second scholar is the Canadian historian of religion Wilfred Cantwell Smith. As an ordained Presbyterian minister Smith develops his understanding of the Qur'an by taking into consideration the historical effect of the Qur'anic message on its followers, since, according to him, what the Qur'an means in itself by reference only to the circumstances of its origin is hardly a relevant question today. More important is what the Qur'an has meant to millions of Muslims over each succeeding century and today.

Within this phenomenological approach, Smith asks, 'Is the Qur'an the Word of God?' Smith, first of all, tries to explain the status of the Qur'an by asking the following: 'Is the Qur'an the word of God?', and points out that both Muslims and non-Muslims answered this question as either 'Yes' or 'No' in the past and also in our modern day without asking and studying it.[7] He stresses that these two different answers can be regarded as prejudgements, since Muslims have insisted that the Qur'an is the *verbatim* speech of God without reading and studying it but by believing it to be so, and in the same way Christians have declared that it is not the Word of God without studying it, but assessing it according to their own predetermined understanding of revelation.[8]

In his *Towards a World Theology*, Smith replaces the above question with a different one: 'Has God spoken to Muslims through the Qur'an across the centuries?'[9] Later on he has clarified this question by stating it as, 'Has the Qur'an been the Word of God for Muslims?', or more concretely, 'Has it served God as a channel for His Word among them?' Then he answers this modified question, after all of his study of Islam and his observations of Muslims among whom he lived for many years, as follows: 'In some cases yes, to varying degrees, in some cases no'.[10] Then he adds that only the following types of people can disagree with him in this answer:

(a) those who are not familiar with Islamic history, and who do not have Muslim friends; (b) those whose prejudices dogmatically rule out any willingness or ability to consider transcendent dimensions of human life and history; (c) those who, although recognizing transcendence and our involvement in it ... are not themselves theist but operate with some other conceptual framework to think and speak of it and yet are unwilling or unable to translate into that framework my theistic vocabulary.[11]

Although there are ambiguities in Smith's answer to the question, 'Is the Qur'an the Word of God?' or 'Has the Qur'an served God as His Word among Muslims?', one cannot conclude that he does not acknowledge the Qur'an as the Word of God. For, in another essay, 'The True Meaning of the Scripture', he makes two suggestions for a better understanding of the Qur'an by non-Muslims. First, he maintains that the Qur'an should be regarded as a separate Scripture, not any other book, before studying it,[12] since, according to him, one cannot appreciate its status and its role in human affairs without taking into account Scripture as a major matter in those affairs, and it is very difficult to develop a scholarly notion of Scripture unless the Qur'an can be acknowledged so.[13] Because of this reason Smith urges non-Muslim students of Islam to accept the Qur'an as a religious document by asking what would its verses convey to them if they acknowledged them as God's words.[14]

Second, Smith argues that if non-Muslims want to understand the status of the Qur'an, they should take into consideration its function in the lives of those whose faith is expressed through it, and then they should acknowledge the Qur'an as Muslims do. He states that:

the Qur'an has meant whatever it has meant, to those who have used or heard it or appropriated it to themselves; that the Qur'an as scripture has meant whatever is has meant to those Muslims for whom it has been scripture. Every passage has meant this or that to so-and-so in such-and-such a place at such-and-such a time ... We leave out nothing that Muslims have seen in it.[15]

Lastly, Smith criticizes western academic intellectuals, who are trying to use the same approaches to studying the Qur'an as are used by New Testament scholars. In this context, he raises three points. First, Smith opposes those western scholars who try to apply a western literary approach to the Qur'an and the Prophet Muhammad by setting up the following analogy between Christianity and Islam. In this analogy, Smith points out that for Muslims the Qur'an is not simply a record of God's revelation, it is that revelation itself. He argues that:

> if one is drawing parallels in terms of the structure of the two religions, what corresponds in the Christian scheme to the Qur'an is not the Bible but the person of Christ – it is Christ who is for Christians the revelation of (from) God. And what corresponds in the Islamic scheme to the Bible (the record of the revelation) is the Tradition (*hadith*) ... the counterpart of the Biblical criticism, which has begun. To look for historical criticism of the Qur'an is rather like looking for a psychoanalysis of Jesus.[16]

Second, Smith argues that those who try to understand the Qur'an by examining the psychology of the Prophet Muhammad, the environment in which he lived, the historical tradition that he inherited and the socio-economic cultural milieu of his followers have never appreciated the true meaning of the Qur'an. For, according to Smith, those scholars have never taken into consideration the religious life of the Muslim *umma* that has been shaped by the Qur'anic message for centuries, and how a great number of Christians and Jews considered the Qur'anic message as a norm for their lifestyle. Third, Smith outlines that those scholars who regarded the Qur'an as a seventh-century Arabian document have failed to discern that the Qur'an is not only a seventh-century Arabian document but 'it is equally a ninth, and a tenth, and a fourteenth, and an eighteenth, and a twentieth-century document'.[17]

My third scholar is Kenneth Cragg, who, as a former Anglican bishop and missionary to Islam, starts his arguments on the status of the Qur'an by defining it as a collection of recorded religious experiences of the Prophet Muhammad.

> The event of the Qur'an lives in an intense personal prophetic vocation. As such it moves with eloquence and poetry in the mystery of speech. It speaks a corporate solidarity, awakening a stirring sense of ethnic identity. These, in their progress, and their climax, are none other than the claim and the vehicle of a total religious demand and surrender.[18]

As can be seen, Cragg, unlike Smith, regards the Qur'an as a religious experience not as a Scripture which came at a particular time and in particular circumstances during the life of the Prophet Muhammad. Hence, he insists that the Qur'an is a document that came from God and his messenger, and its living context was the circumstances in which the prophet lived.[19] Further, he sees the main purpose of the Qur'an as a struggle with idolatry in order to lead pagan Arabs from polytheism to monotheism by claiming that 'the main theme of the Qur'an is to struggle with idolatry; the others are only contributory'.[20] In this sense, he regards the Qur'an 'as a mission to retrieve idolaters to a true worship'.[21]

In explaining the relationship between the Qur'an and the Prophet Muhammad Cragg rejects the traditional Muslim view which considers Muhammad as a mere instrument through which the Qur'an as the *verbatim* speech of God was transmitted. Instead, he argues that to do justice to him as a prophet it is necessary to accept 'a parallel quality of active mind and spirit in both directions of his medial position between the eternal and the temporal, between the word given and the word declared'.[22]

In all his works Cragg tries to prove that the 'matchlessness' and the literary excellence of the Qur'an is very much dependent on the power of poetic language and an active human factor, not on its divinity. For, according to him, the Prophet Muhammad expressed the words of the Qur'an in his own mother tongue by using the daily words of the Arabs. Further, Cragg argues that the language of the Qur'an reflects the living situation of the Arabs at the time of the Prophet Muhammad.[23] It seems that by this argument Cragg implies that the Prophet Muhammad picked the words of the Qur'an from Arabic poetry by using his poetic ability. But, as Watt rightly remarks, most western scholars including Cragg have misunderstood the allusive style of some Qur'anic expressions by assuming those expressions as words of Muhammad.[24]

Cragg further tries to justify his interpretation of the nature of the Qur'an by arguing that the orthodox Muslim view of revelation, 'the celestial dictation', has led to 'a less than lively approach to the sense of the text and to an excessive preoccupation with grammar, parsing syntax'. By doing this he implies that Muslims have underestimated the actual meaning and the content of the Qur'anic message. On the contrary, we would respond that his view that there is a human element and a positive relation between the Qur'an and the Prophet Muhammad's own thinking and feelings, too, does not reduce the value of the Qur'an, but can contribute to its exegesis.[25] Finally, Cragg maintains that Christians can acknowledge the status of the Qur'an as 'the Word of God' in the sense that it is 'the Word *from* God' not in the New Testament sense that 'God was the Word'.[26]

My fourth scholar is Hans Küng, who, as an ecumenical Catholic theologian, prepares the background of his understanding of the status of the Qur'an by pointing out new developments in the process of Christian–Muslim dialogue after the second half of the twentieth century. In all his essays concerning dialogue with Islam, he stresses that after the establishment of Christian–Muslim dialogue, it is no longer possible to return to early Christian polemics about Islam and Muslims.

Küng develops his arguments about the status of the Qur'an as follows. First of all, he articulates the importance of the Qur'an for Muslims by stating that the Qur'an

> has provided Islam with its notion of moral obligation, its external dynamic, its religious depth ... it has also supplied quite specific, lasting doctrines and moral principles: human responsibility before God, social justice, and Muslim solidarity. Thus the Qur'an is the holy book of Islam, and it is such precisely because Muslims understand it as the word that has been written down, the word not of man but of *God*.[27]

After acknowledging that the Qur'an is not only the Prophet Muhammad's but also God's word in this way, Küng moves to answer the following questions: 'What does "God's word" mean? What does revelation mean? Are we to take revelation as something that has fallen straight down from heaven, *inspired or dictated verbatim by God*?' Before answering these questions, he points out the significance of the Qur'an for the Muslim community from the advent of Islam to our modern day, as Smith has done, by stating that the Qur'an

> is not simply a piece of evidence from the seventh century, to be analysed by scholars of religion, but for countless men and women, a twentieth-century document; it is no dead letter, but the most vital text, a source both literary and religious – a book not for study and analysis, but for life and action, and that not only in matters of faith, but of law and morals as well.[28]

Küng argues that instead of discussing the origin of the Qur'an and the Judaeo-Christian influences on it, it would be better in the light of modern exegesis and the challenge of historico-critical method to examine whether the Prophet Muhammad received the Qur'an word by word directly from God or received it as an inspiration and expressed it with his own language.[29] For, according to Küng, whatever result one gets from his/her search of the origin of the Qur'an, 'the important thing is that nowadays the *divine word of the Qur'an* must be understood at the same time ... as the *human word of the Prophet*'.[30] Also, he argues that Christians cannot deny that Muhammad had received revelation, nor can Muslims deny the influence of oral Judaeo-Christian tradition on the Qur'an.[31]

As a strong defender of the application of historico-critical method to both the Bible and the Qur'an, Küng answers the following question: 'To what degree can the Qur'an or the Bible still be revelation and the word of God after a "critical reading"?' by indicating that in the case of the Qur'an or the Bible '*God's word* can be heard only in *human words*; divine revelation is imparted only through human experience and interpretation.'[32] He further clarifies this point in the Qur'anic case by arguing that the Qur'an was revealed as an ideal to the Prophet's mind, and the Prophet, too, expressed it with his own language, Arabic, to the Arabs.

The Status of the Prophet Muhammad

As is well known, in the medieval period, many western scholars claimed that Muhammad was a cardinal who failed to get elected pope and, in revenge, seceded from the Church.[33] They depicted and described him by using the worst terms such as heretic, impostor or sensualist, to disgrace him in the eyes of Christians and in a sense Muslims.[34]

However, after the second half of the twentieth century, many Christian scholars and theologians have started to raise their voices to highlight the importance of the positive appreciation of the Prophet Muhammad. For example Karen Armstrong, Lamin Sanneh and Martin Forward urge non-Muslims to see Muhammad positively by taking into account how God used him 'as a mercy for humankind' to bring peace and civilization to his people.[35] The renowned theologian John Macquarrie in his *Mediators* includes him among the nine great mediators of 'a new or renewed sense of holy being'.[36] William E. Phipps too in his recent work *Muhammad and Jesus* attempts to compare the teaching of Jesus and Muhammad by regarding them as the prophets of the same family.[37]

Montgomery Watt, in his *Muhammad at Medina*, invites Christians to develop an objective view about Muhammad because of the close contacts between Christians and Muslims. He totally rejects the past allegations made against Muhammad and says that the advocate of those allegations regarded Muhammad as an impostor without thinking about 'how God could have allowed a great religion like Islam to develop from a basis of lies and deceit'.[38] Watt begins his own assessment of the status and the prophethood of Muhammad as follows:

> Prophets ... share in (what may be called) 'creative imagination'. They proclaim ideas connected with what is deepest and most central in human experience, with special reference to the particular needs of their day and generation. The mark of the great prophet is the profound attraction of his ideas for those to whom they are addressed.[39]

Furthermore, he notes the differences between Christian and Muslim understanding of the term 'prophet'. Here, Watt indicates that the main specialities of the Old Testament prophets were to be involved in their contemporary public events, and foretell the future. According to the modern historically minded Christians, he argues, the main duty of the prophet is not to foretell the future but to transmit and proclaim God's message to his own people.[40]

Within this context he asks: 'Was Muhammad a prophet?', and answers by pointing out that

> he was a man in whom creative imagination worked at deep levels and produced ideas relevant to the central questions of human existence, so that his religion has had a widespread appeal, not only in his own age but in succeeding centuries. Not all the ideas he proclaimed are true and sound but God's grace has been enabled to provide millions of men with a better religion than they had before they testified that there is no god but God and that Muhammad is his Messenger.[41]

Watt announces his own understanding of the status and the prophet-hood as follows:

> Personally I am convinced that Muhammad was sincere in believing that what came to him as revelation (*wahy*) was not the product of conscious thought on his part. I consider that Muhammad was truly a Prophet, and think that we Christians should admit this on the basis of the Christian principle that 'by their fruits you will know them', since through the centuries Islam has produced many upright and saintly people. If he is a prophet, too, then in accordance with the Christian doctrine that the Holy Spirit spoke by the prophets, the Qur'an may be accepted as of divine origin.[42]

In one of his recent essays, Watt concedes that although in his academic life he always defends the view that the Qur'an was not the prophet Muham-mad's own product but something that came to him from beyond himself, he hesitated to speak of Muhammad as a prophet because of his fear that 'Muslims would have taken this to mean that everything in the Qur'an was finally and absolutely true', which he did not think was the case.

Kenneth Cragg, in his *The Call of the Minaret*, portrayed the personal-ity of Muhammad as being a man of 'a sure monotheism and a prophetic mission in which a divine relationship of revelation, through a scripture, created a community of faith'.[43] Then after asking according to which crite-ria the prophethood of Muhammad is to be evaluated by Christians, Cragg enumerated the following criteria:

> Is it by those of Arabian paganism which would show Mohammad to be a great reformer? Or by those of early Islamic development which would show Mohammad to be one of the rarest potentialities in human history? Or by those of the classical Hebrew prophets which would show in Mohammad a strange and yet unmistakable shift in the whole concept and expression of prophethood? Or by those of the hills of the Galilee and Judea where there are criteria of almost insupportable contrast?[44]

He himself subscribed to the last criterion in answering the question 'How should prophethood proceed?' and made the following contrast:

> The Muhammadan decision here is formative of all else in Islam. It was a decision for community, for resistance, for external victory, for pacification and rule. The decision of the Cross – no less conscious, no less formative, no less inclusive – was the contrary decision.[45]

Here, Cragg's main criterion for the assessment of the phenomenon of Muhammad is the Christian one, and is the direct comparison with Christ as he is portrayed in the Gospels.

When we turn to Cragg's *Muhammad and the Christian*, we realize that he changed his previous approach. At the outset of this work he explains his new approach by indicating that the elements of other religions should be evaluated within their own historical context and not through one's own religious tradition.[46] By stating this, Cragg seems to move away from assessing the phenomenon of Muhammad in the light of Christian teaching and place him in the light of the Qur'an's own teaching. One of the reasons for this moving away could possibly be that some of his Christian colleagues charged him with christianizing Islam.[47]

Concerning the Muslims' demand for acknowledgement of the prophethood of Muhammad by Christians in the process of Christian–Muslim dialogue, Cragg states that a vital part of the Christian's response to this demand concerns Muhammad's inner experience. He points out that

> the ultimate area of Christian response, will be the content of the Qur'an itself. Indeed, the question of a Christian acknowledgement of Muhammad resolves itself into a Christian response to the Islamic Scripture. It is safe to say that Muhammad himself would not have it otherwise. Nor could any faithful Muslim.[48]

Then he maintains that within this context a Christian can consider Muhammad as 'the Prophet of the Qur'an'.[49]

After acknowledging Muhammad as 'the Prophet of the Qur'an', Cragg tries to tie this recognition with the Christian tradition by arguing that this 'must entail a Christian concern for a larger, more loving, comprehension of divine transcendence and, as its sphere, a deeper estimate of human nature and its answer in that which is "more than prophecy"'. And then he adds that that acknowledgement should not mean that

> the Holy Trinity, the divinity of Jesus, the meaning of the Cross, the mystery of the Eucharist, the integrity of the four Gospels, the doctrine of the Holy Spirit, and many contingent matters, are not vital. But it means that they are better left latent here, within the positive and often common themes of Islamic faith and devotion.[50]

Hans Küng remarks that in our pluralistic age it is no longer possible for Christians to accept the distorted medieval images of the prophet Muhammad, such as a false, lying pseudo-prophet, a fortune teller, and a magician. On the contrary, he stresses the necessity of developing a new and positive Christian understanding of Muhammad. To do this, he says it is necessary first of all to take into consideration the historical context of the prophethood of Muhammad and his message within the stream of the religious history of all humanity. From this methodological perspective, he remarks that 'Muhammad is discontinuity in person, an ultimately irreducible figure, who cannot be simply derived from what preceded him, but stands radically apart from it as he, with the Qur'an, established permanent new stands.'[51] Küng argues that there is no one who is more worthy of being called a prophet than Muhammad in the whole of religious history because of his claim that he was no more than a prophet, come to warn people.[52]

Küng draws attention to the similarities between the prophethood of Muhammad and the prophets of Israel in order to expose the significance of Muhammad for Christians.[53] He urges Christians to take into account the effect of Muhammad's teaching on his followers in seventh-century Arabia. He says that by following that message those people

> were lifted to the heights of monotheism from the very this worldly polytheism of the old Arabian tribal religion. Taken as a whole, they received from Muhammad, or rather from the Qur'an, a boundless supply of inspiration, courage, and strength to make a new departure in religion, toward greater truth and deeper knowledge, a breakthrough that vitalised and renewed their traditional religion. Islam, in short, was a great help in their life.[54]

Finally, Küng moves to outline the theological meaning of this recognition of the Prophet Muhammad for Christians. He begins by showing that in the New Testament there are statements which indicate that after Jesus there is the possibility of authentic future prophets. But Küng restricts their mission to witness to Jesus and his message by making it comprehensible for every age and every situation.[55] Within this context, in the last stage of his examination of the status and the prophethood of Muhammad, Küng regards Muhammad 'as a witness for Jesus – a Jesus who could have been understood not by Hellenistic Gentile Christians, but by Jesus' first disciples, who were Jews, because, with this Jesus tradition, Muhammad reminds the Jews that Jesus fits into the continuity of Jewish salvation history'.[56] And he emphasizes that this Muhammad can be a 'prophetic corrective' and 'prophetic warner' for Christians in order to inform them that 'the one incomparable God has to stand in the absolute centre of faith; That associating with him any other gods or goddesses is out of the question; That faith and life, orthodoxy and orthopraxy, belong together everywhere, including politics'.[57]

Evaluation

First of all Muslims must admit that all the Christian thinkers whose views were considered above stressed the necessity of developing a sympathetic and positive Christian attitude towards the Qur'an and the Prophet Muhammad by leaving behind the polemical past. In the light of this significant shift, I would like to highlight first of all those points that, in my opinion, have negative implications for the rapprochement between Christians and Muslims, and then discuss what kind of Christian approach can contribute more to this rapprochement.

As we have observed, apart from Smith, the others studied the status of the Qur'an within the context of their understanding of the nature of the biblical revelation. According to this understanding, revelation in Christian Scripture consists of two elements, namely divine and human. This understanding naturally led them to reject the orthodox Muslim understanding that the Qur'an is *the verbatim speech of God*. According to them, there are both divine and human elements in the Qur'an. Therefore, when the Qur'anic accounts contradict the Gospel accounts, they argue that there are errors and mistakes in the Qur'an. This clearly opens to discussion the sacred nature of the Qur'an. From the dialogical point of view, this cannot lead to Christian–Muslim understanding but can lead to controversy and conflict between them.

Second, except for Smith, all the others argued for the application of modern scientific methods to the Qur'an in order to facilitate Christian–Muslim understanding. Although this can be considered a reasonable demand, it may not facilitate Christian–Muslim understanding. For example, the views of the exponents of the 'literary approach' to the Qur'an definitely do not lead to mutual understanding but controversy, since contrary to the Muslim understanding they claim that the Qur'an was not finally fixed until the early ninth century and was produced in an atmosphere of intense Judaeo-Christian sectarian debate.[58] It seems that if this and similar views are brought to the dialogue table by Christians, the dialogue process will be affected negatively. As Rahman maintains, they can only be defended to make nonsense of the Qur'an[59] not to make a positive contribution to Christian–Muslim understanding. They all mean that from the advent of Islam to our day Muslims do not understand the real status of the Qur'an, and in order to do this they need to apply the methods Christians use to understand their Scriptures. It would seem better to leave it to Muslim scholars to apply modern scientific methods to the Qur'an within the context of their tradition as the Christian scholars applied the modern scientific methods to their own Scriptures within the context of their tradition.[60]

In the light of these points the following question arises: 'If the views of the scholars mentioned have failed to do justice to the Qur'an and thus affect Christian–Muslim relations negatively, what sort of approach is necessary to do justice to Islamic Scripture and affect these relations positively?' In our opinion, Bijlefeld answers this questioning as follows:

> In my opinion we ought to reject the proposition that we have either to accept the Qur'an 'as the work of God or as that of a man' ... There is a third way: to see the Qur'an not just as 'scripture' but as Sacred Scripture, as the Scripture of Muslims and the Muslim community.

Further, he points out that seeing the Qur'an in this way

> is not a 'compromise' between accepting the principles of critical historical scholarship and attempting to avoid giving offence to Muslim sensibilities. It means recognising and taking seriously the fact that the Qur'an was not 'discovered' by Western scholarship, but that it reached us [the Western world] through the Muslim community which did not simply 'preserve' it, but for which it remained reality.[61]

In short, our examination of the above accounts of contemporary Christian thinkers concerning the status of the Qur'an has shown that the Qur'an is no longer considered by them as a product of the Prophet Muhammad's own thinking as it was thought in the past. Instead, they acknowledge that it has a sacred status. In doing this some of them regard the Qur'an as the Word of God for those who follow its message, the others argue that it is a Word of God for all people.

When we turn to Christian scholars' views on the prophethood of Muhammad, first of all we should acknowledge that all of them have tried to deal sincerely and honestly with the question of the status of Muhammad. By doing this they have tried to give theological room to him within the Christian response to Islam. Thus they included him within the rank of the Old Testament prophets by using the title 'prophet' for him. In our opinion, this is indeed a very positive development towards the Christian acknowledgement of the prophethood of Muhammad. But it also raises an interesting and important question about the understanding of the term 'prophet'. For as is well known, Christians and Muslims understand different things by it. The French Catholic scholar J. Jomier states that, according to Christians, a prophet is someone who speaks on behalf of God by divine authority. For that reason, he says, when a Christian considers someone a prophet, he/she should obey what he said. In this sense, he argues that Christians cannot use the title 'prophet' for Muhammad because 'they cannot obey him without reserve'. Further, Jomier clarifies that when Christians use the title 'prophet' for someone, they do not mean that they accept all that he says but admit some of it while rejecting other parts.[62]

Therefore, while there are those who are in favour of a new and positive Christian assessment of the Prophet Muhammad, they do not want to use the title 'prophet' for Muhammad unreservedly. For example, J. Jomier, R. Arnaldez and M. Forward maintain the necessity of a more positive Christian assessment of the Prophet Muhammad. In doing so, while Jomier argues that unless Christians re-examine the question of the status of the Prophet Muhammad positively, it is very difficult 'to take a new step' in Christian–Muslim dialogue,[63] Forward stresses that 'those who seek to cast lustre upon their own religion by darkening another do themselves and their faith little honour and less justice'.[64] But on the other hand, both of them state that because of the differences between Christians and Muslims on the understanding of the term 'prophet' it is better not to use this title for him.[65] For as Forward says: 'Muslims and Christians deceive themselves when they think that, by calling Muhammad a prophet, they mean the same or even a comparable thing.'[66] Because of these reasons, both of them – unlike Watt, Küng and Cragg – regard the Prophet Muhammad as a political and religious genius without using the term 'prophet' for him. Although this attempt of Jomier and Forward seems an honest Christian response to the question of the status of Muhammad, it does not contribute to understanding Muhammad's religious and spiritual vision.[67]

In the case of those whose views were expressed above, it is obvious that contemporary Christian scholarship has generally attempted to go beyond the polemical tradition by accepting Muhammad as a man of religious genius and the messenger of God who affected the course of human history under the sovereign rule of God. Also, when these accounts of contemporary Christian thinkers are compared with the accounts of those who maintained that any theological Christian recognition of the prophethood of Muhammad would be impossible, it becomes obvious that more and more leading Christian scholars regard this issue as a challenging question which deserves to be discussed seriously.[68] But as Antonie Wessels rightly remarks, all Christians are not totally ready to shake off the remnants of the ill-informed medieval distorted images of Muhammad. In this connection, he maintains that 'the task of understanding anew what it means in modern times to say that God spoke to or through Muhammad, as we find reflected in the Qur'an, lies, in my opinion, still ahead'.[69]

In conclusion, I accept that all the scholars whose views have been considered here have tried to give theological room to the Qur'an and the Prophet Muhammad within the Christian theology of religion. In doing so, they emphasized, first, that the Qur'an is no longer considered as a product of Muhammad's own thinking but as God's word which came to him from beyond, and, second, that Muhammad is no longer regarded as only a religious and political genius but as a prophet along the lines of the great Old Testament prophets. Also, except Cragg, the others implied that if Christians want to understand the nature of the Qur'an and the phenomenon of Muhammad for a genuine dialogue with Muslims, they need to observe the contribution of the Qur'anic teaching to the lives of Muslims. In other words, what these thinkers suggest is that instead of discussing whether the Qur'an was an inspiration from God or whether the Prophet Muhammad was inspired by God it is necessary to observe whether the Qur'an or the Prophet Muhammad has an inspiring influence upon Muslims. It seems that this is a very positive development indeed, since it calls non-Muslims not to try to evaluate Islam *a priori* in the light of their own religious traditions.

Notes

1 William Montgomery Watt, 1969, *Islamic Revelation in the Modern World*, Edinburgh: Edinburgh University Press, p. 17.

2 William Montgomery Watt, 1994, *Companion to the Qur'an*, Oxford: Oneworld, first published in 1967, p. 3.

3 Watt, *Islamic Revelation*, p. 8.

4 William Montgomery Watt, 1983, *Islam and Christianity Today: A Contribution to Dialogue*, London: Routledge, pp. 60–1.

5 William Montgomery Watt, 1988, *Islamic Fundamentalism and Modernity*, London: Routledge, p. 82.

6 William Montgomery Watt, 1995, 'Ultimate Vision and Ultimate Truth', in M. Forward (ed.), *Ultimate Visions: Reflections on the Religions We Choose*, Oxford: Oneworld, p. 283.

7 Wilfred Cantwell Smith, 1967, 'Is the Qur'an the Word of God?', in *Questions of Religious Truth*, London: Victor Gollancz, pp. 45–8.

8 Smith, *Questions of Religious Truth*, p. 49.

9 Wilfred Cantwell Smith, 1980, *Towards a World Theology*, London: Macmillan, p. 164.

10 Wilfred Cantwell Smith, 1992, 'Can Believers Share the Qur'an and the Bible as Word of God', in J. D. Gort et al. (eds), *On Sharing Religious Experience: Possibilities of Interfaith Mutuality*, Grand Rapids: Eerdmans, p. 59.

11 Smith, 'Can Believers Share the Qur'an and the Bible as Word of God', p. 60.

12 Wilfred Cantwell Smith, 1980, 'The True Meaning of the Scripture: An Empirical Historian's Nonreductionist Interpretation of the Qur'an', *International Journal of Middle East Studies* 2, p. 489.

13 Smith, 'The True Meaning of the Scripture', p. 490.

14 Smith, *Questions of Religious Truth*, p. 50.

15 Smith, 'The True Meaning of the Scripture', pp. 503–4.

16 Wilfred Cantwell Smith, 1959, *Islam in Modern History*, Princeton: Princeton University Press, p. 18.

17 Smith, 'The True Meaning of the Scripture', pp. 504–5.

18 Kenneth Cragg, 1971, *The Event of The Qur'an: Islam in its Scripture*, London: George Allen, p. 13.

19 Cragg, *The Event of the Qur'an*, p. 16.

20 Cragg, *The Event of the Qur'an*, p. 15.

21 Cragg, *The Event of the Qur'an*, p. 15.

22 Cragg, *The Event of the Qur'an*, p. 19.

23 See Cragg, *The Event of the Qur'an*, p. 107.

24 Watt, *Islamic Revelation*, p. 42.

25 Kenneth Cragg, *Muhammad and the Christian*, London: Darton, Longman & Todd, 1984, p. 95; see also Keith Zebiri, 1997, *Muslims and Christians Face to Face*, Oxford: Oneworld, p. 209.

26 Kenneth Cragg, 1986, *The Christ and the Faiths: Theology in Cross-Reference*, London: SPCK, p. 53.

27 Hans Küng, *Christianity and World Religions*, London: Collins, 1987, pp. 28–9.

28 Küng, *Christianity and the World Religions*, p. 32.

29 Küng, *Christianity and the World Religions*, pp. 34, 30.

30 Küng, *Christianity and the World Religions*, p. 35.

31 Küng, *Christianity and the World Religions*, p. 34.

32 Küng, *Christianity and the World Religions*, pp. 67–8.

33 Daniel, *Islam and the West*, p. 88. [This book has had several editions and publishers and the most recent is Oxford: Oneworld, 2009.]

34 See Daniel, *Islam and the West*, pp. 88ff.; Hourani, *Islam in European Thought*, Cambridge: Cambridge University Press, 1991, pp. 12ff.; see also R. H. Drummond, 1972, 'Toward Theological Understanding of Islam', *Journal of Ecumenical Studies* 9.4, pp. 777–801; Muhammad Benaboud, 1986, 'Orientalism on the Revelation of the Prophet: The Case of W. Montgomery Watt, Maxime Rodinson, and Duncan Black MacDonald', *American Journal of Islamic Social Science* 3.2, pp. 309–26.

35 See Karen Armstrong, 1992, *Muhammad: A Western Attempt to Understand Islam*, London: Victor Gollancz, p. 44; Lamin Sanneh, 1996, *Piety and Power: Muslims and Christians in West Africa*, Maryknoll, NY: Orbis Books, p. 48; 'Muhammad's Significance for Christians', *Studies in Interreligious Dialogue* 1 (1991), pp. 25–9, 36–8; Martin Forward, 1997, *Muhammad: A Short Biography*, Oxford: Oneworld, p. 5.

36 John Macquarrie, 1995, *Mediators*, London: Collins, p. 130.

37 William E. Phipps, 1996, *Muhammad and Jesus: A Comparison of the Prophets and their Teaching*, London: SCM Press.

38 William Montgomery Watt, 1956, *Muhammad at Medina*, Oxford: Oxford University Press, p. 232.

39 William Montgomery Watt, *Muhammad: Prophet and Statesman*, Oxford: Oxford University Press, 1974, p. 238.

40 William Montgomery Watt, 1978, 'Thoughts on Muslim–Christian Dialogue', *Hamdard Islamicus* 1.1, pp. 34–5.

41 Watt, *Muhammad: Prophet and Statesman*, p. 240.

42 William Montgomery Watt, *Muhammad's Mecca*, Edinburgh: Edinburgh University Press, 1988, p. 1.

43 Kenneth Cragg, *The Call of the Minaret*, Oxford: Oxford University Press, 1956, p. 75.

44 Cragg, *The Call of the Minaret*, p. 91.

45 Cragg, *The Call of the Minaret*, p. 93.

46 Cragg, *Muhammad and the Christian*, p. 2.

47 Charles Adams, 1976, 'Islamic Religious Traditions', in L. Binder (ed.), *The Study of the Middle East: Research and Scholarship in the Humanities and Social Sciences*, New York: John Wiley & Sons, ss. 29–95; Jamil Qureysi, 1984, 'Alongsidedness – In Good Faith?', in A. Hussain, R. Olson and J. Qureysi (eds), *Orientalism, Islam and Islamists*, Vermont: Amana Books, pp. 203–48.

48 Cragg, *Muhammad and the Christian*, p. 6.

49 Cragg, *Muhammad and the Christian*, p. 91.

50 Cragg, *Muhammad and the Christian*, p. 139.

51 Küng, *Christianity and the World Religions*, p. 25.

52 Küng, *Christianity and the World Religions*, p. 25; for the Qur'anic verses concerning the claiming of Muhammad he was just a prophet and warner, see *Suras* 49:9; 3:144.

53 Küng, *Christianity and the World Religions*, pp. 25–6.

54 Küng, *Christianity and the World Religions*, p. 27.

55 Küng, *Christianity and the World Religions*, pp. 27–8.

56 Küng, *Christianity and the World Religions*, p. 126.

57 Küng, *Christianity and the World Religions*, p. 129.

58 See John Wansbrough, 1977, *Qur'anic Studies: Sources and Methods of Scriptural Interpretation*, Oxford: Oxford University Press; and 1978, *The Sectarian Milieu: Content and Composition of Islamic Salvation History*, Oxford: Oxford University Press.

59 See Fazlur Rahman, 1985, 'Approaches to Islam in Religious Studies', in Richard C. Martin (ed.), *Approaches to Islam in Religious Studies*, Tucson: University of Arizona Press, pp. 189–202.

60 Heikki Räisänen, 1996, *Marcion, Muhammad and the Mahatma: Exegetical Perspectives on the Encounter of Cultures and Faiths*, London: SCM Press, p. 123.

61 Willem A. Bijlefeld, 1972, 'Islamic Studies within the Perspective of History of Religion', *The Muslim World* 62, p. 5.

62 J. Jomier, 1989, *How to Understand Islam*, London: SCM Press, pp. 146–7.

63 Jomier, *How to Understand Islam*, p. 140.

64 Forward, *Muhammad*, p. 119.

65 See Jomier, *How to Understand Islam*, pp. 146–7; Forward, *Muhammad*, pp. 119–20; see also R. Arnaldez, 1975, 'Dialogue islam–chrétien et sensibilités religieuses', *Islamochristiana* 1, p. 15.

66 Forward, *Muhammad*, p. 120.

67 See Armstrong, *Muhammad*, p. 14.

68 See Willem A. Bijlefeld, 1995, 'Christian–Muslim Studies, Islamic Studies, and the Future of Christian–Muslim Encounter', in Y. Y. Hadadd and W. Z. Haddad (eds), *Christian–Muslim Encounters*, Gainesville: University Press of Florida, p. 20.

69 Antonie Wessels, 1975, 'Modern Biographies of Muhammad in Arabic', *Islamic Culture*, 49, p. 105.

Source: original piece commissioned for this work.

Burdens from the Past, Opportunities for the Future

MARC SAPERSTEIN

I [have] identified four issues in the early church which had powerful repercussions in the history of Christian–Jewish relations – issues pertaining to the Christian definition of identity, scripture, sacred space, and the boundaries of toleration. In assessing the legacy of the past and its impact upon the opportunities for contemporary dialogue and mutual understanding, I shall return to these four issues, considering them in reverse order.

We have seen that for many centuries, the fundamental doctrine controlling the church's position on the toleration of Jews was articulated by St Augustine: the Jews bear God's curse because of their rejection of the Christ, but they must be permitted to live alongside Christians so that their degradation will serve as a constant reminder of the consequences of sin. The two aspects of this doctrine were reasserted throughout the Middle Ages: on the one hand, Jews should not be permitted to flourish; on the other, they should not be put to death. Even during the period of the Holocaust, Christian thinkers appealed to this doctrine, often to oppose the Nazi policies.

The most plausible alternative to this doctrine in the Middle Ages was never that Jews should be allowed to live as equals with Christians, but rather that Jews should either accept Christianity or be expelled from Christian lands. After the Holocaust, however, both the Augustinian doctrine and its historical alternative have been repudiated. Leaders of the Catholic Church at Vatican II wrought a silent revolution when they said in *Nostra Aetate* (1965) that 'Jews should not be presented as rejected or accursed by God, as if this followed from the Holy Scriptures.'[1]

The implications of this statement were further elaborated in the Vatican's 1985 'Notes on the correct way to present the Jews and Judaism in preaching and catechesis in the Roman Catholic Church:' 'We must in any case rid ourselves of the traditional idea of a people punished, preserved as a living argument for Christian apologetic. It remains a chosen people.' This was not, of course, just a 'traditional idea;' it was established doctrine, formulated by the most profound of the church fathers, reiterated by popes over many centuries. Its formal abandonment clears the way for a totally new conceptualization of the church's relationship with the Jewish people.

Protestant groups have also rejected the old theological model in favor of a new one. In 1968, a World Council of Churches report characterized Jewish historical experience not as proof of the dismal fate of the Christ-killer, but as 'a living and visible sign of God's faithfulness to men.' The statement explicitly rejects 'any thought of considering their sufferings during the ages as a proof of any special guilt.' This same statement recognizes that Christians had a hand in much of Jewish suffering, confessing 'the guilt of Christians who have all too often stood on the side of the persecutors instead of the persecuted.'[2] The final step, an affirmation that not only Christians but Christian doctrine has led to persecution of the Jews, is taken in a document 'commended to the churches for study and action' by the Executive Committee of the WCC in 1982: 'Teachings of contempt for Jews and Judaism in certain Christian traditions proved a spawning ground for the evil of the Nazi Holocaust.'[3]

Various denominations have articulated similar ideas. A 1969 committee report of the Lutheran World Federation, expressing anguish over the 'deep and tragic involvement of men of Christian tradition in the persecution of the Jewish people,' called particular attention to 'the cruel and dangerous anti-Jewish attacks in some of the writings of the old Luther.'[4] In 1987, the Presbyterian Church (USA) in a provisional statement on Christian–Jewish relations acknowledged 'in repentance the church's long and deep complicity in the proliferation of anti-Jewish attitudes and actions through its "teaching of contempt" for the Jews,' noting in its explication that this teaching was 'a major ingredient that made possible the monstrous policy of annihilation of Jews by Nazi Germany.' Similarly, the United Church of Christ in a 1987 statement affirms that 'the Church's frequent portrayal of the Jews as blind, recalcitrant, evil, and rejected by God ... has been a factor in the shaping of anti-Jewish attitudes of societies and the policies of governments. The most devastating lethal metastasis of this process occurred in our own century during the Holocaust.'[5]

Such statements move beyond any position taken by the Catholic Church. While the Vatican has repudiated the portrayal of Jews as 'rejected or accursed by God' and has condemned all expressions of antisemitism, it has not, so far as I can tell, drawn a direct connection between traditional church doctrine and anti-Jewish behavior, or admitted that representatives of the church sometimes served as purveyors or instruments of persecution. It has pointedly refused to recognize any possible link between the teaching of contempt and the Holocaust, asserted in the Protestant statements above.

In a moving and powerful statement about the Holocaust made by Pope John Paul II in August of 1987, precisely the opposite lesson is drawn: 'Reflection upon the Shoah shows us to what terrible consequences the lack of faith in God and a contempt for man created in his image can lead.'[6] As for the policy and behavior of the church during the Nazi period, there appears to be little expression of self-criticism at the top. When the storm of controversy erupted over Rolf Hochhuth's play *The Deputy*, Catholic spokesmen not surprisingly rallied to the defense of Pope Pius XII on historical and moral grounds.

Where does this leave us today? I hope to have shown that both questions – the role of traditional Christian doctrine and the policy of the Vatican – are extremely complex. Where carefully nuanced formulations are required, polemical and blatantly inaccurate accusations – such as 'the church did nothing' – often prevail. Where the facts leave room for legitimate difference of interpretation, particularly regarding the subtle interplay of varying motivations, polarization sometimes wins the day. It might be argued that Jewish spokesmen have occasionally shown insufficient sensitivity to the effect of attacks upon the character of either the current pope or one who is still remembered and revered by millions of Roman Catholics. There is also an unfortunate tendency to use the brush too broadly in painting a picture of guilt. *Nostra Aetate*, reversing a tradition almost as old as Christianity itself, proclaimed that responsibility for the crucifixion 'cannot be charged against all the Jews, without distinction, then alive, nor against the Jews of today.'[7] Does not the same principle apply to the responsibility of Christians for the Holocaust?

Nor have Catholic spokesmen always been conscious of Jewish sensibilities in making their case. Here is an example, written by a French writer, Jacques Gommy.

What was there, then, for Pius XII to do? He had warned that the unspeakable horrors of technological warfare could destroy the world. No one listened. Pius XII, consequently, denounced all atrocities, all, including the extermination of the Jews, though he could not condemn only one side when both were equally guilty. In addition, Pius XII did what the West did not in the Hungarian situation, he acted. He did everything in his power to stop human suffering and to save human lives, that is, he did far more than anyone else did. And though in this world we tend to ignore the power of prayer, surely his constant prayers and fatherly concern for all mankind touched the infinite mercy of God and helped bring an end to the homicidal folly. Surely that counted above all.[8]

I will pass by the outright falsification of history in the assertion that only the Pope acted in 'the Hungarian situation' – as if Raul Wallenberg, working for the US War Refugee Board with the cooperation of the Swedish government, never existed! Look at the other statements: the Pope 'did more than anyone else' to stop human suffering. And his constant prayers surely 'touched the infinite mercy of God' and helped end the Holocaust. From a traditionalist Catholic perspective, I suppose this is comprehensible, but think of how it sounds to Jews. The prayers of six million Jewish victims apparently could not move God to halt the bloodbath, but the prayers of the Pope did? A contemporary Jewish thinker has suggested the following working principle for legitimate discourse about the Holocaust: 'No statement, theological or otherwise, should be made that would not be credible in the presence of the burning children.'[9] In my judgment, this particular defense of Pope Pius XII fails dismally by that standard.

A second major question related to the land. The contemporary state of Israel is invariably the subject on which feelings run hottest in inter-faith conferences. On the Jewish side, there used to be a fairly straightforward reality. The experiences of 1948, 1967, and 1973 made Israel a simple touchstone in the minds of most American Jews. While the Jewish people and religion were able to survive almost 1900 years in exile, without a state of their own, the loss of Israel today, so soon after the Holocaust, would be a trauma from which the entire people might never recover. Any religious group that could not recognize the right of Jews to sovereignty over one tiny portion of the earth's surface, or support the threatened state when Egyptian armies mobilized on its borders and tried to sever its economic jugular vein at Sharm a-Sheikh, or when Egypt and Syria initiated a massive surprise attack on Yom Kippur, did not seem to be an appropriate partner for authentic dialogue. If you hesitate and waver over my brother's right to survive, what is there to discuss?

The summer and early fall of 1982 produced a new equation. For the first time, Jews in Israel and in America were deeply ambivalent or sharply divided over the wisdom of policies and actions taken by the Israeli government. These internal divisions intensified with the cycle of violence and repression beginning in December of 1987 and called by Palestinian Arabs 'the uprising.' Yet there appears to be little erosion of the underlying commitment felt by American Jews to the secure survival of Israel, and little dissent that Israel's welfare remains near the top of any authentic Jewish agenda. It is against this background that we need to evaluate the stance of the various Christian groups. I will divide them into three.

The position of the Catholic Church has changed dramatically in theory, considerably less in practice. At the beginning of the century, the church's approach to the idea of a Jewish return to the land of Israel was based on traditional theological foundations. This is clearly demonstrated by the remarks of Pope Pius X in an audience with Theodor Herzl, the leader of the Zionist movement, held on 25 January 1904. The Pope's statements are recorded in Herzl's diary:

> We are unable to favor this movement ... The ground of Jerusalem, if it were not always sacred, has been sanctified by the life of Christ ... The Jews have not recognized our Lord, therefore we cannot recognize the Jewish people ... It is disagreeable to see the Turks in possession of our Holy Places. We simply have to put up with it. But to sanction the Jewish wish to occupy these sites, that we cannot do ... Either the Jews will retain their ancient faith and continue to await the Messiah whom we believe has already appeared – in which case they are denying the divinity of Jesus and we cannot assist them. Or else they will go there with no religion whatever, and then we can have nothing at all to do with them.[10]

According to this account, all of the assumptions of the traditional triumphalist theology are in place. It is the life of Christ that sanctifies the soil of Jerusalem. A Jewish people that either remains traditionally Jewish or becomes secular has no right to return to its ancient homeland. That would violate the doctrine that the Jews must remain scattered and homeless as punishment for their heinous sins. Only when the Jews recognize the true Messiah, who has already come, will they be entitled to a share in the holy land. Until that time, the church can tolerate Turkish control of the holy places, but it cannot approve of a Jewish national return. Herzl reports that the Pope concluded, if a refuge from persecution is needed, let them go anywhere else.

The theological foundations of this negative stance have been abandoned by the church in Vatican II. Yet the church still refuses to extend formal recognition to the state of Israel, and this remains a constant irritant.[11] Various explanations have been given: the Vatican has many interests and agenda items beyond its relationship with world Jewry; it must weigh political considerations such as a fear of retaliation by Arab countries against small Christian minorities in their midst, and the influence of a Catholic Palestinian lobby committed to Palestinian rights. Indeed, in August of 1987, the Vatican stated explicitly that the obstacles to the formal recognition of Israel were not theological but political – apparently implying that if the theological problems have been overcome, the political problems may be easier. Jews hear these explanations as plausible, knowing that Israel does not need the church's approval of its legitimacy.

To many Jews, however, the status quo is still not fully comprehensible. There are some issues of such symbolic importance that they should transcend mundane political calculations. Pope John Paul II's visit to the Great Synagogue of Rome in April of 1986 was a dramatic gesture of respect for the dignity of the Jewish religion. But most Jews today consider the state of Israel to be an integral component of Jewish dignity and survival. Despite protestations to the contrary, something of the attitude expressed by Pius X seems to linger: it is tolerable if Muslims exercise sovereignty over Christian holy places – that is a geo-political fact which even the popes who called for Crusades could begrudgingly accept – but for Jewish soldiers to ensure security at the Church of the Holy Sepulchre – that the church can never endorse. So long as the Vatican refrains from extending full diplomatic recognition to Israel, including full ambassadorial exchange, many Jews will remain unconvinced that the legacy of medieval triumphalist theology is really dead.

American Protestantism divides into two quite different groups on this issue. The most powerful, unquestioning political and economic support for the state and government of Israel comes from the Evangelicals.[12] Particularly at times when Israel is beleaguered and embattled, Jews recognize this and appreciate it. Yet Jews feel considerable ambivalence about the Evangelical position. They remain distrustful of Evangelical motives in their support of Israel, and they fear that to welcome this support while ignoring the eschatological belief-structure undergirding it may be either cynical or naive.

Many Jews suspect that Evangelicals are concerned not about Israel as a reality, but about Israel as a doctrine. The Holy Land tours, which bring tens of thousands of Evangelical pilgrims each year, are of immense economic value to Israel. But when they are limited to the Sea of Galilee, the Church of the Nativity, and the old City of Jerusalem, overlooking all that the Jewish people has accomplished in that land during the past 100 years, is it truly Israel that they are seeing? Finally, at a time when there is considerable dissent both in Israel itself and within American Jewry about policies taken by the Israeli government, the uncritical support of hawkish positions expressed by some Evangelicals, often because of their understanding of eschatological doctrine, is not perceived by all Jews as helpful. All these are issues that deserve to be more fully explored.

On the other hand, Jews share with the mainline and liberal Protestant denominations a legacy of cooperation and communication. Before Vatican II, these groups were the only Christians interested in dialogue. They are unambiguously committed to the principle of religious pluralism in America, and they have forged with Jews the agenda on a wide range of critical social issues. Today they are the most open to healthy dialogue based on mutual respect. But they have serious problems with many of Israel's policies, and their outspoken criticism strikes many Jews as hypocritical and unfair.

Sentiments expressed by Henry Siegman some years ago about a figure from the Catholic radical left seem even more apropos of some liberal Protestant critics: they are 'nourished by a Christian universalism which cannot abide the earthiness of Jewish particularism. They love Jews who are disincarnated, who are suffering servants, who are ghostly emissaries and symbols of an obscure mission. They cannot abide Jews who are flesh-and-blood people, who are men and women like other men and women in all their angularities and specificities, who need to occupy physical space in a real world before they fulfill whatever loftier aspirations they may have. They are distressed by the notion that Jews should want a flesh-and-blood existence as a people in the real geography of this world.'[13]

Few would suggest that any criticism of Israel from Christian sources necessarily reflects an antisemitic bias. There is, however, a fundamental difference between criticism from within and criticism from without. The prophets held ancient Israel to a higher standard of morality than the surrounding nations out of a love for their people that was evident throughout their careers. When the church fathers quoted the prophets out of context to prove to the world the reprobate character of the Jews, their motives were perverse, and the impact of their criticism was potentially devastating.

The same words, when repeated outside the context of underlying commitment, may sound quite different – not the anguished reproach of a lover's quarrel, but the mean-spirited, self-serving attack of those who seek any excuse to embarrass the one whom you treasure. When criticism of particular policies comes from Christians who have established their credentials as supporters and lovers of Israel, not only for its role in some eschatological scheme but for its own sake, Jews can generally accept it as appropriate and legitimate. When it comes from Christians whose underlying position on Israel has always been suspect, the very same words sometimes sound grating and smug.[14]

I will touch upon the final two issues more briefly. We recall that relatively early in its history, the church decided that the Hebrew Bible would remain part of its sacred scripture, and that it would thus in effect share a scripture with the Jewish people. I have argued that the Gnostic alternative might have made the demonizing of the Jewish people even easier for Christians. A common text at least established the possibility of a common ground for communication. Occasionally this produced mutually beneficial common scholarship; more often it led to sterile argumentation.

What about today?[15] Though one frequently hears the assertion that Christians share with Jews a profound commitment to the Bible as the Word of God, a cautionary note is in order. We must not forget that the Hebrew Bible is not the same as the Christian Old Testament, even though it may contain precisely the same books. The old stereotyped Christian reading of scripture still lingers, contrasting the vengeful, zealous God of the Old Testament with the merciful, loving, gracious God of the New.[16] This is certainly not an image Jews would recognize as authentic.

Furthermore, the essential story of the Hebrew Bible as read by Jews is quite different from that of the Old Testament as read by most Christians. For Jews, it is essentially a book of history and of law, providing an account of a people's origin and golden age and the constitution of its legal system. For Christians, it is essentially a book of prophecies and types, a preparation for things to come, important not as history in its own right but as prefigurement and prophecy of a new dispensation which would make the old obsolete. Reading the same words, the content turns out to be quite different.

Often, we do not even read the same words. For the Jew, the Bible is always the Hebrew text. While Judaism has never forbidden translation, as did Islam, and for some time and for very different reasons the Catholic Church, no serious Jewish study of the Bible has ever been separated from the original Hebrew. By contrast, one frequently hears Christians, particularly of the more fundamentalist orientations, quoting 'God's Word' as if the text was originally uttered or revealed in King James English. We should not forget that when we quote an English verse, we are not quoting the Bible; we are merely quoting one translation of the Bible.

This point is not mere academic pedantry. Translation always entails difficult and sometimes arbitrary decisions. A word or phrase in one language often has two possible meanings; the translator must usually render one at the expense of the other. What begins as multivalent and suggestive ambiguity emerges in translation as straightforward simplicity. This is especially pronounced in translation from biblical Hebrew, which has no punctuation, no indications where a quotation ends, hundreds of verbs with unclear subjects and pronouns with unclear referents, an imperfect tense that can mean you must, you may, or you will, and that omnipresent *vav* conversive, which can have at least half a dozen different meanings.

For the Jew, therefore, the Bible, read and studied in Hebrew, is a very different kind of text from that quoted in English. It is fraught with ambiguities and obscurities, forever inspiring new and legitimate interpretations, an open-ended text the meaning of which may be ultimately elusive, which one is left to wrestle with and probe. We are not certain how to translate properly even the first sentence of the book of Genesis. This may be why in theological matters Jews have traditionally had such a marked tolerance for diversity.

Where the Jewish community has tried to impose a measure of conformity upon its members, and this is primarily in the realm of behavior governed by Jewish law, the Bible has been understood and applied through a tradition of rabbinic interpretation. There is no model in traditional Jewish life for appealing directly to the Bible as a source of authority over others. Sola Scriptura is not a live option in the Jewish context, any more than the US Supreme Court today could decide to throw out all the judicial decisions of the past 200 years and adjudicate each case solely on their direct reading of the Constitution. For the traditional Jew, the meaning of the Bible is largely open-ended, but the Bible functions as it has been understood by the rabbis over the past 2000 years. All of this is quite different from the Christian Bible, particularly that of the Protestants.

The final issue, which goes back to the very beginnings of the Christian church, pertains to identity and lines of demarcation. The decision made by what became the normative church was that one did not have to be a Jew to be Christian, and that the major thrust of evangelistic energy would be directed toward the Gentile world. Jews would be permitted to live as Jews, and not baptized under duress, but the conversion of Jews, both as individuals and as an entire people, would remain throughout the centuries as a paramount Christian aspiration and goal.

Perhaps second only to modern Israel, the question of Christian mission to the Jews is today the most vehemently debated in internal Christian circles. Some Christians, particularly Evangelicals, feel unable to compromise on a supersessionist theology which holds that Christianity has taken the place of Judaism. As one spokesman has put it:

> We evangelicals maintain that by the whole Christ-event Judaism qua religion has been superseded, its propaedeutic purpose accomplished. Since the Messiah has come and offered his culminating sacrifice, there is, as we see it, no temple, no priesthood, no altar, no atonement, no forgiveness, no salvation, and no eternal hope in Judaism as a religion.[17]

If that is the starting point, it is obvious that a mission to the Jews remains important; indeed, a renunciation of such a mission would be to abandon Jews to eternal despair.

Other denominations have explicitly abandoned the supersessionist model.[18] The Presbyterians in 1987 stated that 'Christians have not replaced Jews.' Jews are 'already in a covenantal relationship with God,' and remain with Christians 'partners in waiting.' In the same year, the United Church of Christ affirmed that 'Judaism has not been superseded by Christianity; ... Christianity is not to be understood as the successor religion to Judaism; God's covenant with the Jewish people has not been abrogated.'[19] Yet some of those who could support such statements still feel bound by the Gospel's challenge to bring the 'good news' to the entire world and believe that excluding in principle the Jewish people from their witness would be a violation of their responsibility and self-understanding as Christians.[20]

Jewish antipathy toward Christian proselytizing among Jews is powerful and deep. Whether such proselytizing results in a formal severing of all links with the Jewish community or in the dual identity model espoused by 'Messianic Jews,' 'Jews for Jesus,' 'Hebrew Christians,' or any of the other half-dozen names by which such groups are known, the consensus ranging from ultra-orthodox to secular Jews is that the Christian mission must be resisted at all costs.

How might this consensus be explained? Historical memory can be a strong force for an ancient people. It is impossible to eradicate the psychic legacy of sixteen centuries in which Christians, often backed by the power of the state, exerted various kinds of pressure upon Jews to renounce their 'blindness' and accept the 'true faith,' the legacy of generations of Jews who could have made things so much easier for themselves by succumbing to these pressures, yet refused, sometimes at the cost of their lives. Too much has happened in the relationship between the two communities over the centuries for Jews to consider dispassionately the merits of conversion or even of a compromise version that would somehow have the best of both worlds. 1900 years ago, Jewish Christianity may have been a real option; from the Jewish perspective, history has long since rendered it obsolete.

Secondly, the Jewish people today is fighting a demographic battle for its survival. There are still fewer Jews in the world today than there were in 1939. Statistics about reproduction rates, average age, intermarriage, lead many to conclude that the number of Jews in the world will decline significantly over the next few generations. The very existence of a Jewish people 100 years from now is an agonizing question-mark. In such circumstances, the Jewish community simply cannot afford a haemorrhaging to other faith-groups.

In some ways, the claims of the 'Jews for Jesus' that their Jewish identity is fulfilled by accepting a messiah who has already come, though in practice they espouse a rather high christology and an agenda of concerns that hardly reflects that of American Jewry, seem even more insidious.[21] Few would question the right of these individuals to find their own religious way, or the right of the Christians to count them among their own. But those who use traditional Jewish rituals and sancta in affirming Jesus as their savior are not a basis of commonality between Christians and Jews; they are an irritating source of friction.

More complicated is the question whether Jews will insist that a Christian commitment to a universal mission is incompatible with dialogue, destined to produce suspicion and distrust. One of the universally accepted ground rules of dialogue requires that each side recognize the right of the other to define itself in its own terms. How are Jews to respond when they are told that a universal mission is an inherent part of the self-definition of the Christians to whom they are speaking? Do they have the right to argue that a history of persecution requires contemporary Christians to abandon this religious principle as a sign of good will, a pre-condition for communication? This is an issue on which Jews themselves remain divided.[22]

'History is a nightmare from which I am trying to awake,' said Stephen Daedalus to a colleague in *Ulysses*. Though not quite as much as is often assumed, there is much in the history of Jewish–Christian relations that might justify the profound pessimism of this sentiment. But the purpose of this review is not to relive the nightmare, and certainly not to foster feelings either of guilt among the descendants of the persecutors or of self-righteousness among the descendants of the victims. Rather it is to suggest some corrections to prevalent misconceptions about the historical record and some lessons that might be learned from the past: that the marriage of religion and political power often produces the ugly offspring of intolerance and persecution; that the line between faithful devotion and exclusivist fanaticism can be deceptively thin; that any group which believes that it alone knows God's will or that it alone carries God's banner risks perverting God's purpose.

Having wrestled with these lessons and clarified for each other what it is that gives us pain,[23] Jews and Christians can begin to build on a more solid foundation an alliance for a common agenda of action in causes that require concerted effort by all people of good will: an alliance to ensure that human folly and greed will never destroy God's creation through nuclear catastrophe or a poisoning of our physical environment; to end once and for all the scandals of homelessness and hunger in an affluent society; to pursue the elusive goals of social justice and equal opportunity for every one of God's children; to affirm the claims of faith and the ideals of stewardship and accountability before the corrosive challenge of a militantly secular, hedonistic, self-indulgently acquisitive worldview.

Whether because of the vagaries of historical circumstance, the limitations of human understanding and imagination, or the mysteries of divine providence, Jews and Christians have walked widely divergent paths for 1900 years. No one would suggest that the paths can or even should be united today, but perhaps we can ensure that they will lead us in the same direction.

Notes

1 *Nostra Aetate*, in Helga Croner, *Stepping Stones to Further Jewish–Christian Relations*, London and New York 1977, 2. An earlier draft read 'rejected or accursed by God or guilty of deicide;' the last four words were rejected, possibly as a result of political pressures by Arab governments and others; see A. Roy Eckardt, *Your People My People*, New York 1974, 49–51. The Vatican gives a different explanation for this decision: see Walter M. Abbott (ed.), *The Documents of Vatican II*, New York 1966, 666 n. 23. On Jewish reactions to this section of *Nostra Aetate*, see Marc Tanenbaum, in *Twenty Years of Jewish–Catholic Relations*, ed. Eugene Fisher et al., New York 1986, 51–3.

2 Croner, *Stepping Stones*, 78. The phrase 'stood on the side of the persecutors' may signal a reluctance to concede that all too often Christians were the persecutors. The World Council of Churches, like the Catholic church, had to overcome considerable opposition to such statements of friendship toward the Jews. See the report of W. A. Visser't Hooft on the 1954 General Assembly, in Franklin H. Littell, *The Crucifixion of the Jews*, New York 1975, 63–4.

3 'Ecumenical Considerations on Jewish–Christian Dialogue,' Geneva: World Council of Churches 1983, sec. 3.2, p. 9. The phrase 'teachings of contempt' in this and many similar statements shows the enormous influence of Jules Isaac's *The Teaching of Contempt: Christian Roots of Anti-Semitism*, New York 1964.

4 Croner, *Stepping Stones*, 89–90. Cf. the statement by the noted Lutheran scholar Jaroslav Pelikan in his 1971 presidential address to the International Congress for Luther Research: 'The time has come for those who study Luther and admire him to acknowledge, more unequivocally and less pugnaciously than they have, that on this issue Luther's thought and language are simply beyond defense. But any such acknowledgement must be based, theologically, on a much more fundamental conviction, namely, that Judaism is not, as Luther and the centuries before him maintained, a "shadow" destined to disappear with the coming of Christianity even though it stubbornly held on to its existence, but a permanent part of the wondrous dispensation of God in human history.' Quoted in Littell, *The Crucifixion of the Jews*, 105–6.

5 'A Theological Understanding of the Relationship between Christians and Jews,' adopted 'for study and reflection' by the 199th General Assembly (1987) of the Presbyterian Church (USA), 8–9. 'The Relationship Between the United Church of Christ and the Jewish Community;' this was passed as a resolution in the 1987 'Sixteenth General Synod' of the UCC, and it therefore has a more official status than the Presbyterian document.

6 *New York Times*, 20 August 1987, 9.

7 Croner, *Stepping Stones*, 2.

8 Delores and Earl Schmidt, *The Deputy Reader*, Glenview, IL, 1965, 147.

9 Irving Greenberg, 'Cloud of Smoke, Pillar of Fire', in Eva Fleischner, ed., *Auschwitz: Beginning of a New Era? Reflections on the Holocaust*, New York 1977, 23. Note the striking use of this principle by A. Roy Eckardt with Alice Eckardt, *Long Night's Journey into Day: Life and Faith After the Holocaust*, Detroit 1982, 138.

10 *The Diaries of Theodor Herzl*, ed. and trans. Marvin Lowenthal, New York 1956, 428–9. I have not been able to determine whether there is confirmation in Vatican documents for this statement, nor have I been able to find evidence that the Vatican opposition to Zionism was ever officially based on the Augustinian doctrine. Note, however, the reaction of Pope Benedict XV to the Balfour Declaration. Appealing to the sacrifice made by the Crusaders, he concluded, 'Surely it would be a terrible grief for Us and for all the Christian faithful if infidels were placed in a privileged and prominent position; much

more if those most holy sanctuaries of the Christian religion were given to the charge of non-Christians' (cited by Esther Feldblum, *The American Catholic Press and the Jewish State, 1917–1959*, New York 1977, 78.

11 Eugene Fisher has argued (*Commonweal*, 11 January 1985) that the Pope has expressed Vatican recognition of Israel in the following statement from the apostolic letter *Redemptionis Anno* of Good Friday 1984: 'For the Jewish people who live in the state of Israel, and who preserve in that land such precious testimonies to their history and their faith, we must ask for the desired security and the due tranquillity that is the prerogative of every nation.' He maintains that the outstanding issue is only that of the level of diplomatic relations, which, he concedes, is of major symbolic importance to the Jewish community.

12 On American Evangelical support for Zionism and Israel from the nineteenth century through the Six Day War, see Yona Malachy, *American Fundamentalism and Israel*, Jerusalem 1978. Another important study of the theological basis for contemporary support is David Rausch, *Zionism within Early American Fundamentalism 1878–1918*, Lewiston, NY 1980.

13 Henry Siegman, 'A Decade of Catholic–Jewish Relations – A Reassessment,' *Journal of Ecumenical Studies*, 15, 1978, 252.

14 For strong statements by Christian writers of the distinction between criticism from within and from outside, see Littell, *The Crucifixion of the Jews*, 3, and Eckardts, *Long Night's Journey into Day*, 106, 120–2. The Eckardts argue that Jews have the right to set special standards for themselves, but that 'Christians have no right to inflict spiritual and moral requirements upon the Jewish people that may perpetuate or compound Jewish suffering ... As long as the Christian community tries to make Israel something special, to trumpet forth that Israel has obligations greater than or different from those of other human beings, the burden of the Christian past will not be lifted' (106).

15 Some recent treatments of this theme (and here I deal with the Hebrew scriptures alone, not the New Testament, which is primarily an internal Christian issue) include Lawrence Boadt, 'The Role of Scripture in Catholic–Jewish Relations,' in *Twenty Years of Catholic–Jewish Relations*, 1986, 89–108; Bruce Waitke, 'An Evangelical Christian View of the Hebrew Scriptures,' in *Evangelicals and Jews in an Age of Pluralism*, ed. Marc Tanenbaum et al., Grand Rapids 1984, 105–39.

16 David Rausch reports observing an Evangelical seminary graduate writing on the board of a Sunday School class in two columns, JUDAISM/LAW/DEATH/PHARISEES/OLD TESTAMENT and CHRISTIANITY/GRACE/LIFE/SAINTS/NEW TESTAMENT: 'What and How Evangelicals Teach About Judaism,' in *A Time to Speak: The Evangelical–Jewish Encounter*, ed. James Rudin and Marvin Wilson, Grand Rapids 1987, 81. For more subtle traces of this attitude, see Eugene Fisher, 'Research on Christian Teaching Concerning Jews and Judaism,' *Journal of Ecumenical Studies* 21, 1984, 421–36, sec. 1.A., 'A Latent Marcionite Approach to the Hebrew Scriptures.'

17 Vernon C. Grounds, in *Evangelicals and Jews in an Age of Pluralism*, ed. Marc Tanenbaum, 207. The passage continues: 'Harsh and grating expressions as to [Judaism's] salvific discontinuity are called for – abrogation, displacement, and negation. And those expressions are set down here, I assure you, with some realization of how harsh and grating they must indeed sound to Jewish ears.'

18 The phrase refers to the doctrine that Judaism has been superseded by Christianity, and the Jewish people by the 'New Israel,' the Christian church. I was once invited to speak at the Evangelical Gordon-Conwell Theological Seminary in South Hamilton, Massachusetts. After my presentation, a member of the faculty contended that in the Evangelical view, Judaism was like the first stage of a rocket, absolutely necessary to

get the rocket off the ground, but reaching a point where it serves no further purpose. I refrained from reminding him that most rockets have three stages, and from asking about the implications of his analogy for the relationship between Christianity and Islam.

19 For the texts from which these quotations are taken, see note 5 above. Repudiation of supersessionist theology is often made with reference to its historical consequences. The Presbyterian document explains that 'The long and dolorous history of Christian imperialism, in which the church often justified anti-Jewish acts and attitudes in the name of Jesus, finds its theological base in this teaching' (6). Franklin Littell speaks of the 'superseding or displacement myth' as the 'cornerstone of Christian Antisemitism,' which logically leads to genocide (*The Crucifixion of the Jews*, 2, 30).

20 For example, the Presbyterian document of 1987, after repudiating supersessionism, goes on to affirm that 'faithfulness to [our] covenant requires us to call *all* women and men to faith in Jesus Christ' (6, emphasis in the original), and that 'Christians are commissioned to witness to the whole world about the good news of Christ's atoning work for both Jew and Gentile.' The document seems to reveal a tension that it does not claim fully to resolve. Other Christian thinkers would categorically reject any kind of 'mission to the Jews': see Littell, *The Crucifixion of the Jews*, 88; Eckardts, *Long Night's Journey into Day*, 118–19; Paul Van Buren, *Discerning the Way*, New York 1980, 180ff.

21 It is revealing to compare what the 'Messianic Jews' communicate to Evangelical Christians with their appeal intended for Jews. A good example is 'A Messianic Jew Pleads His Case,' by Daniel Juster with Daniel Pawley, *Christianity Today*, 24 April 1981, 22–4. The 'case' which the author pleads is the right of Messianic Jews to be considered as full-fledged Christians despite their Judaizing. He asserts that 'our basic confession is in conformity with mainstream evangelical Protestant denominations,' and affirms 'the basic evangelical concepts of the authority of Scripture, salvation by grace through faith, the triune nature of God, the resurrection of Jesus, the Second Coming, and so on.' Why then do they retain Jewish 'cultural practices'? 'It is first in relating culturally to our own people that we might win them to Jesus. Paul's words ring in our ears with authenticity: "To the Jews I became as a Jew, in order to win the Jews."'

22 For Jewish reflections on this issue, see the statements by Blu Greenberg and Sanford Seltzer on 'Mission, Witness and Proselytization' in *Evangelicals and Jesus in an Age of Pluralism*, 226–54.

23 Cf. the Hasidic tale in Martin Buber's *Tales of the Hasidim*, 2 vols. New York 1951, 2:86, in which Moshe Leib of Sasov learns the meaning of love by overhearing two Gentile peasants drinking in an inn. Various forms of this tale, usually concluding with 'How can you say you love me if you do not know what gives me pain?' have been cited frequently in the literature of dialogue; see, e.g., the 1975 Report of a Lutheran World Federation Consultation in Croner, *Stepping Stones*, 130.

Source: Marc Saperstein, 1989, *Moments of Crisis in Jewish–Christian Relations*, London: SCM Press, pp. 51–64 (chapter 5, 'Burden from the Past, Opportunities for the Future').

16

Eastern Faith Traditions Respond to Christianity

ALAN RACE AND PAUL HEDGES

Introduction

This section provides three passages reflecting from other traditions back on the way Christianity relates to them. The first is from Seshagiri Rao, a well known Hindu scholar and practitioner of interfaith encounter, and whose impressive credentials include being Professor Emeritus of the University of Virginia, the Chief Editor of the *Encyclopedia of Hinduism*, as well as Co-Editor of the journal *Interreligious Insight*, and a trustee of the World Congress of Faiths. Here he reflects, as a Hindu, on the way Christianity has interpreted his own faith.

The other two are based in Buddhist responses. The first is by a Christian theologian of dialogue, Andreas Grüschloß, but shows his understanding of the way two Buddhist figures – a German Buddhist nun, Ayya Khema, and the well-known Vietnamese Zen master, Thich Nhat Hanh – interpret Christianity through the lens of the person of Jesus in the perspective of their own tradition. Although Grüschloß is somewhat critical of their attempts (seeing it as a form of appropriation/interpretation through their own tradition, rather than a genuine empathetic understanding) he nevertheless conveys a good sense of some of the ways Buddhism responds to the Christian tradition – the reader can judge for themselves whether their attempts to measure Jesus are more successful than Christian attempts to measure Buddha. The final piece is by the 14th Dalai Lama, Tenzin Gyatso, who needs no introduction, and shows him in dialogue with a number of figures, most notable of whom is Fr Laurence Freeman, a leading exponent of Christian meditation. In the extracts used, the Dalai Lama, partly through questions directed at him, explains his views on the person of Jesus. While not directly reflecting upon the way that their tradition has been interpreted by Christianity and responding to this, these pieces do, like Rao's, contemplate one very important aspect of the non-Christian response to the Christian faith – the way they understand the figure of Jesus and his presentation and understanding.

Christian Views of Hinduism: A Hindu Response

SESHAGIRI RAO

Introduction

My first acquaintance with Christianity was in the late 1940s, when under the influence of Mahatma Gandhi, students in Indian colleges considered it a fashion to possess a copy of the Bhagavadgita (a popular Hindu scripture; hereafter Gita) and a copy of the Bible. Gandhi never called himself a Christian; but by his life, outlook and methods he aroused a great deal of interest in Jesus Christ among the Hindus. In my college, a few students (including me) used to meet in the evenings for study and discussions on the Gita and the Bible. Our attempts to understand Jesus Christ were our own, unaided and on the basis of our limited knowledge and readings.

Later on in life, in the early 1960s, I accepted a Fellowship from the Gandhi Peace Foundation, New Delhi, to do research on 'Gandhi's Concept of Reverence for all Religions' (Sarvadharmasmabhava). In that connection, I had opportunities to meet leading religious personalities in India and abroad. I also met Christian scholars and leaders of several Christian denominations such as Revd R. R. Keithan, Dr Devanandan, Dr Albert Cuttat, Prof. Robert Slater, Prof. Wilfred C. Smith, Revd Finley P. Dunne, Jr, Revd Stanley Samartha, Revd John Taylor and Revd Marcus Braybrooke, to mention a few.

In the course of my field work, I went to a Christian colony in a South Indian village. I met several Christians and their family members. I came to know that they belonged to seven different churches. I received from them some unfavourable comments against Hinduism and also against one another. That made me wonder whether what had been communicated to them was Jesus Christ or a lot of legalism as well as denominational information and views, much of which scarcely interested them. While they did not know what or where Rome was, they were Roman Catholics; while they did not know where England was, they were Anglicans. Similarly, they professed adherence to Methodist, Presbyterian, Lutheran, congregational and other churches.

I was eager to know about the life and work of Jesus Christ authentically, not as presented or shaped by this or that church. The different churches came into existence in Europe and America for historical reasons. Hindus find it difficult to understand Christ because of the involvement of the churches in crusades, inquisitions, and persecutions. Further, each church considered itself as 'the true faith' and emphasized its differences from others. But how their divisions were useful in communicating Christ to the Hindus in India was the question that troubled me. I thought that these conflicts and ideologies focused on extraneous factors and hindered the vision of Christ. However, in respect of their views on Hinduism, there was not much difference. I had an opportunity to discuss Hindu and Christian attitudes to each other and to Jesus Christ with Fr Bede Griffiths. I stayed with him in his Kurisumala Ashram in Kerala for a week, most of the time following their discipline of silence and work. I could see how he was emotionally and intellectually living and sharing the teachings of Jesus Christ and Vedanta. I shall mention some details of these discussions later on in this section. Anyway, to do justice to the subject, I have distinguished the response of Hindus to Jesus Christ from their response to the views of Christian churches on Hinduism.

Response to Jesus Christ

A Hindu tries to understand the teachings of Jesus by his example. He looks upon Jesus without the appendages of dogma, doctrine and theology. He gives his attention to his life of love and forgiveness. In the majesty of pure living, in the breadth of sympathy, in the sacrificial outlook of his life and in pure disinterested love, he was supreme. What strikes a Hindu, above all, is his complete obedience to the will of God. That is why his words have so much of appeal to the Hindus.

Jesus Christ is seen by a Hindu through his own cultural and religious background; he seeks him for his own spiritual needs and circumstances of life. He has deep interest in and profound respect for him. There are Hindus who believe that Jesus lived in India during the 'missing years' alluded to in the Gospels. It may be true that Hindus have not understood Jesus fully; but who can claim a full understanding of Jesus Christ? In any case, any attempt to keep him within the compounds of this or that church is futile. Those who cannot imagine him working outside the church ignore the operations of the Holy Spirit.

A Hindu sees that Christ stands for divine concern for the whole world. God is for all, for every human being, rich or poor, man or woman, Hindu, Muslim, Christian or follower of any religion. It is not doing justice to the love of God to restrict his love or to make it conditional on a particular rite or ceremony. The fact is that God is the Father of all human beings.

At the beginning of his ministry, Jesus pointed out that Elijah went not to a Hebrew widow, but to a widow in Sidon (Luke 4.25–26); that Elisha did not heal a Hebrew leper, but Naaman of Syria (Luke 4.27). Jesus was almost thrown over a cliff for his larger concept of God (Luke 4.30). It might also be remembered that the Holy Spirit had already worked in the Cornelius family even before Peter got there. It is such a broad understanding of the life and work of Christ that a Hindu likes to cherish.

Responses to Ecclesiastical Views

Compared to the life, activities and teachings of Jesus Christ, Christian churches have functioned at a different level. When the revelation of the founder filtered through the minds of the church leaders, they understood the Master according to their respective needs, capacities and experience. This tendency applies generally to all churches; each believed that it alone had interpreted the revelation correctly, that the truth as understood by each of them is the whole truth, that its followers are the chosen people and the rest of humanity is groping in the darkness. When revelation becomes restricted to this or that church or community, it ceases to be universal Truth, and the message of Christ gets distorted.

Christianity originated as a gentle and self-suffering faith. Within a century of the crucifixion of Christ, this form of gentle faith was also brought to Malabar in South India by St Thomas. These small Syrian Christian settlements adapted themselves well to Hindu society; this Syrian church is even today a living tradition in South India. In its early phase, it did not even proselytize. But in Europe, by about the fourth century, Christianity was transformed into an aggressive creed in which even war was sanctioned and encouraged by the church. Emperor Justinian built a number of churches, but also executed thousands upon thousands of people for being 'heretical Christians and pagans'. The Middle Ages in Europe witnessed the domineering sway of the Christian church and not the gentle, human and divine way of Jesus. Churches are very human institutions, and they have not been free from temptations of self-perpetuation and self-glorification. They do not tolerate differences and dissent. Frequently, they become competitive among themselves to attract more and more followers. 'Jesus preached the coming of the Kingdom of God and what came out was the Church.'

Christianity came into effective contact with Hinduism in India, during the days of colonial expansion of western powers: Portuguese, French, Dutch and British. Their knowledge of Hinduism was poor and distorted. It came mixed with and vitiated by imperialism, colonial domination, a degree of racism and a dose of western culture. Even architecture and music of the churches of the colonies imitated western styles. To a large extent, these historical factors have influenced Christian understanding of Hinduism; and Hindus question the relevance of these factors in understanding their tradition.

Christian Triumphalism

Christian churches saw in Hinduism an opportunity for its replacement with Christianity. They did not respect the faith of others and the dignity of the followers of other religions; Portuguese missionaries destroyed many

Hindu temples and Muslim mosques. Francis Xavier did not even spare Syrian Christians, who had adapted well to the Hindu customs; their valuable manuscripts were burnt. The followers of Hinduism were called 'unbelievers'. They were condemned as 'pagans', 'polytheists' and 'idolaters'. There was an implicit belief that western nations enjoyed a superior religion in Christianity. William Wilberforce said in the British Parliament, 'Our Christian religion is sublime, pure and beneficent. The Indian religious system is mean, licentious and cruel.' Christian churches imposed their own preconceptions on Hinduism. They called it 'superstitious and pernicious'. They believed that Christianity is the true religion and concluded that other religions are false. Karl Barth refused to recognize any revelation of God in other religions; in his *Church Dogmatics* (I. Part 2) he says that they are 'acutely and chronically sick' (p. 315). Hendrick Kraemer's theology of discontinuity and his *The Christian Message in a Non-Christian World* gave great support to evangelism.

The churches used their schools and colleges as well as hospitals and orphanages for the purpose of evangelism. The evangelicals felt that Christianity was the primary tool for 'civilizing' India. Even English education was used for this purpose. Their study of Hinduism was geared to the establishment of the superiority of Christianity; they studied Sanskrit as a means of discrediting Hinduism, and in their work, the missionaries exaggerated the vulnerable problems of Hindu society, such as caste system, untouchability, and unfair treatment of women, and also denigrated Hindu rituals and ceremonies. They had little appreciation for the positive elements in Hindu thought and practice. The objective of these efforts was the conversion of the Hindus to Christianity. The World Conference of the International Missionary Council in Tambaram (1938) stated that 'care should be taken to secure that evangelism has a central place in all medical and educational institutions, their real agenda of conversion of Hindus'.

In Hindu perspective, such views and policies of the churches did not do justice to Hinduism; they distorted and misrepresented Hindu institutions, rituals and practices. The exclusive zeal of the missionaries of this period prevented them from looking at the Hindu tradition objectively. Nor did they do justice to what Jesus said: 'In my Father's house are many mansions: if it were not so, I would have told you' (John 14.2). Again, 'Of a truth I perceive that God is no respecter of persons: But in every nation he that feareth him, and worketh righteousness, is accepted with him.' (Acts 10.34–35, AV). Exclusivism locks out the followers of other faiths and ways of life. It results in alienation from other communities and from God. It prevents free exercise of love across religious frontiers. But God is concerned with all peoples and cultures. The depth and scope of this infinite dealing supersedes all theological and missionary formulations. Further, the proliferation of mutually competing and sometimes opposing churches and denominations had taken the fire out of Christianity. Hindus wonder whether the whole

Truth could be found in the compounds of churches. Mahatma Gandhi wrote, 'The great faiths held by the people of India are adequate for her people. India stands in no need of conversion from one faith to another' (*Young India*, 14 July, 1927).

Hindus do not accept the ecclesiastical view that Jesus Christ is the only son of God or the only instance of God's self-disclosure or that the Bible is the only Scripture. Such totalitarian claims betray pride and self-righteousness. They do not accept the doctrine of 'original sin' or the 'avoidance of hell' as determinative factors in life. To them, realization of God is the goal of life. According to Mahatma Gandhi, 'the great faiths of the world are like many branches of a tree, each distinct from the other, but have the same source' (*Harijan*, 6 April 1939). Hindus accept the Bible and the Scriptures of other religions, along with the Vedas as the word of God. Hindu tradition does not claim that it is the sole repository of truth. Nowhere in the Hindu Scriptures is it said that only Hindus are eligible for salvation. Hindu vision reveals one Supreme Being, unity of humanity, but many households of faith.

With all the hopes and opportunities of the colonial era, Christian triumphalism did not succeed. Christian churches did not make expected headway in the evangelistic work. Christianity continues to be by and large a minority religion in India and in most of Asia. There are no signs of immediate or even distant displacement of Hinduism and other religions by Christianity.

The Crown of Hinduism

There were others who tried to make some accommodation for Hinduism; they considered Hinduism to be preparatory to Christianity, as J. N. Farquhar stated in his widely known book, *The Crown of Hinduism* published in 1913. Disparaging contrasts between Hindu and Christian traditions were given up, and instead Christianity was preached as the 'fulfilment of Hinduism'. They saw in Hinduism human effort to reach God, but they stated that Christianity is 'God's disclosure to humanity'. They saw some truths in Hinduism, but asserted that Christianity is the 'paragon of all religions', and it alone has full truth. They called Hinduism a 'natural religion' and declared Christianity to be a 'revealed religion'. They propagated Christianity as the final stage of humankind's religious development. They judged the Scriptures of other religions as imperfect. They regarded Hinduism as 'life-negating', and affirmed that Christianity is 'life-affirming'. There were Catholic missionaries who even sought to divest the gospel of western cultural trappings to attract Hindus to become Christians by conversion. Certain Hindu practices such as bhajans and kirtans (devotional singing) were used for evangelistic work. For example, Robert de Nobili claimed to be and lived like a Brahmin guru and converted thousands of Hindus to

Christianity. Some others considered that Jesus was a human manifestation of the divine Logos. They said that Hindus are not non-Christians, but
'anonymous Christians', and they are included in 'the unique design of God
in Jesus Christ'. They can only be saved by Christ. This view was upheld
by Karl Rahner in his *Theological Investigations* (vol. V, p. 118). It also
became the official view of the Vatican after the Second Vatican Council.

The catholicity of the Hindu mind and its love of tolerance made it difficult for the Hindus to accept such supercilious and patronizing notions of
their tradition. While the ideal side of the gospel was appreciated, the history
of the churches did not make any strong appeal to the Hindus. To them,
Jesus Christ is one expression of the divine Logos; they say that no religious
tradition can claim that it has the final answer for all others. Such views are
inappropriate to the dignity of other religions. Further, in their view, the
control of the flow of life toward worldly objects and sensate indulgence is
not to be understood as life-negating. Attachment to superficial and fleeting
sense pleasures is to be avoided to live a spiritual life; it is not negating life,
but the affirmation of a deeper view of life. Hindus appreciate the saying of
Jesus: 'He who loves his life shall lose it.'

Hindus are criticized for their treatment of women and for giving them a
secondary status. It is true that many traditions have given undue emphasis
to masculine symbolism and male religious experience. The exploitation of
women in a male-dominated world is a serious issue in all religious traditions. Women have been denied their full participation in the life of many
churches also, but strong movements are underway now to look upon God
as woman or at least to use gender-free language in theology. Woman is
the giver of life, she is the custodian of humankind. God is neither male nor
female; Jesus says that God is spirit. Male and female are two aspects of
infinite consciousness, and their union leads to transcendental consciousness. In the Hindu heritage, the feminine principle is recognized as the
embodiment of the dynamic energy underlying the entire universe. Hindus
worship God in both masculine and feminine symbols and images. This
practice is not peripheral, but is in the mainstream of the tradition. It points
to the importance of the role of the feminine in all levels of life.

Postcolonial Trends

India attained its independence from British Rule in August 1947. Around
the middle of the twentieth century, many Asian countries also gained their
political freedom from western colonial domination. Hindus intensified
their efforts to separate Jesus Christ from colonialism. They rejected ecclesiastical views of their tradition, and began to look at Jesus Christ from a
Hindu perspective.

Jesus Christ is an ineradicable part of modern Hinduism. Hindus adore the Jesus Christ of the Gospels. The influence of Christ is felt by many Hindus in all walks of life. Their responses to him are varied, but they have discovered that the life and teachings of Jesus were in harmony with important aspects of Hinduism. Raja Ram Mohan Roy wrote extensively on Christianity from a Hindu perspective, and he accepted Jesus as a moral teacher. Keshub Chandra Sen refused to accept Christianity on western terms; to him, 'Christ is a true yogi', and he will surely help us 'to realize our natural ideal of a yogi'. He compared the Hindu concept of *sat, cit* and *ananda* (Being, Consciousness and Bliss) with the Christian Trinity. Some others consider him as a *sadguru*, true teacher, and P. C. Mazumdar tried to free Jesus Christ from Christian sectarianism. Mahatma Gandhi, as an orthodox Hindu, showed great reverence and publicly acknowledged his indebtedness to Jesus Christ. Gandhi said, 'Even the blind who do not see the rose perceive its fragrance. That is the secret of the gospel of the rose. But the gospel that Jesus preached is more subtle and fragrant than the gospel of the rose.' Ramakrishna Mission celebrates Christmas in its monasteries; the Mission and its followers adore Jesus Christ as an incarnation of God. To them, spiritual truth is the very light and life of all, and the call of Christmas is a call for 'new birth in spirit'.

Religious Pluralism

A qualitative change in Christian attitudes and approaches to other religions is taking place. Let me support it with my personal experience. I was invited as a guest participant and a Hindu consultant to the World Conference of Mission and Evangelism convened in San Antonio, Texas by the World Council of Churches in May 1989. Revd Eugene Stockwell, Director of the Commission on World Mission and Evangelism of WCC, was a keynote speaker, and I was pleasantly surprised at the tone of his speech. In his address, he deprecated literalism, quantitative obsessions, power play, Christian triumphalism, and so forth. He rejected the cultural pride that branded the followers of other religions 'pagans' and 'heathens'. He said that 'If humanity is to survive, respectful dialogue with the representatives of other faiths is both necessary and Christian imperative.' (See *San Antonio Report*, ed. Fred Wilson, Geneva: WCC Publications, 1998, p. 125.) He also asked Christians to 'open themselves to God's gifts in other faiths'. He reminded them that 'Christians have little standing to decide who will be saved and who will not ... We can leave to God the decision about ultimate salvation.'

Many Christians are realizing that they have no monopoly of Christ; they are finding that an exclusive conception of Christianity is untenable. Professor John Hick writes in *World Faiths Encounter* (no. 28, March 2001): 'The old exclusivist view that only Christians are saved has been abandoned by the majority of Christian theologians and church leaders.' It is now being understood that God is committed to all humans, that God's love embraces the whole world, and that branding the pious people of other religions as 'pagans' is unchristian. Revd Lowell R. Ditzen, the then Director of the National Presbyterian Center, Washington, DC, made a significant speech at the Spiritual Summit Conference in Calcutta (1968), recorded by the editor of *The World Religions Speak* (The Hague: JNV Publishers, 1970). Referring to the activities of the Christian missionaries in the past, Revd Ditzen said,

> Some of them have come to your lands and have been insufferably arrogant in trying to impose the religion of Christianity on your people. Many Christian missionaries have had inexcusably bad manners. There can be no place for chest pounding nor for any attempt to impose one set of beliefs on any one else in the kind of world in which we live. We need, as never before in human history, to communicate with each other, to listen to each other, to have respectful regard for each other, and as world religionists to inspire leaders of government to form the organizational structure needed to carry the human race forward toward peace. (p. 115)

A deeper and a thorough investigation of Christian heritage is being undertaken by some scholars. They are working on theological constructions that would be just to the people of other faiths. They are looking at things in a fresh way. For example, Professor Durwood Foster explores 'the new mood', the chief aspect of which is 'openness to mutual dialogue'; he says, 'Commitment to Christ is commitment to openness ... Committing to his openness, one finds oneself committed to all others, in their truth and most real needs' (see *Visions of An Interfaith Future*, Oxford: International Interfaith Centre, 1994). A movement of unrestricted dialogue and exchange between religious faiths has been initiated by thinkers like Wilfred Cantwell Smith, Paul Knitter, John Hick, and it reveals a new spiritual horizon hospitable to the faiths of others. They advocate religious pluralism; they say that world religions are different, but that they are necessary; they see in them different dimensions of truth. Every religion is strong in some values and weak in some others, no religion is perfect. Diversity of cultures brings richness and beauty to human life; they are complementary. Religious pluralism provides a suitable context, within which each tradition can preserve its unique features, and can act, react, grow and develop. Father Bede Griffiths, in his book *The Marriage of East and West*, (Springfield, IL: Templegate, 1982, p. 190) envisions 'a convergence and a balance between the rational and aggressive West and intuitive and passive East'. He writes in his *Universal Wisdom* (Boston: HarperCollins, 1994), 'Semitic Monotheism overemphasizes the transcendent aspect of God and undervalues God's immanence' (p. 64). Hinduism emphasizes both. Diversity is a fact of our world; it cannot be ignored. Actually, it is the basis for dialogue. He writes in his commentary on the Gita, entitled *River of Compassion* (New York: Amity House, 1987) that

> We are realizing today that no religion can stand alone. We all share a common humanity and need to share the insights of all different religions of the world. A Christian who is open to the message of the Gita will find that it throws new light on many aspects of the Gospel and will see at the same time how the *Bhagavadgita* gathers a new meaning when seen in the perspective of the Gospel. (p. 1)

We are at a crucial turning-point in history. Past modes of thought that considered people as closed groups are no more valid. Categorization of people of other faiths as pagans, heathens, kaffirs and barbarians is not valid. Religious traditions are useful in many ways, but religious exclusivism is close-minded and outdated. Behind us, there is the history of centuries of religious confrontations; before us, the chance of peace, cooperation and dialogue. We have to live in a world that has followers of many religions. Loyalty to our respective traditions should not undermine our loyalty to humanity. Multi-religious society provides suitable context, within which each individual can grow and develop. Attempts are to be made to understand the self-understanding of different religions. Dialogue can bring out the unique message of each religion for the benefit of humanity.

Hindu–Christian Dialogue

Sri Ramakrishna's response to the Bible and Christ illustrates Hindu attitudes to Christianity; it deserves special mention. When he listened to the readings of the New Testament, he began to practise the spiritual disciplines of Christianity. Once he was looking at a painting of the Madonna and the child; suddenly that whole picture became alive to him, and he went into deep ecstasy. This spell continued for three days. On the fourth day, he saw a person of serene countenance approaching him slowly and smiling beautifully; a voice from the depths of his soul rang out, 'Behold Christ, who shed his heart's blood for the redemption of the world.' In Christ, he found the embodiment of love and compassion, his unbounded love for humanity, particularly for those suffering most. He said, 'I look on Him (Jesus Christ) as an Incarnation of God.' He experienced that Sri Rama, Sri Krishna, Allah, and Christ signify him only. He realized that paths are many, but God is one. Water is called by different names in different languages. Differences are in languages and perceptions, not in substance.

Incarnation (Avatar)

Christian churches teach that Jesus Christ is the only incarnation of God. But Hindus consider Jesus Christ as one of many avatars (divine incarnations); he is one expression of the divine Logos. Hindus hold that God descends into the world, whenever there is a serious crisis in history; the purpose of the incarnation is to defeat the evil and protect the good. They see interesting parallels in Hindu and Christian Scriptures on this matter. Lord Krishna says about the purpose of avatar (incarnation of God on earth) in the Gita:

> When righteousness declines and
> Unrighteousness becomes predominant,
> Then I descend upon the earth.
> For the salvation of those who are pious,
> And for the destruction of the wicked,
> And for the reestablishment of the
> Kingdom of righteousness, I come into
> The world age after age
>
> (IV. 7–8)

Mary discloses to Elizabeth God's purpose in the Song of Praise:

> And holy is his name.
> And his mercy is on them that fear him
> from generation to generation.
> he hath shewed strength with his arm;
> he hath scattered the proud in the
> imagination of their hearts.
> He hath put down the mighty from their seats,
> and exalted them of low degree.
> He hath filled the hungry with good things;
> and the rich he hath sent empty away.
>
> (Luke 1.49–53, AV)

Reincarnation and Karma

All religions accept survival beyond bodily death. But not all of them have explained the details of the soul's journey after death; many have left them vague. Generally, Christian churches do not admit the concept of reincarnation. In recent years, some Christian scholars and theologians, remaining firmly within the Christian church, have considered reincarnation as a valid phenomenon. They also show that it was acceptable in Christian tradition in early times. They point to the return of the prophet Elijah in the form of

John the Baptist. They also say that the theory of reincarnation does justice to the Christian God of compassion. An errant child is given enough opportunities to correct its mistakes; God wishes that no soul be lost. To say that 'there is only one chance for a person to achieve salvation, and if the person fails, it is eternal damnation' does not express the divine spirit or even the human spirit. It is not in agreement with Hindu spirit either. Hindus say that the knowledge of the structures and functions of the inner world is the result of prolonged investigations and experimentations. The physical body of a person degenerates and dies, but the soul is imperishable. The mind and its constituents constitute the subtle body, the essence of individuality. It is the subtle body that survives and continues, and it is the storehouse of karma. Mind is the carrier of the individual from one body to the other, and when the subtle body leaves, the gross body collapses.

In Hinduism, spiritual liberation is obtained through the effort of many lives. The subtle body continues to accompany the soul until it is released from bondage. In other words, reincarnation is not the goal of life; it is a fact of inner life. The goal is eternal life, spiritual liberation. Each lifetime is a God-given opportunity for making further spiritual progress. Each person reaps the fruits of his karma – thoughts, words and actions – done in the past. We also generate new causes which bear fruit in present or future lives. Karma is the principle of moral causation. Every event, big or small, has sufficient cause. Sometimes, we may not know the cause. It does not mean that there is no cause. By careful investigation with proper methods, we can find out the cause. 'As you sow, so you reap'; Hindus accept it. They further elaborate that what we are reaping now is the result of what we had sown before. According to a recent Gallup poll, about 27 per cent of Christians in North America and Europe find answers to several of their personal problems in the concept of reincarnation.

In the interpretation of Jesus' life, Hindus pay the highest regard to the quality of his life. They see the unique message of Jesus in the Sermon on the Mount. It deals with the inwardness of morals and rituals. Righteous conduct is an essential part of religion. He exhorted, 'Be ye perfect even as your Father which is in heaven is perfect' (Matt. 5.48, AV). He emphasizes the need for the practice of his teaching, not merely hearing it and believing in it:

Therefore whosoever heareth these sayings of mine, and doeth them, I will liken him unto a wise man, which built his house upon a rock; and the rain descended, and the floods came, and the winds blew, and beat upon the house; and it fell not; for it was founded upon a rock. And everyone that heareth these sayings of mine, and doeth them not, shall be likened unto a foolish man, which built his house upon the sand; and the rain descended, and the floods came, and the winds blew, and beat upon that house; and it fell; and great was the fall of it. (Matt. 7.24–27, AV)

Here is a refreshing statement of human responsibility. The emphasis is on karma, or action. Human moral effort is necessary. Jesus says, 'If ye love me, keep my commandments' (John 14.15, AV). Jesus told Nicodemus that the individual could only be saved by means of self-purification, by regeneration by being reborn of water (total purification) and of the spirit (divine knowledge). He declared, 'Not every one that saith unto me, Lord, Lord, shall enter into the kingdom of heaven; but he that doeth the will of my Father which is in heaven' (Matt. 7.21, AV).

Conclusion

Hindus have never sought nor do they seek to convert humanity to any one set of beliefs. In this sense, they have never been and will never be in competition with Christianity. They only seek friendliness and cooperation with Christians as with people of other faiths. Hindus and Christians have to fight together common enemies of evil and injustice in society. They should involve themselves in humanitarian activities with a holistic approach. Holistic approach relates not only to one's faith community but also to humanity and to God. Interreligious dialogue and engagement is 'our common spiritual journey'.

There is an eternal longing of the individual for the Infinite, the ground of one's own being. Jesus declares: 'God is spirit and those who worship him must worship him in spirit and truth.' Jesus speaks to human beings as human beings, whatever their place and time. His teachings are universal. Sincere seekers of truth should cooperate and communicate at the deeper levels of the spirit. Systems and theologies are outgrown, but not his spiritual message. It is desirable, therefore, that the interpretation of Jesus Christ and his activities should be big enough to be meaningful to the followers of all religions. A Hindu seeks a universal, eternal and living Christ.

Source: original piece commissioned for this work.

The Buddhist Jesus: An Unknown Brother of the Buddha[1]

ANDREAS GRÜSCHLOSS (AYYA KHEMA AND THICH NHAT HANH)

(1) *Ayya Khema* (1923–1997) is the first person to be analyzed here. She was a well known Buddhist nun, who originally came from a Jewish family and who finally managed to escape from Nazi Germany in 1938. Later, she

was trained as [a] Theravada-Buddhist teacher in Burma, Thailand and Sri Lanka. She was ordained as a *bhikkhuni* [in] 1979 and founded and organized several retreat and study centers. She returned to Germany in 1989 where she was active in Buddhist–Christian Dialogues until her death.

Ayya Khema can serve us as a good representative of the Theravada, Pāli Canon-based form of Buddhism. There are two books by her focusing on biblical themes.[2] Not being a convert from *Christianity* to Buddhism, how does she cope with Christianity and Jesus?

In an introduction she states that she is aiming at a better understanding between the traditions, in order to acknowledge the community between the traditions and 'to arrive at a better understanding, especially of the spiritual realm'.[3] Right away she formulates her important guiding thesis: 'that the same is being taught in every religion'[4] – and that is, whether we understand that which has to be done, and whether we practice accordingly.

She can parallel 1 Cor 13 ('Song of Love') and Mt 5,3ff ('Beatitudes') verse by verse with Buddhist associations. A few examples: 'Blessed are the poor in spirit, for theirs is the kingdom of heavens', is paralleled with the Buddha's teaching to empty the mind, to become 'poor in spirit', to focus the mind and to attain calmness of mind (samathabhāvanā) and the consecutive meditative stages (jhānas). The phrase 'kingdom of heavens' is interpreted as alluding to such higher states of consciousness.

The blessing of those without power, of the grieving, of the ones who thirst for justice – all these highly 'realistic' examples of Jesus' Beatitudes are spiritualized by Ayya Khema: 'We have to approach his words on a certain level, which can open spiritual understanding of the question how we can be filled inwardly … since not to experience fulfillment, that's our lot.'[5] In her concluding paragraph on the blessings she writes: This is all about an exercise to let go thinking in favor of some direct experience; only the acceptance of un-fulfillment (i.e. 'suffering') brings remedy; all claims to power have to be overcome in favor of an 'inner richness'; detachment and readiness to give are important.

Thus it becomes obvious, she states again, that all religions teach the same – but 'The Buddha-dhamma additionally informs us of a method to realize this inner growth.'[6] Yet when she runs into passages which are dealing with God – or visions of God – she becomes more hesitant ('the conception of a personal God cannot help us to get closer to the truth'[7]); her commentaries boil down to statements to the effect that God can be understood as 'our true nature,' or 'true love can be called the Divine'.[8] However in some respects Ayya Khema appears to opt for a transcendent, even *mystical* 'ground' of the so-called 'Divine' ('göttliche Natur', 'göttlicher Funke') which lies beyond categorical, rational understanding.[9]

Conclusion. As these few examples can already illustrate, Ayya Kherna is 're-discovering' items of Buddhist wisdom all over the Bible. Concrete remarks about justice, sadness, powerlessness, etc, are always *spiritualized* and *explained as generic inner attitudes*. The element of a personal 'God' is evaded and often appears reduced to cultivation of spiritual awareness – only a transpersonal 'Divine' could perhaps denote something like a (common) deeper layer of religious experience. Finally, the only striking difference between Christianity and Buddhism lies in the fact that the Buddha also taught a way to achieve these common goals and virtues (which can be found in all religions). She never seems to find something new, something different, or something surprising. She constantly alienates Jesus' sayings from their origin and context and appropriates them in a very inclusivist manner through Buddhist eyes and concepts. Although this might not do justice to Ayya Khema's personality and friendly approach, this inclusivism is conceptually nevertheless a form of the 'got the same back home but bigger'[10] attitude, which is typical of all such hierarchical appropriations of the other.

(2) Thich Nhat Hanh (* 1926). The famous Zen-Teacher from Vietnam does not need to be introduced here; he is famous for his personal integration of socio-critical, peace-making efforts and meditative spirituality.[11] Thich Nhat Hanh has written several books on the interrelation between Buddhism and Christianity, and he displays a different approach: He has been *living* with biblical texts for a longer time, he cultivates a personal spirituality with relation to Jesus *and* Buddha – 'the living Buddha' and 'the living Christ', as he says.[12] But in terms of content, his findings are nevertheless similar to Ayya Khema's. He also (re-)discovers mindfulness, a raising of consciousness among Jesus' disciples, peacefulness (the prescription against killing), as well as kindly openness towards all people. Jesus, therefore, is to him explicitly another 'Dharma door'.[13] Jesus' saying; 'Whenever two or three are gathered in my name, I am there', is explained in so far as the eternal Buddha-Dharmakaya and the Christian God have to be understood as the living and ever-teaching 'ground of being'.[14] True religious experience always leads to a de-dogmatizing and de-dualizing; the 'Our Father'-prayer is aimed at the destruction of the human ego (etc.).[15]

Jesus appears as a spiritually advanced *teacher* and as a *social activist*, and as such he is an important 'ancestor' for Thich Nhat Hanh, because Buddha *and* Jesus together are for him spiritual cornerstones in the orientation to a new form of spirituality, which is meditatively centered and also active in fostering peace. The protagonist of 'inter-being' is not afraid of a religious 'fruit salad',[16] but he bases his life actively on two sources: not the *historical* Buddha and the *historical* Jesus, but both teachers as *living realities*, which can manifest themselves in life with other people – as spiritual realities which transcend mere words like 'God'.[17]

Conclusion. Thich Nhat Hanh recollects many virtues and ideals, which have become vital for him in his life – also in the face of the biblical Jesus. However, he would prefer not to have him portrayed on the cross: This image 'does not convey joy or peace, and this does not do justice [to] Jesus.

I hope that our Christian friends will also portray Jesus in other ways, like sitting in the lotus position or doing the walking meditation. Doing so will allow us to feel peace and joy penetrating into our hearts when we contemplate Jesus.'[18]

Notes

1 At various points in his chapter, Grüschloß reproduces some artwork showing Jesus and/or the Buddha; they are not reproduced here and those interested are directed to the original work.

2 In what follows, I focus on Khema (1999) [Ayya Khema, *Das Größte ist die Liebe: Die Bergpredigt und das Hohelied der Liebe aus buddhistischer Sicht*, Uttenbühl: Jhana Verlag]; see also Khema (2000) [Ayya Khema, *Nicht so viel denken, mehr lieben: Buddha und Jesus im Dialog*, Munich].

3 Khema (1999), p. 9f.

4 *Ibid.* p. 12.

5 *Ibid.* p. 45.

6 *Ibid.* p. 46.

7 *Ibid.* p. 62.

8 *Ibid.* p. 60.

9 *Ibid.* p. 62f. – This could be understood as a hint towards her former involvement in mystical strands of the Jewish faith – prior to her decision for Buddhism. Cf. the references to Ayya Kmema in Nathan Katz's contribution to this volume [Nathan Katz, 2008, 'Buddhist–Jewish Relations', in Perry Schmidt-Leukel (ed.), *Buddhist Attitudes to Other Religions*, St. Ottilien: EOS Verlag, pp. 269-93]. I would like to thank Nathan Katz and Perry Schmidt-Leukel, who have convincingly pointed out to me in conversation that there might be more to Ayya Khema's biographical involvement with a kabbalistic essence behind the manifestations.

10 This utterance is said to be a typical statement of Australians visiting London (British rumour).

11 Cf. K. Kiblinger's contribution to this volume [Kristin Beise Kiblinger, 2008, 'Buddhist Stances Towards Others: Types, Examples, Considerations', in Perry Schmidt-Leukel (ed.), *Buddhist Attitudes to Other Religions*, St. Ottilien: EOS Verlag, pp. 24–46]. – CF. also Brück, Lai (1997), pp. 560–568 [Michael von Brück and Whalen Lai, *Buddhismus und Christentum: Geschichte, Konfrontation, Dialog*, Munich: C. H. Beck].

12 Nhat Hanh (1996) [*Living Buddha, Living Christ*, London: Rider]. Cf. also Nhat Hanh (1996b) and (1999) [*Be Still and Know*, NY: Riverhead Trade, and *Going Home: Jesus and Buddha as Brothers*, London: Rider].

13 Nhat Hanh 1996, p. 39.

14 *Ibid.* p. 51.

15 *Ibid.* pp. 179–86.

16 *Ibid.* p. 1f.

17 *Ibid.* p. 21f.

18 Nhat Hanh (1999), p. 46f.

Source: Andreas Grüschloß, 2008, 'Buddhist–Christian Relations', in Perry Schmidt-Leukel (ed.), *Buddhist Attitudes to Other Religions*, St Ottilien: EOS Verlag, pp. 237–68, extract from pp. 253–6 (section, 'The Buddhist Jesus: An Unknown Brother of the Buddha').

The Good Heart

TENZIN GYATSO (HH THE 14TH DALAI LAMA)

The Dalai Lama: When we compare two ancient spiritual traditions like Buddhism and Christianity, what we see is a striking similarity between the narratives of the founding masters: in the case of Christianity, Jesus Christ, and in the case of Buddhism, the Buddha. I see a very important parallel, in the very lives of the masters, the founding teachers, the essence of their teachings are demonstrated. For example, in the life of the Buddha, the essence of the Buddha's teaching is embodied in the Four Noble Truths: the truth of suffering, the truth of the origin of suffering, the truth of the cessation of suffering, and the truth of the path leading to this cessation. These Four Noble Truths are very explicitly and clearly exemplified in the life of the founding teacher, the Buddha himself. I feel this is the same case with the life of Christ. If you look at the life of Jesus, you will see all the essential practices and teachings of Christianity exemplified. Another similarity that I see is that in both the lives of Jesus Christ and the Buddha, it is only through hardship, dedication, and commitment and by standing firm on one's principles that one can grow spiritually and attain liberation. That seems to be a central and common message.

Isabelle Glover: Your Holiness, you mentioned 'rebirth.' In the early days of the Christian church there are many signs that rebirth may have been an accepted belief which is no longer operative in Christian thinking.[1] Could you speak more about that? How important is the teaching on rebirth and karma?

The Dalai Lama: I have heard about this point that you raise, that in the teachings of the early Church there are certain parts of the Scriptures that could be interpreted as implying that a belief in rebirth need not be incompatible with Christian faith. Because of that I have taken the liberty to discuss this point with various Christian priests and leaders – of course, I haven't had the opportunity to ask His Holiness the Pope directly. But otherwise, I've asked many different Christian practitioners and Christian priests about this. I was told by all of them, quite unanimously, that this belief in rebirth is not accepted in Christian doctrine – although no specific reason was given as to why the concept of rebirth would not fit in the wider context of Christian faith and practice. However, about two years ago in Australia, at my last meeting with Father Bede Griffiths (I have met him on several occasions and know him personally), I asked him the same question. I vividly remember the meeting; he was dressed in his *sadhu* saffron-yellow robes, and it was a very moving encounter. He said that, from the Christian point of view, a belief in rebirth would undermine the force in one's faith and practice. When you accept that this life, your individual existence, has been directly created and is like a direct gift from the Creator, it immediately creates a very special bond between you as an individual creature and the Creator. There's a direct personal connection that gives you a sense of closeness and an intimacy with your Creator. A belief in rebirth would undermine that special relationship with the Creator. I found this explanation deeply convincing.

Father Laurence: Your Holiness, I see a connection between the question that Robert Kiely raised and the one that Isabelle just asked, about the relationship between time and eternity, the absolute and the relative. One of the names that Christians give to God is Truth. And all human beings know through experience that truth is something we discover by stages. Truth is emergent; it comes about through phases in an individual's life – whether it is one life or several lives. We also see that there is a historical evolution of religion. There is an absolute core to the teachings of the Buddha and the teachings of Jesus, but the truth of them emerges through history, through reflection. Otherwise, there would be no point in having a Seminar like this one. There is always more truth to be discovered. Would you comment on this idea of truth as something which is here-and-now in its fullness, but also as that which is experienced little-by-little in stages?

The Dalai Lama: Buddhist teachings also address the question of how ultimate truth manifests in stages and has a historical evolution, while at the same time it is absolute or ultimate. There's a particular passage in the *Prajñāpāramitāsūtra*, one of a collection of Buddhist scriptures known as the *Perfection of Wisdom Sutras*, that deals specifically with this concept. The passage states that whether the buddhas of the past or future have come to the world, or whether there is even a buddha existing in the world or not, the truth of the ultimate mode of being of things and events will always remain the same. This truth is ever-present: it is always there. However, this does not imply that all living beings will share in that truth – that is, will attain liberation – spontaneously or without any effort, because individuals must experience that truth in a gradual way. So we must make a distinction between the actual existence of the truth on the one hand, and the experience of that truth on the other. It is here that the point of contact between the historicity and the absolute nature of truth can be understood.

You raised an interesting point. How can an absolute principle like the divine Creator manifest in a historical figure like Christ? What exactly is the nature of the relationship, and what are the mechanics that would explain the relationship of the absolute, which is timeless, and a historical figure, which is time-bound? In the Buddhist context, this question would be regarded in terms of what is known as the doctrine of the *three kāyas*, the three embodiments of an enlightened being. Within this framework, the physical, historical manifestations of enlightened beings are seen, in some sense, as spontaneous emergences from the timeless, ultimate state of the *dharmakāya*, or Truth Body of a buddha.

Robert Kiely: Perhaps another way of thinking about this, especially in terms of day-to-day practice and worship, would be to recall the titles or names that Christians give to Jesus and Buddhists give to the Buddha. One of the seeming paradoxes of Christianity is that we call Jesus our Brother and our Redeemer, or our Brother and our Savior. In personal terms, this can mean that we are invited to love Jesus as a human being, as a brother or spouse. At the same time, we believe that he is our savior, our redeemer, so we also worship him as God. These names remind us that Jesus endows us with the capacity to love him both ways, that he brings his divinity into our hearts. Does this correspond at all to the feelings Buddhists have for the Buddha and the names they give to him?

The Dalai Lama: Given that there is such a diversity even among the Buddhist traditions, we should not have the impression that there is one homogeneous tradition, one definitive path as it were. Personally, I prefer to relate to Buddha as a historical figure and personality – someone who has perfected human nature and evolved into a fully enlightened being. However, according to certain schools of thought in Buddhism, Buddha is not just seen as a historical figure, but also shares a timeless, infinite dimension. In this context, although Buddha is a historical figure, the historicity of Buddha Shakyamuni would be seen as a skillful display of Buddha's compassionate action manifesting from the perfected, timeless state of the *dharmakāya*, or Truth Body. Buddha Shakyamuni as a historical figure is known as the *nirmānakāya*, which means Emanation Body: an emanation that is assumed in order to suit the mental dispositions and needs of a particular time, place, and context. That emanation comes from a preceding emanation, the *sambhogakāya*, or perfect resourceful state, which has arisen from the timeless expanse of the *dharmakāya*. However, if we go into all of these specifics now, we would have plenty of material for headaches and confusion!

The simplest way to regard Buddha Shakyamuni as a historical figure is as follows. For Buddhists – especially for those who are following a monastic way of life – Buddha was the founder of the Buddhist monastic tradition. He is the origin of the lineage of Buddhist monasticism. Fully ordained monks and nuns within that lineage must maintain complete acceptance of their vows of ordination. In order for someone to be a *bhiksu*, a fully ordained monk, or a *bhiksuni*, a fully ordained nun, he or she must be a human being. So if you relate to Buddha as a fully ordained monk then that means you relate to him as a historical, human person.

...

The Dalai Lama: For a Buddhist, whose main object of refuge is the Buddha, when coming into contact with someone like Jesus Christ whose life clearly demonstrates a being who has affected millions of people in a spiritual way, bringing about their liberation and freedom from suffering – the feeling that one would have toward such a person would be that of reverence toward a fully enlightened being or a bodhisattva.

Sister Eileen: Would Your Holiness have certain questions you would like to ask him?

The Dalai Lama: The first question I would ask is, 'Could you describe the nature of the Father?' Because our lack of understanding concerning the exact nature of the Father is leading to so much confusion here!

Sister Eileen: Well, now we think it's both Father and Mother![2]

Father Laurence: Perhaps Mary could be at the meeting as well!

The Dalai Lama: Whenever I see an image of Mary, I feel that she represents love and compassion. She is like a symbol of love. In Buddhist iconography; the goddess Tara occupies a similar position.

Ajahn Amaro: Your Holiness, I don't know if I dare ask another metaphysical question ... But speaking of differences in our traditions, as a Westerner I've always found it hard to accommodate the uniqueness of Jesus Christ, to understand him as a completely unique human being, different from all others that have ever appeared in the world. I wonder if you have any reflections that you'd like to offer, since this idea comes across regularly in the Christian scriptures. How do you relate to the idea of the unique special nature of Jesus?

The Dalai Lama: If you are asking how a practicing Christian should understand the claims of uniqueness of Jesus Christ, then my answer is that it is only by relying on the authoritative scriptures of the spiritual fathers of the past that one may understand the uniqueness that is being described in the Scriptures. But if you are asking my own personal opinion, then I have given it earlier. For me, as a Buddhist, my attitude toward Jesus Christ is that he was either a fully enlightened being or a bodhisattva of a very high spiritual realization.

The following anecdote may not be directly related to your point, but I would like to mention my visit to Lourdes last year as a pilgrim. There, in front of the cave, I experienced something very special. I felt a spiritual vibration, a kind of spiritual presence there. And then, in front of the image of the Virgin Mary, I prayed. I expressed my admiration for this holy place that has long been a source of inspiration and strength that has provided spiritual solace, comfort, and healing to millions of people. And I prayed that this may continue for a long time to come. So my prayer there was not directed to any clearly defined object, like Buddha or Jesus Christ or a bodhisattva, but was simply directed to all great beings who have infinite compassion toward all sentient beings.

Notes

1 It is clear from his *Treatise on First Principles* and his theory of the soul that Origen in the third century thought that reincarnation, which he studied in Greek and Gnostic thought as *metempsychosis*, was worthy of serious debate. Less clear, however, are his own views on it which were raised in his commentary on the gospel text that is often cited as proving the prevalence of such beliefs at the time of Jesus (Matthew 11:14) [it seems quite possible, if not likely, that Origen accepted reincarnation (belief in this was not uncommon in Christian North Africa at this time), however, there is no reasonable scholarly evidence to support the finding of such a teaching in the New Testament – ed.].

2 As the unitary source of all diversity and duality in the world, God is not restrictable to male or female gender while at the same time remaining in some real sense personal. However, the patriarchal roots of Christianity have led to the attribution of maleness to God. This was reinforced by the human maleness of Jesus and his being seen as the 'Son' of the 'Father'. With two of the persons of the Trinity imagined as male, the third, the Holy Spirit, has traditionally been sensed as the feminine side of God [indeed, in both Hebrew and Greek the term for 'Spirit' is feminine, *ruach* and *pneuma*, respectively, while early church councils made clear that God had no gender]. Today, however, feminist theologians are emphasizing the possibility of a feminine perception of the Godhead as well as the wide range of imagery in the biblical tradition available for describing God. See, for example, *She Who Is*, by Elizabeth Johnson [1992, New York: Crossroad].

Source: Robert Kiely (ed.), 1996, *The Good Heart: His Holiness the Dali Lama Explores the Heart of Christianity – and of Humanity*, London: Rider Books, pp. 58–61, 82–4.

Acknowledgements of Sources

The editors, contributors and publisher wish to express their thanks for permission to reproduce published extracts from the following sources:

Eerdmans for J. H. Bavinck, 1965, *The Church Between Temple and Mosque*, Grand Rapids, MI: Eerdmans, pp. 117–28.

Cornell University Press for Alvin Plantinga, 1995, 'Pluralism: A Defense of Religious Exclusivism', in Thomas D. Senor (ed.), *The Rationality of Belief and the Plurality of Faith*, London: Cornell University Press, pp. 191–215, at pp. 191–201.

Vidyajoti, Institute of Religious Studies for Karl Rahner, 1973, 'Christ in the Non-Christian Religions', in G. Gispert-Sauch (ed.), *God's Word Among Men*, Delhi: Vidyajoti, Institute of Religious Studies, pp. 95–104.

ISPCK for Kenneth J. Thomas, 2001, 'The Place of the Bible in Muslim–Christian Relations', in David Emmanuel Singh and Robert Edwin Schink (eds), *Approaches, Foundations, Issues and Models of Interfaith Relations*, New Delhi: ISPCK, pp. 337–46; and Krishna Mohun Banerjea, 'The Relation between Christianity and Hinduism', in K. P. Aleaz (ed. and intro.), *From Exclusivism to Inclusivism: The Theological Writings of Krishna Mohun Banerjea (1813–1885)*, Indian Contextual Theological Education Series 18, Delhi: ISPCK, pp. 594–611.

Missiology for Amos Yong, 2005, 'A P(new)matological Paradigm for Christian Mission in a Religiously Plural World', *Missiology: An International Review* 33.2, pp. 175–91.

T & T Clark for John Hick, 1984, 'Religious Pluralism', in Frank Whaling (ed.), *The World's Religious Traditions: Essays in Honour of Wilfred Cantwell Smith*, Edinburgh: T&T Clark.

Orbis for Aloysius Pieris, *Love Meets Wisdom: A Christian Experience of Buddhism*, New York: Orbis, pp. 83–8 (chapter 7: 'Buddhism as a Challenge for Christians'). Rosemary Radford Ruether, 1989, *Disputed Questions: On Being a Christian*, Maryknoll: Orbis, pp. 55–73; and Gavin D'Costa, 2000, *The Meeting of Religions and the Trinity*, Maryknoll, NY: Orbis, pp. 128–31, 132–3 (chapter 4).

Blackwell for Paul J. Griffiths, 2001, *Problems of Religious Diversity*, Oxford: Blackwell, pp. 10–11, 12–13.

Studies in Interreligious Dialogue for Kate McCarthy, 1996, 'Women's Experience as a Hermeneutical Key to a Christian Theology of Religions', *Studies in Interreligious Dialogue* 6.2, pp. 163–73.

The Journal of Ecumenical Studies for Chung Hyun Kyung, 1997, 'Seeking the Religious Roots of Pluralism', *Journal of Ecumenical Studies* 34.3, pp. 399–401.

Interreligious Insight for Jonathan Sacks and Leonard Swidler, 2004, 'Toward a Dialogue of Civilizations: A dialogue between Jonathan Sacks (Jewish, UK) and Leonard Swidler (Christian, USA)', *Interreligious Insight: A journal of dialogue and engagement* 2.3, pp. 35–46.

Collins for Hans Küng, *Christianity and the World Religions: Paths of Dialogue with Islam, Hinduism, and Buddhism*, London: Collins, pp. 24–8 (section: 'Muhammad: A Prophet?').

Buddhist–Christian Studies for Bonnie Thurston, 2000, 'The Buddha Offered Me a Raft', in Rita Gross and Terry Muck (eds), *Buddhists Talk about Jesus, Christians Talk about the Buddha*, London: Continuum, pp. 118–28 (first published in *Buddhist–Christian Studies* 19 (1999)).

Sheed & Ward for John C. H. Wu, 1951, *Beyond East and West*, New York: Sheed & Ward, pp. 149–88 (chapter 12: 'Religions of China').

Bruce Epperly for Bruce Epperly, 1996, *Crystal and Cross: Christians and New Age in Creative Dialogue*, Mystic, CT: Twenty-Third Publications, pp. 183–4, 185–7, 189–90.

St Mark's Review for David Millikan, 1991, 'Religion and the New Age', *St Mark's Review* 144 (Summer), pp. 6–9, extracts from pp. 8–9.

Random House and Wisdom Publications for Robert Kiely (ed.), 1996, *The Good Heart: His Holiness the Dali Lama Explores the Heart of Christianity – and of Humanity*, London: Rider Books, pp. 58–61, 82–4.

ACKNOWLEDGEMENTS OF SOURCES

EOS for Andreas Grüschloß, 2008, 'Buddhist–Christian Relations', in Perry Schmidt-Leukel (ed.), *Buddhist Attitudes to Other Religions*, St Ottilien: EOS Verlag, pp. 237–68, extract from pp. 253–6 (section: 'The Buddhist Jesus: An unknown brother of the Buddha').

Continuum for Julia Ching, 1999, 'Living in Two Worlds: A Personal Appraisal', in Arvind Sharma and Kathleen M. Dugan (eds), *A Dome of Many Colors: Studies in Religious Pluralism, Identity and Unity*, Harrisburg, PA: Trinity Press International, pp. 15–22; and Roger Haight SJ, 2005, *The Future of Christology*, New York: Continuum, pp. 148, 156–64 (chapter: 'Outline for an Orthodox Christology').

Valentine Mitchell for James Parkes, 1960, *The Foundations of Judaism and Christianity*, London: Valentine Mitchell, ('Epilogue – Two Religions: Two Chosen People').

University of Waterloo Press for M. Darroll Bryant, 1986, 'Meeting at Snowmass: Some Dynamics of an Interfaith Encounter', in John Miller (ed.), *Interfaith Dialogue: Four Approaches*, Waterloo, Ont.: University of Waterloo Press, pp. 1–28.

Index

Note: References to words, names and terms in this index do not necessarily denote a reference to that precise term, i.e. references to Vedanta cover 'Vedantic', 'Vedantin', etc.